Deutsche Sprachinseln weltweit: Interne und externe Perspektiven
German Language Varieties Worldwide: Internal and external Perspectives

German Language Varieties Worldwide: Internal and external Perspectives

Deutsche Sprachinseln weltweit: Interne und externe Perspektiven

William D. Keel
Klaus J. Mattheier
(eds./Hrsg.)

PETER LANG

Frankfurt am Main · Berlin · Bern · Bruxelles · New York · Oxford · Wien

Bibliografische Information Der Deutschen Bibliothek
Die Deutsche Bibliothek verzeichnet diese Publikation in der
Deutschen Nationalbibliografie; detaillierte bibliografische
Daten sind im Internet über <http://dnb.ddb.de> abrufbar.

Gedruckt auf alterungsbeständigem,
säurefreiem Papier.

ISBN 3-631-39025-4
US-ISBN 0-8204-6465-1

© Peter Lang GmbH
Europäischer Verlag der Wissenschaften
Frankfurt am Main 2003
Alle Rechte vorbehalten.

Printed in Germany 1 2 3 4 6 7

www.peterlang.de

Contents

William D. Keel
University of Kansas
Lawrence, Kansas

Introduction: Global Perspectives of German Language Varieties

Judging from the title of the first essay in this volume, the reader might have the initial impression that this collection of essays on German language varieties around the world is the final word on a dead subject. That is, however, far from the case. On the contrary, it is only now—at the beginning of the twenty-first century—when faced with the nearly certain demise of an incredibly rich array of German settlement dialects from Kazachstan to Kansas that we are discovering the treasure trove of linguistic and sociolinguistic data in these vanishing *Sprachinseln*.

The essays in this volume resulted from a conference held from March 29 to April 1, 2001, at the Max Kade Center for German-American Studies at the University of Kansas on German speech island research. Researchers of German settlement dialect varieties found in the United States, Brazil, Mexico, Hungary, Romania and the former Soviet Union discussed and debated a number of current issues in our discipline.

Setting the tone for the volume is the essay on speech island death by Klaus Mattheier. Despite the prospect of the ultimate demise of the large array of (German) linguistic enclaves around the world, Mattheier argues that this very situation is an incredible opportunity for linguists and sociolinguists to study the very process and context of language death and thus gain significant insights for the theory of linguistic change per se. He also places speech island research within the larger context of international minority studies. For Mattheier, the point in the life of a speech island at which stability turns to instability is the key to understanding the life cycle of such linguistic enclaves.

Mattheier's call for more research on this point is echoed in the final essay of the volume by William Keel. Many researchers looking at the linguistic assimilation of urban and rural German-Americans during the twentieth century have appealed to the impact of the two world wars, especially the anti-German hysteria surrounding the First World War. Keel questions both the negative impact of the wars and the generally assumed positive role of the German churches in maintaining German language enclaves.

A number of our contributors address issues relating to one of the longest surviving German dialect communities in the New World, the Pennsylvania Germans. Joachim Raith describes the complexities of the speech community "Big Valley" in central Pennsylvania, with subgroups exhibiting a variety of states of diglossia and bilingualism. He also confirms the division into "plain" and "nonplain" varieties of Pennsylvania

German and predicts the ultimate demise of the latter varieties. The "plain" varieties, however, will continue to exist with ever increasing tendencies to borrow from English.

Taking his perspective from recent research visits to the "Big Valley" in Pennsylvania, Ludwig Eichinger contemplates the near impossibility of developing an adequate methodology for sociolinguistic research in such complex speech communities. The linguist using the traditional method of direct interview is faced with the dilemma of having to observe and record without partaking in the life of the community. And, even the researcher who devotes the time to, in effect, become a part of the community remains limited by the roles taken by each individual in the community.

Mark Louden reflects on the observations of Johann David Schöpf, an eighteenth-century physician who accompanied "Hessian" troops sent to fight for the British during the Revolutionary War. Schöpf wrote extensively about the Pennsylvania Germans and their language behavior. Louden finds much in Schöpf's survey to support the view that language contact with English has characterized the sociolinguistic situation of the nonsectarian speakers of Pennsylvania German since at least the end of the eighteenth century. Achim Kopp, on the other hand, takes a look at attitudes about Pennsylvania German expressed by the members of that speech community with a detailed study of the members of six Pennsylvania German families, both sectarian and nonsectarian. And, the final study of Pennsylvania German in this volume, by Steven Keiser, outlines the origins and development of a midwestern variety of Pennsylvania German.

As can be seen from the Pennsylvania German essays in this volume, a central concern for this international group of scholars is the differentiation between transfer processes in language contact situations and the phenomenon of language attrition, simplification or decay in the last phases in the death of a language variety—in this case German dialect varieties in contact with varieties of American English, Mexican Spanish, Brazilian Portuguese, Russian or Hungarian. Obviously any speech island is by definition placed in a context of language contact with another speech variety due to its separation from its linguistic homeland. Normally, languages in contact tend to borrow not only vocabulary but also structure. And, normally the directionality of the linguistic influence is from the more prestigious, powerful or majority language, but not necessarily so.

Phenomena of language decay for such varieties in linguistic isolation include the breakdown of grammatical categories (e.g., the loss of case distinctions in the noun phrase, the loss of tense or aspectual distinctions in the verb), loss of hypotaxis, lack of morphological integration of borrowed forms, phonological distortion and hypercorrection and simply the inability to remember lexical items. An extreme state of decay is reached in agrammatism: the total disintegration and confusion of the phonological, morphological and syntactic systems (Sasse 1992; Mesthrie and Leap 2000; Wolfram 2002).

Both contact-induced change and linguistic decay may involve the loss of linguistic categories. In such a scenario it may not be at all easy to assign the reduction of some grammatical category with certainty to decay or contact. In those cases where a dying language exhibited a certain grammatical category prior to the decay phase and the dominant language did not, the loss of that category by the dying language during the period of linguistic decay could be explained by both theoretical models. Support for either explanation would have to appeal to evidence outside of the languages in question.

Several contributors to this volume address the issue of contact-induced versus internal causes in the attrition of case distinctions in the varieties of German found in a number of speech islands in the United States, Russia and Brazil. Looking at the loss of the dative case (marked typically by the definite or indefinite article) in the noun phrase and in pronouns, Glenn Gilbert and Janet Fuller re-examine the data collected several decades ago for the atlas of Texas German (Gilbert 1972). They conclude that the evidence does not support a transfer from English and believe the loss of the dative case reflects an internal development. To the extent that language contact favors simplification, it could be argued that such developments accelerate in a language contact environment.

The view of Gilbert and Fuller is sustained in Renate Born's investigation of similar phenomena in the variety of German spoken in Frankenmuth, Michigan (Born 1994). However, Born sees this simplification in the context of language regression—loss of grammatical categories in the reverse order of their acquisition. She also argues that the loss of case in the Frankenmuth variety reflects a similar situation in the area of origin of the dialect in Franconia in the German homeland. A final word on this topic comes from Peter Rosenberg. Drawing on a broad range of research in German speech islands in Russia and Brazil, Rosenberg urges caution in rushing to the conclusion that "linguistic convergence" is the explanation for the changed linguistic systems found in speech islands. Future research in this area will require the comparative investigation of such phenomena in multiple speech islands in different contexts.

And, precisely this type of comparative work is outlined by Nina Berend, who brings her knowledge of German dialect varieties in Russia, particularly the Volga German dialects, to offer different perspectives on a series of phonological, morphological and lexical phenomena from her interviews with Kansas speakers of Volga German. She urges a more intensive comparative research effort to elucidate aspects of linguistic change and to offer new insights on a variety of linguistic phenomena. A major contribution in this regard is the essay by Göz Kaufmann, who analyzes in detail the sequence of verbal elements in Mennonite Low German or *Plautdietsch* in speech communities in Texas (USA) and Rio Grande do Sul (Brazil). His larger study, on which this essay is based, will include communities of Mennonites in Canada, Mexico, and Paraguay.

Peter Wagener and Elisabeth Knipf-Komlósi report on German speech communities separated by the Atlantic Ocean and thousands of miles. Yet, the linguistic situation of German dialect speakers in Wisconsin and Hungary, respectively, is amazing similar. Both groups are faced with the loss of functionality in their German varieties for everyday communication and ultimately the death of those varieties. As Wagener notes poignantly, the German dialects might have had a chance to survive if there had been a need for it. Different in the two groups is the role of Standard German for the speakers of German dialects in Hungary. Here the possibility of substituting Standard German for the dialect exists, but even that as a possibility is placed into doubt by Knipf-Komlósi.

A common thread running through the German dialect varieties faced with extinction, at least in a number of communities in the American Midwest, is the attempt to salvage what can be saved through heritage activities. Social clubs, singing societies, amateur theatrical productions and other activities featuring a number of German dialect varieties have sprung up across the Central Plains of the United States. In his essay, Philip Webber describes one such group in north central Iowa: The East Frisian Low German play *Sien gefohrl'ke Voertelstuenn* produced by a group of heritage speakers in Wellsburg, Iowa. And, to round out the volume, Kurt Rein presents a digital aid for future speech island researchers, the Dialect Identification Program or DIP. By matching pertinent dialect data to a set of binary questions, the researcher traces a path that leads to a characterization of the German dialect variety in question.

The editors would like to especially acknowledge the support of the *Sprachinselkonferenz 2001* by several offices at the University of Kansas: The Graduate School, the College of Liberal Arts and Sciences, the Department of Germanic Languages and Literatures, and, primarily, the Max Kade Center for German-American Studies. The conference was also supported by the Topeka Chapter of the American Historical Society of Germans from Russia and a generous grant from the Max Kade Foundation, Inc., New York. Support for the publication of this volume has come from the Hall Center for the Humanities at the University of Kansas and Peter Lang Publishers, Frankfurt, Germany. We would also like to acknowledge the editorial assistance of Noelle Giuffrida, Hall Center for the Humanities.

References

Born, Renate. 1994. *Michigan German in Frankenmuth: Variation and Change in an East Franconian Dialect.* Columbia, SC: Camden House.

Gilbert, Glenn. 1972. *Linguistic Atlas of Texas German.* Marburg: Elwert; Austin: University of Texas.

Mesthrie, Rajend, and William L. Leap. 2000. "Language Contact 1: Maintenance, Shift and Death." In *Introducing Sociolinguistics,* ed. Rajend Mesthrie, Joan Swann, Andrea Deumert and William L. Leap, 248-78.

Sasse, Hans-Jürgen. 1992. "Language Decay and Contact-Induced Change: Similarities and Differences." In *Language Death: Factual and Theoretical Explorations with Special Reference to East Africa*, ed. Matthias Brenzinger, 59-80. Contributions to the Sociology of Language, 64. Berlin: Mouton de Gruyter.

Wolfram, Walt. 2002. "Language Death and Dying." In *The Handbook of Language Variation and Change*, ed. J. K. Chambers, Peter Trudgill and Natalie Schilling-Estes, 764-87. Malden, MA: Blackwell Publishers.

Klaus J. Mattheier
Ruprecht-Karls-Universität
Heidelberg, Germany

Sprachinseltod:
Überlegungen zur Entwicklungsdynamik von Sprachinseln

Sprachinseltod—damit ist die soziolinguistische, linguistische und teilweise auch dialektologische Entwicklung angesprochen, durch die eine Sprachinsel eingegliedert wird oder sich eingliedert in die neue Kontaktgesellschaft, in die es die Sprachinselgemeinschaft verschlagen hat. Und Sprachinseltod, das scheint das Schicksal aller Sprachinseln zu sein, wie etwa der australischen Sprachinseln, die weitgehend schon ausgestorben sind und wahrscheinlich auch der Sprachinseln in Kansas, die alle wohl "in den letzten Zügen" liegen. Wenn dem so ist, lohnt es sich dann überhaupt, sich mit solchen gesellschaftlich und sprachlich im wahrsten Sinne abgelegenen Themen zu beschäftigen (Mattheier 1994, 336)?

Indem ich diese Bedenklichkeiten aufnehme, werde ich zu zeigen versuchen, dass die systematische Beschäftigung mit dem Sprachinseltod interessante Forschungsergebnisse verspricht und schon erbracht hat im Bereich der Minoritätenforschung ebenso wie in der Kontaktlinguistik, der Dialektologie und besonders der Sprachwandelforschung. Dabei werde ich in diesem Beitrag von zwei Thesen ausgehen, die hoffentlich die Brisanz der Erforschung von Sprachinselauflösungsentwicklungen erkennbar werden lassen:

1. Das Sterben von Sprachinseln und ihren Sprachen ist ein Prozess, der sowohl linguistisch als auch soziolinguistisch in das Zentrum der theoretischen Modellierung von Sprachwandel führt und der daher als Laboratorium für die Erforschung von sprachlichen Veränderungen dienen kann.

2. Von Sprachinseltod kann man nur sprechen, wenn man das Konzept der Sprachinsel auf einen sozialhistorisch sehr engen Bereich von Migrationsentwicklungen im ländlichen Bereich beschränkt. Nur bei diesen Sprachinseln kann man heute von einem Sprachinselsterben sprechen. Die städtischen Sprachinseln sind in der Regel längst untergegangen. Parallel dazu erleben wir aber derzeit einen massiven "Sprachinselgeburtsprozess," um im Bild zu bleiben. Die großen Bevölkerungsverschiebungen, die seit den 1960er Jahren etwa die europäischen Wirtschaftsräume umstrukturieren, lassen überall neue, aber diesmal eher städtische und industrielle Sprachinseln entstehen, über deren Geschichte wir bisher noch wenig wissen.

Eine dritte These betrifft die Internationalität der Beschäftigung mit Sprachinseln und ihren Veränderungsprozessen. Sprachinseln sind nur scheinbar ein in erster Linie germanistisches Problem. Sprachinselbildung und Sprachinseltod gab es zu allen Zeiten und überall in der Welt. Man denke etwa an die Sprachinselbildung im Zusammenhang mit der indischen Auswanderung im 19. Jahrhundert nach Südafrika, in die Karibik und in den Pazifik (Moag 1977). Nur werden diese Entwicklungen von der anglo-amerikanischen Forschung in der Regel der Minderheitenforschung zugerechnet, wobei der spezielle Charakter von Sprachinseln, nämlich die Rückbindung in ein sprachliches Mutterland, in dem die Sprachinselsprache oftmals sogar Nationalsprache ist, nicht angemessen berücksichtigt wird.

Diesen Überlegungen zur Dynamik von Sprachinselentwicklungen werde ich in zwei Schritten nachgehen: zuerst werde ich die übergreifende Problemstellung des Sprachtodes allgemein und seiner Erforschung nachgehen, die in den letzten Jahren erhöhte Aufmerksamkeit in der soziolinguistischen Forschung gefunden hat (Dorian 1998). Danach werde ich versuchen—ausgehend von einem Normaltyp einer Sprachinsel—einige Aspekte einer Typologie von Sprachinselverfallsprozessen herauszuarbeiten. Schließen werde ich mit einigen Überlegungen zum "Sprachinsellebenslauf."

Bevor ich aber in die Überlegungen zu einer Theorie der Sprachinselentwicklung eintrete, möchte ich ein kleines Schaubild diskutieren, in dem ich versuche, die verschiedenen Forschungsansätze, die man im Bereich der Sprachinselforschung unterscheiden kann, in einen systematischen Zusammenhang zu bringen und zugleich der Erforschung von Sprachinselsterben, um die es hier gehen soll, einen Platz im Gesamtbereich der Erforschung von Sprachinseln zuzuweisen. Wissenschaftliche, oder manchmal auch pseudowissenschaftliche Forschung zum Phänomen der Sprachinsel, gibt es schon etwa seit der Mitte des 19. Jahrhunderts, als man zuerst in der auf das Mittelalter zurückreichenden Sprachinsellandschaft Siebenbürgen Fragen stellte über die sprachliche Heimat der deutschstämmigen Dialekte dieser Region (Scheiner 1896, 1971).

Die vielfältigen Forschungsansätze, die sich seit dieser Zeit im Bereich der Sprachinselforschung herausgebildet haben, lassen sich systematisch am besten gliedern, wenn man sie hinsichtlich von drei Kategorien einander zuordnet: dem sprachlichen Gegenstand, dem Interessenfeld und der Perspektive, unter der Sprachinseln betrachtet werden. In der Sprachinselforschung gibt es zwei sprachliche Objekte: das Spektrum der autochthonen Varietäten, also etwa das Pennsylvania-German und das Bibelhochdeutsch der Old Order Amish (OOA) und die allochthone Kontaktvarietät bzw. Kontaktvarietäten, also bei den OOA das Englische. Dann gibt es in der Sprachinselforschung drei Interessenfelder: das strukturlinguistische Feld der Beschreibung der Sprachlichkeit auf den verschiedenen Sprachrängen und das soziolinguistische Interesse der Beschreibung der Wechselwirkungen zwischen Sprache

Übersicht über die Forschungsätze im Bereich der Sprachinselforschung

	Varietätenlinguistik		Kontaktlinguistik	
	Statik	Dynamik	Statik	Dynamik
Strukturlinguistik	Sprachinselphonologie Sprachinselgrammatik Sprachinsellexikologie	Ausgleichsvarietäten-bildung, Driftprozesse	Strukturelle Analyse des Kontakts mit der Umgebungssprache	Kontaktinduzierter Wandel der Sprach-inselsprache
Soziolinguistik	Autochthones Kommuni-kationsprofil einer Sprachinsel	Soziolinguistische Struktur des soziolinguistischen Varietätenausgleichs; Koineisierung	Soziolinguistische Globalanalyse einer Sprachinsel und ihrer Kontaktsprachen	Sprachverlust und Spracherhaltanalysen
Dialektologie	Sprachinseldialektatlanten	Heimatbestimmung durch Dialektvergleiche	Dialektgeographie des Kontaktraumes zwischen der Sprachinselvarietät und der Kontaktsprache	Dynamische Deutung eines Sprachkontaktraumes im Umfeld einer Sprachinsel

und Gesellschaft. Hinzu kommt als drittes Arbeitsfeld der Sprachinselforschung die Region, der Raum, in dem sich Sprachinseln auf dialektgeographische Differenzierungen entfalten. Und weiterhin gibt es zwei Forschungsperspektiven, unter denen man die Untersuchungen ansetzen kann: die statische Perspektive der Beschreibung und Funktionsanalyse von Sprache im gesellschaftlichen Umfeld der Sprachinsel sowie die dynamische Perspektive, unter der Sprachinseln und die in ihnen verwendeten Varietätensysteme im Prozess der Entstehung, des Sich-Entwickelns und des Verfalls bzw. des Verschwindens gesehen werden.

Fügen wir diese kategorialen Dimensionen zusammen, dann ergeben sich zwölf Forschungsfelder, die zumindest für die auf deutsche Sprachinseln bezogene Forschung alle bisher erprobten und ausgearbeiteten theoretisch-methodischen Ansätze und noch weitere, nicht erprobte Forschungsansätze, erfasst. So findet sich etwa die Schirmunskische Theorie der primären und sekundären Merkmale im Bereich der linguistischen Aspekte des Varietätensystems der autochthonen Varietäten einer Sprachinsel und zwar als Beschreibung der Entwicklungsdynamik solcher Sprachinseln und der von Schirmunski postulierten Ausbildung von "Neudialekten" wie des Neufränkischen, des Neuschwäbischen und des Neuhessischen (Mattheier 1993, 41-45). Der in letzter Zeit unter dem Einfluss der sich entwickelnden Soziolinguistik häufiger zu beobachtende Ansatz der Herausarbeitung eines Kommunikationsprofils der autochthonen Varietäten einer Sprachinsel lässt sich unter die Kategorien "Varietätenkontakt—Soziolinguistik—statisch" einordnen. Und die Erforschung der Abbau- und Veränderungsprozesse der autochthonen Varietäten unter dem Einfluss bzw. in Auseinandersetzung mit den Kontaktsprachen ist unter "Sprachkontakt—linguistisch und Dynamik" einzuordnen. Unser Gegenstand—der Sprachinseltod—thematisiert im Bereich des Kontaktes zwischen Sprachinsel- und Kontaktsprache den soziolinguistischen Aspekt und zwar unter dynamischer Perspektive der ablaufenden Entwicklungen und Veränderungen.

Nun zu einigen Festlegungen, die das Phänomen der Sprachinsel allgemein betreffen. Ich gehe hier aus von dem Definitionsvorschlag, den ich vor einiger Zeit publiziert habe. Danach ist eine Sprachinsel eine als Sprachminderheit von ihrem Sprachmutterland geographisch getrennte und durch eine sprachlich/ethnisch differente Kontaktgesellschaft umschlossene und/oder überdachte Kommunikationsgemeinschaft, die sich von der Kontaktgesellschaft durch eine Reihe von die Sonderheit der Sprachinselbewohner begründenden objektiven Faktoren abgrenzt bzw. abgegrenzt wird, die eine besondere soziopsychische Sprachinseldisposition oder Sprachinselmentalität entstehen lassen, die ihrerseits wiederum die Ursache für eine verhinderte oder verzögerte sprachlich-kulturelle Assimilation an die Kontaktgesellschaft darstellt. Eingehen möchte ich jedoch nur auf einige Problembereiche, die Konsequenzen für den Verfallsprozess von Sprachinseln haben.

Es geht einmal um die Frage nach dem Umfang von Sprachinseln. Da ist etwa die Rede von "der deutschen Sprachinsel" in Siebenbürgen oder in Texas. In neueren Forschungen werden jedoch in der Regel kleinere ländliche Siedlungsgemeinschaften als Sprachinseln bezeichnet. Die Definition wählt das Gumperzsche Konzept von der Kommunikationsgemeinschaft als einen angemessenen Rahmen für eine Sprachinsel. Dabei steht bekanntlich das geteilte System soziokommunikativer Regeln und Normen im Vordergrund. Hinzu kommt jedoch—insbesondere in Sprachinseln—die Identitätskomponente. Sprachinseln werden nicht zuletzt gebildet in einem Diskurs der Menschen, die mit diesen Sprachinseln zu tun haben. Und dieser Diskurs bestimmt auch, was noch zur Sprachinsel gerechnet wird und was zu einer anderen benachbarten Sprachinsel gehört. Dieser Ansatz führt dann in der Regel zu kleineren dörflichen Gemeinschaften oder Gruppierungen von zwei bis drei Dörfern, die von ihren Sprechern und auch von der allochthonen Umgebungsgesellschaft als Sprachinseln bezeichnet werden. Deshalb ist etwa auch von "den" texasdeutschen oder den südungarischen "Sprachinseln" die Rede, die zwar durchaus sprachliche Ähnlichkeiten aufweisen, aber trotzdem nicht als eine Kommunikationsgemeinschaft identifiziert werden.

Ein anderes Problem der Sprachinseldefinition im Zusammenhang mit dem Verfall—dem Sterben—von Sprachinselnist die Beziehung des Phänomens "Sprachinsel" zu dem zentralen kontaktlinguistischen Konzept "Minorität"/ "Minderheit" bzw. Minderheitensprache (Haugen a. o. eds., 1981). Denn die Diskussion um den Sprachtod wird im allgemeinen ausschließlich im Bereich der Minoritätensprache geführt. Sprachinseln sind offensichtlich Minoritäten-sprachgemeinschaften. Das zeigt sich schon daran, dass in fast allen außerdeutschen Forschungsbereichen das Konzept der Sprachinsel nicht speziell kategorial erfasst wird und keinen besonderen Namen hat. Gehen wir von einem neueren Versuch zur Typisierung von Sprachminoritäten, dem Konzept von John Edwards (1990) aus, so ist zunächst einmal zu unterscheiden zwischen indigenen Minoritäten und Immigrantenminoritäten. Diese sehr einleuchtende Differenzierung unterscheidet Sprachminoritäten wie die Friesen, die Basken, die Bretonen und die Sorben eindeutig von Minoritäten, die aufgrund von Einwanderung entstanden sind, wie etwa die deutschen Sprachinseln in Russland. Blickt man genauer hin, dann hat diese Trennung aber durchaus ihre Probleme. So sind die inselhaften Siedlungen von Deutschsprachigen im slavisch besiedelten Schlesien um 1200 ohne Zweifel unter die Immigrantenminoritäten zu rechnen. Aber was ist mit den deutschen Restsiedlungen in Schlesien nach der Vertreibung von 1945. In diesem Fall wird man sicherlich von indigenen Minderheiten sprechen. Trotzdem wird man Sprachinseln in der Regel zu den Immigrantenminoritäten rechnen. Edwards formuliert nun in seinem Typisierungsversuch vier Kategorien, anhand derer er verschiedene Typen von Minoritäten/Sprachminoritäten unterscheidet:

+/- unique
+/- cohesive
+/- adjoining
local/nonlocal

Mit "unique" ist gemeint, dass eine Sprache/Varietät ausschließlich in einer Region und sonst nirgends vorkommt. So ist etwa das Sorbische unter diese Kategorie zu rechnen, aber auch das Friesische oder das Bretonische. Sprachinseln sind in der Regel nicht "unique," da sie sowohl in den Inselsiedlungen als auch im Sprachmutterland vorkommen. Mit der zweiten Kategorie "cohesive" ist gemeint, dass eine Minderheit nicht vereinzelt lebt, sondern gemeinsam in einer größeren oder kleineren Region. So bilden etwa die südungarischen deutschstämmigen Sprachinseln einen tendenziell zusammengehörigen Raum, selbst wenn es dort dazwischen auch kontaktsprachige Siedlungen gibt. Die dritte Kategorie "adjoining" ist für die typologische Erfassung von Sprachinseln besonders wichtig. "Adjoining" meint hier, dass die Minorität in Verbindung steht zu einer anderen Minderheit in einem anderen Land oder zu einer Region, einem Land, in dem diese Sprache keine Minderheitensprache ist. Das ist bei allen Sprachinseln der Fall. Überall gibt es ein Sprachmutterland, zu dem es von Fall zu Fall engere oder geringere Beziehungen gibt. Hinzu kommt, dass Sprachinseln oder "immigrant enclaves," wie Edwards sie nennt, immer "local only" sind, das heißt, im Rahmen von örtlichen Siedlungen Kommunikationsgemeinschaften bilden.

Fasst man die kategorialen Zuordnungen zusammen, so ist eine Sprachinsel nach Edwards dadurch definiert, dass sie eine Immigrantenminderheit darstellt, die miteinander in Zusammenhang stehende lokale Kommunikationsgemeinschaften bilden, die jedoch Sprachen umfassen, die auch außerhalb der Sprachinseln verwendet werden und die mit diesen Sprachbereichen in Verbindung stehen.

In einer auf diese Weise strukturierten Sprachinselgemeinschaft interessiert uns in erster Linie der Prozess, in dem über eine gewisse Zeit hinweg die Sprachlichkeit der Sprachinsel aufgegeben wird oder an die umgebende Kontaktsprache assimiliert. Solche linguistischen bzw. soziolinguistischen Entwicklungen, in denen Varietäten oder Sprachen aus einem Varietätenspektrum ausscheiden, sind in den letzten Jahrzehnten in der Nachfolge der richtungsweisenden Arbeiten von Nancy Dorian (1981) unter dem Terminus "Sprachtod" immer häufiger Gegenstand wissenschaftlichen Interesses gewesen (vgl. Dorian 1989). Im allgemeinen wird auf diesem Forschungsfeld unterschieden zwischen Sprachtod (Lg. Loss) und Sprachverlust (Lg. Attrition) (Seliger Vago 1989; Andersen 1982). Von Sprachverlust ist eher in psycholinguistischen Zusammenhängen die Rede, wenn es um das Verlieren einer Erst- oder auch einer Zweitsprache aus dem Kompetenzspektrum eines Sprechers geht. Sprachtod ist dagegen primär eine soziolinguistische bzw. kontaktlinguistische Kategorie, bei der es um den

Wegfall einer Varietät oder einer Sprache des Varietätenspektrums einer Sprachgemeinschaft und auch des Kompetenzspektrums eines Sprechers geht.

Je nach Ablauf des Prozesses der Sprachaufgabe werden in der Forschung verschiedene Typen von Sprachtod unterschieden. Dabei ist der sogenannte "plötzliche Tod," der "sudden death," besonders spektakulär, wenn auch heute glücklicherweise immer seltener. Hier steht der Sprachtod oftmals mit dem Aussterben einer ethnischen Gruppe oder sogar mit dem Genozid in Zusammenhang. So stirbt etwa 1911 Ishi, der letzte Sprecher von Yahi, einer Indianersprache aus Nordkalifornien, ohne Kenntnisse des Englischen. Hier stirbt die Sprache gleichzeitig mit ihren letzten Sprechern, ohne dass ein Sprachverlagerungsprozess über eine binguale Phase eingesetzt hat. Ähnlich spektakulär ist auch der Tod von Sprachinseln, die mehr oder weniger intakt waren, durch den Wegzug der Sprachinselbewohner. Dann kann man zwar nicht von Sprachtod reden, da die Sprache ja an anderer Stelle weiterverwendet wird, aber eine Sprachinsel geht verloren, wie wir derzeit an den Entwicklungen in den russischen und den rumänischen Sprachinseln des Deutschen sehen.

Ein zweiter Typ von Sprachtod wird in der Forschung "radical death" (Campbell/ Muntzel 1989, 184) genannt. Hier geben die Minderheiten ihre Sprache aufgrund massiven politischen und sonstigen Drucks der Mehrheitsgesellschaft quasi als ein Akt der Selbsterhaltung auf. Campbell/Muntzel führen hier als Beispiel einige Indianersprachen aus El Salvador an, die nach den massiven Massakern an diesen Indianern in den 1930er Jahren von den Überlebenden vollständig aufgegeben wurden, um zu verhindern, dass sie als Indianer erkannt wurden. Es wäre jedoch zu fragen, ob nicht die Sprachentwicklung vom I. zum II. Weltkrieg in den U.S.A. und auch in Kanada durch den massiven Druck, der auf alles Deutsche ausgeübt wurde, einen ähnlichen "radical death" von Deutsch—insbesondere in den mehr städtischen Siedlungsräumen—ausgelöst hat. In Hunderten von Berichten über diese Zeit und ihre Auswirkung auf die Deutschen in und außerhalb von Sprachinseln ist immer wieder davon die Rede, dass man das Deutsche möglichst zu verbergen suchte, und dass hier der Ansatzpunkt für den endgültigen Verlust des Deutschen gesehen wird (Mertens 1994, 312-21).

Der eigentliche Normaltyp von Sprachtod ist jedoch weder der "sudden death" noch der "radical death." Es ist ein Prozess, den man am besten als "language shift," als Sprachverlagerung oder Sprachverschiebung bezeichnen kann. Campbell/Muntzel (1989, 184f.) sprechen hier von "gradual death." Bei diesem Typ von Sprachverlust verläuft die Entwicklung innerhalb einer Sprachgemeinschaft oder auch in der Sprachkompetenz der einzelnen Sprecher über drei Phasen. Es beginnt mit einer monolingualen Phase der gesamten Gruppe. Dann folgt eine mehr oder weniger ausgedehnte "binguale" Phase. In dieser Phase können wir sowohl auf der Ebene der linguistischen Struktur als auch innerhalb der soziolinguistischen Verbreitung der Varietäten einen Trend hin zu den Kontaktsprachen feststellen und beschreiben. Und am Ende haben wir wiederum eine monolinguale Phase. Die Ausgangssprache ist vollständig oder in einzelnen Varietäten verlorengegangen. In dem bilingualen Feld des Übergangs zwischen der autochthonen Ausgangssprache und der allochthonen Zielsprache setzen nun auch die zahlreichen Forschungsansätze an, mit denen versucht wird, diese Entwicklung in einem theoretischen Modell zu fassen. Einige dieser Ansätze seien hier erwähnt.

Einmal lässt sich bei der *language-loss*-Forschung deutlich ein soziolinguistischer von einem strukturlinguistischen Ansatz unterscheiden. Die strukturlinguistischen Forschungen, die heute allgemein mit dem entwickelten Instrumentarium der Kontaktlinguistik betrieben werden, suchen die sprachlichen Veränderungen zu erfassen, die sich in der Ausgangssprache über die Zeit hinweg einstellen und die—so eine Forschungsthese—zu einer kontinuierlichen Simplifikation der Struktur führen. Dabei wird die Leistungsfähigkeit dieser Sprache nur erhalten durch intensive Entlehnungen aus der Kontaktsprache. Doch zeigen hier schon erste empirische Untersuchungen, dass die strukturellen Ab- und Umbauprozesse wesentlich komplizierter sind (Thomason/Kaufman 1988), und dass es durchaus Sprachen gibt, die ohne strukturelle Einschränkung bestimmte Teilsysteme bis zu ihrer Aufgabe beibehalten.

Die zweite Entwicklungsrichtung von *language-shift*-Forschung ist soziolinguistisch. Durch den Übergang von einer zu einer anderen Sprache wird sowohl das Sprachverhalten des einzelnen Sprechers als auch das der gesamten Sprachgemeinschaft über mehrere Stufen hinweg verändert. Sasse unterscheidet hier in seinem Versuch einer Theorie des Sprachtodes drei sich inkludierende Schritte. Ausgangspunkt des Sprachtodes ist immer ein komplexer Zusammenhang externer Faktoren. Er denkt dabei an allgemeine historische bzw. sozialhistorische Prozesse wie den Nationalismus, den Imperialismus, den Kolonialismus und auch an die Migration. Durch diese und ähnliche Entwicklungen werden Ausgangskonstellationen für die Aufgabe von Sprachen erzeugt. So führt die spanische Eroberung in Mittelamerika zum Sprachtod der Indianersprachen, die nationalistische Ideologie "ein Staat—eine Sprache" zur Ausrottung anderer Sprachen, etwa in den U.S.A. nach 1914, die Kolonisierung Australiens zum Sprachtod von vielen Aboriginessprachen und die durch die Migration aus Europa ausgelösten Mehrsprachigkeits- und Assimilationskonstellationen etwa zur Aufgabe der deutschen Sprache in Amerika. Diese externen Faktoren lösen innerhalb des Sprachverhaltens von einzelnen Sprechern und auch von Sprachgemeinschaften, also etwa von Sprachinseln, systematische Veränderungen aus. Und diese Veränderungen im Sprachverhalten haben nun wiederum Auswirkungen auf die Struktur der verwendeten Sprache in der Art, wie sie angedeutet worden ist.

Die Aufgabe des Soziolinguisten ist dabei in erster Linie, die Veränderungen im Sprachverhalten und in der Sprachbewertung zu erfassen. Beschreibungen derartiger Übergangsprozesse von einer Sprache zur anderen haben immer wieder vier Entfaltungsdimensionen erkennen lassen, über die eine Gemeinschaft von einer neuen

Sprache/Varietät erfasst wird. Im Vordergrund steht dabei die diastratische Dimension, in der es um die Auswirkungen von gesellschaftlichen Gruppierungen bei der Aufgabe einer Sprache geht. Hier ist immer das Alter genannt worden, das die Sprachverdrängung steuert. Alte Leute behalten die Ausgangssprache noch bei, während die jungen Leute schon die neue Sprache übernehmen. Auch wird behauptet, dass Frauen eher die neue Sprache übernehmen als Männer, oder dass die neue Sprache in den höheren bzw. gebildeten sozialen Schichten zuerst übernommen werden. Doch hat andererseits Anne Betten vor kurzem gezeigt, dass gerade die gebildeten vertriebenen Juden aus Deutschland in Israel das Hochdeutsche am meisten gepflegt und bewahrt haben (Betten 2000).

Eine zweite Entfaltungsdimension für Neuerungen in einer *language-shift-*Konstellation ist die diaphasische. Hier geht es um die verschiedenen Verwendungssituationen für die alte und die neue Sprache sowie das Muster der Reihenfolge, in der die alte Sprache diese kommunikativen Funktionen aufgibt. Immer wieder wird hier die berufliche Sphäre genannt, über die während des Assimilationsprozesses die Kontaktsprache Eingang erhält in die Sprachlichkeit der Sprachinsel. Und in den streng konfessionellen Sprachinseln zeigt sich eine deutliche Dichotomie zwischen Binnenfunktionen mit autochthonen Varietäten und Außenfunktionen in der Sprachverwendung mit allochthonen Varietäten. Andere religiöse Minderheiten haben die autochthone Sprache schon fast ganz aufgegeben. Nur in bestimmten kirchlichen Zusammenhängen behält diese Varietät noch eine Funktion. Hier ist etwa das Hochdeutsche bei den Hutterern oder den Old Order Mennonites zu nennen. Aber ein festes Raster von Situationen und Funktionsbereichen, nach dem immer wieder die Ausgangssprache aufgegeben wird, hat sich noch nicht beschreiben lassen. Eine dritte Entfaltungsdimension für eine Kontaktsprache in Minderheiten ist die diatopische Dimension, die bisher oftmals vernachlässigt worden ist. Die Regionen etwa, in denen Minderheitensprachen zuerst abgebaut und aufgegeben werden, sind in der Regel die ökonomischen und industriellen Zentren, während man an einer Karte der letzten noch vorhandenen Sprachminderheiten zugleich auch die gesellschaftliche, ökonomische und kulturelle Isolation ablesen kann. Eine vierte Dimension erfasst die mediale Verteilung von alter und neuer Sprache. In Minoritätenregionen ist die aktive und primäre Kontaktsprache in der Regel auch die Schriftsprache und die autochthone Sprache hält sich meist noch länger auf der sprechsprachigen Ebene. Aber etwa die passive Position des geschriebenen Hochdeutschen bei den Amischen zeigt, dass es auch gegenläufige Fälle gibt.

Integriert in die vier Entfaltungsdimensionen, von denen eben die Rede war, ist eine Reihe von Entwicklungsfaktoren, die von der Forschung in den letzten Jahren immer wieder vorgeschlagen und modifiziert worden ist. Dieses Faktorenbündel führt entweder zu einem Aufgeben der Minoritätensprache (*loss*-Faktor) oder es führt demgegenüber zu einer Erhaltung der Minoritätensprache, also zu einer *language-*

maintenance-Konstellation. Oder aber es erweist sich als ambivalent, indem es je nach Gesamtkonstellation die Sprachaufgabe fördert oder verhindert (vgl. dazu Kaufmann 1997). So ist etwa die in den diaphasischen Bereich gehörende Übernahme der Kontaktsprache in den schulischen Bereich in jedem Fall eine Zurückdrängung der Minoritätensprache, insbesondere in den folgenden Generationen. Eine starke konfessionell motivierte Isolation, die in den diastratischen Bereich gehört, führt dagegen zur Erhaltung der Minderheitensprache. Und eine aggressive Antiminderheitenpolitik der Kontaktgesellschaft kann entweder zur schnellen Sprachaufgabe führen, sie kann aber im Gegensatz dazu auch Identitätsbildungsprozesse innerhalb der Minorität und dadurch die Erhaltung dieser Varietät auslösen, wie das etwa in Südtirol zu beobachten ist (vgl. dazu jetzt Egger/Lanthaler 2001).

Während des Sprachaufgabeprozesses verändert sich nicht nur die Struktur der Ausgangssprache. Es wandelt sich auch das Ausmaß der Sprechfähigkeit über die Generationen hinweg. Gonzo und Saltarelli haben hier 1980 ein *Caskade*-Modell vorgeschlagen, nach dem die Sprachaufgabe innerhalb von drei bis vier Generationen abläuft. In der ersten, der Migrationsgeneration, erfolgt der Abbau der autochthonen Sprache nur dadurch, dass bestimmte Wörter nicht mehr verwendet werden und dass dafür neue Wörter, Wörter aus der Kontaktsprache entlehnt werden. Die zweite Generation, also die erste, die in der neuen Heimat Sprache lernt, hat bei ihren Lernvorbildern—der ersten Generation—schon ein in gewisser Weise reduziertes Modell der Migrantensprache vor Augen. Von diesem Modell erwerben sie jedoch wiederum nur einen Teil. In der dritten Generation wird das Sprachmodell auch wieder nur teilweise übernommen. Und es liegt nur ein reduziertes Modell zur Übernahme vor. Durch die doppelte Reduktion, die sich in jeder Generation verstärkt, wird eine Migrantensprache—in der Regel in drei bis vier Generationen—vollständig aufgegeben.

Die unterschiedlichen Grade der Sprachfähigkeit und ihren Wandel sucht Dorian 1981 in ein Modell zu fassen. Sie geht aus von dem "älteren fließenden Sprecher," bei dem in einer Minoritätengemeinschaft noch kein Anzeichen eines Einflusses der Kontaktvarietät zu erkennen ist. Davon abgehoben wird eine Gruppe der "younger fluent speakers," die jedoch schon einige Ansätze des Einflusses zeigen. Deutlich unterschieden werden davon die "semi-speaker." Bei diesen Sprechern ist die linguistische Kompetenz in der Minoritätensprache schon deutlich eingeschränkt. Die soziokommunikative Kompetenz ist jedoch noch voll entwickelt, indem der semi-Sprecher extensiven Gebrauch von Entlehnungen macht. Als vierte Gruppe nennt Dorian die "passive bilinguals," die keine aktive Sprachfähigkeit mehr haben, sich jedoch, wenn sie—etwa von Wissenschaftlern—gefragt werden, noch an Formen oder Formsegmente erinnern können. Campbell/Muntzel nennen diese Gruppe die "rememberers."

Soweit die Überlegungen zum Abbau von Sprachinseln allgemein und zum Phänomen des Sprachtodes in seiner bisherigen wissenschaftlichen Erschließung. Ich

22

werde jetzt auf dieser Grundlage paradigmatisch einige Sprachinselkonstellationen skizzieren, in denen sich Entwicklungstendenzen in Richtung auf die Kontaktsprache zeigen. Und abschließend werde ich dann versuchen, diese Exempel in den Zusammenhang eines "Sprachinsellebenslaufes" einzuordnen.

Beginnen wir unsere *tour d'horizont* über die Sprachinseln mit dem, was man mit Blick auf Nord- und Südamerika, aber auch auf Australien als den Normaltyp einer Sprachinselentwicklung nicht nur für deutschsprachige Siedlungen ansprechen kann: den durchweg ländlichen Charakter dieser Siedlungen. Städtische Sprachinseln gab es zumindest im 19. Jahrhundert durchaus. Sie unterliegen aber einem wesentlich schnelleren Akkulturationsprozess und folgen dabei auch anderen Entwicklungszügen (vgl. dazu Louden 2001, 14-16). Die ländlichen Sprachinseln, deren Entwicklung wir für einen Normaltyp von Sprachinseln ansehen, sind so gut wie alle bis zum 19. Jahrhundert im Zuge der großen—in erster Linie ökonomisch bedingten—Migrationsbewegung entstanden. Bei all diesen Sprachinseln spielen besondere konfessionsbedingte Lebensformen für die Sprach- und Kulturentwicklung keine Rolle. Diese Sprachinseln treten noch in ihrer Konsolidierungsphase, die etwa den Nachzug berücksichtigt, in einen komplexen sozialhistorischen Entwicklungsprozess ein, der bestimmt ist durch zwei gegeneinander wirkende Faktorenbündel, die einerseits die Assimilation und Akkulturation fördern, andererseits zur Erhaltung der Sprachinselkonstellation beitragen: die *language loss* und die *language-maintenance*-Faktoren. Auf die Differenzierungen innerhalb der Faktorenbündel, auf unterschiedliche Gewichtungen, auf ambivalenten Charakter und auch auf das Problem der objektiven und der subjektiven Faktoren soll hier nicht eingegangen werden. Für die Beschreibung der Entwicklungsprozesse der "Sozialgeschichte" einer Sprachinsel dieses Typs ist wichtig, dass sich die sozial- und sprachhistorischen Rahmenbedingungen, die in den Faktorenbündeln wirksam werden, nach Maßgabe der allgemeinen sozialhistorischen und historisch-politischen Entwicklungen wandeln, und zwar der historischen Entwicklungen nicht nur in der neuen Umgebungsgesellschaft, sondern auch im Mutterland der Sprachinseln. Das ist mit Blick auf andere Sprachinselkonstellationen durchaus ungewöhnlich. So wirkt sich die historische Entwicklung in Deutschland zwischen 1770 und 1900 sicherlich über lange Zeit nirgends in den russlanddeutschen Sprachinseln aus. Dagegen hatte die Nationalbewegung auf die Amerika-Auswanderer des 19. Jahrhunderts großen Einfluss.

Die Sprachinselgeschichte unseres Normaltyps zerfällt in zwei Phasen: in die Stabilitätsphase nach der Konsolidierung der Besiedlung und in die Assimilationsphase, die mit dem Sprachinseltod endet. Nur in der ersten Phase können wir im eigentlichen Sinn von Sprachinseln sprechen. Die ökonomischen und sozialen Netzwerke werden noch durch die autochthone Kultur/Sprache dominiert. Die Siedlungen neigen teilweise sogar zur ökonomischen und kulturellen Isolation. Die allochthonen sozialhistorischen Strukturen der Kontaktgesellschaft wirken sich in erster Linie deshalb nicht aus, weil sie überhaupt noch nicht vorhanden sind. So orientieren sich etwa die Lutheraner noch lange an deutschen Synoden, weil sich das amerikanische Synodenwesen erst im Laufe des Jahrhunderts bildete und konsolidierte. Und auch die verschiedenen Ebenen allochthonen administrativen Handelns (Schule usw.) greifen in den Regionen des Mittleren Westens erst in den letzten Jahrzehnten des 19. Jahrhunderts. Inwieweit sich auch das entstehende Nationalbewusstsein im Mutterland—etwa durch die 48er Bewegung und die Reichsgründung—auf einen autochthonen deutschen Nationalismus in den USA ausgewirkt hat, der wiederum eine angloamerikanische nationalistische Gegenreaktion ausgelöst hat, wird noch erforscht werden müssen. In jedem Fall werden solche Entwicklungen nicht auf dem Lande, sondern allenfalls in den deutschgeprägten städtischen Zentren Wisconsins und Minnesotas gegriffen haben.

Sprachlich und sprachsoziologisch haben wir in dieser statischen Phase mit folgenden Entwicklungen zu rechnen. Einmal baut sich bei einer Gruppe von Sprachinselbewohnern, die wir als "Vermittler" oder "gate keeper" bezeichnen könnten, eine Randkompetenz in der Kontaktsprache auf. Die eigentliche Sprachinsel bleibt jedoch durchaus auch in der zweiten Immigrantengeneration (der ersten dort Geborenen) noch monolingual in der autochthonen Sprache. Innerhalb dieser Sprachinselvarietät kommt es ansatzweise zu Ausgleichsentwicklungen, zur Bildung von überlokalen Verkehrsvarietäten. Die deutsche Standardsprache hat in den ländlichen Sprachinseln anfangs nur eine periphere Bedeutung. Gegen Ende des 19. Jahrhunderts nimmt sie an Bedeutung zu, da auch der Alphabetisierungsgrad zunimmt. Sie wird jedoch weitgehend ausschließlich im Schriftsprachigen verwendet, worüber die vielen überlieferten Auswandererbriefe des 19. Jahrhunderts Auskunft geben (Macha 1994). Berichtet wird darüber, dass Sprachinseln mit verschiedenen autochthonen Sprachen, wie etwa das Norwegische und das Deutsche, sich schon früh des Englischen als lingua franca bedienten (Haugen 1989).

Die durch Sprachinselstabilität gekennzeichnete Phase der Entwicklung wird um die Jahrhundertwende zum 20. Jahrhundert abgelöst durch eine Assimilations- oder auch Akkulturationsphase. Diese Phase wird häufig mit den Wirkungen des I. Weltkrieges in Verbindung gebracht, die besonders die Sprachinseln mit "der Sprache des Gegners" betroffen haben. Doch gibt etwa Einar Haugen in seiner Geschichte der Norweger in den USA Hinweise darauf, dass die Konstellation wohl komplexer sein muss. Er weist nämlich für die Gruppe der Norweger ganz ähnliche Entwicklungen nach wie für die Deutschen. Es müssen also noch andere Faktoren als das Feindmotiv von Bedeutung gewesen sein. Am ehesten ist dabei zu denken an das sich allgemein im 19. Jahrhundert und in den USA insbesondere in den letzten Jahrzehnten ausbildende angelsächsisch geprägte Nationalbewusstsein, das auch von allen nicht Englisch Sprechenden eine Integration in die amerikanische Leitkultur verlangte. Weiterhin haben wir um die Jahrhundertwende mit einem Ausbau der allgemeinen administrativen, sozialen und ökonomischen Struktur in der Kontaktgesellschaft zu rechnen. In diesem Zusammenhang ist etwa der Aufbau des amerikanischen Schulsystems zu nennen, das überall die im Entstehen begriffenen Ansätze für ein autochthones Schulsystem weitgehend zerstörte. Die Wirkungen der beiden Weltkriege kamen zu diesen schon ins 19. Jahrhundert verweisenden Entwicklungen hinzu. Die Entwicklung, die in dieser Assimilationsphase in den Sprachinseln des Normaltyps anläuft, zeigt überall eine ähnliche Struktur. Auf kontaktlinguistischer Ebene haben wir es mit einem Abbau der autochthonen Sprachinselvarietät und der Hochdeutschkenntnisse, soweit vorhanden, zu tun, über dessen linguistisch/ kontaktlinguistischer Charakter die Meinungen durchaus noch auseinandergehen. Mit einer einfachen Reduktions- oder Simplifikationsthese kommt man, das zeigen neuere Untersuchungen, wohl nicht sehr weit. Auch ist offen, ob es etwas wie saliente Merkmale gibt, die eher abgebaut werden als andere. Und insbesondere wissen wir noch wenig über die Integration von kontaktsprachigem Sprachgut und die Regelhaftigkeiten, denen dieser Prozess folgt.

Soziolinguistisch wird man den Verdrängungsprozess der autochthonen Varietät, nach dem die Kontaktsprachenkompetenz aufgebaut ist, mindestens nach drei oder vier Dimensionen getrennt untersuchen müssen, von denen schon die Rede war: diastratisch nach den progressiven und retardiven gesellschaftlichen Gruppierungen, diaphasisch nach den jeweiligen Sprachsituationen bzw. Sprachfunktionen, aber auch diatopisch hinsichtlich des jeweiligen Grades der Ländlichkeit und diamesisch nach den in den Medien Schriftlichkeit und Mündlichkeit verwendeten Varietäten. Am Ende steht dann eine tote Sprachinsel. Es gibt nur noch wenige ältere Sprecher in ländlichen Regionen, die jedoch über die Sprache—nur selten noch fließend—meist auf "semi-speaker" Niveau verfügen. Oftmals handelt es sich schon um die berüchtigten Altenheim-Sprachinseln, von denen auch Clyne für Australien spricht (Clyne 1994). Es gibt keine regelmäßig auftretenden Sprechsituationen für die autochthone Varietät mehr. Folkloristische Versuche zur Belebung der Sprachlichkeit scheitern meist, indem man den heimatlichen Identitätsbereich der Kontaktsprache öffnet. Sprachinseln sind hier eher Folkloreinseln oder Kulturinseln, in denen jedoch die autochthone Sprache keine Rolle spielt. Ansatzpunkte zu einer Umkehr des Verfallsprozesses gibt es selbst in Gemeinden mit starken folkloristischen Interessen—wie etwa dem Oktoberfest in Frankenmuth, Michigan—auf die Dauer nicht (Born 1994).

Ich werde nun in wenigen Strichen einige Varianten zu diesem Normaltyp von Sprachinselentwicklungen skizzieren. Da sind einmal die älteren Sprachinseln, die nicht erst im Zuge der allgemeinen Migrationsbewegung im 19. Jahrhundert entstanden sind, also Pennsylvania, Russland, Ungarn aus dem 18. Jahrhundert, oder auch noch ältere Sprachinseln wie etwa Siebenbürgen, wo die deutsche Besiedlung bis ins 13. Jahrhundert zurückreicht (vgl. Scheiner 1896/1971). Alle diese Sprachinseln weisen erheblich längere Stabilitätsphasen auf als der Normaltyp. Eine weitere und noch interessantere Gemeinsamkeit ist die lange Entwicklung dieser Sprachinseln ohne eine schon ausgestaltete deutsche Standardsprache als Orientierungspunkt für die sprachliche Entwicklung. Das führt bei solchen Sprachinseltypen zur Ausbildung von charakteristischen Ausgleichsvarietäten, die als eigentlicher Standardvarietätenersatz angesehen werden. Auf diese Weise entstehen das Pennsylvaniadeutsch, aber auch das Siebenbürgische und die verschiedenen ungarischen und russlanddeutschen Ausgleichssprachen, für deren Entwicklung Viktor Schirmunski (jetzt in 1992) oder Claus J. Hutterer soziolinguistische und linguistische Entwicklungsmodelle vorgeschlagen haben.

Eine weitere Entwicklungsvariante von Sprachinseln findet sich etwa in Ungarn, aber auch in Westpolen/Schlesien, in Rumänien und in Südafrika. Diese Sprachinseln haben gemeinsam, dass sich innerhalb des Varietätenspektrums der autochthonen Sprache Verschiebungen zeigen. In diesen Sprachinseln herrschten ursprünglich Immigrantendialekte vor, so in Ungarn etwa im Bergland bairische Dialekte und in der schwäbischen Türkei osthessisch-fuldische Dialekte (Bassola 1995). Seit den 1950er Jahren gehen diese Dialekte, wie alle Dialekte in den europäischen Industrienationen, verloren. Sie werden in erster Linie durch das Ungarische als Kontaktsprache ersetzt, was zur Assimilation führt. Es gibt aber auch eine Tendenz zum Ausbau des Hochdeutschen, die insbesondere über das ausgezeichnete Minderheitenschulwesen abläuft. Und diese Hochdeutschvarietät wird zumindest durch zwei Faktoren gestützt: einmal ist das Deutsche unter ökonomischen Gesichtspunkten in diesen Regionen von Bedeutung—man kann damit Geld verdienen. Wichtiger ist aber vielleicht, dass das Deutsche auch in der jüngeren Generation als Indiz für die ansonsten nicht mehr vorhandene deutsche Identität angesehen und auch gepflegt wird. Ob diese doppelte Absicherung jedoch ausreichen wird, das Hochdeutsche als Zweitsprache neben dem Ungarischen zu sichern, ist noch nicht zu entscheiden. Auch in den anderen genannten Sprachinselregionen, also in Südafrika, in Polen und in Siebenbürgen, aber auch in Chile tritt an die Stelle der deutschstämmigen Sprachinseldialekte die deutsche Standardsprache.

Eine ganz besondere und bisher selten beobachtete Form von Sprachinseltod und Sprachinselgenese kann man seit ca. 10 bis 15 Jahren in Europa verfolgen: den Sprachinseltod durch Wegwanderung und die Bildung von sprachinselähnlichen Gebilden in den Aufnahmegebieten der Rückwanderer. Sprachinseltod durch Wegzug gibt es insbesondere in Rumänien und in Russland. In Rumänien steht dieser Prozess kurz vor dem Abschluss und es gibt keinerlei Anstrengungen, eine solche Entwicklung zu verhindern. In Russland ist auch schon eine große Anzahl von Sprachinseln durch Wegzug aufgelöst worden. Und ob dort Sprachinseln deutscher Herkunft erhalten bleiben, ist unklar. In der Sprachheimat Deutschland werden diese Rückwanderer grundsätzlich, auch juristisch abgesichert, aufgenommen. Rumäniendeutsche ziehen jedoch in der Regel nicht in Siedlungsgemeinschaften, sondern assimilieren sich schnell an die Kontaktgesellschaft. Russlanddeutsche bringen neben einer teilweise schwachen

Kompetenz in Russlanddeutsch oftmals eine gute in Russisch und fast nie eine in Hochdeutsch mit. Was sich hier an Entwicklungen ergibt, hat Nina Berend (1998) vor einigen Jahren gezeigt. Es gibt keinen Ausbau des Russlanddeutschen, selbst in einer Region, die dialektale Ähnlichkeiten mit der jeweiligen russlanddeutschen Dialektgruppe aufweist. Dagegen wird das Hochdeutsche oftmals mit einem russischen Akzent ausgebaut, und was überraschend ist, wird das Russische als gruppeninterne Alltagssprache weiterverwendet. Ob diese Tendenzen der nächsten Generation erhalten bleiben, ist unklar.

Während wir uns bis jetzt nur mit Modellen des Sprachinseltodes beschäftigt haben, werden wir nun einen kurzen Blick auf Fälle richten, in denen die Sprachinsel nicht stirbt, sondern erhalten bleibt. Für deutschstämmige Sprachinseln lassen sich hier vier nennen: das Hunsrückisch in Brasilien, der bairische Dialekt der Hutterer in den USA und Canada, das Pennsylvaniadeutsch der OOA und der OOM in den USA und evtl. auch noch das Plautdietsch der konservativen Mennoniten in verschiedenen Weltgegenden. Bei den konfessionell bedingten Sprachinseln, also den konservativen Mennoniten, den Hutterern und den Amischen, ist die besondere Sprachlichkeit natürlich durch die konfessionelle Bindung und ihre gesellschaftlichen Implikationen festgelegt. Bei den pennsylvaniadeutschsprechenden Sprachinseln wird sich dieser Faktor in der kommenden Generation wahrscheinlich noch verschärfen, wenn alle Nichtsektierer das Pennsylvaniadeutsch aufgegeben haben, so dass es ausschließlich Konfessionsmerkmal ist, wie bei den Hutterern und den konservativen Mennoniten. Das Hunsrückische in Südbrasilien ist eine weitgehend stabile Sprachinsel aufgrund der ökonomischen und auch administrativen Isolation und des extrem ländlichen Charakters der deutschstämmigen Bevölkerung, wie übrigens auch bei italienischen Nachbarsprachinseln (Damke 1997).

Ich werde meinen Beitrag mit einer kurzen Zusammenfassung schließen, einer Zusammenfassung in Form einer Modellskizze des Lebenslaufes von Sprachinseln. Der Lebenslauf einer Sprachinsel beginnt mit der Bildungsphase, die in der Regel in Zusammenhang mit bedeutsamen allgemein- oder sozialhistorischen Prozessen steht. Die Migrationstheorie unterscheidet hier sozio-ökonomisch bedingte Migration, von konfessionell-weltanschaulich bedingter sowie ethnisch-nationaler und schließlich kriegsbedingter Migration. Die Bildungsphase einer Sprachinsel ist im allgemeinen abgeschlossen, wenn Nachzüge in größerem Ausmaß aufhören. Es beginnt dann eine Konsolidierungsphase, in der die oftmals aus verschiedenen Herkunftsgebieten stammenden Sprachinselbewohner durch Mischungs-, Angleichungs- und Ausgleichsprozesse zu einer Sprachinsel zusammenwachsen, eine eigene Identität entwickeln, die meist über die besondere Sprachlichkeit symbolisiert wird. Es folgt dann die Stabilitätsphase einer Sprachinsel, eine Phase, in der der Kontakt mit der Umgebungssprache und Umgebungskultur stabil ist, und in der sich in vielen Fällen weitere eigene kulturelle und auch gemeinsame sprachliche Eigenheiten bilden. Die

Entwurf eines Sprachinsel-Lebenslaufmodells

Ausgangskonstellation ◄── soziohistorische Entwicklungen, die
      │   Bevölkerungsbewegungen in größerem Ausmaß auslösen
      ↓

                     Migrationsphase
Konstituierungsphase
einer Sprachinsel   gruppenhafte Ansiedlung (wobei die Gruppen sich
      │   teilweise erst in der Migrationsphase bilden)
      ↓

Konsolidierungsphase   linguistische Mischungs-, Angleichungs- bzw.
                    Ausgleichsprozesse; soziolinguistischer Abschluss der
                    Gruppenbildungsphase (Integration von Nachwanderern);
      │   Ausbildung einer Gruppenidentität bzw. Anpassung der
      │   mitgebrachten Gruppenidentität an die neue Umgebung

      │   kommt es nicht zur Identitatsbildung, muß man
      │   mit schneller Assimilation rechnen
      ↓

Stabilitätsphase   es gibt keine oder nur minimale Sprachverlustfaktoren
      │
      │   von dieser Phase aus kann es auch zu
      │   Sprachausbreitungsprozessen (language spread)
      │   kommt
      ↓

Zwischen der Stabilitätsphase und der Assimilationsphase muss es in der Sprachinsel
oder in ihrer Umgebung zu einer soziokulturellen Wandlung kommen.

                     Umschlagpunkt

Assimilationsphase   oftmals in Form eines nachgeholten
      │   Dreigenerationen-Assimilationsprozesses
      │
      │   Sprachinselverfall
      ↓

Sprachinseltod   Spätphasen einer Sprachinsel sind die Kulturinsel oder
                     auch die Touristenattraktion

Dauer dieser Phase kann sehr unterschiedlich sein, wenn man einerseits etwa an das Jahrhunderte alte Siebenbürgen denkt und andererseits an die russlanddeutsche Sprachinsel in Topeka, Kansas die erst nach der Jahrhundertwende entstanden ist. In dieser Phase der Entwicklung eines Sprachinsellebenslaufes gibt es noch eine andere Entwicklungsmöglichkeit. So hat sich etwa in den Niederländisch sprechenden Sprachinseln am Kap der Guten Hoffnung im 18. und 19. Jahrhundert in Auseinandersetzung mit den Umgebungs- bzw. Überdachungssprachen eine neue Varietät, das Afrikaans, herausgebildet. Dieses Afrikaans ist jedoch keine Sprachinselsprache geblieben, sondern hat sich aufgrund bestimmter sozialhistorischer Prozesse ausgebreitet bis zu einer eigenen Nationalsprache. Hier haben wir nicht *language-loss* und auch nicht *language-maintenance*, sondern *language-spread* (Cooper 1982) vor uns. Und wir müssen uns wohl auf die Ausbreitung des Englischen in den USA über weite Regionen als einen *language-spread*-Prozess vorstellen, der jeweils ausgeht von einzelnen englischen Sprachinseln in andersprachigen Umgebungsgesellschaften.

Wenig weiß man bisher über den Umschlagpunkt, an dem eine stabile Sprachinselkonstellation übergeht in die Verfallsphase, in der sich die meisten deutschstämmigen Sprachinseln heute befinden. Sicherlich wird man durchgehend feststellen können, dass vorhandene isolationistische Tendenzen innerhalb der Sprachinseln abgebaut werden. Die allgemeine gesellschaftliche Modernisierung, die alle Gesellschaften seit dem 20. Jahrhundert umstrukturiert, führt in Sprachinseln in der Regel zu einer Assimilation an die Umgebungsgesellschaft. Hinzu kommen jedoch in der Regel noch spezielle sozialhistorische Entwicklungen, wie in den USA und Canada etwa die Entwicklung eines eigenen Nationalismus und die administrative Durchorganisierung des Landes. Und drittens muss man mit punktuellen historischen Prozessen, wie etwa den Weltkriegen, rechnen, die nicht nur in den USA und Canada von entscheidender Bedeutung für die Zurückdrängung des Deutschen waren.

Der Abbauprozess der Sprachinsel und ihrer Sprache selbst erfolgt nach den oben skizzierten Modellen, die bisher noch keineswegs erforscht sind. Wann wir im Verlauf dieses Ersetzungsprozesses der autochthonen Sprachlichkeit durch die der Kontaktgesellschaft vom Tod der Sprachinsel sprechen können, ist gar nicht leicht festzulegen. In den Altenheim-Sprachgemeinschaften, wie sie Michael Clyne schildert und wie sie auch in Kansas beobachtet werden können, finden sich noch Reste von aktivem, kommunikativem Handeln auch dann, wenn nur noch "jokes" in der alten Sprache gemacht werden. Wenn nur noch "rememberer" leben, die von Forschern aktiviert werden, dann ist die Todeslinie wohl überschritten. Doch bleibt nach dem Tode einer Sprachinsel oftmals die Kulturinsel und teilweise auch eine Tourismusinsel noch lange erhalten. Und auch sprachliche Substrate aus der Sprachinselsprache halten sich noch lange (vgl. hier Kopp). Ganz am Ende der Entwicklung werden wir nur noch quasi archäologische Reste der Inseln auf den Friedhöfen und im Namensschatz finden. Dann, eines Tages, wird der letzte oder die letzte sterben, die noch etwas von Sprachinseln wussten, erst dann ist eine Sprachinsel endgültig tot.

Literatur

Andersen, R. 1982."Determining the Linguistic Attributes of Language Attrition." In *The Loss of Language Skills*, hrsg. R. Lambert und B. Freed, 83-118. Newbury House, Rowley, MA.

Bassola, Peter. 1995. *Deutsch in Ungarn in Geschichte und Gegenwart.* Heidelberg.

Berend, Nina. 1998. *Sprachliche Anpassung: Eine soziolinguistisch-dialektologische Untersuchung zum Russlanddeutschen.* Tübingen.

Betten, Anne. 2000."'Vielleicht sind wir wirklich die einzigen Erben der Weimarer Kultur': Einleitende Bemerkungen zur Forschungshypothese 'Bildungsbürgerdeutsch in Israel' und zu den Beiträgen dieses Bandes." In *Sprachbewahrung nach der Emigration–Das Deutsch der 20er Jahre in Israel. Teil 1, Band 2: Analysen und Dokumente,* hrsg. Anne Betten und Miryam Du-nour Miryam, 157-80. Tübingen.

Born, Renate. 1994. *Michian German in Frankenmuth: Variation and Change in an East Franconian Dialect.* Columbia, SC: Camden House.

Campbell, Lyle, und Muntzel, Martha C. 1989. "The Structural Consequences of Language Death. In *Investigating Obsolescence: Studies in Language Contraction and Death,* hrsg. Nancy Dorian, 181-96. Cambridge: Cambridge University Press.

Clyne, Michael. 1994. "What Can We Learn from Sprachinseln?: Some Observations on 'Australian German.'" In *Sprachinselforschung,* hrsg. Nina Berend und Klaus J. Mattheier, 105-22. Frankfurt.

Cooper, Robert L., hrsg. 1982. *Language Spread: Studies in Diffusion and Social Change.* Bloomington: Indiana University Press.

Damke, Ciro. 1997. *Sprachgebrauch und Sprachkontakt in der deutschen Sprachinsel in Südbrasilien.* Frankfurt.

Dorian, Nancy. 1981. *Language Death: The Life Cycle of a Scottish Gaelic Dialect.* Philadelphia, University of Pennsylvania Press.

Dorian, Nancy, hrsg. 1989. *Investigating Obsolescence: Studies in Language Contraction and Death.* Cambridge: Cambridge University Press.

Edwards, John. 1990."Notes for a Minority-Language Typology: Procedures and Justification."*Journal of Multilingual and Multicultural Development* 11: 137-51.

Egger, Kurt, und Frank Lanthaler, hrsg. 2001. *Die deutsche Sprache in Südtirol.* Einheitssprache und regionale Vielfalt. Wien.

Gonzo, Susan, und Mario Saltarelli. 1979. "Pidginization and Linguistic Change in Emigrant Languages." Paper presented at the Symposium on the Relationsship between Pidginization, Creolization and Language Acquisition, LSA Annual Meeting.

Haugen, Einar, Derrick J. Mc Clure, Derrick Thompson, hrsg. 1981. *Minority Languages Today.* Edinburgh: Edinburgh University Press.

Haugen, Einar. 1989. "The Rise and Fall of an Immigrant Language: Norwegian in America." In *Investigating Obsolescence. Studies in Language Contraction and Death*, hrsg., Nancy C. Dorian, 62-73. Cambridge.

Kaufmann, Göz. 1997. *Varietätendynamik in Sprachkontaktsituationen: Attitüden und Sprachverhalten rußlanddeutscher Mennoniten in Mexiko und den USA*. Variolingua Bd. 3. Frankfurt.

Kopp, Achim. 1999. *The Phonology of Pennsylvania German English as Evidence of Language Maintenance and Shift*. Selingsgrove, Susquehanna University Press.

Louden, Mark L. 2001. "The Development of Pennsylvania German Linguistics Within the Context of German Dialectology and Linguistic Theory." In Seifert, Lester, W. J., *A Word Atlas of Pennsylvania German*, hrsg. Mark L. Louden, Howard Martin und Joseph C. Salmons, 7-52. Madison, University of Wisconsin Press.

Macha, Jürgen. 1994. "'... ich will nich Ueber Ammireka nicht stronsen...': Briefe von Eifel- Auswanderern als sprachhistorische Quelle." In *Geschichtliche Landeskunde: Regionale Befunde und raumübergreifende Perspektiven: Georg Droege zum Gedenken*, hrsg. Marlene Nikolay-Panter u.a., 516-33. Köln.

Mattheier, Klaus J.1993."Sprachinselsoziolinguistik: Beobachtungen und Überlegungen an deutschsprachigen Sprachinseln." In *The German Language in America 1683-1991*, hrsg. Joseph C. Salmons, 38-61. Madison Wisconsin.

Mattheier, Klaus J. 1994. Theorie der Sprachinsel: Voraussetzungen und Strukturierungen. In *Sprachinselforschung: Eine Gedenkschrift für Hugo Jedig*, hrsg. Nina Berend und Klaus J. Mattheier, 333-48. Frankfurt.

Mertens, Birgit. 1994. *Vom (Nieder-)Deutschen zum Englischen: Untersuchungen zur sprachlichen Assimilation einer ländlichen Gemeinde im mittleren Westen Amerikas*. Heidelberg.

Moag, Rodney. 1977. *Fiji Hindi*. Canberra Australian National University Press.

Scheiner, A. 1896. *Die Mundart der Siebenbürger Sachsen*. Stuttgart; 2. Aufl., Wiesbaden, 1971.

Schirmunski, Viktor M. 1992. *Linguistische und Ethnographische Studien 1926-1931*, hrsg., von Claus J. Hutterer. München.

Seliger, Herbert und Robert M. Vago, Hrsg. 1989. *First Language Attrition*. Cambridge, Cambridge University Press.

Thomason, Sarah Grey, und Terrence Kaufman. 1988. *Language Contact, Creolization and Genetic Linguistics*. Berkeley: University Press of California.

Ludwig M. Eichinger
Institut für Deutsche Sprache
Mannheim, Germany

Der unexotische Blick auf das Fremde: Soziolinguistische Überlegungen zu Datenerhebung und -interpretation

1. Plan

Die Erforschung von deutschen Sprachinseln bringt einen als Forscher aus dem historischen "Mutterland" der Vorfahren dieser Sprecher in eine kulturelle Differenz ganz spezifischer Art. Ich spreche hier nicht nur abstrakt, sondern konkret auch von den Erfahrungen bei einigen Erhebungsaufenthalten im "Big Valley"/Pennsylvania, das durch die weitgehende Besiedlung durch Amische der Alten Ordnung gekennzeichnet ist.

Es weht einen der Hauch einer längs vergangenen Gegenwart an, die einem vertraut und fremd zugleich ist.[1] Es ist, als wäre ein Stück der eigenen Vergangenheit in eine Umgebung gesetzt, die ihrerseits als die Speerspitze der zivilisatorischen Entwicklung auf dieser Welt gilt.

Wenn man nicht willens ist, ob dieser Diskrepanzen einfach ärgerlich zu sein, das Beharren auf der eigenen ungleichzeitigen Kultur als unaufgeklärtes Bewusstsein bei Seite zu schieben, dann hat man zwei Optionen. Entweder hat man den Zoo-Effekt zu gewärtigen. Man bestaunt eine merkwürdige Population, die zur Unterhaltung des modernen Menschen aufgefahren wird. Sehen möchte man etwas, was der Religionsersatz des modernen Menschen darstellt, die Natur. Dass hier mit Zwang die Momente des zivilisatorischen Fortschritts vor der Tür gehalten werden, wird zu einer Geschichte stilisiert, die von Natürlichkeit handelt. Das ist natürlich paradox, hat aber gute Tradition. Auch die ganzen Traditionen eines einfachen Landlebens, die in Europa gepflegt werden, sind Konstruktionen über der Realität des 19. Jahrhunderts, als die Städter in größerer Menge aufzutreten begannen, und überhaupt erst ein Blick auf das Land geworfen wurde. Der Reiz der Exotik ist eine Fiktion, weniger provokant vielleicht: das Ergebnis einer kulturell verträglichen Konstruktion.

Daher hat man als Wissenschaftler nur die Alternative, das gesellschaftliche Symbolisierungssystem in seinem internen Funktionieren und in seiner Einbettung in die dieses System begrenzende Umgebung zu analysieren. Nun ist es aber bekanntlich schwer, jenen Standpunkt außerhalb der beobachteten Welt zu finden, der einem erlaubt, einen gerechten Blick auf diese Objekte des wissenschaftlichen Interesses zu werfen. Wenn sowohl die internen wie die externen Strukturen nach ungewohnten

Regeln verlaufen, ist es schwer, sich eine andere als die Meinung zu bilden, die einem die eigenen Vorurteile nahe legen. Wiewohl man nicht leugnen wird, dass jeder Typ von gesellschaftlicher Interaktion letztlich in Übereinkünften über die objektive Realität ihre Grenzen findet, bleibt trotzdem wahr, dass wir uns in der Kommunikation zunächst auf der Ebene normativer Festlegungen und Berechtigungen der Erfassung der Welt annähern. Das gilt viel grundlegender als man gemeinhin denkt: das Funktionieren einer kommunikativen Gemeinschaft ist immer eine Systemstabilisierung im Hinblick auf benachbarte und übergeordnete Optionen. Daher bekommen Verhaltensweisen, die ursprünglich einen anderen Sinn hatten, nun einen neuen symbolischen Wert— und das gerade deshalb, weil die Gruppen, um die es uns geht, ihre Lebens- und Sprechweise kaum als historisch verstehen können. Es gibt eigentlich keine Möglichkeit zum Wandel. Wenn alles gottgewollt und gut ist, so wie es ist, dann kann jeder Wandel nur Verschlechterung und Verfall sein. Für den Beobachter kann das natürlich nicht gelten. Wie kann man die historische Entwicklung nicht vergessen und trotzdem das gegenwärtige System aus sich beschreiben? Was kann daraus soziolinguistisch werden?

2. Der amerikanische und der europäische Blick

Soziolinguisten können sich zweifellos für verschiedene Dinge interessieren: im Kern geht es ihnen jedenfalls um die Feststellung sprachlicher Variation unter gesellschaftlichen, bei unserem Beispiel vielleicht wirklich besser: sozialen, Bedingungen. Sozialen Bedingungen vielleicht deshalb, weil die Konzeptualisierungen im öffentlichen Leben der Gemeinschaften, von denen wir hier sprechen, weniger in einem abstrakten europäischen Sinn als gesellschaftliche Beziehungen zu fassen sind, sondern dem unter den Bedingungen der US-amerikanischen Demokratie entwickelten Geflecht von Gruppenbeziehungen entsprechen.

Von früh auf ist das amerikanische Modell vom Empirismus geprägt, während das kontinentaleuropäische Modell mit rationalistischen Deduktionen zur Volkssouveränität brilliert (cf. Sartori 1992, 60ff.). Entsprechend sind auch die zentralen Begriffe eines demokratischen Selbstverständnisses unterschiedlich gelagert: in beiden Fällen handelt es sich zwar um die Fahnenwörter der Französischen Revolution, Freiheit, Gleichheit und Brüderlichkeit. Im amerikanischen Selbstverständnis sind, wie als erster Alexis des Tocqueville erstaunt bemerkt hat, aber Freiheit und Brüderlichkeit in gewisser Weise Epiphänomene der Gleichheit. Dabei geht es logischerweise nicht um eine Gleichheit der Ergebnisse, denn natürlich gibt es reichere und ärmere, einflussreichere und unbedeutendere Mitglieder der Gesellschaft.

Gleichheit meint vielmehr zwei andere Dinge: zum einen sozusagen die gleiche Differenz zum Gegenpol des Individuums, der Regierung, und zum zweiten die Gleichheit der Möglichkeiten ("equality of opportunities"). Vor allem diese zweite Konzeption führt unmittelbar zu einem entsprechenden Freiheitsbegriff, der nicht so sehr die Freiheit von Unterdrückung in einem nicht demokratischen System meint, was ja nicht das Problem der USA ist, sondern die Freiheit des Individuums zu seiner—nicht zuletzt wirtschaftlichen, Entfaltung ("pursuit of happiness") Ein solches Verständnis dieser beiden Konzeptionen lässt die Brüderlichkeit aus dem öffentlichen Raum zurücktreten, verweist sie auf die kleinräumigeren Aggregationen innerhalb des politischen Aufbaus. Diese Idee, die ja so direkt auf in sich geschlossene Gemeinschaften wie die *Old Order Amish* zu passen scheint, betrifft tatsächlich das Aussehen der Gesellschaft als Ganzer, wie die Auseinandersetzung zwischen Libertarians und *Communitarians* im letzten Jahrzehnt nachdrücklich gezeigt hat, wo die Frage nach den Grenzen der Variationsmöglichkeiten und den Voraussetzungen von gemeinsamen Bindungen ins Zentrum des Interesses geriet (cf. Taylor 1995).

Denn in der liberalistischen Organisation des US-amerikanischen Staatswesens hat die Vielfalt gesellschaftlicher und ethnischer Gruppen, die nebeneinander leben, einen wichtigen Platz. Von Anfang an erscheint die Vielfalt aufgrund der hohen Disparatheit der Herkunftskulturen jener Menschen, die USA bilden sollten, als Garant für einen letztlich doch vernünftigen Ausgleich des Ganzen, jenes Ganzen, das sich im Zentrum der Regierungshauptstadt Washington bündelt und das seinerseits dafür die Staaten und auch die Gemeinden weitgehend unbehelligt lässt. In jener polemischen Auseinandersetzung um die amerikanische Verfassung, die sich in den 1787 und 1788 erschienenen *Federalist Papers* von Alexander Hamilton, James Madison und John Jay niederschlägt, liegt "Entwurf und Rechtfertigung eines politischen Systems [vor], das liberal nur noch den institutionellen Rahmen für individuelles Glücksstreben vorgibt" (Zehnpfennig 1993, 1). Dort heißt es von der "Föderativen Republik der Vereinigten Staaten":

> Während sich hier alle Autorität von der Gesellschaft ableitet und von ihr abhängig ist, ist die Gesellschaft selbst in so viele Teile, Interessen und Schichten von Bürgern aufgesplittert, daß den Rechten Einzelner oder der Minderheit nur wenig Gefahr von Interessenzusammenschlüssen der Mehrheit droht. In einer freiheitlichen politischen Ordnung muß die Sicherung für bürgerliche Rechte dieselbe sein, wie für religiöse Rechte. Im einen Fall besteht sie in der Vielfalt der Interessen und im anderen in der Vielfalt religiöser Sekten. Der Grad der Sicherheit hängt in beiden Fällen von der Anzahl der Interessen und Sekten ab; und diese Anzahl wiederum wird vermutlich von der Ausdehnung des Landes und der Zahl der Menschen abhängen, die unter derselben Regierung zusammengefaßt sind. (*Federalist Papers* 1993, 322)

Dieser Text stammt aus der Zeit der amerikanischen Revolution. Schon weit vorher hatte William Penn das seine dazu getan, um zumindest einen erheblichen Teil religiöser Vielfalt in dem von ihm besiedelten Pennsylvania zu implantieren und gleichzeitig durch "Peuplierung" (vgl. Wehler 1987, 348) das Gebiet Pennsylvanias wirtschaftlich nutzbar zu machen.

Zum Kontrast ist noch darauf hinzuweisen, dass die so entstehende, ja geförderte religiöse Vielfalt im strikten Widerstreit zu den religiösen und staatlichen Verhältnissen in Europa steht, wo Tendenzen der Gleichordnung von Konfession und politischer Organisation zu den leitenden Entwicklungen im 17. Jahrhundert geworden waren. Dadurch war der Druck auf weniger "staatsnahe" Konfessionen erheblich, welche diese "Konfessionalisierung" (vgl. Schilling 1991) nicht mittragen können und wollen.

Man kann aus diesen Voraussetzungen schon ableiten, dass und warum traditionelle normative Gesichtspunkte unter diesen Voraussetzungen zumindest theoretisch kaum eine Rolle spielen können. Es geht nicht darum, wie man möglicherweise abstrakt die widerstreitenden Interessen ausgleichen und Erscheinungsformen angleichen könnte, vielmehr geht es um einen Modus, um ihr Miteinanderleben zu organisieren. Das hat sprachlich zur Folge, dass eigentlich kein Homogenisierungsdruck auf die beteiligten Gruppen ausgeübt wird. Der Druck in Richtung einer Mehrheitsnorm wird eher dadurch erzeugt, dass ihre Befolgung im individuellen Vorteil liegt oder zumindest zu liegen scheint. Die in der alltäglichen gesellschaftlichen Praxis liegenden Regeln sollen durch ihren Erfolg zur Entwicklung entsprechender normativer Konzepte führen.

Diese Konstellationen sind natürlich auch die ideale Voraussetzungen dafür, dass sich zusammenhängende kleine Gruppen, die ihre Individualitäten großenteils als Gruppenidentität verstehen, und ihre Konzepte von Brüderlichkeit im sozialen Netzwerk der eigenen Gruppe aufheben, als idealer Bestandteil einer solchen Gesellschaft verstehen können. In der europäischen Konzeption stehen solche Gruppen unter einem wesentlich höheren Öffnungsdruck. Das hat damit zu tun, dass sich in den USA der Bürger innerstaatlich eher als Gegenpol der Regierung versteht, während im kontinentaleuropäischen System eine starke Konvergenz von Staat und Gesellschaft besteht, so dass die Menge der Bürger den Staat darstellt und lediglich seine Vertretung an die Politiker delegiert.

Von daher wird auch davon ausgegangen, dass sich gemeinsame Symbolisierungsformen finden, in denen die Bürger sich wiedererkennen. Das macht bei aller Vielgestaltigkeit im Einzelnen das gesamte Bild der europäischen Staaten doch homogener. Das ganz Andere begegnet einem kaum. Und durch die Jahrhunderte langen Traditionen des Zusammen- oder Nebeneinanderlebens stellen sich auch feste Bilder dessen ein, was man voneinander zu erwarten hat. Höhere Distanz wird als altertümlich, als merkwürdig empfunden, eine soziale Interpretation von Ungleichheit gilt nicht als in irgendeiner Weise sekundär, sie ist vielmehr der Aufruf zu Aktivitäten öffentlicher Wohlfahrt. Die Individualisierung wird hier erkauft durch die Delegation der Brüderlichkeitsanforderungen an die Gesellschaft.

3. Und Minderheiten

Was hilft uns das, wenn wir uns an die Sprachinsel als eine sinnhafte und sinnvolle Einheit des symbolischen Lebens annähern wollen? Wir können jedenfalls nicht darüber hinweg sehen, dass bei gleichen Sachverhalten einem vergleichbaren symbolischen Verhalten ein unterschiedlicher Sinn zuzuschreiben ist, so dass sie einem unterschiedlichen Geflecht normativ fundierter Behauptungen entsprechen und dass diese Behauptungen in ein unterschiedliches Netz inferentieller Beziehungen eingebunden sind. Es sind nicht dieselben Behauptungen, die als Gründe und als Folgen normativer Behauptungen verstanden werden. Daraus ergeben sich Aufgaben für die wissenschaftliche Beobachtung, Aufgaben dahingehend, die Alterität der anderen Symbolwelt nicht wegzuerklären, aber dennoch interpretative Geschichten von innen und von außen zu rekonstruieren, um so der Lage der Sprachinsel als einer sozialen Entität, und nicht einer Sprache äußernden Maschine, Rechnung zu tragen. Daher ist auch bei den Methoden der Erhebung darauf zu achten, welchen Teil des symbolischen Gefüges sie eigentlich zu untersuchen unternehmen.

Wir können dabei unterscheiden zwischen dem Vorgehen in einer exploratorischen Phase und dem Vorgehen im Zentrum der Untersuchung: das macht logischerweise für den sachlichen Informationsstand und für die soziale Akzeptiertheit des Forschers einen entscheidenden Unterschied.

In der exploratorischen Phase wird man zunächst einmal versuchen, alles zu lesen zu bekommen, was es zu dem untersuchten Objekt zu lesen gibt. Dabei steht man als jemand, der sich mit der sozialen Interaktion der Amischen der Alten Ordnung beschäftigt, in einem methodischen Dilemma. Viele der Publikationen sind entweder aus einer Insider-Perspektive geschrieben oder sie tragen zur Folklorisierung der fremden Erscheinungen bei. Wer das nicht glaubt, sollte bei einer der gängigen Internet-Suchmaschinen das Stichwort "Amish" eingeben. Ein dritter Teil ist einem Typus der Wissenschaftlichkeit verpflichtet, der soziale Phänomene allenfalls als Störfaktoren in den Griff bekommt. Viele dialektologisch, aber auch strukturell orientierte linguistische Untersuchungen sind von dieser Art.

Bei allen drei Arten von Publikationen ist Vorsicht geboten. Bei den ersten beiden Typen steht ein häufig unzuträglicher Grad an Empathie der Intersubjektivierbarkeit der Erkenntnisse im Weg. Im letzten Fall ist es wohl eher der Mangel an Empathie, der Strukturen nicht sehen lässt, die nicht die des wissenschaftlichen Interesses sind, und die müssen nicht viel mit dem Selbstverständnis der beobachteten Gruppe zu tun haben, und das heißt mit der Rekonstruktion von sinnvollen Strukturen. Dennoch, vor allem wenn man das weiß, ist keine Untersuchung so belastet, dass man nicht Nutzen aus ihr ziehen könnte. Häufig lernt man mehr noch aus defensiven als aus positiv darstellenden Passagen, wo kritische Stellen in dem entwickelten Außen- oder Innenbild bestehen: diesen Punkten kann man dann sicherlich nachgehen.

4. Der Rahmen der Kommunikation

4.1. Gelassenheit

Aufgrund der Vorkenntnisse, die man sich aus verschiedenen Quellen beschaffen kann, sieht man, welche Erscheinungen und Handlungsweisen die unaufgebbare Differenz der Sprachgemeinschaft der *Old Order Amish* zu der Umgebungsgesellschaft, der "Welt" ihres Lebens, signalisieren (cf. Raith 1982).

Es sind das alles Ausbuchstabierungen einer Grundhaltung, die gegenüber dem individualistischen Tätigkeitsdrang des *mainstreams* westlicher Gesellschaften durch das Grundkonzept der "Gelassenheit" zu kennzeichnen wäre, eine Gelassenheit, auf der Einbettung in der Gruppe beruht. Doris Kupferschmidt (1994, 81) hat die zentralen Elemente, an denen sich auch Integrationskonflikte entzündet haben, zusammengestellt. Dabei schlägt sich diese "Gelassenheit" in vier Dimensionen nieder, sie zeigt sich auf der Ebene der Persönlichkeit und der Werte, auf der Ebene des Ritus, auf der Ebene der sozialen Struktur der Gruppe und letztlich, oder, von der Wahrnehmung her gesehen vielleicht sogar vor allem, auf der Ebene der Symbole.

4.2. Sozialisationsinstanzen

Für die Wahrung der Identität der Gruppe, damit für die Tradierung einer gelassenen, schlichten Lebensweise und der damit verbundenen Ordnungsvorstellungen ist das Funktionieren der entsprechenden Sozialisationsinstanzen von enormem Belang. Die zentralen Sozialisationsinstanzen stellen die Familie, die schulische Erziehung, die religiöse Gemeinde, die berufliche Praxis des Alltags und " als temporäre Option " die *peer-group*, dar. Diese Bereiche lassen sich mit den Phänomenen eines gelassenen Lebens korrelieren, die in den Ebenen von Ritus, Gruppenstruktur und sozialer Symbolik oben angesprochen worden waren.

4.2.1. Die Familie im großen Haus

Was strukturelle Eigenheiten dieser Kleingruppengemeinschaft angeht, so sind nicht verhandelbare *essentials* die Familienstruktur und -größe. Bei ihnen handelt es sich um Elemente, die sozusagen die Selbstreferentialität des Systems sichern. In diese systemabgrenzende Eigenheit eingebaut sind bestimmte Autoritätsstrukturen, zwischen den Geschlechtern und zwischen den Generationen, die es erlauben, symbolische Konventionen gegen den Druck der Außenwelt durchzusetzen.

Historisch schließt diese Einheit an die traditionelle Form des "großen Hauses" als Wirtschaftseinheit an, die in der Herkunftsregion der Amischen schon im Verlaufe des 18. Jahrhunderts an Bedeutung verliert. Schon durch die Größe und Strukturiertheit dieses Kernbereichs wird gesichert, dass eine Trennung von der Welt überhaupt eine lebbare Möglichkeit darstellt. Die Basis für ein solches distante Leben wird weiter verbreitet durch eine Nachbarschaftshilfe, die über die religiöse Bindung funktioniert— und so die Unabhängigkeit von öffentlichen Eingriffen sichert. Täuferische Tradition ist ja die Existenz keiner übergeordneten Organisationsform,—außer befreundeten Gemeinden ("affiliation")—daneben die Rekurrenz auf nicht professionell geführte kleine Einheiten. Das symbolisch dominante Verkehrsmittel—*horse and buggy*—ist von daher mehr als ein Bestandteil eines symbolischen Inventars, es ist vielmehr der praktische Garant für die Begrenztheit der persönlichern Aktionskreise. Was eine heutige Praxis angeht, so sind die damit verbundenen Beschränkungen auch für die *Amish people* relativ leicht zu überwinden. Vertrauenswürdiger *driver* in einem amischen Umfeld zu sein, ist, wie wir erfahren haben, eine wahrhafte Vollbeschäftigung (vgl. auch Vossen 1994).

4.2.2. Nützliches und überflüssiges Wissen

Der Sicherung einer Identität, die in einem Leben in diesem Umfeld seine Ruhe findet, ist selbst bei räumlicher Abgeschiedenheit und Konzentration im Raum moderner westlicher Gesellschaften nicht ganz einfach. Vielmehr bedarf es bewusster und konsequenter Strategien, um einer Überlagerung der gruppeninternen durch die generellen gesellschaftlichen Sozialisiationsinstanzen in den Weg zu treten. Dem dient ganz offenkundig und an hervorgehobener Stelle die Durchsetzung der Forderung nach einem eigenen Schulsystem, das nicht über die achtjährige Pflichtschulzeit hinausgeht, und bei dessen Abschluss auf die Ausstellung von Abschlusszeugnissen verzichtet werden darf. Diese deutliche Zurückweisung der enkulturierenden Wirkung gemeinsamer Bildung repräsentiert ja einerseits natürlich ein Merkmal der voraufklärerischen europäischen Historie solcher Glaubensgemeinschaften (cf. Eichinger 1997), ist aber, wie die entsprechenden gerichtlichen Auseinandersetzungen im 20. Jahrhundert zeigen, mit dem durchgreifenden Wirksamwerden der allgemeinen Schulpflicht zu einem der zentralen Punkte der Stabilisierung der eigenen Gemeinschaft geworden. Das heißt übrigens nicht, dass professionelle Leistung nicht anerkannt und daraus stammender wirtschaftlicher Erfolg geringgeschätzt würde. Aber das ist etwas, was sich im Leben so ergibt, Bildung und als ihr konkretes Symbol die Abschlusszeugnisse und Diplome, die von den Bildungseinrichtungen vergeben und in der modernen Gesellschaft als Qualifikationsmerkmale anerkannt werden, sind dagegen ein möglicher Anlass zu Stolz, einer der dramatischsten Sünden, ein Zeugnis der menschlichen Eitelkeit, im wahrsten Sinne des Wortes. Dass dem so ist, zeigt das Interview, das wir mit einem über 90-jährigen "Austragsbauern" von den *Yellow Toppers* geführt haben, der uns in einer stillen Minute und im vertrauten Gespräch sein altes Schulzeugnis—aus der damals noch öffentlichen Schule—zeigt, es ist ein gutes Zeugnis, und er verbindet das mit dem Geständnis, dieses Zeugnis sei die einzige Gelegenheit in seinem Leben gewesen, bei der er eitel gewesen sei. Man sollte weit entfernt sein davon, darüber zu lächeln: es zeigt nur, wie weit das ganze Leben von den Werten und Vorstellungen der Gemeinschaft geprägt ist.

4.2.3. Machtstrukturen und gesellschaftlicher Wandel

Im Umfeld der Schulfrage zeigt sich auch mancherlei Geschlechtsspezifisches; die relative Geringschätzung des Lehrerberufes teilen die *Amish people* mit den Traditionen ihrer Herkunftsorte und -zeiten, aber auch durchaus mit der Einschätzung der modernen US-amerikanischen Gesellschaft. So ist es denn nicht verwunderlich, dass nicht nur Frauen diese Beschäftigung ausüben, sondern unverheiratete Frauen, die oder solange sie zu nichts Besserem zu gebrauchen sind, und dass einer der wesentlichen rechtlichen Streitfälle in diesem Kontext darum ging, dass keine Mindestlöhne für diese Tätigkeit akzeptiert wurden. Die Geschlechterrollen sind als Macht- und Aufgabenrollen im Sinne einer vormodernen Arbeits- und Pflichtenverteilung festgelegt: auch diese Festlegung geht aber weit darüber hinaus, ein historisches Relikt zu sein; es gehört zu den Konstanten der konstruierten Wirklichkeit. Manchmal konstruiert aber die Welt selbst eine stärkere Wirklichkeit, die dann die innersektererischen Geschichten als das erscheinen lassen, was sie sind, Selbstrechtfertigungen. Diese Tatbestände werden in den letzten Jahrzehnten zunehmend gerade bei den strengsten Denominationen, in unserem Falle den *Nebraska-Amish* oder *White-Toppers*—nach der Farbe der Dachbespannungen ihrer *buggies*—deutlich. Die zunehmenden wirtschaftlichen Probleme, die sich gerade dieser asketischsten Richtung stellen, führen dazu, dass andere Mitglieder die dem Hausvater zustehende Machtposition partiell übernehmen. Und so verdienen die Frauen mit Schneidern, mit Quilten, mit Verkauf auf der "Vendue," dem örtlichen Markt, ein Erhebliches zum Lebensunterhalt, und, mehr noch, sie agieren in der Außenkontaktposition. Auch hier haben wir etliche Beispiele aus dem Kreis der Nebraskas, die erkennen lassen, dass die Rolle von Mann und Frau denn doch mehr die Rolle von Mann und Frau in ländlichen wirtschaftlichen Strukturen spiegelt, denn spezifisch religiös bedingt ist. Diese Verschiebungen betreffen neben dem Geschlechterverhältnis auch das für diese patriarchalisch gedachte Gemeinschaft ideologisch wichtige Eltern-Kind-Verhältnis, noch spezifischer das Verhältnis zwischen Vätern und Söhnen. Die extreme Weltferne dieser strengsten Denominationen innerhalb der von uns untersuchten Gemeinschaft, können das berufliche Fortkommen der nächsten Generation kaum mehr intern sichern, da schon in den letzten Generationen der mangelnde wirtschaftliche Erfolg der bäuerlichen Tätigkeit zu einer weiteren Minderung seiner Basis durch Realteilung bei der Erbschaft gezwungen hat. So sind denn gerade die jungen Mitglieder dieser Subgemeinschaft dazu gezwungen, ihr Auskommen in den örtlichen Sägewerken, Palettenfabriken und ähnlichen Arbeitsstellen, die religiös noch verträglich sind, zu suchen. Sie bringen in Folge dieser Arbeit Geld in einer Menge in den familiären Kontext ein, wie es mit der prinzipiell von Subsistenzideen geprägten landwirtschaftlichen Tätigkeit in diesem Umfeld nicht beizubringen ist. Daneben erhöht sich für sie auch der Druck zur Benutzung des Englischen ganz erheblich. Beides in seiner Kombination führt logischerweise zu einer Gefährdung der Macht- und Image-Verhältnisse in der Familie.[2]

4.2.4. Teilhabe an der Deutung der Welt

Unverzichtbar, und für den Selbsterhalt wohl ein ganz zentraler Punkt ist der Tatbestand, dass die ideologische Deutungskompetenz, also die Führung der Kirchengemeinde nicht der Professionalisierung unterliegt, die ja für viele Lebensbereiche ein Kennzeichen der Moderne ist. Die Bischöfe, die anderen Diener und die Prediger stammen aus der Mitte der Gemeinde, ihre relative Macht kennt keine externe Motivation. Dadurch kann man auch mit Auseinandersetzungen um den richtigen Weg zu einem angemessenen Leben leichter fertig werden: über der Gemeinde ist keine weitere Instanz; andererseits bedarf es einer ganz erheblichen psychischen Kraft, wenn man sich aus einer so kleinen und sozial so eng verbundenen Gruppe absetzen will. Das ist ganz offenkundig, wenn man sich ins Gedächtnis ruft, dass zu den zentralen Elementen der Selbstdefinition die sogenannte Meidung gehört.[3] Und noch einmal andersherum gesehen, lässt sich, wenn es denn sein muss, eine neue Gruppe dieser Größe auch relativ leicht neu einrichten.

Die Sozialisationsinstanz der Kirchengemeinde lässt ihre Stellung darin aufscheinen, wie ausführlich, umständlich und strikt ihre Riten sind. Dazu gehören auf der ersten Ebene die ebenso aufwendigen wie von repetitiven und extrem langsamen Strukturen geprägten vierzehntägigen Gottesdienste, deren hochgradig symbolischer Wert so offenkundig ist, dass eigentlich nicht gesondert darauf hingewiesen werden muss. Das beginnt bei den melismatischen Gesängen des *slow tones*:

Die Gesänge haben einen langsamen, ecclesiastischen Charakter, der an gregorianischen Choräle erinnert. Die Lieder beziehen sich inhaltlich häufig auf die Märtyrerthematik des frühen Täufertums. (Vossen 1994, 101)

Und es geht bis zu den Predigten, die den besprochenen Bibeltext in einer Sprachform paraphrasierend deuten, die zumindest den im Hintergrund anwesenden Frauen der Gemeinde kaum verständlich ist. Mit einem ähnlichen rituellen Aufbau kann man auch bei anderen gesellschaftlichen Ereignissen rechnen, etwa bei Hochzeiten, wo es offenbar großräumiger eine Gesangabfolge bestimmter Lieder aus dem *Ausbund* gibt. Eine Steigerung erfährt die rituelle Strenge in der Ordnungsgemeinde, wo die

Ordnung der Lebensweise unmittelbar thematisch wird, und daher auch die Frage der Sanktionen nach Verstößen. Daher spielen hier auch andere Textformen eine wichtige Rolle: Glaubensbekenntnis, Zeugnis und Ähnliches. Die Härte der letzten Strafe, der "Meidung," hat an Härte selbst da nicht verloren, wo der Austritt aus der amischen Gemeinschaft in wohlgeordnete soziale Verhältnisse führt. Die Tochter eines Bischofs bei den Nebraska-Gemeinden, die einen Mennoniten geheiratet hatte, wurde von ihrer Mutter nicht an ihr Sterbebett gelassen, da durch diesen Bruch der Meidung auch das eigene Seelenheil gefährdet gewesen wäre.

4.2.5. Exzentrik als Schutz

In den Kontext der religiösen Sozialisation gehören auch die Kleidungs-Symboliken; so hat z.b. die Huttragepflicht[4] letztlich zu einer Ausnahme von der Pflicht, bei bestimmten Arbeiten Schutzhelme zu tragen, geführt. Damit ist die Ebene der Erscheinungen erreicht, die auf der rein symbolischen Ebene das Konzept von gelassener distanzierter, dörflich akzentuierter Lebensweise repräsentieren. Auf die Kleiderordnung im einzelnen einzugehen, lohnt nicht, der zentrale Punkt ist ja wohl wie bei vielen der besprochenen Erscheinungen, dass durch Konstanz und Unauffälligkeit jede Gefahr von Individualität und Lebensstilorientierung ausgeschlossen werden soll. Wiewohl denn auf der anderen Seite es dann genau diese Merkmale sind, die ihren jeweiligen Träger in der modernen Gesellschaft als vom Gewöhnlichen abweichend und exzentrisch er scheinen lassen.

Zu diesen Merkmalen, die auch dem eindeutigen sozialen Wiedererkennen dienen, gehört auch das zumindest bei den striktesten Gruppen befolgte Gebot der bewussten Gleichgültigkeit gegenüber den Normalerwartungen der Gesellschaft. So werden zum Teil Formen einer rituellen Unhöflichkeit kultiviert. Der Bischof einer Gemeinde, die uns dann zu ihrem Gottesdienst zugelassen hat, unterhielt sich mit uns, indem er dezidiert in eine andere Richtung blickte, unmittelbar neben unseren Füßen auf den Boden spuckte und dergleichen in westlichen Gesellschaften unter unbekannten Erwachsenen eher abweichendes Verhalten mehr. In diesen Kontext gehört auch der Grad, in dem auf "ordentliches" Aussehen geachtet wird.

4.3. Symbolik und praktischer Wert der Sprache

4.3.1. Demonstration, Beziehung und Interaktion

Zu einer symbolisch angemessenen Innen- und Außenrepräsentation trägt auch der Sprachgebrauch bei (cf. Huffines 1994a). Das Deutsche in der Form des Amischen Hochdeutsch, das nur in ritueller Funktion vorkommt, weist den Weg zu den Quellen und Rechtfertigungen des eigenen Lebenszuschnitts, ist von daher von hoher ideologischer—und zweifellos geringerer praktischer—Bedeutung.[5]

Das Hochdeutsche hat hochgradig rituellen Charakter, es dient dazu, ein fixes Korpus von Texten abzurufen. Vielleicht wird diese Funktion in Verbindung mit der melismatischen Ferne der musikalischen Gestaltung bei den Liedern, die bei den Gemeinden, aber auch bei den Festen gesungen werden, besonders deutlich. Zu diesem Zweck haben wir uns von einem Sattel- und Zaumzeugmacher der strengsten Denomination, der sogenannten *Nebraska-Amish*, der zudem Vorsänger in seiner Gemeinde ist, das Kirchenlied "Wachet auf, ruft uns die Stimme" vorsingen lassen. Hier ist schon die Artikulation im *slow tone* Zeichen genug, dass es nicht um Textverständnis, sondern um das Abrufen von Einverständnis geht. Je exzentrischer die Mittel, desto mehr ist das Einverständnis damit natürlich sozial wert. Dabei ist auch noch im Auge zu behalten, dass diese Texte in Situationen gebraucht werden, die nicht für den Kontakt mit der Außenwelt gedacht sind.

Wenn das auch im Prinzip bei den Texten der Heiligen Schrift nicht anders sein mag, ist es zumindest bei dem Teil der Gemeinden, die sich intensiver damit beschäftigen und die nicht die extreme Bildungsfeindlichkeit der Nebraskas pflegen, auch aufgrund der Komplexität der Texte doch etwas differenzierter zu sehen. Hier kann man bei der Beobachtung große Differenzen feststellen, was die Beherrschung dieser Sprachform angeht. Diese Unterschiede haben mit vielen Umständen zu tun, z.B. mit dem weniger beschränkten Leben bei den nicht so strikten Denominationen, mit der Art der Schulbildung—die früheren öffentlichen Schulen brachten offenbar insgesamt eine höhere Lesefähigkeit zustande—und ähnlichem. Das in einer anderen unserer Aufnahmen enthaltene Beispiel der Lektüre aus der Bibel, wo uns ein ca. 80-jähriger Black-Topper vorliest, vermag eine recht hohe Fertigkeit in diesem Bereich zu dokumentieren. Hier ist außer der typischen lautlichen Veränderung, die von der Vorstandardsprachlichkeit der tradierten Formen der deutschen Sprechsprache und von der Adaptation an die Umgebungssprache zeugen, nichts besonders Auffälliges zu vermelden.

Dem sei gegenübergestellt die Lektüre eines rituellen Gebets durch den etwa 10-jährigen Sohn aus einer *Car-Amish*-Familie, das heißt einer Gruppe, die sich selbst noch zu den *Amish* rechnet, aber schon Autos, elektrisches Licht, Telefon usw. benutzt, so dass sie von sehr strikten Denominationen der *Amish* schon als nicht mehr eine der ihren betrachtet wird. Bei der Leseperformanz in dieser Aufnahme, bei der nur noch bruchstückweise deutsche Elemente erkennbar sind, kommt sicherlich manches zusammen; ganz offenkundig ist, dass zwischen der alltäglich gesprochenen Sprachform und dem hier abgeforderten Lesen eines rituellen Textes kaum ein Zusammenhang herzustellen ist. Auch in diesem relativen Misslingen wird der soziale und rituelle Charakter der mit dem Text intendierten Kommunikation besonders deutlich. Gerade an den Rändern der Gemeinschaft wird es immer wichtiger, die Symbole der Zugehörigkeit zu pflegen (cf. Enninger 1988).

Wenn man so will, stellt sich gerade von dieser rituellen hochdeutschen Sprachform her das Sprachgebrauchsmuster als Fall von Triglossie dar; wobei dann die funktionale Verteilung nicht einfach eine Erweiterung einer Diglossiesituation um eine weitere Dimension ist, sondern eine Sprachgebrauchssituation eigener Art ergibt. Die dezidiert bildungsferne und ländliche Organisation des Lebens und der erwünschten Kommunikation erfordert eine andere Art der Verteilung der sprachlichen Varietäten. Vor allem gibt es keine richtige *High*-Varietät, das Englische ist genau das nicht, sondern die exolektale Gebrauchssprache, mit einem umgangssprachlich zentrierten Spektrum an Verwendungsmöglichkeiten. Aus privaten Briefwechseln mit uns kann man sehen, dass die schriftliche Kommunikationstechnik auch in dieser Varietät auf einer sehr ungeübten Stufe stehen bleibt.

Dem steht als endolektale Gebrauchssprache das "Deitsch," also das *Pennsylvania-Dutch* gegenüber. Diese Varietät ist einerseits die gruppeninterne Gebrauchssprache, die aber auch darüber hinaus gerne benutzt wird, wenn an irgendwelchen symbolischen Hinweisen sichtbar ist, dass die Person, z. B. ein Mennonit mit *Amish*-Nähe, in der Lage ist, diese Sprache zu verstehen.

Die Beherrschung der schriftlichen Ritual-Varietät ist im Bewusstsein der Sprecher deutlich verbunden ist mit der gleichzeitigen Benutzung des *Pennsylvania-Dutch* als kolloquialer Nähe-Variante; beiden zusammen wird ein hoher Identitätswert für die eigene Gruppe zugewiesen. Dabei sind die Verhältnisse nicht immer so klar gesehen, wie im Fall eines *Nebraska-Amish*-Paars, die uns freundlich und ausführlich als Gewährsleute für diese Fragen zur Verfügung standen. In einem längeren Gespräch mit diesen Beiden kamen wir auch auf die Frage, mit wem sie Deutsch und mit wem sie Englisch sprechen würden: Englisch, heißt es da, werde gesprochen, wenn man bei den Englischen sei. Im folgenden kann man nebenher einen netten Interferenzeffekt beobachten; wenn gefragt wird, *wer die Englischen seien*, versteht unser Partner offenkundig *where*—also *wo*—und antwortet daher auch *We han lots von Englische harum so die Weger.* Vor allem in Belleville, dem Zentralort des Tals, gebe es solche, wo die Frau auch jeden Mittwoch auf dem Markt einen Stand hat. Sie mischt sich an dieser Stelle auch ins Gespräch ein und erläutert, dass man Deutsch mit Leuten rede, die an der Kleidung als Amische erkennbar wären. Dann geht es letztlich um Leute, die Amish gewesen seien, dann *gechanged*, d.h. die religiöse Zugehörigkeit gewechselt, hätten und schon noch deutsch könnten, ohne dass man es ihnen ansehen würde. Auf die Nachfrage, wie das mit der Abwanderung, dem *changen* aus dem Amischen sei, wird zögerlich eher abgebrochen und dann explizit bestätigt: *Amish und deitsch is the same. Mir heisse se amish un mir heisse se deitsche Leit.* Nach einem kurzen Exkurs wird zudem angemerkt, dass in der anschließenden Snyder-County auch viele Englische gut deutsch geredet hätten. Man kann aus diesen verschiedenen Äußerungen schließen, dass im Idealfall Deutsch reden zum Symbolinventar der Amischen gehöre, dass die ideale Kookkurrenz aber durch mancherlei Überlagerungen gestört sei. Zentral für die eigene Identität ist offenbar die rituell distanzierende Verwendung der hochsprachlichen religiösen Texte. An einer weiteren Stelle des gerade behandelten Gesprächs kam die Rede darauf, dass wir mit einer Gruppierung Kontakt hatten, die sich am Rande des Amisch-Spektrums sieht, worauf die Frau des Paars relativ heftig einwirft, mit welchem Recht sich solche Leute *Amish* nennten, wo sie doch in der Gemeinde—d.h. in der religiösen Praxis—nicht mehr das Deutsche verwendeten.

An anderen Stellen können wir sehen, dass die in der individuellen Lage ansonsten nicht ungefährdete Zugehörigkeit zu den *Amish* auch mit diesem symbolischen Mittel zu sichern gesucht wird. Der Vater des Jungen, der sein Gebet so mühselig las, beantwortete unsere Frage zum Verhältnis zwischen *Amish*-Sein und Deutsch-Sprechen ganz dezidiert: wer nicht Deutsch sprechen könne, sei auf keinen Fall ein *Amish*. Und vielleicht ist es kein Zufall, dass das Gespräch, das dauernd zwischen Deutsch und Englisch hin und her wechselt, an dieser Stelle auf Deutsch weitergeführt wird. Gegenüber den Mennoniten, die, wie an dieser Stelle des Gesprächs ebenfalls betont wird, in diesem Tal nicht originär sind, sondern alle ehemals aus *Amish*-Familien stammen und daher oft noch *Pennsylvania-Dutch* sprechen, wird nun als Kriterium angegeben, nur wer das Deutsche an seine Kinder weitergebe, sei Amish. In dieser Funktion als gruppeninterne Alltagssprache sind auch Entlehnungen aus dem Englischen der Umgebung unproblematisch, bleiben oft unentdeckt; an bestimmten Stellen kann der Wandel bewusst gemacht werden.

Daneben hat die gesprochene Varietät des Deutschen aber auch eine hohe ideologische Bedeutung. Sie und das Amisch-Hochdeutsche sind die Shibboleths der Zugehörigkeit zu der eigenen Gruppe. Eher der hohen symbolischen Wertung ist zuzurechnen, dass Differenzen, Dialektunterschiede innerhalb dieser Varietät eher nicht wahrgenommen oder akzeptiert werden. Dabei gibt es sie ganz sicher, zumindest schon aufgrund der unterschiedlichen Nähe zum Englischen. Durch den wirtschaftlichen Druck, der vor allem auf den strengsten Denominationen lastet, sind viele der jüngeren Mitglieder dieser Gemeinden gezwungen, einen Beruf außerhalb des engsten familiären Umfelds zu ergreifen. Dabei spielt der Kontakt zum Englischen eine erheblich erhöhte Rolle. Noch dazu, da diese Welt den Gebrauch des Englischen unter bestimmten Bedingungen geradezu fordert. Uns liegt ein Arbeitsvertrag einer von Mennoniten geleiteten Firma in dem Untersuchungsgebiet vor, in dem der Gebrauch des Englischen am Arbeitsplatz vorgeschrieben bzw. der Gebrauch des *Pennsylvania-Dutch* untersagt wird. Zwischen den beiden deutschen Varietäten steht in gewissem Maße die Kenntnis eines Lese-Deutsch für alltägliche Gegebenheiten, das durchaus parallel zu einem Lese-Englisch zu stellen ist. Diese Fähigkeit wird vor allem aktiviert für die Lektüre der Zeitungen, die in der eigenen Gemeinschaft herausgegeben werden, vor allem der *Botschaft* und des *Budget*.

In diesen amischen Zeitungen und Zeitschriften finden sich Beiträge zum christlichen Familienleben, landwirtschaftliche Hinweise, ausführliche Krankheitsberichte amischer Gemeindemitglieder und Informationen über deren Genesungsprozess, Beiträge zur Geschichte der Amischen, Bibelzitate, Veranstaltungshinweise und ausführliche Familiennachrichten. (Kupferschmidt 1994, 69-70)

Im Hinblick auf diese Ebene macht der sprachliche Unterschied des Englischen und des Deutschen praktisch keinen Unterschied in der soziolinguistischen Stellung. In der jüngeren Generation scheint das in gewissem Umfang auch für gesprochene Varietäten zwischen dem Englischen und dem "Deitschen" zu gelten, die den eher konservativen Dialekt der Älteren bedrängen. Dem Deutschen sicher zugehörig und von hohem ideologischem Wert, aber eigentlich eher ein Akrolekt als eine *High-Variety* haben wir im *Amish*-Hochdeutschen vor uns, dessen Gebrauchsbereiche oben schon erwähnt wurden. Es hat in vielerlei Hinsicht eine fast virtuelle Realität. Insbesondere die beobachteten Predigten waren außerordentlich schwer einer Sprachform zuzuordnen, und auch bei den Gemeindemitgliedern schwankt der Verständnisgrad erheblich. Da es zum Selbstverständnis gehört, dass es keinen privilegierten Zugang zu diesen Texten gibt, so dass jedes " zumindest männliche " Mitglied der Gemeinde sie lesen können sollte, sind Aussagen zu diesem Bereich schwer zu gewinnen; ähnlich schwer wie zu dem Bereich, was nun wirklich kommunikativ mit aus der Gemeinde ausgeschiedenen Mitgliedern geschieht. Auf jeden Fall ergibt sich eine Gliederung der sprachlichen Varietäten, die nur zum Teil von ihrer kommunikativen Wirksamkeit und den Beschränkungen ihres Gebrauchs gesteuert ist.

4.3.2. Kompromisse der Praxis und Distanz aus Prinzip

4.3.2.1. Sprachen des Alltags

Für das normale Mitglied der Gemeinden gilt zunächst einmal das Grundschema: Es gibt zwei der sprachlichen Meisterung des Alltags dienende Formen, das *Pennsylvania-Dutch* und das Englische, sie werden zentral in gesprochener Form realisiert. Der gute Erhaltungszustand des *Pennsylvania-Dutch* ergibt sich aus der Einbindung dieses symbolischen Elements in die gesamte Bindungsstruktur, wie sie oben geschildert worden ist. Wie bei allen anderen symbolischen Distanzmerkmalen ist zu beachten, dass Kontaktphänomene zum Englischen so lange nicht als problematisch gelten, so lange die kommunikative Distanz gewahrt bleibt. Es scheint allerdings so zu sein, dass für die Regelung dieses Sachverhalts kein so starkes Bewusstsein besteht wie für die in der Ordnung geregelten anderen Dinge.

So werden entsprechende Erscheinungen in den Gesprächen zwar manchmal mit Überraschung aber ohne ein eigentliches Gefühl der Gefährdung festgestellt. Schon in dem oben angesprochenen Gespräch gab es eine Vielzahl von Fällen, bei denen die Sprachform Elemente des Deutschen und des Englischen verbindet. Englische Elemente wären z.B: *Lots of Englische; de amish dressed sin; watch awer, was du sagst in German; changen* 'Glauben wechseln'; *you know* als Partikel; *same; some, nich so viel, once in a while; se hen about ned Englisch schwätze kenne.*

Es gibt darüber hinaus in den Gesprächen, die wir geführt haben, auch immer wieder Partien, die sich explizit auf dieses Phänomen beziehen. So erzählt uns jener Nebraska-Amish, der für uns gesungen hat, von Dingen, die man früher anders genannt habe, so habe das Austauschen von Milchkannen früher *wechseln* geheißen, jetzt *changen*; die jetzt *cookies* genannten Kekse hätten *Küchlen* geheißen, bei der Alternative *breakfast* gegen *Morgenessen* entscheidet er sich für beide, und erläutert, daß man früher für das Mittag eingenommene Mahl *Awendesse* ('Abendessen') gesagt habe; an einer Stelle äußert er, *man spürt besser* im Sinne von 'man fühlt sich besser.' Daneben erwähnt er etliche Wörter, die aus der speziellen Lebenspraxis der *Amish* stammen, so z.B. *Mosch* ('Mus; Brei'), *Welschken* ('Welschkorn; Mais'). Ähnliche Erscheinungen finden sich, als zwei alte Yellow-Toppers ihre Familiengeschichte Revue passieren lassen, wo sie vom Verhältnis der Wörter *Roofer* und *Dachdecker* sprechen; *was wäre der Deutsch Weg für sell socha*, fragt uns an einer Stelle unser Gesprächspartner, mit erkennbar allerlei auch syntaktischen Interferenzen.

Schon an diesen Beispielen wird klar, dass natürlich die hier jeweils angesprochenen Erscheinungen ganz unterschiedlichen Status haben. Das geht von ad-hoc-Entlehnungen zu festen Lexikonelementen, von Lehnsyntax bis hin zu konvergenten eigenständigen Entwicklungen in den gesprochenen Varietäten des Deutschen und des Englischen. Man muss an dieser Stelle nicht nur den Einfluss des Englischen sehen, über den man nicht zu streiten braucht, in den letzten Jahren ist aber in der Sprachwissenschaft erst so recht klar geworden, dass auch die gesprochenen Varietäten des Deutschen eine Reihe von Trends zeigen, die wesentlich analytischer, d.h. "englischer" sind als das Standarddeutsche (cf. Keel 1994; Louden 1994; Salmons 1994). Zu Recht ist verschiedentlich darauf hingewiesen worden (vgl. Coulmas 1981; Polenz 1994), dass die Norm der Standardsprache, insofern sie auf unser Sprechen zurückwirkt, den Sprachwandel verlangsamt und verschiebt. Unter diesem Aspekt ist so manche Veränderung im amischen Deutsch auch intern durchaus "natürlich" im Sinne typologischer Aspekte. Zudem ist umgekehrt die Prägung durch englischsprachige Schriftlichkeit unverkennbar—wir haben ja schon gezeigt, dass das Hochdeutsche in dieser Gemeinschaft nicht den standardsprachlichen Ansprüchen einer funktionierenden Schriftsprache genügt. Vielleicht ist es daher zu wenig oder zu viel, wie Marion Huffines (1994b, 49) zu sagen

. . . a strict diglossia within the seperatist groups does not exist. The use of English within the seperatist groups steadily increases, even within more intimate domains, a progression which seems to be accelerating.

Natürlich gibt es keine Diglossie, wenn—mehr und mehr—kein grundsätzlicher Übergang an der ursprünglich genetisch-historischen Sprachtrennung von Deutsch und Englisch gespürt wird, sofern man nicht die reine Existenz der Ritualsprache so bewerten möchte. Ein weiterer Teil der Aufnahme des oben behandelten Paars von *Nebraska-Amish*, also einer eher strengen Denomination, mag vielleicht den sprachlichen Befund dazu illustrieren. Es geht im ersten Teil der Aufnahme um die Fische im Aquarium, die ein Geschenk des Sohns in Ohio zu Weihnachten ("*Christdag*") waren. Sechs große Fische habe es darin gehabt, und sie habe sie lange gehabt; eine Phase später sagt sie dann, dass der Tod der Fische wohl damit zu tun habe, dass man das Wasser nicht oft genug gewechselt habe (139): *I figure we hens not oft genug gechanged.* In dieser Partie kann man nach dem ersten expliziten Sprachwechsel sehen, dass es sich hier um eine gesprochene Innenform handelt, die einen Kompromiss aus den relevanten Varietäten der Umgebung darstellt, deren eigenständige Bestandteile der Identitätsformung und der Binnenkommunikation dienen.

4.3.2.2. Rituelle Sprache und Schriftlichkeit

Auf der anderen Seite steht das im wesentlichen geschriebene akrolektale *Amish-Hochdeutsch*; auch die gesprochenen oder gesungenen Varianten dieser an den historischen Texten orientierten Varietät können als Realisierungen eines prinzipiell geschriebenen Codes verstanden werden. Die Lesefähigkeit in diesem Bereich ist sozial hoch gewertet. So geht denn dieses Kriterium doch in die Abwägung ein, wer denn Bischof oder Prediger werden solle. Mehrere Gewährspersonen haben erläutert, dass nur "die männlichen Mitglieder einer Gemeinde, deren Familie sich streng an die Ordnung hält und die gut die deutsche Bibel lesen können, . . . als geeignete Kandidaten betrachtet" (Kupferschmidt 1994, 25) werden. Auf einem anderen funktionalen und sozialen Blatt stehen die Lese- und Schreibfähigkeiten in einem modernen Deutsch und im Englischen, die beide als funktionale Fertigkeiten genutzt werden, und insofern nicht geschieden sind. Allerdings kann man sich fragen, inwieweit durch eine deutschsprachige Praxis, die ja ihre Normen selbst definieren muss, eine für die Gruppe sensitive schriftliche Form des Deutschen entsteht, bzw. einfach die Schriftfertigkeit im Deutschen abnimmt. So ist es denn auch nicht so leicht, das Leben und Sprechen der hier in Frage stehenden Gruppen zu beurteilen. Und es ist wohl nicht die ganze Wahrheit, wenn ein deutscher Amerikanist an den Amischen kritisiert, dass sie ein schlechtes Deutsch schrieben:

Ebenso richtig ist aber, daß die Muttersprache der Immigranten von der Macht des Englischen überwältigt wird. . . . Dies gilt sogar für Sprechergruppen, die relativ abgeschieden von der englischsprachigen Mehrheit lebten. Die Zeitschrift *Herold der Wahrheit* der Amish-Sekte in Iowa ist in einem seltsamen Mischmasch aus englischer Syntax und Mennonitendeutsch abgefaßt:

"Das ewige Leben in Christo Jesu ist was wir alle streben dafür. Wenigstens wir hoffen, das sei der Fall . . . Und ohne die Liebe und die Frucht, ist es mir bange, wir sind verlorene Seelen." (Raeithel 1992, 2: 403)

Auch hier scheint es nicht nur um eine Anpassung an ein "normales" Hochdeutsch zu gehen, sondern um den Versuch, das rituelle Schreiben der Symbolpraxis des Alltags so weit anzunähern, dass mit Verständnis gerechnet werden kann. Wie weit das gelingt und welche Wege zu diesem Ziel es geben wird, wird man sehen.

5. Und die Realität

5.1. Kann sein, was nicht sein darf?

Die Befunde, die wir bisher angedeutet haben, können bei dem interessierten Soziolinguisten zwei ganz verschiedene Reaktionen hervorbringen. Beide haben damit zu tun, dass die Bedingungen der Existenz dieser so auf sich selbst bezogenen Gruppe, und die Erforschung ihrer allgemeinen Rahmenbedingungen, eine einfache Errechnung des Verhaltens des jeweiligen Einzelnen—man ist bestrebt das Wort Individuum zu vermeiden—zu erlauben scheint. Da kann man sich entweder freuen, dass die Arbeit schon zu Ende ist, oder man kann sich Sorgen machen, wie man hier möglicherweise die Wand zwischen Sein und Schein methodisch einbrechen könnte. Direkte Befragung, das könnte ich mit Ausschnitten aus entsprechenden Versuchen belegen, ist zweifellos nicht die beste Idee, da die Aussagen eigentlich nicht miteinander verglichen werden können; vielmehr hängt es im Einzelfall von der Frage ab, inwieweit ein Vertrauens- oder ein Vertrautheitsverhältnis zu den Gewährspersonen entstanden ist, das es erlaubt, jenseits der Vorschriften, die ja eigentlich keine Optionen offen lassen, über die Praxis, ihre Ambivalenzen und ihren Wandel zu räsonieren. Teilnehmende Beobachtung im weitesten Sinne steht andererseits vor dem Problem, dass bestimmte kommunikative Konstellationen nicht für Personen zugänglich sind, die nicht ohnehin in sie involviert sind. Das spielerische Einnehmen von Rollen ist nicht der Gestus, den solche relativ strikt in sich geschlossenen Gemeinschaften pflegen würden, und selbst relativ einfache Dinge, wie die Beobachtung freier Kommunikation unter Frauen, die ja in das religiöse Sprachsystem eine Stufe weniger einbezogen sind, bedarf zumindest ganz erheblicher methodischer Präkautelen, und ist von männlichen Exploratoren nicht zu leisten.

5.2 Begleitung des "guten Lebens"

Diese Anmerkungen zeigen, dass diese beiden Methoden, die als die Königswege der modernen Befragungstechnik gelten, und auf die man daher zweifellos nicht verzichten kann, nur dann Sinn machen, wenn sie in einem Deutungsrahmen operieren, der die gesellschaftlichen Eigen- und Fremddeutungen aufzunehmen erlaubt. Daher bedarf es zunächst einer intensiven Eingewöhnungsphase, um dann einen Beobachtungsleitfaden zu erstellen, der die genannten Bereiche eines guten Lebens in diesen Gesellschaften erfasst, und dessen kritische Stellen dann in Einzelinterviews, die wie normale Gespräche geführt werden, abgefragt werden können.

Anmerkungen

[1] Die entsprechenden Forschungen wurden zwischen 1992 und 1999 mit verschiedenen Sachbeihilfen des DAAD und der DFG gefördert; diesen Institutionen sei hiermit gedankt.

[2] Auch Hostetler (1993, 131) weist auf die nachteiligen Folgen dieser Entwicklung hin.

[3] Zur historischen Stellung und heutigen Praxis dieser weitreichenden Maßnahme vgl. Vossen (1994: 87 und 113ff.).

[4] Zu ihrem prototypischen Charakter vgl. z.B. Plancke (1984, 18); zum Umgang mit eigen- und fremdkulturellen symbolischen Elementen insgesamt vgl. z.B. Enninger (1988, 92ff.).

[5] Dem widerspricht nicht, dass es einen wichtigen Baustein in der kommunikativen Ausstattung einer Gemeinde darstellt: sein Verschwinden und damit sein Ersatz im religiösen Kontext wirft für die Gemeinschaften sicher bald auch praktisch die Frage auf, warum man sich eine strikt getrennte Gruppensprache leisten soll; vgl. Huffines (1994b).

Literatur

Bischoff, Volker, und Marino Maria. 1991."Melting Pot: Mythen als Szenarien amerikanischer Identität zur Zeit der New Immigration." In *Nationale und kulturelle Identität*, hrsg. Bernhard Giesen, 513-36. Frankfurt.

Blume, Helmut. 1979. U.S.A.: *Eine geographische Landeskunde*. Bd. 2. Darmstadt.

Coulmas, Florian. 1981. *Über Schrift*. Frankfurt.

Eichinger, Ludwig M. 1997. "Deutsch in weiter Ferne." In *Variation im Deutschen* (IdS Jahrbuch 1996), hrsg. G. Stickel. Berlin.

Enninger, Werner. 1988. "Coping with Modernity: Instrumentally and Symbolically." In *Internal and External Perspectives on Amish and Mennonite Life 3*, hrsg. Werner Enninger, Joachim Raith und Karl-Heinz Wandt, 16-51. Essen.

Hamilton, Alexander, James Madison und John Jay. 1993. *Die Federalist Papers*. Übersetzt, eingeleitet und mit Anmerkungen versehen von Barbara Zehnpfennig. Darmstadt.

Hostetler, John A. 1993. *Amish Society*, 4. Aufl. Baltimore.

Huffines, Marion Lois. 1994a."Amish Languages." In *Old and New World Anabaptists: Studies on the Language, Culture, Society and Health of the Amish and Mennonites*, hrsg. James R. Dow, Werner Enninger und Joachim Raith,21-32.Essen.

Huffines, Marion Lois. 1994b. "Directionality of Languages Influence; The Case of Pennsylvania German and English." In *Sprachinselforschung*, hrsg. Nina Berend and Klaus J. Mattheier,47-58. Frankfurt.

Kauffman, Duane S. 1991. *Mifflin County Amish and Mennonite Story 1791-1991*. Elverston.

Keel, William D. 1994. "Reduction and Loss of Case Marking in the Noun Phrase in German--American Speech Islands: Internal Development or External Interference?" In *Sprachinselforschung*, hrsg. Nina Berend und Klaus J. Mattheier, 93-104. Frankfurt.

Kupferschmidt, Doris. 1994. "Tradierung von Lebensformen in einer modernen Gesellschaft: Die Amischen in Pennsylvania als Subkultur der USA." Diplomarbeit, Universität Passau.

Louden, Mark L. 1994. "Syntactic Change in Multilingual Speech Islands." In *Sprachinselforschung*, hrsg. Nina Berend und Klaus J. Mattheier, 73-92. Frankfurt.

Plancke, Fritz. 1984. "The Evolution of Clothing Trends Among the Amish: An Interpretation." In *Internal and External Perspectives on Amish and Mennonite Life*, hrsg. Werner Enninger, 12-23. Essen.

Polenz, Peter von. 1994. *Deutsche Sprachgeschichte*, Bd. 2. Berlin.

Raeithel, Gert. 1992. *Geschichte der nordamerikanischen Kultur*. 3 Bde. Weinheim.

Raith, Joachim. 1982. *Sprachgemeinschaftstyp, Sprachkontakt,Sprachgebrauch: Eine Untersuchung des Bilinguismus der anabaptistischen Gruppen deutscher Abstammung in Lancaster County, Pennsylvania*. Wiesbaden.

Salmons, Joseph. 1994. "Naturalness and Morphological Change in Texas German." In *Sprachinselforschung*, hrsg. Nina Berend und Klaus J. Mattheier, 59-72. Frankfurt.

Sartori, Giovanni. 1992. *Demokratietheorie*. Darmstadt.

Schilling, Heinz. 1991. "Nationale Identität und Konfession in der europäischen Neuzeit." In *Nationale und kulturelle Identität*, hrsg. Bernhard Giesen, 192-254. Frankfurt.

Taylor, Ch. 1995. *Philosophical Arguments*. London.

Vossen, Joachim. 1994. *Die Amishen Alter Ordnung in Lancaster County Pennsylvania. Religions- und wirtschaftsgeographische Signifikanz einer religiösen Gruppe im Kräftefeld der amerikanischen Gesellschaft*. Berlin.

Wehler, Hans-Ulrich. 1987. *Deutsche Gesellschaftsgeschichte 1700-1815*. München.

Wehler, Hans-Ulrich. 1995. *Deutsche Gesellschaftsgeschichte 1849-1914*. München.

Joachim Raith
Universität/Gesamthochschule Essen
Essen, Germany

The Speech Island "Big Valley" as a Speech Community

> Das Bild der Insel impliziert ein *Territorium* und die
> *Wesensverschiedenheit* vom umgebenden Meer, als Teil
> des Festlandsockels oder als Rest eines versunkenen
> Festlands. Kann die Wesensverschiedenheit primär
> sprachlich begründet sein—gibt es *sprachlich motivierte
> Inseln*? (Stölting-Richert 1994, 179)

When or if people immigrate, then they tend to assimilate as a rule within about three generations, at the latest. The Old Order Amish and other (Conservative) Mennonite groups in Pennsylvania and other locations in the U.S. have retained their Palatinate-based dialect as their vernacular and a Lutheran biblical High German as their religious ritual language for more than 300 years. By means of language contact (and economic contact) the local variety of American English was adopted. For sociolinguistic research into language contact this provides an almost "ideal" language laboratory situation to investigate pertinent questions: from a linguistic point of view to investigate contact induced phenomena, from a sociolinguistic point of view to describe the functional distribution of the varieties and the rules and regulations of their use. The coincidence of religious and social community and the isolation from the mainstream culture facilitates this undertaking. Or, as Stölting-Richert (1994, 181f.) puts it, "die Konkurrenzerfahrung führt zum Implikationsschluss: von Religionszugehörigkeit wird auf Sprachbeherrschung geschlossen und umgekehrt; dies wird gefördert durch die sprachlichen Konsequenzen von Konfessionsunterschieden …"

Some years ago the Amish were in the focus of public interest, enhanced by the interest in alternative forms of living. This was—in part—initiated by the film of the anthropologist director of *Witness*, Peter Weir. This film which deals in a rather serious mode with the "otherness" and "exotic nature" of the Old Order Amish also tries to illustrate their nonverbal, semiotic behaviour: As a means of transportation in "General Motors" country they do not use (or rather possess) motor cars but horse-drawn buggies in various forms and shapes according to group membership. For the daily field work (the dominant profession is farmer) they use horses and mules, some more progressive sectarians use tractors with steel rims or with full rubber tires. They do not wear western "casual wear" despite the fact that Levi's is around the corner, but uniform, "old-fashioned" pieces of clothing. In the home country of AT&T they use neither (private) telephones nor the news provided by CNN, the news channel, nor the local radio station sponsored by McDonald's. In addition they do not use electricity by public energy providers, but try to make use of other sources of energy, such as wind and water.

And their linguistic behaviour separates them from the surrounding culture, too: Pennsylvania German (or Pennsylvania Dutch) instead of English as the main means of communication and Bible German as their ritual language. These are some reasons why the Amish have become a tourist attraction, at least in Lancaster County, Pennsylvania, with all the semitrue, distorting stereotypes.

Exkursus: Big Valley as a Physical "Speech Island"

The Big Valley, or Kishacoquillas Valley (the name comes from an eighteenth-century Shawnee Indian chief), when judged by its geographical make-up, comes as close to a nonmaritime island as is possibly imaginable. It is situated in the Appalachian Ridge and Valley Region in central Pennsylvania. The valley which runs on a northeast-southwest axis is borderlined by two parallel mountain ridges. On one side of the valley we find Jacks Mountain with its long twenty-mile gapless span. This mountain range is at its maximum elevation about 2,000 feet high. The Big Valley lies on the northwest side of Jacks Mountain. The northeastern edge of the valley is formed by another mountain range, Stone Mountain, whose elevation of 2,250 feet is the highest in Mifflin County. The Big Valley is five miles wide at its lower end and less than two miles across at its upper end. Hostetler characterizes this "island without water" as follows: "Protected by mountains on either side, this valley, thirty miles long, is a complete unit with natural entrance only through gaps. Within these walls is an agricultural landscape never more beautiful than in spring or harvest time. Viewed from the tops of Jacks Mountain, hundreds of fields in various shades of green and yellow form a patchwork which could not be duplicated by the Amish inhabitants, famous for their beautiful quilts" (1948, 226). An abundance of limestone contributed to the valley's rich soil, and this is what the original Amish settlers, so one says, smelled for a hundred miles (Kauffman 1991, 41). The soil with the greatest potential for productivity in the area was the limestone area of the Kishaquocillas Valley. Another resource worth mentioning is timber: hardwoods such as chestnut, hickory, oak, and walnut predominated, but pine and hemlock were also found. The only main road that cuts through the valley near its lower end is route 322 which goes through Reedsville and Milroy.

Big Valley in the 20th Century

In the Big Valley, Pennsylvania, there are twelve religious groups that can be traced back to the Old Order Amish (henceforth OOA). All groups can be traced back to those Amish groups which came from southeast Pennsylvania and settled there from 1791 onwards. These groups can be classified vis à vis the U.S. society into "high" and into "low" churches, the criterion being the degree of assimilation, whereby "low" means that the old traditions and mores have been retained. Around 1900 there were three OOA groups in the Big Valley: The "Old Church" ("Alt Gmee"), the "Old School" ("Nebraskans") and the Peachy Amish. The three groups still exist today.

As the Amish groups often name themselves after their bishops, some of the labels have changed in time. As some of their bishops were Bylers, the "Alt Gmee" ("Old Church") was called Byler Church. The Bylers regard themselves as the core Amish of Mifflin County, from whom all other Amish groups (and Mennonite groups) in the Big Valley can be derived. The Byler Amish as a group have proved to be the most stable. Only a few families changed to the "New Amish" who ceased to exist in the valley in 1986. The Byler Amish are also called "Yellow-toppers" because of the color of their buggy tops or, sometimes, "Bean-soupers" because it is their custom to serve bean soup after their Sunday service. This, in fact, they have in common with the "White-toppers." The "Yellow-toppers" are conservative. The men wear their hair so that it covers their ears, they wear white shirts on formal occasions, otherwise predominantly blue shirts. They wear one suspender. The women wear brown bonnets and the traditional "Mantel." Their houses are simple but attractive and well kept. Curtains on the lower half of the windows are permitted, but there are no woven carpets. Tractors and other technical aids are permitted. But tractors may not be used in the fields, only for belt power. Today there are about 110 members of the "Alt Gmee," in two church districts around Belleville. In 1948 the Bylers started an affiliation with the Rennos ("Black-toppers"), i.e., they encourage interaction, they exchange preachers.

The "Old School" or Nebraska Amish separated in 1881 from the "Old Gmee": "Various reasons for the split have been given. Some said it was a dispute over cloverseed. Others claimed controversy over steam engines caused the break. Issues pertaining to the length of men's hair, buggy styles, and fashions and type of clothing material were also factors" (Kauffman 1991, 119). The Nebraska Amish wanted to go back to their old *Attnung* ('order') of 1830. Their name goes back to an Amish settlement in Nebraska who helped the Mifflin County group with the selection of their preachers. They are very conservative and allow but a very few innovations. They are probably the strictest Amish. The men wear their hair almost shoulder-length, William Penn style. They wear white shirts and brown denim trousers, no suspenders, their trousers are laced up in the back. Their hats have very wide brims. If necessary, they put on long overcoats, always grey. The women wear black bandanas or the flat straw hat, bonnets are not permitted. They prefer dark, solid materials. Until about 1940 wheat was threshed with horse power. Their houses are inconspicuous, even shabby. They do not display any exterior trimmings, curtains and carpets are forbidden. The barns are not painted. The tops of their buggies are white, therefore the label "White-toppers." In 1933 a schism occurred in the Nebraskan community: a member of the group bought a house from a person outside the fellowship and refused to cut off the protruding end of the gable. Some families followed. Christian Zook was their leader, therefore they were called "Zook Old School." The original Nebraskans continued as "Yoder Old School." In 1985 a somewhat more "progressive" group favoured the use of automatic pick-up balers and some other technical innovations. Thus a new faction, the "Back Mountain District" came into being. At present, there are two Yoder Amish districts and three Zook Amish districts in the Big Valley. The two Nebraska Amish groups have a slightly different order and exchange no preachers. Although, theoretically, in a fellowship relationship they are, practically, in an affiliation relationship. The Nebraska Amish are the fastest growing Amish group.

The Peachy Amish group, the biggest of the Amish groups in the Big Valley, is also named after the founder bishop. The reason why they split away from the "Alt Gmee" consisted in an apparently different interpretation of the mode of baptism: baptism in a room inside a house vs. baptism in a river. In the past 50 or 60 years the group is also called Renno Amish; Renno was also a long-serving bishop. The tops of their buggies are black, hence the name "Black-toppers." Their *Attnung* is similar to that of the Byler and Nebraska Amish. They practice strict shunning and emphasize nonconformity. In the field only horses and mules are allowed, tractors and engines may be used for belt power. Their barns are normally red, their houses white. Carpets and indoor plumbing are allowed, also curtains on the lower half of the windows. The clothes they wear are similar to those of the Byler Amish ("Yellow-toppers"). Married women wear dresses in dark solid colours, dark bonnets and white, starched prayer coverings and a *Halsduch*. The men have a full *Täuferbart*, the hair just about covers the ear. They wear one suspender, the colour of the trousers is black. The hat is either a black felt hat or a rather broad-brimmed straw hat. The brim is somewhat narrower than that of the Nebraskans. Today there are seven Renno Church districts in the Big Valley.

In 1911 a schism occurred in the Peachy Church ("Black-toppers"). As a result there was a fourth Amish denomination in the valley: The Zook-Speicher Amish, from 1962 onwards called the Valley View Amish Mennonites. The "Beachy Amish," as they were also called, stressed their Amish identity, but their attitude was less restrictive than that of the other Amish in the valley. The men wear two suspenders, the range of permitted materials and colours increased, the brims of hats became more narrow, the beards shorter; in addition cardigans and jackets with zips could be worn. At the end of the 1940s electricity became an issue. Finally the Beachy Amish church permitted the use of commercially produced electricity in 1948. Tractors with rubber tires were allowed before 1954. In 1954 the Beachys, after a long controversy, allowed the possession of motor cars: The colour of the cars had to be dark and solid. This decision to permit motor cars increased the distance to the other Amish in the valley. Other consequences were the increased mobility, and thus increased possibilities as regards jobs, etc. The Beachys built churches, promoted Sunday school, emphasized prosyletising and practiced shunning very moderately. In 1962 they adopted the name Valley View Amish Mennonite church.

Die Beth-El Mennonite church is the result of the split of the Allensville Mennonites. Remnants of characteristic clothing are still visible: Black stockings and cape dresses for women, collarless jackets, no ties for men.

1958 saw the emergence of a new sect, the Holdeman group who show a steady increase in membership ever since. Basic principles are prosyletising and the assurance of salvation. Their dress code is plain, but shows distinct features compared to other Anabaptist sects: men wear beards and moustaches, women characteristic dresses. Cars and modern farm technology are permitted.

In 1972 another new group appeared on the scene, the so-called "New Amish," a split off of the Renno and Byler Churches. "Incarnation" and "assurance of salvation" were their foremost principles. The New Amish held their religious services at home and opposed commercial electricity, motor cars and tractors in the field. After manifold arguments the New Amish movement in the Big Valley ceased to exist in 1986.

The Allensville Mennonite Church is a somewhat more "liberal" group, affiliated to the Allegheny Conference of the Mennonite Church, the biggest group of Mennonites in the U.S. Remnants of the formal dress code for women are recognizable: white prayer coverings and bonnets.

The Locust Grove or Conservative Mennonite Church was founded in 1898 as a conservative spin off of the Belleville and Allensville Mennonites. This *Gmee* belongs to the Conservative Mennonite Conference. The once distinctive dress code can hardly be found today.

The Brethren in Christ Church, a "revivalist" group gained members from the Beachy Amish from 1959 onwards. The emphasis of the group lies on repentance and conversion. No distinct code dress is recognizable.

The Maple Grove Mennonite Church, established in 1868, now a member of the Allegheny Conference of the Mennonite Church is perhaps the most "progressive" in the valley. They were the first to permit attendance in colleges and universities, their pastors are theologically educated persons. Prosyletising is high on the agenda. They are the "highest" Mennonite church in the Big Valley.

These twelve groups of Anabaptist origin in our language island represent various aspects of Amish-Mennonite culture. The OOA groups are nonmissionary and to a high degree endogamous. The Mennonite groups are prosyletising but do not try to convert other Mennonites, only the Holdeman-Mennonites and the Brethren in Christ-Mennonites are active converters.

Systems of Signification

As the short survey of the religious complexity of our language island "Big Valley" indicates: The universe of our social isolate or island is verbally and nonverbally highly coded. Independent of other social categories that are coded, the borderline between one's own world and the world out there is always marked. Forms of signification, as Enninger calls them, play an important role in "high context" cultures. They provide the basis of verbal communication in the appearance phase. To quote Stone (1962, 90):

> Appearance then, is a phase of the social transaction which establishes identifications of the participants. As such, it may be distinguished from discourse, which we conceptualize as the text of the transaction—what the parties are discussing. Appearance and discourse are two distinct dimensions of the social transaction. The former seems more basic. It sets the stage for, permits, sustains, and delimits the possibilities of discourse by underwriting the possibilities of meaningful discussion.

In the Big Valley there are—as mentioned above—three OOA groups, one Beachy Amish group and at least six different Mennonite groups. The OOA own no motor cars, however, they use any means of transportation except the airplane for travel outside their settlement area. Inside their settlement area they exclusively use horse and buggy as a means of transportation. Thus, horse and buggy becomes a salient borderline marker vis à vis the "other" world. Corresponding to the three horse and buggy groups there are three types of buggy which stand in opposition to the cars of all other groups. The three OOA groups overtly signify their group membership through the colour of the buggy top: yellow for the Byler Amish ("Yellow-toppers"), white for the Nebraska Amish ("White-toppers") and black for the Renno Amish ("Black-toppers"). This seemingly outward variation reflects partly the history of Amish schisms where disagreement about normal things of the *Ordnung* led to splits in the groups.

In the Big Valley we find the following contrasts as regards means of transportation, thus setting the appearance stage of social encounters: Buggy vs. Car (black, dark) vs. Car (any colour); this contrast signifies/symbolizes the distinction: Amish ("daidsch") vs. Beachy Amish (intermediate position) vs. "plain" Mennonites/"fancy people." Before beginning a social interaction participants marked by their means of transportation can reduce their mutual insecurity by social identification. They also know which rules of opening an encounter are appropriate as they signify each other:

- whether they operate in the network of their own community (*Gmee*, church district) where interaction is encouraged;
- whether they operate in the fellowship network (same order) where interaction is recommended;
- whether they operate in the affiliation network (basis "Dordrecht and Schleitheim Confessions of Faith") where interaction is permitted;
- whether they belong to communities where at least one church district disallows interaction with the other;
- whether they belong to the mainstream culture where only transactional relationships are permitted.

Hats, beards, suspenders place a male person in his social space: thus, the Nebraska Amish wear no suspenders (the trousers are laced up in the back), the Renno Amish and the Byler Amish wear one suspender, the Beachy Amish two suspenders. The hats of the Nebraskans have a broader brim than those of the Byler Amish and the Renno Amish. Rennos and Bylers, however, have broader brims than the Beachys. The Nebraskans wear their hair notched and their hair almost reaches their shoulders. The Byler Amish also have a notched hairstyle, but their hair is shorter. This is also true for the Rennos. The Beachy Amish wear their hair even shorter and not notched. The Nebraskans wear a beard before baptism, the Rennos only after baptism. The Holdeman Mennonites are the only ones who wear full beards, inclusive of moustache. In a similar way women signify their place in the social space of the "island": how they dress, wear and cover their hair, etc.

Speech Island, Speech Community, Language Change

For Klaus Mattheier, speech island research, to pick up the German terminology, is primarily a laboratory to evaluate sociolinguistic theories of language change. The situation of attrition in which the German dialects find themselves all over the world represent . . . phases, stages of a general process of change . . . The U. S. and Canada are of particular importance in this context, as we can find the various types of speech islands in these two countries (Mattheier).

How can we define our speech island Big Valley in terms of sociolinguistics? The generally accepted criterion, "eine in einem größeren Siedlungsraum, zumindest aber in einer dorfartigen Gemeinschaft lebenden Gruppe von Menschen, die sich durch eine oder mehrere Sprachvarietäten in ihrem Repertoire von der Mehrheitsgesellschaft unterscheidet" (Mattheier), is true of our speech island Big Valley; at least for the

OOA groups: the Nebraskans, for instance, settle in a relatively homogeneous area where only a few of the other denominations settle. Enninger, however, has already pointed out in his research in Pennsylvania German speech islands, or settlements, that the criterion of a homogeneous, closed settlement area is seldom met. Better suited for the work with religiously defined groups, so Enninger, was a definition of speech islands via denomination, family relations, friendship, via a so-called"'mental map." This is the only way in which certain OOA settlement areas (where only a few OOA are actually present) could be defined as speech islands in Lancaster County.

These interaction networks on the basis of social networks may consist of religious or economic or ethnic interests, and "wird von der gemeinsamen Sprachlichkeit dann in der Regel gestützt oder sogar symbolisiert" (Mattheier). A speech island, then, according to Mattheier:

- is a linguistic minority geographically separated from its homeland;
- is a communication community surrounded or superseded by a linguistically and ethnically different contact community/or society;
- is set off from the contact community/society by a number of objective criteria which define its special status;
- gives rise to a particular socio-physical disposition—a so-called speech island mentality;
- owes its existence to the obstructed or delayed linguistic and cultural assimilation vis à vis the contact community/society.

Stölting-Richert (1994, 181) points to a weak point in the definition of speech islands when he says: "Mit der Beherrschung und Verwendung auch der Sprache der Umgebung ist aber der sprachliche "Insel"-Charakter untergraben; tradiert wird/werden die Eigensprache(n) der Gemeinschaft durch die Stärke religiöser, ethnischer und sozialer Faktoren, die die Gemeinschaft primär zusammenhalten . . . " Mattheier summarizes the central question of speech island research:

Der dominierende und strukturierende Entwicklungsprozess innerhalb jeder Sprachinsel ist, wie auch bei jedem einzelnen fremdsprachigen Immigranten, soziolinguistisch und sprachlich ein Assimilationsprozess. Das Besondere an der Sprachinselforschung ist, dass der Prozess nicht "normal" verläuft, sondern durch bestimmte Faktoren verzögert wird: "language loss" ist also in jeder

Sprachinselkonstellation das "Normale" und "language maintenance" ist das Erklärungsbedürftige.

Hagiolect, Language Maintenance, Sociolinguistics

How can we explain the more than 300 years of language maintenance in the Big Valley? Which are the factors that delay assimilation? Which general developments as regards language change can we observe? Are these in line with the processes of language change in other Pennsylvania German areas?

The Anabaptists provide good examples for two diverging developments: on the one hand, despite an identical genesis there is a deliberate process of language maintenance (cf. Enninger 1991, 144), i.e., the ritual language "Bible German" is retained as a nonproductive, fossilized hagiolect, thus protecting the German-based vernacular (this is the case with the OOA but also with the Hutterites); and, on the other hand, there is a deliberate loss of the inherited varieties which can only be explained extralinguistically (this is the case with the "liberal" Mennonite groups).

Exkursus: Role of the Hagiolect

The hagiolect or the ritual language is the marked variety within a linguistic repertoire of a group. It is coded in a written form, but normal members of the religious group would, if they did not master the written form, only achieve, if at all, a kind of listening comprehension, as they are only exposed to reading passages or quotes (from the Bible). This strengthens the markedness of this code and leads, ultimately, to the use of the hagiolect as a restricted code (Raith 1982, 198). This is one of the developments in the religious repertoire communities of the Anabaptists outside the German language area (cf. Stölting-Richert 1994, 184f.), as only the "preachers" have a more or less active command of the ritual language. The hagiolect is based on Standard German but displays strong group-specific features, i.e., sermon Hutterite, Mennonite Standard German, Amish High German to name but a few. As there is no explicit theology, the Bible is the only authority, an interpretation and discussion of the religious principles is out of the question, even regarded as detrimental to the foundations of the respective faith. As Moelleken (1987, 166) puts it:

Die Gemeinde hat niemals die Möglichkeit den Text zu diskutieren oder darüber Fragen zu stellen. Zyniker in der Gemeinde behaupten, dass diese Art des Spracherwerbs von der Kirche unterstützt wird, um die Gläubigen dumm zu halten. Zu viel Wissen führe zu unaufhaltsamen strukturellen Veränderungen innerhalb ihrer Gemeinden, sprich Kirchengemeinden, die nicht im Interessse des mennonitischen Glaubens seien.

Something sociolinguistically important happened in the Big Valley at the end of the 19th century: the Amish Mennonites of Maple Grove and Allensville changed their ritual language, introduced bible studies on Sunday night, and Sunday School, in order to attract the young folks and to gain new members. In Belleville, German was used as hagiolect until 1896. Around 1900 all Sunday School classes were held in English. This also applied to the Allensville Amish Mennonites. In 1893 J. K. Hartzler gives a pragmatic description of this process:

> Here in the valley we are not blessed as those of many places with the privilege of hearing the word preached according to the faith in our English language. Our numbers here, to a great extent, use the English language in their everyday conversation and consequently German has to some extent been neglected and the young people do not understand German preaching as well as they should to get the most benefit from it. (Kauffman 1991, 130)

This transition to English of the Mennonites and Amish Mennonites had a twofold consequence: First, the loss of Bible German as their ritual language led to the circumstance that the vernacular PG, lost its support (*Überbau*), i.e., in the families of the non-Amish PG slowly loses its function. The process of language loss sets in. Second, the principle of prosyletising asks for the giving up of the rather inaccessible "secret language" Bible German and the related vernacular PG. The discussion amongst the Mennonites about the introduction of prosyletising (between 1870 and 1900) ultimately led to the abandoning of German as their sacred language for ". . . the language breach has usually prevented a program of active evangelism and outreach" (Bender 1973, 290). The reason for abandoning the minority language(s) was, thus, to emphasize the principle of expanding religious aims.

Social relationships and friendship networks of the OOA are strictly specified. The inherited varieties serve to demarcate these endogamous groups. Face-to-face interaction is only part of the constitution of the group. Equally important is the congruity of social and religious interaction, the participation in the same social and religious norms, the "cognitive" constitution of the groups. This, however, is illustrated by the four socio-religious interactional networks in which the OOA take part:

First, the "church district network," more precisely the *Gmee*, which is defined theologically by the same order (*Attnung*), regionally by buggy distance and spatially by the fact that all members of the *Gmee* assemble in one house where the church service is being held. This is a face-to-face group which shares the common everyday knowledge and sticks to common norms of behaviour, the verbal repertoire is identical. Co-occurrence of personal, social and religious relations. Interaction between participants is encouraged, if not enforced.

Second, the "fellowship network" which consists of church districts which have by and large the same order, i.e., they share essentially the same religious and social norms. These are not necessarily face-to-face groups, but there is regular interaction at the level of the leaders of the community (bishop, preacher, deacon). The linguistic repertoire is identical. Interaction is encouraged. In Big Valley the Byler and the Renno Amish participate in a fellowship network, they exchange preachers and attend each other's *Gmee*.

Third, the "affiliation network" which consists of church districts of different orders whereby the highest authority, the Schleitheim and Dordrecht Confessions of Faith, is generally recognized. Thus, in Lancaster County, the OOA communities are in affiliation with the Conservative Mennonites and the Mennonite Church Mennonites. Common indices of appearance are reduced: a few remnants of a once similar dress code survived. The once common linguistic repertoire is also reduced as most of the Mennonite communities have given up the inherited German varieties. Interaction within the affiliation network is permitted. In the Big Valley the two Nebraskan Amish groups do have roughly the same order, but they do not exchange preachers nor do they attend each other's *Gmee*. Their relationship is not really one of fellowship but rather one of affiliation.

Fourth, the "mainstream network" whereby the relationships for the OOA is marked by the principle of "separation of this world" where only transactional business relations are permitted, where hardly any face-to-face contact exists. The linguistic repertoire is different.

Our *Sprachinsel* Big Valley consists thus, as we have seen, of overlapping "interactional networks." These "social networks," as John Gumperz (1977, 87) calls them, are a means to investigate the relationships of members of a local network with co-inhabitants of the respective area, in order to point to the socio-ecological factors which influence the linguistic repertoire of speakers. The substrate speech community in our speech island Big Valley consists of a number of basic units, the "networks," in which a member of a community participates to various degrees and in more than one function. In this context it is worth mentioning that the network concept does not explicitly specify the type of interaction. Linguists doing field work who use this concept constantly hypothesize about the make up of these networks in which they carry out empirical research.

In the Big Valley this also poses some problems: The Nebraskan Amish have roughly the same order, but do not exchange preachers and do not attend each other's service. Do they interact within the fellowship network or the affiliation network? Or the Byler Amish and the Renno Amish: although their order is slightly different, is there regular interaction, exchange of preachers, visiting patterns? John Gumperz calls this the "self-recruiting force" of the networks under investigation, i.e., not a priori definitions of the field worker are constitutive for the network structure but how a person places and interprets himself/herself in space and time.

The socio-religious situation of the *Täufer* may serve to illustrate the consequences of language contact situations: to show, how, on the one hand, some groups have retained, over centuries, their German-based bi- or multilingualism in diglossic distribution and, on the other hand, how linguistic assimilation, i.e., the convergence of linguistic repertoires, has led to the language death of a native variety "ohne dass jedoch der Wegfall des sprachlichen Minoritätenstatus . . . mit der Aufgabe des religiösen Minoritätenstatus verknüpft ist" (Enninger 1991, 143). If "isolative" motives were decisive then the functional use and the diglossic separation contributed to language maintenance. Stölting-Richert also stresses the point that the more isolative speech communities are with respect to religion and ethnicity vis à vis their immediate environment and vis à vis their original homeland the more they develop into an ethnodenominational group where shared origin and shared religion coincide for longer periods of time as the social and religious community also survives as an economic community: thus, we can speak of a state within a state (1994, 186). If, however, "integrative" motives prevailed, then we find, as a rule, rapid assimilation.

Bilingualism and Diglossia

In the Big Valley we can, tentatively, distinguish three sociolinguistic situations: First, the so-called conservative sectarians, i.e., the OOA (Bylers, Nebraskans, Rennos): their sociolinguistic situation can be described as a stable bilingual/diglossic state, i.e., every fully socialized member of this group knows the contact varieties English, Pennsylvania German (and Bible German, in a restricted way). PG and AE are acquired from childhood. Mark Louden calls this "ambilinguism." One thing is worthy of note: the spoken English of the OOA and Mennonites. The Big Valley shows different contact phenomena compared to Lancaster County or the Big Valley descent from "indigenous" Amish groups whose language acquisition patterns have changed relatively late and the necessity of an "ethnic" marking does not exist in this specific speech island situation, the spoken English of the socio-religious groups comes up with less "German" interferences or other contact induced features. An exception seems to be the Nebraskan Amish: because of their stricter separation from their neighbourhood their English seems to vary from those of the co-territorial Amish. The vernacular PG is used in the domains of family and friends in informal contexts. In the *Gmee* and at more formal occasions, particularly in the school context a higher form of PG is being used (connected with quotations from the Bible). Domains of English are: members of the family who have left their faith (symbolic value of PG), friends, written language, official school language. In this context it is interesting to see what the different groups understand under the term "Deidsch." "Amish un deidsch is the same. Mir heese se amish un mir

heese se deidsche Leit" (cf. Eichinger 1999, 7), or "unser (Satt) Leit." "Klar ist . . . ,
dass man wissen muss, dass das Wort *deutsch*, das man verwendet, wenn man diese
Sprachgemeinschaften als deutsche Sprachinseln bezeichnet, eine historische Bedeutung
hat und nicht den Kern der Selbstdefinition der Gruppen trifft. Die kulturell
'deutscheste' Korrelation, die sich ergibt, die protestantische Tradition mit der
Lutherbibel, spielt nur in einem sehr abgeschlossenen Bereich innerhalb der
Gemeinschaften eine Rolle" (Eichinger, 1999, 10). This fits in very well with the all-
pervading duplicity of keep-the-distance from the outside world and keep-the-solidarity
with your own group. Thus, the OOA form a "community of practice," a practice that
is based on a fundamental protestantism which regards the Luther bible and some
other traditional songs and texts (as the *Ausbund*) as promoting their group identity. It
is obvious that to speak German has a highly symbolic value for the Amish and that
those people who do not use German in the *Gmee*, i.e., who have given up the hagiolect
Bible German, are neither Amish nor *deidsch*. Thus, for the Amish the Mennonites are
no longer *deidsch*, maybe they are not really "English" either, but certainly not *deidsch*
any longer. This is rather astonishing as the separation cuts through families in the Big
Valley who were originally all Amish. We cannot but agree with Huffines (1994, 49)
that "a strict diglossia within the separatist groups does not exist. The use of English
within the separatist groups steadily increases, even with more intimate domains, a
progression that seems to be accellerating."

Second, the Beachy Amish call themselves *deidsch*. They occupy an intermediate
position as regards their linguistic repertoire and the admission of technological novelties.
The OOA no longer accept the Beachy Amish as *deidsch*. The church service is
occasionally still held in German. In the Big Valley there are attempts by one group to
go back to the in-house religious service, from church Amish to house Amish. As
regards distinctive dress patterns and means of transportation they also occupy an
intermediate position. The linguistic situation: a bilingualism which is not entirely
stable any longer, remnants of diglossia are still there.

Third, in the case of the more liberal Mennonite groups who roughly correspond
to Louden's nonsectarians. Here we find a situation of instable bilingualism, the
functional/diglossic separation does no longer exist, whereby PG or English can
dominate. Both are learned at childhood, but not to the same degree: either PG is
dominant or English is dominant (loss of PG, first language attrition). PG does no
longer occupy functional domains and is used—if used at all—by older speakers. All
domains are now English. The Amish regard them as *Englische*.

As for general tendencies of language change I believe that Louden's predictions
will be right: All three groups show a strong tendency in their PG to borrow from
English. The OOA show a strong tendency towards syntactic and semantic convergence,
at the same time retaining PG phonology. The Mennonites who have given up German

show, at least occasionally, phonological impositions of PG on English and a tendency to retain syntactic and semantic features. Perhaps it is true what Mattheier predicts:

Nach allen vorliegenden Entwicklungsprognosen wird das Pennsylvania-Deutsch unter den nonplain people . . . in den nächsten Generationen völlig aufgegeben. Die plain people bewahren es jedoch relativ stabil. Es zeichnet sich also eine Konstellation ab, in der Pennsylvania Deutsch nur noch von den plain people und nicht mehr von den nonplain people verwendet wird. dadurch gewinnt aber das Pennsylvania-Deutsch eine erhebliche sozialsymbolische Funktion hinzu, die es heute erst ansatzweise in wenigen Regionen hat. Durch das Pennsylvania-Deutsch können die *plain people* ihre "Sonderheit" eindeutig symbolisieren.

This use of a Palatinate-based variety of German serves as an appropriate means of communication, which, at the same time, functions as a keep-the-distance code vis-à-vis the surrounding mainstream culture. The loss, however, of this keep-the-distance function would jeopardize the coherence and ultimately the existence of the speech island "Big Valley." Or, as Stölting-Richert (1994, 190) puts it:

Die universell werdende Konfession, die Nationalstaatlichkeiten und die Nationalsprachlichkeiten haben in der westlichen Hemisphäre ihre Rollen konfliktarm verteilt oder sind auf dem Weg dorthin: Es sind die politischen und sozialen Antagonismen der internationalen Migration, die zu sprachsoziologischen Veränderungen führen. Hier gibt es nur noch diskontinuierliche Schichtungen, keine Inseln mehr.

References

Bender, Harold S. 1973. "Language Problems." *Mennonite Encyclopedia* 3:290-92.

Eichinger, Ludwig M. 1999."Das europäische Erbe einer amerikanischen Religionsgemeinschaft: Zum Sprachgebrauch der Amish-people im Kishacoquillas Valley/Pennsylvania." Unpublished manuscript.

Enninger, Werner. 1991. "Offensive und Defensive (Sprach-) Minderheiten."*Akten des 7. Essener Kolloquiums über Minoritätensprachen/Sprachminoritäten" vom 14.-17.6.1990 an der Universität Essen*, ed. J. R. Dow and T. Stolz, 145-51. Bochum.

Enninger, Werner, and Raith, Joachim. 1988. "Varieties, Variation, and Convergence in the Linguistic Repertoire of the Old Order Amish in Kent County, Delaware." *Variation and Convergence: Studies in Social Dialectology*, ed. P. Auer and A. di Luzio, Berlin. 259-92.

Gumperz, John J. 1977. "Social Meaning in Linguistic Structures." In *Language in Social Groups: Essays by John J. Gumperz*, ed. A. S. Dil, 274-310. Stanford.

Hostetler, John A. 1948. "Life and Times of Samuel Yoder." *The Mennonite Quarterly Review* (October).

Hostetler, John J. 1993. *Amish Society*, 4th ed. Baltimore.

Huffines, Marion Lois. 1994. "Directionality of Language Influence: The Case of Pennsylvania German and English." In *Sprachinselforschung*, ed. N. Berend and K. J. Mattheier, 47-58.

Kauffman, S. Duane. 1991. *Mifflin County Amish and Mennonite Story 1791-1991*. Belleville.

Louden, Mark L. 1992. "Old Order Amish Verbal Behavior as a Reflection of Cultural Convergence." *Diachronic Studies on the Languages of the Anabaptists*, ed. K. Burridge and W. Enninger, 264-78.

Mattheier, Klaus J. no date. "Sprachinselsoziolinguistik: Beobachtungen und Überlegungen an deutschsprachigen Sprachinseln." Typescript. Heidelberg.

Moelleken, W. W. 1987. "Die russlanddeutschen Mennoniten in Kanada und Mexiko: Sprachliche Entwicklung und diglossische Situation."*Zeitschrift für Dialektologie und Linguistik* 54.

Raith, Joachim. 1981."Phonologische Interferenzen im amerikanischen Englisch der anabaptistischen Gruppen deutscher Herkunft in Lancaster County (Pennsylvania) unter Berücksichtigung von Sprachgemeinschaftstyp und Erwerbskontext." *Zeitschrift für Dialektologie und Linguistik* 48: 35-52.

Raith, Joachim. 1982. *Sprachgemeinschaftstyp, Sprachkontakt, Sprachgebrauch*. Wiesbaden.

Raith, Joachim. 1992. "Diachronic and Synchronic Aspects of Status Change: The Case of the Old Order Amish and Related Groups."*Status Change of Languages*, ed. U. Ammon and M. Hellinger, 457-86. Berlin.

Rein, Kurt. 1977. *Religiöse Minderheiten als Sprachgemeinschaftsmodelle*. Wiesbaden.

Stölting-Richert, Wilfried. 1994. "Glaube und Sprache: Die Rolle der Konfessionen bei sprachsoziologischen Wandlungen in deutschen Sprachinseln." In *Sprachinselforschung*, ed. N. Berend and K. J. Mattheier, 179-92.

Stone, Gregory P. 1962. "Appearance and the Self." *Human Behavior and Social Processes: An Interactionist Approach*, ed. A. Rose, 86-118.

Mark L. Louden
University of Wisconsin-Madison
Madison, Wisconsin

An Eighteenth-Century View of Pennsylvania German and Its Speakers

1. Introduction

As is familiar to students of the history of Pennsylvania German (PG), the dialect emerged in colonial Pennsylvania during the eighteenth century through the synthesis of varieties of German spoken by emigrants from the central and southern German-speaking areas of Central Europe, mainly those from the Rhenish Palatinate. To this day, PG resembles most closely the modern dialects of the southeastern Palatinate, the *Vorderpfalz*. Until recently, most linguistic research on PG was of a traditional dialectological character, with scholars focusing on the rigorous description of Pennsylvania German phonology and vocabulary, patterns of intradialectal variation according to geography, and parallels between the sounds and words of PG and those of its modern cousin dialects in the Palatinate in order to shed light on the dialect's genesis some two centuries ago. Over the last two decades, Pennsylvania German linguistics has seen a shift in focus toward the sociolinguistic circumstances of PG speakers with a special emphasis on differences between the two major social subgroups, the so-called sectarians (mainly members of Old Order Mennonite and Old Order Amish communities) and the nonsectarians, other PG speakers, usually of Lutheran or (German) Reformed background.[1]

The most obvious sociolinguistic difference between sectarian and nonsectarian Pennsylvania Germans has to do with maintenance of the dialect. Whereas PG is today nearly extinct among nonsectarians, it continues to be naturally transmitted from Old Order Mennonite and Old Order Amish parents to their children such that virtually all sectarian Pennsylvania Germans can be said to speak the dialect and English with equal facility. In order to account for these differential patterns of maintenance of PG, researchers point mainly to the fact that the dialect has ceased to fill any major sociolinguistic need among nonsectarians, while among sectarian speakers PG serves important symbolic functions as both a connection to the past and as a marker of distance between themselves and their non-Old Order counterparts. A logical question to ask at this point is, if PG is sociolinguistically superfluous for today's nonsectarians, why did they maintain it for over two hundred years?

In my view, the root causes of attrition away from PG, that is, shift toward English monolingualism, have been present since the emergence of the dialect during the eighteenth century. As I have discussed elsewhere (Louden 2001, 15-16), the maintenance of PG among nonsectarians has throughout its history been correlated with the low social and geographic mobility of its speakers. A child who learned PG from her parents was more likely to continue speaking the dialect through adulthood and to pass it on to her own children if she lived most or all of her life in a rural area among mainly other nonsectarian Pennsylvania Germans, had limited formal education, and married another PG speaker. Only under such circumstances has the dialect had a sociolinguistic function as an oral medium of informal daily communication. Conversely, Pennsylvania German speakers who have moved to larger communities where English is the norm, achieved higher levels of formal education, and married non-Pennsylvania Germans have in virtually every case either themselves shifted to using English predominantly during adulthood and/or have not passed the dialect on to their children. These fundamental factors underlying the attrition away from PG were masked somewhat during the nineteenth century by the natural increase in the population of nonmobile, nonsectarian Pennsylvania Germans, but the major social and demographic changes of twentieth-century American society (including large population shifts due to urbanization, the movement away from small-scale farming, and the conscription of large numbers of males during World War II) made the rapid decline of PG among them all but inevitable.

Given the hypothesis, then, that the root causes for the decline of PG are to be traced back to the formation of the dialect over two hundred years ago, any direct attestation of the sociolinguistic situation of the earliest Pennsylvania Germans is valuable.[2] Although descriptions of eighteenth-century Pennsylvania society abound, including the lives of its German-speaking members, references to the everyday verbal behavior of Pennsylvania Germans during this period are relatively rare. The classic 1789 pamphlet of Dr. Benjamin Rush (1875), while containing much of interest about early Pennsylvania German life, devotes but one paragraph to their linguistic situation (Rush 1875, 54-55). But there is a secondary source of major importance, namely, the work of James Owen Knauss, Jr. (1922), based on information drawn mainly from German-language newspapers published in Pennsylvania before and shortly after the Revolution. Knauss in fact devoted an entire chapter (Knauss 1922, 104-18) to the subject of language that contains much of relevance for the present study.

In this essay I focus on what appears to be the most extensive contemporary firsthand description of the sociolinguistic situation of German in Pennsylvania, that of an eighteenth-century polymathic German physician named Johann David Schöpf (Schöpf 1788). Schöpf was born in Wunsiedel, near Bayreuth in northern Bavaria, in 1752, and earned his medical degree in 1776 at the University of Erlangen (Morrison 1910, Lloyd 1992). Soon after completing his degree, in 1777 Schöpf was sent to America as the chief surgeon for the Hessian soldiers fighting on behalf of the British crown. Before returning to Germany in 1784, Schöpf undertook an extensive, eleven-month tour of the eastern United States and the Bahamas, making detailed descriptions of the natural situation of the regions he visited, including their inhabitants, both human and animal. The result of Schöpf's journey was a two-volume account that remains an important reference work for those interested in the natural history of early America. Schöpf spent much of the summer and fall of 1783 in Philadelphia and rural southeastern Pennsylvania, providing us with a trove of interesting facts about early Pennsylvania German life.

Five pages of the first volume of Schöpf's account are devoted exclusively to the linguistic situation of (Pennsylvania) German as he observed it (Schöpf 1788, 156-161); these pages, along with a translation, are reprinted in an appendix. In what follows, I discuss Schöpf's various observations in the light of what we know about PG in the eighteenth century from other sources (such as those Knauss 1922 drew on), as well as the facts of the more recent situation of the dialect among nonsectarians. At this point, it should be mentioned that Schöpf's writings under discussion here have not gone unnoticed by others. Already in 1792, Knauss mentions that the *Neue Unpartheyische Lancäster Zeitung* cited Schöpf's observation that "the language of the Germans in Pennsylvania was a fearful mixture of German and English" (Knauss 1922, 108). Further, in the first serious linguistic study of PG, Samuel S. Haldeman (1872, 28) mentions that Schöpf's remarks on PG had also been quoted earlier in that century in reference works on German dialects. And certainly Alfred J. Morrison's 1911 translation of much of Schöpf's book (see also his 1910 article in *German American Annals*) has done much to make English speakers aware of Schöpf's importance. Thus Schöpf's observations about language are not significant for their novelty, but for their relevance in clarifying the situation of PG among nonsectarians from the earliest time right up to the present.

A further remark on the timing of Schöpf's observations needs to be made before considering them in detail. As mentioned above, PG emerged during the eighteenth century; we know this from the fact that by 1800, secondary settlements of PG speakers were established outside of Pennsylvania (e.g., in Ohio and Ontario; Louden 2001, 14). In part on the basis of Schöpf's text (and supported by Knauss's eighteenth-century sources), it seems we can push this *terminus ante quem* for the development of PG back even further, to around 1780. In the introductory chapter to his 1937 doctoral dissertation, Buffington (1937, 1-8), following Strassburger (1934), divides the settlement history of German-speakers in colonial Pennsylvania into three periods: 1683 (the founding of Germantown) to 1710 (the arrival of the Swiss Mennonites); 1710 to 1727 (the passage of a law requiring all immigrants to swear an oath of loyalty to Britain); and 1727 to 1775, at which point immigration from Europe was effectively suspended. The peak of German immigration likely occurred at about mid-century, after which, according to Knauss (1922, 23), there was a sharp decline; he estimates only six thousand German-speakers arrived between 1765 and 1785 (compare this with Wokeck's [1999, 45-6] estimate of a total of 81,000 German immigrants to North

America by way of the port of Philadelphia). It is quite likely, then, that the crucial period in the formation of PG occurred between 1760 and 1780. Schöpf, basing his remarks on experiences of 1783 and 1784, would therefore have witnessed the Pennsylvania German situation immediately after the dialect's coalescence.

2. Schöpf on German-English Contact, Its Structural Consequences, and Its Valuation

To begin, the most obvious fact about the German spoken in Pennsylvania, Schöpf observes, is that is strongly characterized by contact with English and that the result of this "confusion" (*Verwirrung*), linguistic "nonsense" (*Unsinn*), is perceived in a strongly negative way.

Die Sprache, derer sich unsere deutsche Landesleute bedienen, ist ein erbärmlich geradebrechter Mischmasch der englischen und deutschen, in Ansehung der Worte sowohl, als ihrer Fügungen. [1]

Indeed, these two facts, that PG is affected to some extent by contact with English, and that this contact is stigmatized, have been constants throughout the history of the dialect. Virtually every popular treatment of PG has either reiterated these views, often in a ridiculing way, or has defended the image of the dialect in the face of them. The popular (nonlinguists') view of language contact as in some way "unhealthy" is certainly familiar to those who study linguistic varieties strongly affected by contact, including those that emerge in colonial or immigrant situations. Einar Haugen, a pioneer in the study of immigrant languages in the United States, made the following observation in his monumental study on the varieties of Norwegian spoken by immigrants and their descendants in the Upper Midwest:

Many have been the scornful expressions used by observers about the "mongrelian" languages, as the popular publicist Brander Matthews once called them . . . This opinion has been shared to a high degree by the more educated members of each immigrant group, who have lashed their less fastidious countrymen for their treatment of the native tongue. Each critic has usually been familiar with his own group only, and has assumed that some personal or national perversity was the underlying cause. Observers fresh from overseas have been the most vehement in their critique, for to them the phenomenon has often seemed particularly conspicuous. It is noticeable that some years of sojourn among their fellow bilinguals have usually softened many of these judgments, and led even the most puristic to temper their speech to the winds of mongrelianism. (Haugen 1953, 12)

Schöpf would certainly qualify in Haugen's terms as an "observer fresh from overseas," but whether he would have "tempered" his views on PG in any way after spending more time in Pennsylvania remains an open question.

It is interesting to note that Schöpf assesses German-English bilingualism as a form of what some have called "double semilingualism," that is, having incomplete knowledge of two languages:[3]

> In allen Gerichtsgesezlichen- und Staatsangelegenheiten bedient man sich blos der englischen Sprache. Diese wird dahero den deutschen Familien nothwendig, und durch Umgang und Nachahmung geläufig, so, daß sie auch unter sich vielfach, bald elend deutsch, bald noch elender englisch schwäzen, denn sie haben den besondern Vorzug vor andern Nationen, daß sie im eigentlichen Verstand weder der einen noch der andern vollkommen mächtig sind. [4]

This is another common folk linguistic myth regarding bilingualism and one that has been frequently applied to PG speakers as falling between the chairs of German and English. It is true that some nonsectarian speakers speak a form of English with an accent attributable to phonological interference from their PG that differs from the regional varieties spoken by their English monolingual neighbors in Pennsylvania. That fact may support the assessment of the "dutchified" English of nonsectarians as in some sense "imperfect," hence their image as "semispeakers" (Dorian 1981, 106-10) of English. On the other hand, the only way in which nonsectarian Pennsylvania Germans could be viewed as true semispeakers of PG is if they acquired the dialect incompletely during childhood or underwent first-language attrition as adults. Such individuals would then of necessity be fluent English speakers. There has never been an individual reported who is semispeaker of both PG and English, in essence a feral Pennsylvania Dutchman. Nonsectarian speakers of PG typically fall into one of two categories: (1) those who are PG-dominant and speak accented (imperfect, "dutchified") English; and (2) those who are English-dominant and speak imperfect PG, either through incomplete acquisition or first language attrition. The nonsectarian situation thus contrasts with that of most sectarians, who have in effect fully acquired both PG and English. But Schöpf and others would view PG itself as an inherently deficient linguistic system for its difference from Standard and other European varieties of German; therefore anyone who speaks PG, fluently or not, would count for them as a semispeaker of (Standard) German.

As "pitiful" and "ugly" as this early form of PG is to Schöpf, he points out (correctly) how the genetic affinity between German and English facilitates transfer from the latter to the former, as well as the naturalness with which this transfer happens in colloquial speech:

Die nahe Verwandtschaft, die die englische mit der deutschen Sprache hat, hilft die Verwirrung befördern. Wenn jemand nicht sogleich das benöthigte deutsche Wort finden kann, nimmt er ohne Bedenken das nächste beste englische dafür, und viele englische Worte sind ihnen schon so geläufig, daß sie solche zuverlässig für ächt deutsche halten. [3]

What Schöpf is describing are two phenomena that are typical of verbal behavior in bi- or multilingual speech situations, namely code-switching and lexical borrowing. Though not all nonsectarian PG speakers have displayed the same degree of balanced bilingualism between the dialect and English as that of their modern sectarian counterparts, for all PG speakers switching between the two varieties is a natural part of everyday discourse. Furthermore, many words have become fully integrated into the PG lexicon, though not nearly as many as the popular stereotypes might indicate.

One further point about Schöpf's assessments of the implications of German-English contact in Pennsylvania merits mentioning. He notes that contact affects both PG vocabulary (*Worte*) as well as its *Fügungen*. I have translated the latter term as "syntax" (Morrison [1910] uses "syntaxis"), though Schöpf likely meant here to refer to word order, and not syntax in the modern linguistic sense of "(a) grammar." Though a very limited degree of contact-induced change in the direction of English can be observed in certain areas of modern PG syntax, word order is not one of those areas. I revisit this point in section 5, in which I analyze the putative examples of linguistic *Mischmasch* Schöpf cites.

3. Schöpf on Patterns of Language Maintenance and Shift

The contact situation Schöpf describes between German and English in eighteenth-century Pennsylvania, while evidently natural from a sociolinguistic point of view, is not static. Schöpf notes patterns of shift away from German-English bilingualism and toward English monolingualism that are consistent with the situation of virtually all non-English-speaking immigrant groups in the United States. The pressure to become English-dominant is clearly strongest among urban dwellers and those born in America, though the immigrants themselves move in this direction too.

Erwachsene Personen, welche aus Deutschland hinüber kommen, vergessen ihre Muttersprache zum Theil, indem sie eine neue zu lernen sich vergeblich bemühen; die eingebornen lernen ihre Muttersprache fast niemalen ordentlich und rein. Die Kinder der Deutschen, besonders in Städten, gewöhnen sich aus dem Gassenumgang ans Englische; von ihren Eltern werden sie in der einen Sprache angeredet, und sie antworten ihnen in der andern. [2]

The asymmetry of language use between parents and children (i.e., parents addressing their children in German, who may respond in English) Schöpf mentions is also a common phenomenon among non-English-speaking communities undergoing shift toward the dominant language.

The major reason for the shift away from German (of whatever form) Schöpf cites is the dominance of English in commercial and legal affairs, something that would naturally affect upwardly mobile immigrants and their descendants in cities and towns (such as Philadelphia) more than those in the countryside.

Es sind einige wenige abgesonderte Ortschaften, und einzelne wohnende Landleute im Gebürge, die weniger Umgang mit Engländern pflegen, und dahero zwar zuweilen ganz und gar kein Englisch verstehen, aber deswegen doch auch nicht besser deutsch sprechen. [6]

Schöpf is clearly referring here to the ancestors of today's last nonsectarian PG (i.e., "bad" German) speakers living in rural southeastern Pennsylvania. But the relative intensity of the need to use English is not the only factor in the maintenance or loss of (Pennsylvania) German; the ineffectiveness of institutional support for German is clearly relevant also. Schöpf mentions both the pulpit and the press in this regard.

Die einige Gelegenheit, wo die Deutschen einen ordentlichen Vortrag in ihrer eignen Sprache hören, (denn Lesen ist nicht ihre Sache) ist in der Kirche. —Aber auch während der deutschen Predigt, unterhalten sie sich einander in ihrem Bastard-Kauderwelsch. [5][4]

Nicht genug aber, daß man elend spricht, man schreibt und druckt ebenso erbarmenswürdig. Die deutsche Buchdruckerey des Melchior Steiners, (und ehemals des Christoph Sauers) liefert wöchentlich ein deutsches Zeitungsblatt, welches eben so häufige, als traurige Beweise der erbärmlich verunstalteten Sprache unserer amerikanischen Landsleute enthält. Es sind hauptsächlich nur Uebersetzungen aus englischen Blättern, aber so steif, und so englisirt, daß sie ekelhaft werden. Die beyden deutschen Geistlichen und Herr Steiner selber besorgen das Blatt. Wenn ich nicht irre, erhält Herr **Kunze** allein 100 Pfund Pens. für seine Arbeit. Wenn wir sie rein deutsch schrieben, entschuldigen sich die Verfasser, so würden sie unsere amerikanische Bauern weder verstehen noch lesen wollen. [12]

Schöpf's reasons for the shift away from German find support in Knauss's (1922) assessment of the language situation in eighteenth-century Pennsylvania derived from information in German-language newspapers. Knauss (1922, 75-76; 108-9) points out that about mid-century, there was a movement in England to found free schools for the children of German immigrants to Pennsylvania with the ostensible goal of making them proficient in both English and German. This movement met with initial protest, however, from those German-speakers who saw it as a covert way of trying to make the children English monolinguals. But Knauss notes that between the 1750s and the Revolution, this "spirit of suspicion was gradually replaced by one of mutual respect and goodwill" (Knauss 1922, 109). He notes (1922, 110-11) several factors that combined to promote English monolingualism, including: intermarriage with non-Germans; commercial interests; political unity in the cause against England; a sharp decline in the number of immigrants from Germany between 1755 and 1781; suspension of contacts between Pennsylvania and Europe during the Revolution; and the poor quality of the German-language press (including the fact that the news appeared more quickly in English newspapers). Further, Knauss points out that the fact that a stigmatized Pennsylvania German colonial dialect clearly distinct from Standard German had arisen during this period became an added factor: "Many of the common people, ridiculed by their English friends and conscious that their language was far from being the German which their ministers were preaching in the pulpits, became ashamed of their dialect and attempted to speak the language which their English neighbors used" (Knauss 1922, 111-12).

Reminding ourselves of the question posed in the introduction, how PG was able to survive for as long as it has among nonsectarians in the face of the pressures from English, Knauss (1922, 116-18) cites the protective influence of rural isolation already mentioned. As this isolation, geographic and social, diminished, PG was to meet with the same fate as in cities and towns. Writing from the perspective of the early twentieth century, Knauss notes:

> Thus the influences which were rapidly causing the German language to disappear in Philadelphia had not yet seriously affected its vitality in German inland counties. Here the struggles for the preservation of the language were destined to be repeated during the entire nineteenth century, always with the same ultimate outcome, so that now in the second decade of the twentieth century, the time seems not far distant when the last vestige of the remarkable Pennsylvania-German dialect will have vanished. (Knauss 1922, 118)

Today it seems inevitable that Knauss's prediction will hold true for nonsectarians, though PG will have endured for about one hundred years beyond the time he made it.

Schöpf held out the tepidly optimistic possibility that from the perspective of the time at which he was writing, the mid-1780s, renewed immigration from from Europe might counteract the decline of German (either to Pennsylvania German or extinction):

> Es war zwar nicht zu besorgen, daß die deutsche Sprache, auch bey iher häßlichsten Ausartung, jemals, oder wenigstens nicht so bald ganz in Verfall und Vergessenheit hätte kommen können. Durch den Gottesdienst, die Bibel und den gepriesenen Calender, würde sie sich doch auf mehrere Geschlechter fortpflanzen, wenn auch nicht neue deutsche Emigranten sie von Zeit zu Zeit auffrischten. Vielleicht aber gewinnt sie Verbesserung und Aufnahme durch den gegenwärtigen erneuerten freyen und unmittelbaren Verkehr zwischen dem Mutterlande und Amerika. [13]

Though the German-speaking immigrants to colonial Pennsylvania were indeed followed by successive waves of "fresh" speakers from Europe, these newcomers largely avoided integration into Pennsylvania "Dutch" society, mainly settling in cities and towns where, as we have seen above, English played the leading role. This is an important sociolinguistic fact that makes the Pennsylvania German situation quite different from that of other German-American communities, motivating Kloss (1966), for example, to make a clear distinction between German speech islands of "colonial stock" and those produced by nineteenth- and twentieth-century immigration.

4. Schöpf's "Examples" of Pennsylvania German Speech

I mentioned above that Schöpf is quoted in the first published academic treatment of PG, Haldeman 1872. Haldeman (1872, 28) points out that one of the putative examples of PG Schöpf cites is in fact not representative of native-speaker norms. It is worth considering, then, how closely all the data Schöpf cites match modern PG. We begin with the five full sentences he "quotes" (from [8] and [9]). Below each is the contemporary PG equivalent in italics;[5] in both versions, English derived words (including calques) are in boldface.

(1)   Ich hab' wollen mit meinem Nachbar **tscheinen** und ein Stück **geklaret** Land **purtschasen**.
*Ich hab welle mit meim Nochber **joine** un en Schtick **gecleart** Land **kaafe**.*

(2)   Wir hätten **no doubt**, ein' guten **Barghen** gemacht, und hatten können gut **darauf ausmachen**.
*Mir hette **no doubt** en guter **Bargain** gmacht un hette kenn(d)e gut **ausmache druff**.*

(3) Ich war aber net **capable** so'ne Summe Geld **aufzumachen,** und konnt nicht länger **expekten.**
*Ich war awwer net **able** so viel Geld uff(zu)mache un hab net lenger expecte kenne.*

(4) Das thät mein Nachbar net **gleichen,**[6] und fieng an mich übel zu **yuhsen,** so dacht' ich, 's ist besser du thust **mit aus.**
*Sell deet mei Nochber net gleiche (sell hot mei Nochber net gegliche?) und hot aagfange, mich wiescht (zu) **use,** so hawwich gedenkt, s'is besser, du duscht **unni** (mitaus).*

(5) Mein **Stallion** ist über die **Fehnß getsche[m]pt,**[7] und hat dem Nachbar sein' **Whiet** abscheulich **gedämätscht.**
*Mei Hengscht is iwwer die **Fence** getschumpt un hot 'm Nochber sei Weeze schlimm gedamatscht.*

Not surprisingly, there are differences between Schöpf's "examples" and actual PG forms. First, the number of English-derived lexical items is overstated (Haldeman made this very same point regarding sentence 5). The historical tendency to exaggerate English influence on PG by critics (in all senses of the word) of the dialect has been mentioned above.[8] Second, some expressions of past time (e.g., in 3 and 4) employ preterite (simple past) verbal forms. Except for *waar* ('was')-forms of *sei* ('to be'), only present perfect forms have been attested in reliable secondary sources on the dialect. Other differences are more minor (such as the existence of final *-n* in plural and infinitival verbal forms, *wir* for PG *mir* 'we', *das* for PG *sell* demonstrative 'that', etc.). Returning to Schöpf's first sentence regarding the "broken mishmash" character of PG syntax (as well as words), he gives no evidence of it here. As mentioned earlier, PG word order has been unaffected in any significant way by contact with English. Though extraposition (*Ausklammerung*) of certain constituents, especially embedded infinitivals, is more productive in PG than in Standard German (as in sentence 1), this is a well-known fact of spoken varieties of European German, especially regional dialects.

Aside from the sentences Schöpf provides, in (10) and (11) he correctly identifies the two major types of influence from English on the PG lexicon: (1) borrowings (e.g., *serwe* 'to serve [as in a meal]'); and (2) calques (e.g., in modern PG, *abdrehe* = 'to turn off' in all senses, as with a light or a person). Also, the semantic shift of German-derived words that are phonologically similar to English ones does occur, but not as frequently as Schöpf would have us believe here. Referring to the examples in (11), the normal PG verb corresponding to English *belong* is *heere* (cf. German *(ge)hören*), not *belange(n)*; on the other hand, PG *gleiche* (= English *like*) is very much characteristic of

PG (as well as apparently most other varieties of American German and Yiddish). Finally, though, Schöpf's belief that the distribution of the PG modal verb *due* matches that of English *do* (in emphatics and negatives) is spurious; this verb typically marks habitual or iterative aspect, as in: *Ich du Bicher lese* 'I (habitually) read books'.

5. Conclusions

Taking stock of what we have seen, we can say that much of what Johann David Schöpf has to say about German and its speakers in Pennsylvania during the latter half of the eighteenth century, at the very point when the Pennsylvania German dialect had developed, confirms what other sources have observed and is in line with what we know about the sociolinguistic situation of PG in nonsectarian society later, in the nineteenth and twentieth centuries. Specifically, PG has, from the very start, always been in contact with English. Further, nonsectarian PG speakers have only been able to avoid the shift to English monolingualism if they were geographically and socially isolated from the English-speaking mainstream. The dialect's lack of overt prestige (not to mention the outright discrimination its speakers have suffered, especially in schools), as well as the absence of support from being the L-variety in a diglossic relationship with Standard German, have only reinforced the motivation for speakers either to give up speaking the dialect in adulthood and/or to not pass it on to their children (cf. Huffines 1980 for a good description of the currently moribund status of PG among nonsectarians). At the same time, the inherently unstable sociolinguistic (external) situation of PG, has nothing to do with any structural (internal) inadequacy within the dialect itself. Contrary to the old and persistent view of language contact as a kind of infection, the influence of English evident in PG is in no way destabilizing. In any case, a close look at the grammar of PG reveals that in the core areas of structure (phonological and morphosyntactic), evidence of contact-induced change is virtually nonexistent. Such change has been effectively restricted to lexical semantics, including borrowed vocabulary.[9]

The basic accuracy of Schöpf's observations about PG reinforces the hypothesis described at the outset regarding the constancy of the sociolinguistic situation of nonsectarian speakers. But what about the sectarians? Why does Schöpf make no mention of them and why is their situation so different from their nonsectarian counterparts? To begin with, it must be recognized that the percentage of sectarian speakers within the greater Pennsylvania German-speaking population has only recently become significant due to the dual factors of rapid language shift among nonsectarians and the near-exponential growth in the numbers of sectarians. For example, a reliable estimate of the total number of PG speakers in southeastern Pennsylvania in the 1940s is 300,000 (Frey 1949). At that time, the Old Order Amish, the largest sectarian group today, numbered only about 3,000 in Lancaster County (where the nearly all Amish in southeastern Pennsylvania lived; Hostetler 1997, 93), or roughly 1% of total PG-speaking population. There is no reason to assume that the ratio of sectarians to nonsectarians was any different in the eighteenth century. Fogelman (1996, 104-5) estimates that there were approximately 265 original Amish immigrants to the American colonies during the eighteenth century. Comparing that figure with Wokeck's (1999, 45-6) estimate of 81,000 German-speaking immigrants to Pennsylvania during that same time, the Amish would have comprised three tenths of one percent of the total input population. Fogelman (ibid.) estimates 3,207 sectarians total were among the German-speaking immigrants settling in Pennsylvania between 1717 and 1775, still comprising only 4% of the 81,000 cited by Wokeck.

The second part of the question, why the sectarian sociolinguistic situation differs from that of nonsectarians, is easily answerable when one considers the former group's social circumstances. For spiritual reasons sectarians have chosen to remain apart from the social mainstream, one tangible consequence of which is the symbolic function of PG as an outward marker of difference referred to in the introduction. But although they live almost exclusively in rural areas and generally limit formal education to eight grades, this has not resulted in their isolation from English (as it did for generations of rural, nonmobile nonsectarian Pennsylvania Germans). Just the opposite, their increasing economic interconnectedness with the larger society (cf. Kraybill 2001) has if anything led to increased use of English in everyday sectarian life, but crucially *not* at the expense of PG. A detailed discussion of the sociolinguistic circumstances of Pennsylvania German sectarians is beyond the scope of the present article (cf. Louden 1994), but their stable bilingual situation stands in clear contrast to the situation of nonsectarians, who, as Schöpf's account supports, have always been more vulnerable to shift in the direction of English monolingualism.

Appendix

Below are J. D. Schöpf's remarks in full (Schöpf 1788, 156–61) on the situation of German in eighteenth-century Pennsylvania. The spelling and punctuation in A follow the original; the translation in B is my own and differs somewhat from that of Morrison (1910). The numbers in brackets mark quotes referred to in the text above.

A.

[1] Die Sprache, derer sich unsere deutsche Landesleute bedienen, ist ein erbärmlich geradebrechter Mischmasch der englischen und deutschen, in Ansehung der Worte sowohl, als ihrer Fügungen. [2] Erwachsene Personen, welche aus Deutschland hinüber kommen, vergessen ihre Muttersprache zum Theil, indem sie eine neue zu lernen sich vergeblich bemühen; die eingebornen lernen ihre Muttersprache fast niemalen ordentlich und rein. Die Kinder der Deutschen, besonders in Städten, gewöhnen sich aus dem Gassenumgang ans Englische; von ihren Eltern werden sie in der einen Sprache angeredet, und sie antworten

ihnen in der andern. [3] Die nahe Verwandtschaft, die die englische mit der deutschen Sprache hat, hilft die Verwirrung befördern. Wenn jemand nicht sogleich das benöthigte deutsche Wort finden kann, nimmt er ohne Bedenken das nächste beste englische dafür, und viele englische Worte sind ihnen schon so geläufig, daß sie solche zuverlässig für ächt deutsche halten. [4] In allen Gerichtsgesezlichen- und Staatsangelegenheiten bedient man sich blos der englischen Sprache. Diese wird dahero den deutschen Familien nothwendig, und durch Umgang und Nachahmung geläufig, so, daß sie auch unter sich vielfach, bald elend deutsch, bald noch elender englisch schwäzen, denn sie haben den besondern Vorzug vor andern Nationen, daß sie im eigentlichen Verstand weder der einen noch der andern vollkommen mächtig sind.

[5] Die einige Gelegenheit, wo die Deutschen einen ordentlichen Vortrag in ihrer eignen Sprache hören, (denn Lesen ist nicht ihre Sache) ist in der Kirche. — Aber auch während der deutschen Predigt, unterhalten sie sich einander in ihrem Bastard-Kauderwelsch.

[6] Es sind einige wenige abgesonderte Ortschaften, und einzelne wohnende Landleute im Gebürge, die weniger Umgang mit Engländern pflegen, und dahero zwar zuweilen ganz und gar kein Englisch verstehen, aber deswegen doch auch nicht besser deutsch sprechen. [7] Das reinste und schönste Deutsch erhält sich in den Colonien der Mährischen Brüder. — Zur Probe will ich meinen Lesern wörtlich mittheilen, was mir als einem Deutschen, ein deutscher Bauer auf deutsch erzählet hat:

[8] "Ich hab' wollen, sagte er, mit meinem Nachbar tscheinen (*join*) und ein Stück geklaret (*cleared*) Land purtschasen (*purchase*). Wir hätten *no doubt*, ein' guten Barghen (*bargain*) gemacht, und hatten können gut darauf ausmachen. Ich war aber net capable so'ne Summe Geld aufzumachen, und konnt nicht länger expekten. Das thät mein Nachbar net gleichen, und fieng an mich übel zu yuhsen, (*use one ill*) so dacht' ich, 's ist besser du thust mit aus (*to do without*). — — Oder ein dito: [9] Mein Stallion ist über die Fehnß getsche[m]pt, und hat dem Nachbar sein' Whiet abscheulich gedämätscht." D. h. Mein Hengst ist über den Zaun gesprungen, und hat des Nachbars Weizen ziemlich beschädigt. — Aber es ist nicht genug, daß sie ganz englische Worte für deutsche an und aufnehmen; [10] als Schmart seyn (*smart*, thätig, klug) — serben, geserbt haben (*serve*, dienen) sondern sie übersezen andere wörtlich und brauchen sie so; als **absezen**; statt abreisen, sich auf den Weg machen, vom englischen *set off*; **einen auf den Weg sezen**, einen auf den rechten Weg bringen, vom englischen *put one in the road*; **abdrehen**, sich vom Weg abwenden, vom englischen *turn off*; **aufkommen mit einem**, jemanden auf dem Weg einholen, vom englischen *come up with one*. — [11] Oft nehmen sie ein gleichlautendes deutsches Wort, für ein englisches, das ganz einen andern Sinn hat; als, **das belangt zu mir**, das gehört mir, nach dem englischen *this belongs to me*; da doch das deutsche **belangen** und das englische *belong*, ganz verschiedenen Sinn bezeichnen. Oder: "**Ich thue das nicht gleichen,**" vom englischen *I do not like that*, anstatt: das gefällt mir nicht. — Es ist nicht der Mühe werth, mehr dergleichen Unsinn anzuführen; von welchem noch vielen meiner Landsleute die Ohren gellen. — [12] Nicht genug aber, daß man elend spricht, man schreibt und druckt ebenso erbarmenswürdig. Die deutsche Buchdruckerey des Melchior Steiners, (und ehemals des Christoph Sauers) liefert wöchentlich ein deutsches Zeitungsblatt, welches eben so häufige, als traurige Beweise der erbärmlich verunstalteten Sprache unserer amerikanischen Landsleute enthält. Es sind hauptsächlich nur Uebersetzungen aus englischen Blättern, aber so steif, und so englisirt, daß sie ekelhaft werden. Die beyden deutschen Geistlichen und Herr Steiner selber besorgen das Blatt. Wenn ich nicht irre, erhält Herr **Kunze** allein 100 Pfund Pens. für seine Arbeit. Wenn wir sie rein

deutsch schrieben, entschuldigen sich die Verfasser, so würden sie unsere amerikanische Bauern weder verstehen noch lesen wollen.

[13] Es war zwar nicht zu besorgen, daß die deutsche Sprache, auch bey iher häßlichsten Ausartung, jemals, oder wenigstens nicht so bald ganz in Verfall und Vergessenheit hätte kommen können. Durch den Gottesdienst, die Bibel und den gepriesenen Calender, würde sie sich doch auf mehrere Geschlechter fortpflanzen, wenn auch nicht neue deutsche Emigranten sie von Zeit zu Zeit auffrischten. Vielleicht aber gewinnt sie Verbesserung und Aufnahme durch den gegenwärtigen erneuerten freyen und unmittelbaren Verkehr zwischen dem Mutterlande und Amerika. Da man in Amerika, in Absicht auf deutsche Litteratur, bey 30–40 Jahren zurück ist, so wäre es vielleicht eine feine Spekulation, unsere ungelesene und vergessene Dichter und Prosaisten ihrer Gefängnisse in Buchläden zu entlassen und nach Amerika zu transportiren, wie man sonst von England aus, anderes unnüzes Gesindel hinüber schaffte.

B.

[1] The language used by our German countrymen is a pitifully broken mishmash of English and German, with regards to words, as well as syntax. [2] Adults coming over from Germany partially forget their native language in the process of trying unsuccessfully to acquire a new one; the nativeborn practically never learn the mother tongue properly and purely. The children of the Germans, especially in cities, pick up English from the streets; when they are addressed by their parents in the one language, they respond in the other. [3] The close historical relationship between English and German reinforces the confusion. If a speaker cannot immediately think of a German word, he chooses without hesitation the nearest English equivalent, and many English words are already so familiar to the Germans that they actually consider them to be truly German. [4] In all legal and administrative affairs English is used solely. For that reason it becomes a necessity for German families. English has become so familiar through social contact and imitation that even among themselves they chatter away sometimes in miserable German, at others in even more miserable English, giving them the singular distinction among other immigrant groups of having complete knowledge of neither one nor the other language. [5] The only opportunity Germans have to hear a decent speech in their own language (since reading is not their "thing") is in church. — But even during the sermon they converse with one another in their bastard gibberish. [6] There are a small number of isolated communities and scattered individual countrymen in the mountains who have less contact with Englishmen, and therefore sometimes understand no English at all, but despite that they still do not speak German any better. [7] The purest and best German is preserved in the colonies of the Moravian Brethren. — As a sample I would like to share with my readers verbatim what I as a German was told by a German farmer in German:

[8] "I wanted to *join* my neighbor and *purchase* a piece of *cleared* land. We *no doubt* would have made a good *bargain*, and could have worked it out well. But I wasn't capable of raising such a sum of money, and couldn't have *expected* the deal to be extended [?]. My neighbor didn't like that and started to *use* me ill, so I thought, It's better you do without. — — Or similarly: [9] My *stallion jumped* over the *fence* and *damaged* the neighbor's *wheat* terribly. — But it is not enough that they take totally English words to be German ones and start using them as such; [10] for example, *schmart* [< *smart*] — *serben, geserbt haben* [< *serve*], but they

also translate others directly into German and use them like as they would in English [i.e., they calque English words], for example, *absezen* (< lit. *set off*) instead of *abreisen*; *einen auf den Weg sezen*, (< lit. *put one in the road*); *abdrehen* (< *turn off*); *aufkommen mit einem* (< *come up with one*). — [11] Often they use a [near]homophone of an English word with a totally different meaning, for example, *das belangt zu mir* (< *that belongs to me*), where German *belangen* and English *belong* have entirely different meanings. Or *Ich thue das nicht gleichen* (< *I do not like that*). — It is not worth the effort to present more examples of such nonsense, which would make the ears of many of my countrymen ring. — [12] But it is not enough that people speak so miserably, they also write and print just as pitifully. The German printing company of Melchior Steiner (and earlier Christoph Sauer) puts out weekly a German newspaper that contains just as frequent as sad examples of the pitifully disfigured language of our American countrymen. It consists mainly of translations from English papers, but so stiff and anglicized as to be sickening. The two German preachers and Mr. Steiner themselves run the paper. If I am not mistaken, Mr. Kunze [one of the preachers] himself earns 100 Pennsylvania pounds for his work. "If we wrote pure German," the publishers explain, "our American farmers would neither understand nor read the paper."

[13] It was indeed not to be expected that the German language, even in its worst expression, could ever, at least not so quickly, fall into such decay and be forgotten. Through church services, the Bible, and the laudable farmer's almanac the language could be passed on for several generations, if it were not also freshened up from time to time by new immigrants. Perhaps it will improve and spread because of the free and direct contact now renewed between the mother country and America. Since America is about 30 to 40 years behind the times as far as German literature goes, it might make a fine business to free our unread and forgotten poets and prose writers from their bookstore-prisons and transport them to America, just as England once shipped over their useless riffraff.

Notes

[1] For an overview of the history of Pennsylvania German linguistics, see Louden 2001.

[2] The basic continuity of the sociolinguistic situation of PG among nonsectarians is supported by the study of Achim Kopp (2000), who examines the persistence of stereotypes about Pennsylvania Germans, including those dealing with the dialect itself, from the eighteenth century to the present. The earliest primary source Kopp cites dealing extensively with the PG linguistic situation is the 1829 account of the German Jonas Heinrich Gudehus republished in English translation in 1980 (Gudehus 1980).

[3] See Romaine 1995, 260-73 for an overview of the various views on "semilingualism."

[4] Schöpf's mention of the exception of the Moravian Colonies regarding the state of German is interesting: "Das reinste und schönste Deutsch erhält sich in den Colonien der Mährischen Brüder." [7].

[5] Modern sectarian and nonsectarian renderings would likely be identical in terms of morphosyntax, save for the use of the dative case and simple *zu* 'to' as an infinitival marker in nonsectarian PG. In sectarian PG, the dative case is no longer productive; *zu* + infinitive is now ø + infinitive for most speakers, though

Buffington (1937, 275) notes that many nonsectarian speakers also drop the *zu*. Therefore, I have chosen to put the *zu* in parentheses.

⁶ Here it is not clear what Schöpf's original is supposed to mean. This clause as it stands is formulated in something close to the PG present subjunctive, but a past indicative expression would make more sense in the context; hence the alternate rendering in parentheses.

⁷ This sentence is the one quoted by Haldeman (1872, 28), who also points out the evident typographical error in Schöpf's original in the past participle of the English-derived verb *tschumbe* (< *jump*).

⁸ Parallel to the exaggerated stereotype of PG as being excessively influenced by English are the ridiculous "examples" of "Dutchified English" attested only on tea towels and trivets in tourist shops in Pennsylvania.

⁹ Of course if the percentage of loanwords in a language were any kind of measure or linguistic "inadequacy," English, with its roughly three-quarters non-Germanic vocabulary, would fare quite poorly in the estimation of language purists.

References

Buffington, Albert F. 1937. "A Grammatical and Linguistic Study of Pennsylvania German." Diss., Harvard University.

Dorian, Nancy C. 1981. *Language Death: The Life Cycle of a Scottish Gaelic Dialect.* Philadelphia: University of Pennsylvania Press.

Fogelman, Aaron Spencer. 1996. *Hopeful Journeys: German Immigration, Settlement, and Political Culture in Colonial America, 1717-1775.* Philadelphia: University of Pennsylvania Press.

Frey, J. William. 1949. "Who Speaks Pennsylvania Dutch and Where?" *The Pennsylvania Dutchman* 1,7:1.

Gudehus, Jonas Heinrich. 1980. "Journey to America (translated from the 1829 German original by Larry M. Neff)." *Ebbes fer Alle—Ebbes fer Dich / Something for Everyone—Something for You: Essays In Memoriam Albert Franklin Buffington*, 184-329. Publications of The Pennsylvania German Society 14. Breinigsville, PA: The Pennsylvania German Society.

Haldeman, S. S. 1872. *Pennsylvania Dutch: A Dialect of South German with an Infusion of English.* London: Trübner & Co.

Haugen, Einar. 1953. *The Norwegian Language in America.* Philadelphia: University of Pennsylvania Press.

Hostetler, John A. 1993. *Amish Society*, 4th ed. Baltimore: The Johns Hopkins University Press.

Huffines, Marion Lois. 1980. "Pennsylvania German: Maintenance and Shift." *International Journal of the Sociology of Language* 25: 43–57.

Kloss, Heinz. 1966. "German-American Language Maintenance Efforts." *Language Loyalty in the United States*, ed. Joshua A Fishman, 206–52. The Hague: Mouton.

Knauss, James Owen, Jr. 1922. *Social Conditions among the Pennsylvania Germans in the Eighteenth Century as Revealed in the German Newspapers Published in America.* Lancaster: The Pennsylvania German Society. (Reprinted and edited by Don Heinrich Tolzmann as *The Pennsylvania Germans: James Owen Knauss, Jr.'s Social History*, Bowie, MD: Heritage Books, Inc., 2001.)

Kraybill, Donald B. 2001. *The Riddle of Amish Culture*, 2d ed. Baltimore: The Johns Hopkins University Press.

Kopp, Achim. 2000. "Of the Most Ignorant Stupid Sort of Their Own Nation": Perceptions of the Pennsylvania German in the Eighteenth and Twentieth Centuries. *Yearbook of German-American Studies* 35: 41-55.

Lloyd, Joel J. 1992. "Johann David Schöpf, Hessian Traveler." *Earth Sciences History* 11: 88-89.

Louden, Mark L. 1994. "Patterns of Sociolinguistic Variation in Pennsylvania German." In *The German Language in America, 1683-1991*, ed. by Joseph C. Salmons, 284-306. Madison: Max Kade Institute.

Louden, Mark L. 2001. "The Development of Pennsylvania German Linguistics within the Context of General Dialectology and Linguistic Theory." *A Word Atlas of Pennsylvania German* by Lester W. J. Seifert, 7-52. Madison: Max Kade Institute.

Morrison, Alfred J. 1910. "Doctor Johann David Schoepf." *German American Annals*, new series 8: 255-64.

Romaine, Suzanne. 1995. *Bilingualism*, 2d ed. Oxford: Basil Blackwell.

Rush, Benjamin. 1875. *An Account of the Manners of the German Inhabitants of Pennsylvania, Written 1789, by Benjamin Rush, M.D. Notes Added by Prof. I. Daniel Rupp*. Philadelphia: Samuel P. Town.

Schöpf, Johann David. 1788. *Reise durch einige der mittlern und südlichen vereinigten nordamerikanischen Staaten nach Ost-Florida und den Bahama-Inseln unternommen in den Jahren 1783 und 1784*. Vol. 1. Erlangen: Johann Jacob Palm. (Translated and edited by Alfred J. Morrison as *Travels in the Confederation*, Philadelphia: W. J. Campbell, 1911; reprinted 1968, New York: Bergman.)

Strassburger, Ralph B. 1934. *Pennsylvania German Pioneers: A Publication of the Original Lists of Arrivals in the Port of Philadelphia from 1727 to 1808*, ed. Wiliam J. Hinke, 3 vols. Proceedings of The Pennsylvania German Society, 42-44. Norristown, PA: The Pennsylvania German Society.

Wokeck, Marianne S. 1999. *Trade in Strangers: The Beginnings of Mass Migration to North America*. University Park, PA: The Pennsylvania State University Press.

Achim Kopp
Mercer University
Macon, Georgia

Language Attitude across Society and Generations in a Pennsylvania German Speech Island[1]

1. Introduction

In his influential 1966 study on "German-American Language Maintenance Efforts," Kloss offers fifteen factors (such as religious insulation, existence of parochial schools, number of speakers, and education of the speakers, to name just a few) as either favorable to, or ambivalent for, language maintenance. While Kloss does not list language attitude as one of the fifteen factors, he repeatedly addresses the topic in his discussion of individual factors (Kloss 1966, 207; 209; 211; 212) and in his remarks on Pennsylvania German (Kloss 1966, 215-23). Over the last few decades, the study of language attitude has emerged as an important instrument in its own right to explain or predict language change (Shuy and Fasold 1973, Ryan and Giles 1982; Louden 1991; cf. Kopp 1999).

The attitudinal patterns found in language islands can be complex: They normally consist of the attitudes of the speakers of the minority language toward their own linguistic variety as well as toward the surrounding majority language. Likewise, the linguistic and cultural attitudes present in mainstream society come into play. The question of language maintenance or shift is determined by the interplay of two sociolinguistic factors, namely the overall attitudinal patterns and the language use patterns, with the linguistic patterns prevalent in the language island (cf. Kopp 1999, in which Pennsylvania German English phonology serves as an example).

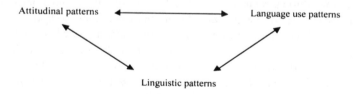

Interplay of three factors determining language maintenance or shift

In response to a recent manuscript of mine on language attitude in eighteenth- and twentieth-century Pennsylvania, an anonymous reader suggested that "if [he or she] were in the field interviewing native speakers about their attitudes—an in-depth study which surely is needed—[he or she] would be asking straight out questions about their attitudes concerning Pennsylvania German." In addition, the reader advised that "a real profile on each informant" be developed. This well-taken statement made me decide to undertake such a study myself, especially since I was sitting on a mountain of unevaluated data that matched the above description exactly.

From October 1989 to May 1990 I had interviewed fifty members of six multi-generational families in central Pennsylvania, at the northern edge of the Pennsylvania German area. Three of the families were nonsectarian Pennsylvania German, two were sectarian, and one was non-Pennsylvania German. All members of the nonsectarian families lived in the Mahantango Valley (around Klingerstown, Pennsylvania), where their ancestors had originally settled during the eighteenth century. Most were members of the local Lutheran or Reformed congregations. While the older family members typically had a public-school education, some younger ones had college degrees, reflecting a recent trend to greater geographical and social mobility. The members of the two sectarian families included in the study (one Old Order Mennonite, the other one New Order Amish) had migrated from Lancaster County to Buffalo Valley (the area around Mifflinburg, Pennsylvania) in the 1960s. The sectarians distance themselves from mainstream society through life in tight-knit religious communities, abstention from some aspects of modern technology (such as electricity, telephones, television, or radio, depending on degree of conservatism), reliance on horse and buggy for transportation, and use of their own eight-grade parochial schools for education. The members of the sixth family, which was non-Pennsylvania German, lived in larger towns in the area, such as Lewisburg and Berwick, Pennsylvania. Although some of their ancestors may have been Pennsylvania German, intermarriage with English, Welsh, and other families had eliminated a distinct ethnic affiliation. In their lifestyle these informants were exposed to the greatest ethnic diversity of all the families in the study. Altogether, the informants ranged from 5 to 81 years of age. The interviews usually consisted of two sessions of approximately one and a half hours each, in which the informants talked about life in Pennsylvania Dutch country, answered questions about their language use patterns, and were administered a matched-guise test on their language attitudes. I analyzed the above components of the questionnaire in my 1999 monograph on *Pennsylvania German English as Evidence of Language Maintenance and Shift*.

One section of the questionnaire that had not been used for the above study comprised 161 questions on language attitude. Most of the questions were to be answered on a five-grade differential scale, usually comprising the possible answers "definitely yes," "yes," "neutral," "no," "definitely no."

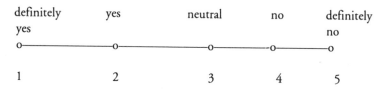

Five-grade differential scale

Twenty-one of the 161 questions were open-ended. Thirty-seven informants actually completed this part of the interview, which proved to be largely unsuitable for smaller children. Eight of these informants belong to the so-called "a-generation," all fully bilingual members of the three nonsectarian families, who were raised with Pennsylvania German as native language and acquired English in early childhood. These informants range in age from 60 to 79. The second group of informants is called the "b-generation" and consists of those nonsectarians who are the first generation in their family to be raised in English. Many of the eight informants (37 to 83 years of age) have near-native competence in Pennsylvania German, usually acquired by interaction with their grandparents. The c-generation includes the members of the second generation to have English as their native language. The age range of this group of seven informants is 23 to 54 years. While some members of this group have a passive command of Pennsylvania German, others are practically monolingual. Since this portion of the questionnaire was unsuitable for children, the d-generation (which is the third nonsectarian generation to be raised with English as native language) consists of only two members, two young adults of 27 and 31 years of age, who both of whom are monolingual speakers of English. While the nonsectarian families shifted from Pennsylvania German to English as native language during the 1930s and 1940s, all members of the sectarian families are fully bilingual to the present day. For the purposes of the present study, it is therefore not necessary to differentiate between generations or denominations. The sectarian group is comprised of five informants ranging from 27 to 57 years of age. Similarly, the non-Pennsylvania German group is linguistically homogeneous, i.e., monolingual English-speaking. The seven members of this group range in age from 30 to 63 years of age.

Informant	Family	Generation	Age	Sex	Native Variety
1	1	a	77	m	PG
2	1	a	77	f	PG
3	1	a	77	f	PG
4	2	a	71	m	PG
5	2	a	68	f	PG
6	2	a	74	f	PG
7	3	a	79	f	PG
8	3	a	60	f	PG
9	1	b	57	f	E
10	1	b	54	m	E
11	1	b	53	F	E
12	2	b	83	F	E
13	2	b	49	m	E
14	2	b	54	m	E
15	3	b	61	m	E
16	3	b	37	f	E
17	1	c	35	m	E
18	1	c	30	m	E
19	1	c	30	f	E
20	1	c	26	m	E
21	1	c	23	f	E
22	2	c	54	f	E
23	3	c	37	m	E
25	2	d	31	f	E
26	2	d	27	f	E
29	M	(a)	57	m	PG
30	M	(a)	55	f	PG
31	M	(b)	37	m	PG
32	M	(b)	27	f	PG
36	A	(a)	52	m	PG
42	N	(b)	63	m	E
43	N	(b)	50	m	E
44	N	(b)	52	f	E
45	N	(b)	54	m	E
46	N	(b)	52	f	E
47	N	(c)	31	m	E
48	N	(c)	30	f	E

List of informants with social data

2. Analysis of Language Attitudes

Question 161, the very last question posed to the informants in this part of the interview, gave them one last chance to summarize their idea of the Pennsylvania German character. The question asked: "How would you describe a typical Dutchman or Dutchwoman?[1] Please name a few of his / her characteristics."

Even the most superficial look at the responses teaches us something we have to bear in mind in all further analyses: The informants do not necessarily associate the same people with the term "Dutchman or Dutchwoman." While the nonsectarians have their own group in mind, both the sectarians and the non-Pennsylvania Germans think of the sectarians as typical Pennsylvania Germans. This becomes evident through responses such as "plain dress," "barn raisings," "horse and buggies," "beard," "straw hat," "suspenders," "bare feet," etc.

Regardless of this difference in association, the characteristic most frequently named by all groups is "hard-working" (twenty-six times). Other prevalent positive attributes include "honest," "religious," "bilingual," "family-oriented," "traditional," "conservative," "dependable," "friendly," "concerned for others," "generous," "punctual," "sincere," "loyal," "humorous," "sociable," "stable," "not extravagant," "pragmatic," "tolerant," "not materialistic," "frank," "trusty," and "sensitive." Far fewer depictions had negative connotations: "less educated," "speaking with an accent," "clannish," "stubborn," "selfish," "ambitious," "narrow-minded," "not warm," "opinionated," and "tight with money." In addition, Pennsylvania Germans are described as "hefty (good eaters)," "talkative," "good cooks (the women!)", "getting up early," "farmers," "good business people," "having little crime," "happy," "musical," "no nonsense," "strict," "obedient," and "aloof to outsiders."

Based on this dichotomy between positive and negative character traits associated with the Pennsylvania Germans, I identified six clusters of questions on either side whose results should facilitate a comparison of the attitudes prevailing in the six informant groups. The questions evoking some of the positive characteristics circle around the six topics ethnic pride, bilingualism, honesty and trust, nostalgia and humor, religion, and efforts of preservation. The six topics addressing the negative aspects of the Pennsylvania German image include lack of linguistic prestige, "dutchified" English, self-consciousness, language acquisition and ethnic marking, real-life repercussions, and the "dumb Dutchman" stereotype.

2.1. Positive Factors

Ethnic Pride

Question 135 concerned itself with ethnic pride:

Question 135: Are you proud of being Dutch?	1 = definitely yes 5 = definitely no
Nonsectarian a	1.12
Nonsectarian b	1.12
Nonsectarian c	1.33
Nonsectarian d	1.50
Sectarians	1.80
Non-Pennsylvania Germans	(1.33)

All informants expressed a high level of pride in their Pennsylvania German heritage. In the nonsectarian group there is a slight but steady decrease from the a- to the d-generation. The sectarians, while still indicating a degree of ethnic pride, are at the end of the continuum. Their identity is defined less by their being Pennsylvania German than by their membership in their respective religious communities. In addition, the use of the word "proud" in the question (which has a negative connotation for most sectarians, who consider the cultivation of humility a guiding principle) may have caused some of these informants to deny a more positive attitude toward Pennsylvania German ethnicity. The non-Pennsylvania Germans' identification with a Pennsylvania German heritage has to be taken with a grain of salt. The results are based on the responses of two members of this group, while all other informants ruled this question inapplicable. The two non-Pennsylvania Germans to respond positively may have thought of some distant single Pennsylvania German ancestors in their families.

The goal of question 136 ("What does it mean to you to be Dutch?") was to elicit narrative responses to find out what the components of a Pennsylvania German identity might be in the various groups. In the nonsectarian a-generation, three informants specifically refer to their proficiency in two languages as a distinct feature of their ethnic identity. Other responses express an appreciation of the hard work of the early Pennsylvania German settlers who prepared the land for cultivation and enabled their descendants to enjoy freedom and independence. While the latter answer is also quite common in the b-, c-, and d-generations, the monolingual nonsectarians also list positive character traits of their ancestors that they perceive as being continued in their own group: diligence, discipline, honesty, obedience. Two younger informants mention their pride in being of German descent rather than "English," as they perceive most of the non-Pennsylvania Germans to be. Two factors seem to be dominant in the sectarians' perception of their ethnic identity: As bilinguals they are proud of their proficiency in two languages. At the same time, two informants express a clear priority of the Christian aspects of their identity over their being Pennsylvania German: "We need to be more concerned about being Christian than what language we speak." While the non-Pennsylvania Germans typically express some admiration of the positive character traits of their Pennsylvania German neighbors, they do not normally include themselves in this group. Only two informants wondered whether they had some Pennsylvania German blood in them.

The responses received for question 137 generally confirm the findings for questions 135 and 136:

Question 137: Do you feel closer to Germany because of your heritage than to the other European countries (e.g. Britain)?	1 = definitely yes 5 = definitely no
Nonsectarian a	1.50
Nonsectarian b	1.51
Nonsectarian c	1.16
Nonsectarian d	1.00
Sectarians	1.80
Non-Pennsylvania Germans	4.00

All Pennsylvania German subgroups say they feel closer to Germany than to other European countries. Interestingly enough, this sentiment becomes stronger in the younger nonsectarian groups. Although present, it is less pronounced among the sectarians. By contrast, the non-Pennsylvania Germans deny any closer emotional ties to Germany as compared to other countries.

Bilingualism

Question 1 asked about the informants' attitude toward individual bilingualism and was directed to bilingual speakers only. The results attest a highly favorable view of bilingualism in this group:

Question 1 (bilinguals only): Are you glad that you can speak two languages, Dutch and English?	1 = definitely yes 5 = definitely no
Nonsectarian a	1.00
Nonsectarian b	1.00
Nonsectarian c	1.00
Nonsectarian d	-
Sectarians	1.40
Non-Pennsylvania Germans	-

To find out about the attitude toward individual bilingualism among the monolinguals, the following hypothetical question posed to the monolinguals rendered still positive, although somewhat less overwhelmingly favorable results:

Question 2 (monolinguals only): Do you sometimes wish you could speak Dutch as well as English?	1 = always 5 = never
Nonsectarian a	-
Nonsectarian b	-
Nonsectarian c	2.20
Nonsectarian d	2.00
Sectarians	-
Non-Pennsylvania Germans	2.14

With the help of the next two questions, both of which elicited narrative answers, I tried to establish what the informants perceived to be the advantages of knowing Pennsylvania German (question 3) and English (question 4).

Question 3 ("Which are the advantages of knowing Dutch?") almost universally triggered the answer "to be able to communicate with the older local people" in the nonsectarian a-generation. This answer was also common in the nonsectarian generations b, c, and d, with additional remarks on the value of Pennsylvania German in dealing with the Amish and when traveling in Germany. To the sectarians, the answer seemed self-evident: "This is the language we speak." Two of the sectarian informants emphasized their ability of reading the Bible in German, although one maintained that "High German would be more important." The non-Pennsylvania Germans typically would like to know the German dialect to communicate with their "Amish and Mennonite neighbors." Their reference to sectarian rather than nonsectarian Pennsylvania Germans reflects the fact that the image of the prototypical "Pennsylvania Dutchman" is by no means homogeneous. While for the nonsectarians this term evokes a member of their own group, the sectarians and non-Pennsylvania Germans are more likely to associate the Amish or Mennonites with it.

The standard response to question 4 ("Which are the advantages of knowing English?") implied that one has to know English in order to succeed in mainstream American society. One member of the nonsectarian b-generation emphasized that English is the language one needs to communicate with children—an indication of the fact that Pennsylvania German is dying in the nonsectarian community. The sectarians stressed the importance of English for communication with "outsiders," while the remark "to speak with people," which I received from a non-Pennsylvania German, points to the relative unimportance of Pennsylvania German as a means of communication in the mind of this group.

Honesty and Trust

Honesty and trustworthiness are among the Pennsylvania German characteristics most frequently received in question 161. The results for question 37 show that a person's membership in the Pennsylvania German community for most ethnic informants has a positive effect on his or her trustworthiness:

Question 37: Do you trust a stranger more when you find out that he / she can speak Dutch?	1 = definitely yes 5 = definitely no
Nonsectarian a	1.75
Nonsectarian b	2.00
Nonsectarian c	2.28
Nonsectarian d	1.50
Sectarians	2.20
Non-Pennsylvania Germans	3.85

Overall, the nonsectarian informants are the ones for whom membership in the Pennsylvania German ethnic group most readily evokes a feeling of trust. This feeling is even shared by the monolingual nonsectarians. The sectarians exhibit the same tendency, although somewhat less clearly. By contrast, the non-Pennsylvania Germans do not believe that Pennsylvania Germans are automatically more trustworthy than members of the majority population.

Nostalgia and Humor

Questions 73 and 74 as well as 60 through 63 concerned themselves with the role of topic or subject matter. Questions 73 and 74 were aimed at the aesthetic perception the informants might have of the Pennsylvania German language:

Question 73: Are there some things that sound better in Dutch than in English?	1 = definitely yes 5 = definitely no
Nonsectarian a	1.87
Nonsectarian b	1.42
Nonsectarian c	2.57
Nonsectarian d	2.00
Sectarians	2.00
Non-Pennsylvania Germans	3.57

The clearest expression of an aesthetic preference for Pennsylvania German comes from the nonsectarian b-generation, closely followed by the nonsectarian bilinguals. Even the nonsectarian c- and d-generation as well as the sectarians answer the question with yes. The non-Pennsylvania Germans, unrestrained by any pressures of ethnic loyalty, are the only group to tend toward the denial of an aesthetic superiority of Pennsylvania German in certain situations.

Examples for "things that sound better in Dutch than in English" were collected with the help of question 74. Situations most often mentioned by the nonsectarians include jokes (five times), old sayings (four times), poetry and songs (four times), colloquialisms and picturesque sayings (four times), stories about the past (twice), and swearing (once). The common denominator of all these responses is a certain degree of limitation in scope, most often to humor, isolated sayings, or contents pertaining to the past. While the sectarians' responses did include "phrases," greetings," and "some sayings that rhyme," this group was the only one to mention "talk in the family and at church" and "farming," i.e., topics whose discussion assumes active competence and everyday use of Pennsylvania German. No response was received from the non-Pennsylvania Germans.

Question 60 asked about Pennsylvania German in certain linguistic situations:

Question 60: Are there certain situations or topics that ought to be dealt with in Dutch?	1 = definitely yes 5 = definitely no
Nonsectarian a	2.75
Nonsectarian b	2.12
Nonsectarian c	3.00
Nonsectarian d	5.00
Sectarians	2.00
Non-Pennsylvania Germans	4.20

The most resounding "yes" to this question comes from the sectarians, whose use of Pennsylvania German and English is clearly structured according to domains. Certain situations dictate the use of a variety, e.g., Pennsylvania German in church and with group members, English in school and with outsiders. On the basis of this domain-driven system of language use the sectarians tend toward the notion that certain topics also trigger the use of Pennsylvania German. The nonsectarian a- and b-generations express this view as well, if somewhat more cautiously. Although equally bilingual, the nonsectarian a-generation exhibits much less of a domain-driven language use pattern than the sectarians. The interlocutor's proficiency in Pennsylvania German plays a much greater role in the choice of language for the nonsectarian a-generation. While the cgeneration is undecided, the monolinguals (nonsectarian d-generation and non-Pennsylvania Germans) strongly reject the notion that certain topics ought to be discussed in Pennsylvania German.

Question 61 asked the informants to state the situations or topics that ought to be dealt with in Pennsylvania German. The sectarians almost unanimously name family, sectarian community, and church. One informant, however, states that English should be used in the home domain if an "English" person, i.e., a nonsectarian, is present. The nonsectarian bilinguals list farming, things that happened a long time ago, and things you want to hide from your children as topics for which Pennsylvania German is more suitable. In the b-generation, the most prevalent occasions named include telling jokes, Pennsylvania German sayings, describing Pennsylvania German food, plays at the family reunions, and the annual *Fersomlinge*. These answers reflect a shift toward more sporadic and humorous uses of Pennsylvania German, i.e., the reduction of Pennsylvania German to a variety that serves only very specialized, non-everyday, almost nostalgic purposes. Nostalgia also plays a role in the answers gleaned from the c-generation: Two informants suggest that Pennsylvania German ought to be used at the annual home butchering and at funerals of older Pennsylvania German speakers (since Pennsylvania German would be more comforting to the bereaved).

In question 62, the focus shifted toward English:

Question 62: Are there certain situations or topics that ought to be dealt with in English?	1 = definitely yes 5 = definitely no
Nonsectarian a	2.16
Nonsectarian b	2.12
Nonsectarian c	2.42
Nonsectarian d	3.00
Sectarians	1.40
Non-Pennsylvania Germans	1.00

The results differ only somewhat from those received for question 60. Unsurprisingly, the non-Pennsylvania German monolinguals are most clearly determined about the use of English in certain situations. The fact that the sectarians are almost equally vocal in this demand is less plausible only at first sight. As stated above, this group's strict adherence to domains in their language use predestines certain situations for conduct in English. The nonsectarian bilinguals and their children also exhibit this tendency, but much less clearly. With the c- and d-generations the trend goes even more toward an undecided attitude, which shows that for lack of active proficiency in Pennsylvania German (while at the same time being a member of their ethnic group) these informants do not really have any strong feelings one way or the other.

Question 63 elicited narrative answers as illustration of the above statistical data by asking the informants to list the situations or topics that ought to be dealt with in English. The sectarians' responses are in line with their strict adherence to domains: All five informants maintain that English should be used for interaction with "strangers" (i.e., nonplain), or even if "outsiders" are simply present. The latter response reflects the sectarians' sense of politeness toward people who do not understand their native language. One sectarian informant mentions the second important domain of English:

school. The non-Pennsylvania Germans and the members of the nonsectarian c- and d-generations show almost complete unanimity in their reaction to question 63. According to them, English should be used for all situations and topics—an answer that reflects the lack of proficiency in Pennsylvania German in these groups. The members of the nonsectarian a- and b-generations exhibit a similar degree of courtesy as their sectarian counterparts: Two informants say that English should be used in the presence of people who cannot understand Pennsylvania German. Topics that should be discussed in English include medical problems (mentioned twice), science (three times), business (once), school (twice), and church and religion (three times). One isolated answer was rather instructive: According to one a-generation informant, "something that's written in English should be discussed in English." This response reflects the fact that on an everyday basis Pennsylvania German is not and has never been used as a written medium. Lack of standardization of Pennsylvania German and dominance of English in schools and newspapers curtailed the use of the German dialect as a written medium. The use of written Pennsylvania German in literary texts and "Dutch" newspaper columns is a relatively recent phenomenon, closely associated with attempts to preserve the ethnic language and culture.

Religion

Religion plays an important role in the lives of many informants in this study, not only the sectarians, but also the nonsectarians and the non-Pennsylvania Germans. Repeatedly religion and faith were named as one of the important characteristics of Pennsylvania Germans in question 161. It seems therefore fitting to look at the connection in attitudinal patterns between the Pennsylvania German language and the church (questions 40 through 42). Questions 40 and 41 asked about the use of Pennsylvania German in the worship service and in private interaction with the minister:

Do / Would you like your minister to use Dutch 40: - in church? 41: - privately?	1 = definitely yes 5 = definitely no	
	40	41
Nonsectarian a	3.25	1.87
Nonsectarian b	2.81	1.87
Nonsectarian c	3.71	3.71
Nonsectarian d	3.00	4.00
Sectarians	1.00	1.00
Non-Pennsylvania Germans	4.14	5.00

Nonsectarians are overall undecided about the issue of Pennsylvania German as language in church. This result reflects reality in this group: While regular services are conducted in English, annual services in Pennsylvania German enjoy great popularity in many congregations. The existence of such special services may have prompted some informants at least to consider the possibility of regular use of Pennsylvania German in church. The results are more defined for question 41: The more proficiency nonsectarians have in Pennsylvania German, the more likely they are to desire private interaction with their minister in Pennsylvania German. Sectarians and non-Pennsylvania Germans offer quite different points of view. For the sectarians, the language of the worship service is German (more specifically, a mix of Bible High German and Pennsylvania German; cf. Enninger and Raith 1982). Likewise, interaction with ministers, all of whom are members of the sectarian community, is conducted in Pennsylvania German. As monolinguals, non-Pennsylvania Germans are clearly opposed to the use of German in the church domain.

Question 42 asked about the use of Bible High German in church:

Question 42: Do / Would you like your minister to use High German in the service?	1 = definitely yes 5 = definitely no
Nonsectarian a	4.12
Nonsectarian b	4.12
Nonsectarian c	4.14
Nonsectarian d	4.50
Sectarians	1.60
Non-Pennsylvania Germans	5.00

The results are rather unsurprising. While the nonsectarians reject the use of a language in which they have, at best, traces of proficiency, the sectarians, who put great emphasis on learning Bible High German at school, at home, and in Bible class, and who use this variety as a spoken medium along with Pennsylvania German in sermons and hymns, embrace it as a variety used in their service. The non-Pennsylvania Germans, on the other hand, are opposed to the use of Bible High German in church.

Efforts of Preservation

Question 19 addressed the rather emotional topic of the more or less impending death of Pennsylvania German:

Question 19: Would you regret if Dutch was spoken less in the next few years?	1 = definitely yes 5 = definitely no
Nonsectarian a	1.50
Nonsectarian b	2.00
Nonsectarian c	2.33
Nonsectarian d	1.50
Sectarians	1.40
Non-Pennsylvania Germans	2.71

The two groups of native speakers of Pennsylvania German (nonsectarian a-generation and sectarians) express the strongest regret over the decline of their first language. They are joined by the nonsectarian d-generation, whose two representatives seem to display a high degree of nostalgia. Even though all informant groups would regret the loss of Pennsylvania German, this sentiment generally declines with distance from Pennsylvania German as native language. At the end of this continuum, the non-Pennsylvania Germans are almost indifferent (2.71).

Questions 147 through 149 were concerned with efforts to preserve the Pennsylvania German culture and language through Pennsylvania German societies and *Fersomlinge*. Question 147 asked about the desirability of such activities:

Question 147: Do you think it is / would be a good idea to have Pennsylvania German societies and / or *Fersomlinge* in this area?	1 = definitely yes 5 = definitely no
Nonsectarian a	1.75
Nonsectarian b	1.25
Nonsectarian c	1.42
Nonsectarian d	1.50
Sectarians	2.20
Non-Pennsylvania Germans	1.00

Overall, there is an almost unanimous call for organized cultural and linguistic maintenance efforts. Surprisingly, the strongest support comes from the non-Pennsylvania German informants, all of whom answered question 147 with "definitely yes." Even an unlikely target group like the sectarians, most of whom are prohibited by church rules from attending *Fersomlinge* or similar secular gatherings, expresses its general approval of such activities. As would be expected, an even clearer positive attitude is found among the nonsectarians, whose fellow group members form the majority of the participants at the *Fersomlinge*. Although the typical *Fersomling* audience includes mostly bilingual nonsectarians, support for such activities is even stronger from the b-, c- and d-generations.

Question 148 was concerned with the potential success of institutionalized cultural activities:

Question 148: Are these activities (talks, *Fersomling*, etc.) successful in maintaining the Dutch language and culture?	1 = definitely yes 5 = definitely no
Nonsectarian a	1.75
Nonsectarian b	2.62
Nonsectarian c	2.71
Nonsectarian d	3.50
Sectarians	1.80
Non-Pennsylvania Germans	1.57

The informants are far more skeptical in their evaluation of the actual effect on the maintenance of the Pennsylvania German culture and language. Sectarians and non-Pennsylvania Germans, both informant groups prone to being rather unfamiliar with *Fersomlinge* and similar events, believe that such activities represent quite successful maintenance tools. The assessment within the nonsectarian group appears to be more realistic, possibly because of the active involvement of many of these informants in the events. There is, however, a marked difference between the various nonsectarian generations: While the bilingual informants are convinced of the positive effect, the subsequent generations are progressively less sure that institutionalized efforts will be able to stop cultural and linguistic shift.

Question 149 ("What should be done in the future?") asked for the informants' input into ways to preserve Pennsylvania German culture. All suggestions for future activities come from the nonsectarian informants. They include more *Fersomlinge*, Pennsylvania German church services, skits, evening language classes, and language instruction in high school. While two bgeneration informants suggest speaking Pennsylvania German to little children (along with English), two members of the c-generation find the same rather unrealistic: "There is no way to preserve the culture and language as it was; I regret that." Another c-generation informant comments: "It won't be maintained, but it won't die out completely." This ambivalent attitude, marked by skepticism about linguistic and cultural maintenance on the one hand and by the insight that cultural identity cannot be prescribed, appears to be prevalent among the younger nonsectarians. A member of the d-generation puts it this way: "You can't force it, but more activities might create some interest, and people might choose to be part of the culture. Make Pennsylvania German prestigious." A member of the same subgroup suggests that women be included in the *Fersomlinge*. This comment reflects a clash between an institution once devised to save a dying culture and the thinking of a new generation that will be instrumental for the survival of that culture.

2.2. Negative Factors

Lack of Linguistic Prestige

Question 80 addressed the notion of Pennsylvania German not being a "real" language or having an inferior syntactical structure:

Question 80: Which of the two, Dutch or English, is more sophisticated in grammar and vocabulary?	1 = Dutch 5 = English
Nonsectarian a	3.42
Nonsectarian b	3.75
Nonsectarian c	4.28
Nonsectarian d	5.00
Sectarians	4.00
Non-Pennsylvania Germans	3.42

Overall, the informants' answers reflect the common stereotype of Pennsylvania German not being a "real" language, having "no grammar," and being "neither German nor English" (cf. Kopp 1999, 244ff.). All subgroups attribute a higher level of lexical and syntactic sophistication to English than to Pennsylvania German. Among the nonsectarians, the pattern is very smooth: the less proficiency in Pennsylvania German, the more clear-cut the view of its functional deficiency. While the a-generation is merely mildly convinced, the d-generation unreservedly believes in the linguistic superiority of English, the progression gaining in speed steadily. The sectarians, despite their shared native competence in Pennsylvania German, are more convinced of its linguistic inferiority than their nonsectarian bilingual counterparts. The result for the non-Pennsylvania Germans is rather surprising: While giving the edge to English, they do so only barely and with much reservation. It may be that their complete unfamiliarity with Pennsylvania German and their inability to compare this language to Standard German prevents them from sharing the ethnic informants' bias about the linguistic inferiority of Pennsylvania German.

Questions 81 and 82 asked about the status Pennsylvania German has among insiders and outsiders:

How high a status or prestige has Dutch 81: - among the Dutch people themselves? 82: - among outsiders?	1 = very high 5 = very low	
	81	82
Nonsectarian a	2.12	4.00
Nonsectarian b	2.62	3.62
Nonsectarian c	2.57	3.71
Nonsectarian d	2.50	4.50
Sectarians	1.80	4.00
Non-Pennsylvania Germans	2.28	4.42

Without exception, all the subgroups believe that Pennsylvania German enjoys higher prestige among the Pennsylvania Germans themselves than in surrounding mainstream society. The discrepancy is most clearly felt by the sectarians and the members of the nonsectarian a-generation. By contrast, nonsectarian generations b and c, while following the overall trend, do not perceive as clear-cut a difference in the prestige Pennsylvania German enjoys among insiders and outsiders.

"Dutchified" English

Question 102 addressed the issue of Pennsylvania German interference in the speakers' variety of English:

Question 102: Do Dutch people have a different English than non-Dutch people?	1 = definitely yes 5 = definitely no
Nonsectarian a	1.87
Nonsectarian b	2.75
Nonsectarian c	1.33
Nonsectarian d	1.00
Sectarians	1.20
Non-Pennsylvania Germans	1.42

Generally speaking, the informants sense a strong difference between the English varieties spoken by the Pennsylvania Germans and those of other speakers. Sectarians, non-Pennsylvania Germans, and the younger nonsectarian generations seem to perceive this difference the most. The nonsectarian a- and, in particular, the b-generation are somewhat less certain about this issue.

Questions 103 through 108 asked about the degree of Pennsylvania German interference in various generations:

Does your family's English sound dutchy? 103: - great-grandparents' generation 104: - grandparents' generation 105: - parents' generation 106: - children's generation 107: - grandchildren's generation 108: - great-grandchildren's generation	1 = very dutchy 5 = not dutchy at all					
	103	104	105	106	107	108
Nonsectarian a	-	1.00	1.12	3.37	4.25	5.00
Nonsectarian b	1.00	1.14	1.37	3.71	4.60	5.00
Nonsectarian c	1.25	2.33	3.33	4.40	-	-
Nonsectarian d	-	1.00	2.00	-	-	-
Sectarians	1.00	1.60	2.00	3.00	3.33	-
Non-Pennsylvania Germans	1.50	4.00	4.50	5.00	5.00	-

Each group of informants senses a steady decrease of interference from generation to generation, including the sectarians and the non-Pennsylvania Germans. In the latter group, the biggest discrepancy is between questions 103 and 104, i.e., great-grandparents and grandparents' generations. However, the result for question 103 is based on only two responses from informants who believe that some of their ancestors were of Pennsylvania German descent. Not surprisingly, the nonsectarian a-generation perceives the greatest difference in degree of interference to be between their parents and their children (questions 105 and 106). An actual decrease in interference would in retrospect justify their decision to raise their children in English, which was motivated by the sentiment that Pennsylvania German as native language causes "bad" English. On the other hand, the a-generation's responses to questions 106, 107, and 108 as well as the responses from other groups show that the shift to English as native language alone did not immediately eliminate all Pennsylvania German interference. According to the informants' perception it takes about three generations until no interference is present. The nonsectarian b-generation (the first to be raised in English) also shows the greatest decrease in perceived interference between their parents' and their children's generations.

The answers to question 109 show how the informants perceive their own speech:

Question 109: Do you speak dutchy English?	1 = very dutchy 5 = not dutchy at all
Nonsectarian a	1.25
Nonsectarian b	2.50
Nonsectarian c	3.66
Nonsectarian d	5.00
Sectarians	2.60
Non-Pennsylvania Germans	5.00

Once again, the informants' self-perception mirrors linguistic reality quite well. From nonsectarian generation a through d there is a decline of perceived interference. The sectarians see their English about as "dutchy" as the nonsectarian b-generation informants rate theirs, and the non-Pennsylvania Germans perceive no German interference in their English at all. As a comparison with questions 105 and 106 shows, the nonsectarian a-generation perceives the degree of interference in its own variety of English (1.25) more on the level of that of its parent generation (1.12) than on that of its children's generation (3.37). The nonsectarian c-generation shows a similar pattern (3.33 to 3.66 to 4.40), while the numbers for the b-generation are more evenly distributed (1.37 to 2.50 to 3.71). The largest decrease in interference between parents and one's own generation is claimed by the members of the nonsectarian d-generation (2.00 to 5.00).

Self-consciousness

Questions 8 through 11 tried to establish whether speakers might ever be self-conscious about using Pennsylvania German and for what reasons. Question 8 was directed to the bilinguals:

Question 8 (bilinguals only): Are you ever embarrassed to speak Dutch?	1 = always 5 = never
Nonsectarian a	4.50
Nonsectarian b	4.00
Nonsectarian c	4.00
Nonsectarian d	-
Sectarians	4.20
Non-Pennsylvania Germans	-

The responses constitute an almost unanimous denial of any personal feeling of embarrassment, which is strongest among the two groups of native speakers (nonsectarian a-generation and sectarians). However, the relatively few answers received for question 9 ([bilinguals only]: "If yes, under which circumstances and why?") do give an indication of what might cause any embarrassment for using Pennsylvania German. As two members of the nonsectarian b-generation remarked, people who cannot speak the dialect might make fun of those who use Pennsylvania German around them.

Question 10: Do you know people who are embarrassed to speak Dutch?	1 = many 5 = none
Nonsectarian a	4.00
Nonsectarian b	2.75
Nonsectarian c	2.85
Nonsectarian d	2.00
Sectarians	3.20
Non-Pennsylvania Germans	5.00

When the question is phrased in a less personal way, asking about signs of embarrassment in other speakers of Pennsylvania German, the results are quite different. While the members of the a-generation do not really perceive others to be embarrassed about their use of the German dialect, their children, grandchildren, and great-grandchildren do sense a certain degree of self-consciousness. As this sentiment is strongest in the youngest generation (which is completely monolingual), it appears that the perception of discomfort in others increases with decreasing language proficiency. In a sense, the younger informants cannot help judging others by their own standards. On the other hand, even the bilingual sectarians report a stronger sense of embarrassment in other speakers than in themselves. Interestingly enough, the non-Pennsylvania German informants completely denied any sign of self-consciousness in speakers of Pennsylvania German. It seems that the admiration for the Pennsylvania German heritage and the bilingualism of many Pennsylvania Germans counteracts any negative perceptions. As the answers to question 11 ("If yes, under which circumstances and why?") indicate, speakers of Pennsylvania German are perceived to be linguistically self-conscious when interacting "with professionals who are better educated," "with strangers," "in public situations," "at college," and "when English speakers are around." Thus, there appears to be a consensus among the informants that Pennsylvania German is an inadequate medium in the public and professional spheres.

Language Acquisition and Ethnic Marking

Questions 20 through 26 were concerned with the informants' opinion about whether and how Pennsylvania German should be learned and if it has any effect on a speaker's variety of English. Question 20 asked whether children should be taught Pennsylvania German as a first language:

Question 20: Should parents teach their children Dutch as a first language?	1 = definitely yes 5 = definitely no
Nonsectarian a	2.62
Nonsectarian b	4.00
Nonsectarian c	4.00
Nonsectarian d	5.00
Sectarians	1.20
Non-Pennsylvania Germans	4.28

The results indicate a clear division between native speakers of Pennsylvania German and the rest of the informants. The sectarians advocate the use of Pennsylvania German as native language practically without reservation. The nonsectarian a-generation would also like to see Pennsylvania German as a native language, although less unanimously. The other groups all reject this idea, most categorically the members of the nonsectarian d-generation. The answers to the question whether children should be taught Pennsylvania German as a second language turned out to be much more homogeneous and positive:

Question 21: Should children learn Dutch from their grandparents or other relatives?	1 = definitely yes 5 = definitely no
Nonsectarian a	1.75
Nonsectarian b	1.37
Nonsectarian c	2.00
Nonsectarian d	1.50
Sectarians	1.40
Non-Pennsylvania Germans	1.57

To find out about the motivations for the attitudes ascertained with the help of the preceding two questions, questions 22 and 23 tried to elicit narrative answers. Question 22 was directed to older nonsectarians only, asking them why they did not or do not speak Pennsylvania German to their children. Of the eight a-generation informants, five explicitly state that they raised their children in English because they wanted them to be able to speak that language when they started school. Many answers imply that a child that did not know English, which was the only language of instruction used at the schools at the time, would have been "handicapped." While none of the a-generation informants denies their shift to English as native language, two of them state that their husbands and other relatives initiated it. The attempt to establish the motives of the a-generation is probably the closest one can get to a first-hand explanation for an extraordinary event that took place in the 1930s and 1940s, when a whole speech community almost simultaneously and unanimously, after close to two centuries of raising its offspring in Pennsylvania German, shifted to English as a first language for their children, thus initiating the slow process of extinction of Pennsylvania German in the nonsectarian group. The answers provided by the following generations (b and c) follow two main lines: Some informants state that they simply did not know enough Pennsylvania German themselves to pass it on as a native language. At the same time, the responses reflect a certain sense of guilt, as the informants begin to understand the consequences of the shift ("I didn't know better. I was too young").

The answers to question 23 shed light on the prevailing attitudes from a different perspective. Directed toward the nonsectarian b-, c-, and d-generation, question 23 asked why the informants' parents did not or do not speak Pennsylvania German to them. The majority of answers points to the English-speaking schools as the main reason ("They wanted us to learn the English language for school. It was hard for them to learn English in school"). Starting with the c-generation, however, other explanations are offered as well: "It wasn't fashionable. They were trying to fit in with mainstream America. There were anti-German feelings in the post-war period." One succinct answer by a c-generation informant is particularly revealing: "They were ashamed of it." While a feeling of the inferiority of Pennsylvania German is implicit in the responses citing English as the language used in the schools, no member of the older generations ever expresses it explicitly.

Question 24 examined one possible reason why Pennsylvania German as a native language might be considered shameful for a speaker:

Question 24: Does Dutch cause bad English?	1 = definitely yes 5 = definitely no
Nonsectarian a	1.75
Nonsectarian b	3.00
Nonsectarian c	1.85
Nonsectarian d	3.50
Sectarians	1.80
Non-Pennsylvania Germans	2.42

The two groups raised with Pennsylvania German as their native language most clearly support the view that their first language adversely affects their English. Somewhat surprisingly, they are joined by the nonsectarian c-generation. Although less determined, the non-Pennsylvania Germans also sense a negative impact of one variety on the other. The two groups that are at best undecided or even opposed to such an assessment are the nonsectarian b- and d-generation. Could it be that their nostalgic yearning for the preservation of the Pennsylvania German language and culture causes these informants to deny any negative side effects?

Questions 25 and 26 asked about school as a possible domain for Pennsylvania German:

Question 25: Should Dutch be taught at school (as a subject)?	1 = definitely yes 5 = definitely no
Nonsectarian a	1.87
Nonsectarian b	2.25
Nonsectarian c	2.00
Nonsectarian d	2.00
Sectarians	5.00
Non-Pennsylvania Germans	2.71

In all groups except for the sectarians there is support for making Pennsylvania German a subject at school. Even the non-Pennsylvania Germans, albeit somewhat less enthusiastically than others, would be in favor of such a plan. In fact, a small number of younger nonsectarians had taken occasional night classes in Pennsylvania German. By contrast, the idea of formal classes in Pennsylvania German is rigorously rejected by the sectarians, for whom English is the language of school.

When asked whether Pennsylvania German should be the language of instruction at school, the informants were almost unanimous in their rejection:

Question 26: Should Dutch be spoken at school in all subjects?	1 = definitely yes 5 = definitely no
Nonsectarian a	3.50
Nonsectarian b	4.50
Nonsectarian c	4.14
Nonsectarian d	4.50
Sectarians	4.40
Non-Pennsylvania Germans	4.42

As no group finds the use of Pennsylvania German as the language of instruction desirable, it appears that the nonsectarian informants are realistic enough to understand that lack of proficiency among the younger generations prevents such action. The sectarians are opposed for a different reason: To ensure their children's proficiency in English, they follow a strict policy of English as the language of instruction.

Real-life Repercussions

Question 111 inquired about possible repercussions of a high level of Pennsylvania German interference in one's variety of English:

Question 111: Do you think that children speaking dutchy English have more difficulties at school or later in life?	1 = definitely yes 5 = definitely no
Nonsectarian a	3.25
Nonsectarian b	2.75
Nonsectarian c	3.14
Nonsectarian d	3.00
Sectarians	2.60
Non-Pennsylvania Germans	2.00

Although rather cautiously, non-Pennsylvania Germans and sectarians sense a societal disadvantage for speakers of ethnically marked English. The nonsectarian informants all hover around 3.00, i.e., are not sure whether there is any negative impact.

Question 113 reformulated 111 and approached the issue from the perspective of the surrounding mainstream society:

Question 113: Do you think that non-Dutch people generally tend to look down on people who speak dutchy English?	1 = definitely yes 5 = definitely no
Nonsectarian a	2.15
Nonsectarian b	1.87
Nonsectarian c	1.57
Nonsectarian d	1.50
Sectarians	2.20
Non-Pennsylvania Germans	2.28

While the results for the sectarians and non-Pennsylvania Germans are not significantly different from those received for question 111, the nonsectarians have a much stronger opinion than they showed in question 111. All groups say that outsiders look down on people speaking Pennsylvania German English. This sentiment is strongest in the nonsectarian d-generation and only slightly decreases from generation d through a. The children, grandchildren, and great-grandchildren of those who have the greatest degree of interference are the ones who perceive the ridicule from outsiders the most.

A sample from the narrative answers received for question 114 ("If yes, why do you think is that so?") will illustrate why, in the view of the informants, outsiders might look down on speakers with German interference. Many responses focus on the assumed rural lifestyle and resulting lack of education of the Pennsylvania Germans: "They consider them rural, not well educated." "They can't understand the Dutch elements, customs, and rural lifestyle." "The people from the coal region call the school in the Pennsylvania German area 'the farmers' school.' They sing at sports events: 'The

Farmer in the Dell.'" Other informants, especially the sectarians, emphasize the linguistic aspect of the stereotype: "Dutch is the language of the plain people. They look down on the plain farmers." "Because they don't speak the correct English." At the same time, there is a shared suspicion that negative remarks are evoked by a certain amount of jealousy: "Maybe they wish they could speak Dutch themselves." Two informants expressed the opinion that ethnic stereotypes are on the decline: "It's less than it used to be. People are more aware of their ethnic difference."

The "Dumb Dutchman" Stereotype

Questions 139 through 141 concerned themselves with the stereotype of the "dumb Dutchman."

Question 139: "The Pennsylvania Germans are dumb Dutchmen. Just listen to the way they speak English." Is this statement correct?	1 = definitely yes 5 = definitely no
Nonsectarian a	3.50
Nonsectarian b	4.37
Nonsectarian c	4.42
Nonsectarian d	5.00
Sectarians	4.60
Non-Pennsylvania Germans	4.57

While all the subgroups denounce the view that Pennsylvania Germans are stupid, there are some interesting trends visible in their answers. Among the nonsectarians, the denial of the validity of the "dumb Dutchman" stereotype becomes steadily stronger from the a- to the d-generation. In fact, the a-generation is close to being undecided, thus expressing a certain degree of self-deprecation. After all, it is this group that exhibits the highest degree of Pennsylvania German interference in its English, thus being most clearly marked as Pennsylvania German through its speech. By contrast, the members of the d-generation, whose English variety is virtually unmarked and who have no proficiency in Pennsylvania German, take the clearest stance in denying the validity of the stereotype. Sectarians and non-Pennsylvania Germans are equally determined in their rejection of the "dumb Dutchman" stereotype. In a way, both of these groups are on the outside of this issue. While the non-Pennsylvania Germans do not at all associate themselves with the "victims" of the stereotype, the sectarians—as we have seen—put far more emphasis on religion as the marker of their ethnic distinctiveness than on the fact that they are Pennsylvania Germans.

Question 140 ("Who says things like that?") sought to elicit information about the perceived source of the "dumb Dutchman" stereotype. As would be expected, the group to which the dissemination of the stereotype is most readily attributed are the "outsiders." At closer look, these include "people who don't understand Dutch," people who "can talk English more fluently and have a better education," "other ethnic groups," "people with an English background," "people from the cities," "people from the coal region" (an area adjacent to the Mahantango Valley whose population has hardly any Pennsylvania German background), "people who are not Dutch, usually younger people," and even "Southern people." The most important finding, however, is that it is only in the nonsectarian a- and b-generation that the informants include their own among those who hold the stereotype of the "dumb Dutchman." This confirms the quantitative results for question 139, where the nonsectarian a-generation was identified as the one to be the most undetermined in its rejection of the stereotype.

Question 141 ("What do you feel when you hear people say things like that?") was concerned with the emotional impact of the "dumb Dutchman" stereotype. By and large, the responses distinguish the three ethnic informant groups. Most nonsectarians, regardless of membership in a certain generation, fall into three large categories: Nine informants express pain or anger, eight say that those who call Pennsylvania Germans "dumb" are misinformed and / or that they feel sorry for them, and six informants take such opinions as a joke or do not let themselves be bothered. The sectarians' reaction to the "dumb Dutchman" stereotype is far more homogeneous. Without exception, all five informants state that they are not really offended by such an attitude or that the appropriate remedy is forgiveness. This reaction reflects the strong religious convictions of love of one's neighbor and tolerance prevalent in this group. The responses received from the non-Pennsylvania Germans indicate their relative remoteness from the issue. Answers such as "I laugh. I don't care" and the hypothetical "I would get upset" show that these informants do not see themselves as victims of the "dumb Dutchman" stereotype.

3. Interaction of Attitudes, Use, and Language

Whenever immigrants bring their native language into the context of a majority language, they are exposed to various pressures. On the one hand, tradition and loyalty to their origins tell them to maintain their old culture and language. On the other hand, outside pressures and the resulting desire for assimilation pull them toward the majority culture and language. The Pennsylvania Germans are no exception. Sheer numbers, settlement patterns, religious insulation, and other factors have made the Pennsylvania Germans the group of German immigrants to preserve their ethnic variety the best and the longest. Pennsylvania German is in its fourth century on the American continent, and, at least among the sectarians, very much alive. Yet Pennsylvania German has been under attack from the very beginning. As a non-standardized, non-written variety of German, it has never enjoyed high overt prestige. Moreover, the rural setting of its speakers has contributed, not just since Benjamin Franklin, to an image of vulgarity, lack of education, and even stupidity (cf. Kopp 2000).

The data of the present study show that the old dichotomy between positive and negative language attitudes is still present today (cf. Huffines 1990 and the results of a matched-guise test that I describe in Kopp 1999, 210-75). The old view of the uneducated "Dutch" has been perpetuated in the stereotype of the "dumb Dutchman." The commercial exploitation of this image by the local restaurant and tourism industry is relatively unthreatening to modern-day Pennsylvania Germans. Linguistically, however, this stereotype is at the root of the general shift from Pennsylvania German to English as native language, which the nonsectarian community underwent during the 1930s and 1940s and which will lead to the death of the last native speaker of Pennsylvania German in this group within a decade or two. On the other hand, both sectarian and nonsectarian Pennsylvania Germans, if for different reasons, consistently express pride in their German origin. Even if the language itself is threatened by extinction, as in the case of the nonsectarians, numerous preservation efforts (*Fersomlinge*, Pennsylvania German newspaper columns, church services, radio programs, night classes, etc.) show that there is a positive attitude toward the Pennsylvania German culture and language in this group. In fact, it appears that the threat of extinction is instrumental in the strengthening of the positive language attitudes. In the younger nonsectarian generations the negative attitudes still harbored by the a-generation are being replaced by more positive attitudes based on nostalgia. This development is an example of language attitudes being reversed by changes in language use patterns (in this case a shift from Pennsylvania German to English as native language). Such nostalgic feelings are largely absent in the sectarian communities of this study. Here Pennsylvania German continues to be used as native language and is therefore not in danger of extinction.

Since the four nonsectarian generations differ from each other in acquisition patterns and language proficiency (the a-generation being the last one to have native command of Pennsylvania German), the attitudinal examination has to be put into the framework of a larger study of linguistic differences and differences in language use between the subgroups. On many occasions it is the nonsectarian a-generation which exhibits the strongest adherence to the "dumb Dutchman" stereotype. At the same time, this generation shows by far the highest degree of Pennsylvania German interference in its English phonology (Kopp 1999, 63-133). This combination of attitudinal and linguistic patterns led this generation to make a radical change in its language use patterns by raising its children with English as a first language starting in the 1930s. By contrast, the members of the b-, c-, and even the d-generation are the ones who exhibit a fairly positive attitude toward the Pennsylvania German language and culture. They are among the most fervent supporters of the various maintenance efforts, trying to reverse an irreversible development: the impending loss of Pennsylvania German as native language within their community. Ultimately, this attitudinal pattern has linguistic consequences: It appears that particularly members of the c-generation, who have no active command of Pennsylvania German, resort to Pennsylvania German features in their English phonology to mark their ethnic identity (Kopp 1999, 262-71). Sectarians, on the other hand, have no need to mark their group identity through English. On the contrary, they strive to teach their children interference-free English in their parochial schools. In this study, their attitudinal patterns often revealed an identity with their religion (i.e., being Amish or Mennonite) rather than their being Pennsylvania Germans. Finally, the non-Pennsylvania Germans, as outsiders, are often much less involved in attitudinal dilemmas. While fostering the "dumb Dutchman" stereotype, they mean no harm and are extremely benevolent toward the Pennsylvania Germans. For them, however, Pennsylvania German is synonymous with sectarian, a group that through its extreme difference is non-threatening to them.

In sum, an analysis of the attitudinal patterns in the light of language use data and linguistic evidence shows that the Pennsylvania German speech community is certainly not uniform: Sectarian bilinguals differ from nonsectarian bilinguals, nonsectarian monolinguals from non-Pennsylvania Germans. In addition, the old negative image of the Pennsylvania Germans caused the compartmentalization of the nonsectarians, who sociolinguistically are the most interesting group at this time. Their shift away from Pennsylvania German as native language has set in motion a rapid change in their language use patterns over the last decades. This process has triggered both attitudinal and linguistic changes in the younger generations, which reflect a desire to stop or at least delay language death. Nevertheless, the new positive attitude toward the ethnic culture and language appears to come too late to prevent the loss of Pennsylvania German in the nonsectarian group.

Notes

[1] Following popular language use of the area, the term "Dutch" was used in the questions instead of the more scholarly phrase "Pennsylvania German."

References

Enninger, Werner, and Joachim Raith. 1982. *An Ethnography of Communication Approach to Ceremonial Situations: A Study on Communication in Institutionalized Social Contexts: The Old Order Amish Church Service*. Wiesbaden: Steiner.

Huffines, Marion Lois. 1990. "Pennsylvania German in Public Life." *Pennsylvania Folklife* 34: 117-25.

Kloss, Heinz. 1966. "German-American Language Maintenance Efforts." In *Language Loyalty in the United States*, ed. Joshua A. Fishman, 206-52. The Hague: Mouton.

Kopp, Achim. 1999. *The Phonology of Pennsylvania German English as Evidence of Language Maintenance and Shift*. London: Associated University Presses.

Kopp, Achim. 2000. "'. . . Of the Most Ignorant Stupid Sort of Their Own Nation': Perceptions of the Pennsylvania Germans in the Eighteenth and Twentieth Centuries." *Yearbook of German-American Studies* 35: 41-55.

Louden, Mark L. 1991. "The Image of the Old Order Amish: General and Sociolinguistic Stereotypes." *National Journal of Sociology* 5,2: 111-42.

Ryan, Ellen B., and Howard Giles, eds. 1982. *Attitudes towards Language Variation: Social and Applied Contexts*. London: Edward Arnold.

Shuy, Roger W., and Ralph W. Fasold, eds. 1973. *Language Attitudes: Current Trends and Prospects*. Washington: Georgetown University Press.

Steven Hartman Keiser
Marquette University
Milwaukee, Wisconsin

The Origins and Maintenance of Dialect Differentiation in Midwestern Pennsylvania German

1. Introduction

The time to study regional differentiation in *Deitsch* (a.k.a. Pennsylvania German and Pennsylvania Dutch) is now. Recent research on German speech islands on other continents has revealed fluid patterns of dialect convergence and divergence as circumstance and attitude bring speakers from different speech islands into and out of contact with each other (e.g., Rosenberg 1998 in Russia and Brazil). However, the interactions between the ever-growing number of *Deitsch* speech islands in North America have largely escaped attention.

Researchers studying *Deitsch* as a speech island variety in North America have generally focused on disentangling the roles of language contact (i.e., convergence toward English) and language internal factors in effecting linguistic change in *Deitsch*. Previous descriptions of regional variation have been restricted to varieties in Pennsylvania (e.g., Frey 1985 [1942],88-89, Reed and Seifert 1954, Seifert 2001). In recent years the investigation of social variation (again largely within Pennsylvania) has taken center stage with claims of divergence between the language of sectarian groups, that is, Old Order Mennonites and Amish, and that of the non-sectarian groups—a difference sometimes rephrased as plain vs. non-plain (e.g., Huffines 1989).

These areas of inquiry have been immensely fruitful, and gatherings such as Sprachinselkonferenz 2001 serve as testimony to their ongoing productivity. Yet what emerges from these studies is a continuing perception of *Deitsch*, in particular *Deitsch* outside of Pennsylvania, as relatively undifferentiated—or simply unknown.[1]

In addition, researchers have tacitly assumed that changes observed in one speech island have no connection to change or lack thereof in other speech islands. But the interaction between speakers from different speech islands forms a locus for the spread of linguistic change, for dialect convergence, and for the emergence of a cultural identity beyond the local speech island.

This is an attempt to redress the absence of recent inquiry into regional variation in *Deitsch* and the relationships between *Deitsch* speech islands. In it, I explore the emergence of a regional *Deitsch* dialect in Amish communities in the American Midwest—a dialect that is distinct from varieties in Pennsylvania and that today unifies

117

dozens of speech islands across distances of over one thousand miles. I also explore the extent to which this Midwestern *Deitsch* serves as a salient marker of regional identity for the Amish.[2]

I begin by defining the geographic region "Midwest" as it applies to *Deitsch* usage. Then I trace the history of Amish settlements in the American Midwest and note the economic and social factors which shaped early patterns of regular and intense interaction between these widely scattered speech islands. These patterns of interaction were not unique to the Amish, but existed among their "Englisch" settler neighbors as well and set the stage for the diffusion of a common set of linguistic features (in both *Deitsch* and English) across great geographic distances. I show how similar patterns of interaction persist among the Amish to this day, though with significantly less intensity. Next, using data from two *Deitsch* speaking communities in the Midwest and two in Pennsylvania, I propose an inventory of the linguistic features of Midwestern *Deitsch* and demonstrate that these features are socially diagnostic across *Deitsch* speech islands. Finally I discuss the complex factors that have led to the emergence of these dialect features in the Midwest. These factors include notions of natural sound change, settlement history, and contact between speech islands. I conclude with suggestions for future research in the dialectology of *Deitsch* speech islands.

2. Defining the "Midwest" as It Applies to *Deitsch*

In its broadest geographic definition the Midwest consists of the states stretching between the Appalachian and Rocky mountains and lying north of the Ohio River and north of an imaginary line extending west from the Ohio's confluence with the Mississippi.[3] The oldest and largest Amish settlements outside of Pennsylvania are in this broadly defined region, in Ohio, Indiana, Illinois, Iowa, and Kansas—states generally considered historically, culturally, and geographically Midwestern. It is these communities—and by extension their numerous recent daughter settlements—that I consider here.

3. Amish Settlements in the 18th Century: The Beginning of the Isolation of Lancaster County, Pennsylvania

The earliest Amish presence in the Midwest coincided with the general Euro-American expansion into the region in the early 1800s. But the seeds of social, geographical, and eventually linguistic division between the Amish settlements in Pennsylvania and the Midwest may have been sown long before any Amish ever crossed the Appalachians: during the early settlement history of the Amish in colonial Pennsylvania.

In the years following the first documented arrival of Amish in North America in 1737, the largest settlement was at Northkill in northern Berks County, Pennsylvania.[4] Northkill remained the largest Amish settlement until after the Revolutionary War when its people made the choice either to move south to better farmland in Lancaster County, or to head west to the new frontier in Somerset County, Pennsylvania. As inconsequential as it may have appeared at the time, the departure from Northkill serves as a watershed point in the history of the Amish in North America.

Those who moved to the Lancaster area in the late 1700s found an agricultural paradise and most never left.[5] Those who chose to move to Somerset County formed the vanguard of Amish settlers in the Midwest. As Euro-American expansion continued west making available more and cheaper land, the Amish of Somerset followed. It is out of and through Somerset that most of the Midwest Amish settlements were founded.[6]

Thus the moves to Lancaster County and to Somerset County effectively and quite literally divided the North American Amish "family tree" into two main branches, and there are, in fact, certain surnames which are found almost exclusively in one or the other areas.[7]

We cannot know for certain the linguistic profiles of these two groups of early American Amish in the years when *Deitsch* was in its formative stages. We cannot know what varieties of German were spoken in Somerset and in Lancaster and by how many speakers, nor the patterns of interaction between speakers. But it is possible that the set of input dialects was slightly different in these two settlements.

To be sure, as Amish moved from Somerset to the Midwest during the 19th century, they carried with them a linguistic heritage in many ways similar to that of the Lancaster Amish. Still, throughout the 19th century ties of family and friendship were forged and strengthened between the Midwestern Amish, while ties with the east weakened.

4. Amish Settlements in the Midwest in the 19th Century

Even as many Amish from Somerset began moving further west in the early 1800s, the Lancaster Amish contributed relatively few participants to the westward expansion. The result was continued isolation of Lancaster from the emerging Midwest: isolation which set the stage for linguistic divergence.

The settlement of the Holmes County area in Ohio is an example of the importance of the Somerset Amish in the Midwest settlements. Beginning in 1809, several dozen extended family groups from Somerset County arrived in Holmes County. By one estimation 90% of Holmes County Amish trace their origins to Somerset County.[8]

Arrivals from the old southeastern Pennsylvania communities were few. So few, in fact, that when several families from Lancaster settled in Holmes County in the years 1826-48, they are described as "a little island of Lancaster County culture" (Kaufman and Beachy 1990,18).

As Amish moved further west, this pattern remained basically the same with one significant variation: recent European immigrants joined the Somerset Amish in settling the frontier. Nearly all of these European Amish, however, bypassed the old Lancaster settlement and were acculturated to North American Amish ways of speaking and living by residing in Somerset for a period of time.[9] The Arthur, Illinois settlement, founded in 1864, in particular illustrates the growing interconnectedness of midwestern Amish communities as its early settlers came from Somerset County as well as Iowa, Indiana, and Ohio.[10]

Linguistic data from the 19th century are scarce, so it is difficult to assess the degree to which Midwestern Deitsch was emerging as a separate entity. Still, economic, religious, and social divisions between the frontier Midwest and the established Eastern Amish were emerging by the mid 1800s. Lancaster arrivals to Holmes County in mid-century are described as exhibiting wealth as well as a distinctive stone architecture, furniture design, and folk art (Kauffman and Beachy 1990). Too, the Midwestern Amish generally had a greater tolerance for diversity in religious practice: experimenting with non-traditional hymnals, the building of meetinghouses, and lessstrict baptism and shunning practices.[11] The relatively more moderate religious stance of Midwestern Amish may have been due both to a pragmatic frontier spirit and to the influence of the large numbers of more progressive European Amish immigrants in the Midwest.

5. Patterns of Interaction between Amish Communities

By the middle of the 19th century, dozens of new Amish settlements were established from Ohio to Kansas. Patterns of interaction within these settlements as opposed to within Lancaster, Pennsylvania, point to two possible sources of dialect divergence: in Pennsylvania, contact with non-Amish neighbors and in the Midwest contact with a new wave of European Amish immigration. I will not attempt here to provide a specific account of these contacts, but suggest them as topics for future research. Furthermore and more important, patterns of interaction *between* Midwestern settlements suggest that the highly mobile nature of many Amish families aided the diffusion of linguistic variants across the Midwest.

5.1. The Mobility of Amish in the 19th Century

Frequent moves often linked Amish families to multiple Midwestern communities. This was particularly true in the first half of the 19th century when as one historian notes, "families might move three times in as many decades." (Nolt 1992, 99). Many did so of necessity given that most new Amish settlements failed eventually, forcing families to move on in search of land and church community.[12]

The Keim and Miller families are but two examples of the Amish instinct to migrate. Joseph N. Keim was born in Somerset and moved to Kalona, Iowa, around 1850 where he was ordained. In 1864 friction in the church precipitated a move to Indiana and from there to Arthur, Illinois. His son Joseph W. Keim was born in Iowa in 1859, and after living in Indiana and Illinois, moved to Holmes County, Ohio, where he married in 1880 and where his son began a prosperous lumber company (Kauffman and Beachy 1990, 44, Lind 1994, 119). A half-century later the pattern continued as the William Miller family moved from Holmes County to Madison County, Ohio, in 1908, then lived in Indiana from 1911 until 1916 when they returned to Ohio even as other relatives moved to Arthur, Illinois.[13]

These types of stories crop up again and again in family histories from the 19th century.[14] But this quasi-nomadic lifestyle was not unique to the Amish. Throughout the Midwest families were on the move throughout the 1800s in search of more and cheaper land. One example is the Ingalls family of *Little House on the Prairie* fame. Laura and her family, over the course of one decade, lived in Wisconsin, Kansas, Iowa, Minnesota, and South Dakota.

5.2. Current Patterns of Interaction

The family ties in the Midwest, together with economic and church connections, remain intact, though less intense, in the 21st century. These ties can be illustrated by a survey of the current migration of Ohio Amish to other states, by individual stories, and by surveys of Amish travel destinations.

A representative survey of the addresses of adult children listed in the Holmes County, Ohio, Amish Directory indicates that the Amish are somewhat more sedentary than their 19th century forbearers. Few (about 5%) are listed as having left their home community.[15] Although this suggests a limited degree of current migration between Amish communities, it is significant to note when Amish do leave Holmes County, the vast majority (over 90%) resettle elsewhere in the Midwest.[16]

Lancaster Amish have founded numerous settlements within Pennsylvania, yet very few Ohio Amish have joined them. What is more, Lancaster Amish have begun settling in the Midwest, too, but they remain, in the words of one historian "'Lancaster Amish' in dress, ordnung, and orientation" (Steve Nolt, p.c.). The reluctance of Pennsylvania Amish and Midwest Amish to mix in new settlements is affirmed by a Holmes County historian: "they don't think alike…one or other would have to change [the style of their] buggies" (Leroy Beachy, p.c.). Apparently family ties and community practices are different enough to help squelch partnership between eastern and Midwestern Amish pioneers in the 21st century.

But permanent moves are only one means of inter-island contact. Amish young people have, over the years, visited other Amish communities, and young men in particular often find work for a season or longer away from home. For Midwestern Amish, this meant traveling to other Midwestern communities. In the early 1900s young men from Holmes County, Ohio, traveled regularly to Indiana to do carpentry work, and often spent the harvest season in Illinois Amish communities husking corn at the lucrative wage of forty cents per hour (Leroy Beachy, p.c.).

Reports in the Sugarcreek (Ohio) *Budget*—a national newspaper for the Amish with correspondents contributing from Amish communities all over the world—indicate that the visiting patterns of Amish are relatively unchanged.[17] Correspondents often report on the travels of persons from their community, and 90% of travelers from the Midwest are destined for other Midwest locales—usually to visit relatives on the occasion of a wedding or funeral. These current travel patterns reflect the high degree of mobility of the Amish in the 19th century when families moved frequently and established ties in multiple Midwestern communities.

These current travel patterns are further corroborated by persons who offer taxi services to Amish. Drivers from Holmes County frequently make out-of-state trips to other Midwestern states, but report traveling to Lancaster only once or twice a year. One driver from a Lancaster settlement reports making few out-of-state trips.[18]

The enduring interaction between Midwestern Amish, albeit at a lower level of intensity, and the ongoing relative isolation of the Lancaster Amish continues to be reflected in cultural differences between the two regions. Differences include marrying age, and season for marriage, preaching style, clothing styles, and even naming practices (Hostetler 1992, 98-105; Louden 1997, 83). Too, Midwesterners perceive Pennsylvania Amish as being aggressive in business and social dealings. The image of the aggressive Easterner and the laidback Midwesterner is of course, an enduring stereotype in American culture.

The early isolation of Lancaster, Pennsylvania, from Midwestern Amish communities and the significant mixing of Amish in the new 19th settlements in the Midwest then sets the stage for a discussion of the linguistic reflexes of this social interaction.

6. Features of Midwestern *Deitsch*

Louden (1997, 82) is the first researcher to identify features which explicitly contrast *Deitsch* in the Midwest with *Deitsch* in Lancaster, Pennsylvania. Louden lists the following features (see table 1):

Table 1. Louden's (1997) Features of Midwestern *Deitsch*

feature	Pennsylvania	Midwest	Earlier Deitsch
/aɪ/ e.g., *Deitsch* 'German'	[aɪ]	[eː]	[aɪ]
/r/ e.g., *Ohre* 'ears'	[ɹ] retroflex *r*	[r] tapped *r*	[r] tapped *r*
/l/ e.g., *Balle* 'ball'	[ɫ] "dark" *l*	[l] "clear" *l*	[l] "clear" *l*
future auxiliary verb	*zeele/zelle*	*figgere*	none

In addition to Louden's list of primarily phonetic differences, speakers I interviewed identified several lexical contrasts (see table 2).

Table 2. Lexical features of Midwestern *Deitsch*

	Pennsylvania	Midwest
'the bucket'	*der Kiwwel*	*der Eemer*
'the autumn'	*der Harebscht*	*'s Schpohtyaar*
'the lawn'	*'s Hefli*	*der Hoch/Hof*
'through'	*darich*	*deich*
Composition of the lexicon	fewer English borrowings	more English borrowings

The patterns of dialect differentiation in *Deitsch* follow those of the regional dialects of American English: differences are marked primarily by phonetic and lexical contrasts, and there are relatively few contrasts at the level of morphology or syntax.

Some of these differences have been previously reported as local social variants within Lancaster County. Raith (1992, 160-61) observes that the phonetic realization of intervocalic /r/ as the American retroflex [ɹ] (e.g., *sie waare* 'they were') and syllable-final /l/ as "dark" [ɫ] (e.g., *der Balle* 'the ball') separate the Lancaster County Old Order Amish from their neighboring Mennonites and nonplain speakers.[19]

It is not the case that one region or the other is progressive or conservative with respect to older norms for *Deitsch*. One might argue that the *Deitsch* of Pennsylvania shows more signs of borrowing sounds from English (i.e., American [ɹ] and [ɫ]), but, on the other hand, it appears Midwestern *Deitsch* is more advanced in the monophthongization of /aɪ/ and has borrowed more English vocabulary. This last finding is unexpected. Since lexical borrowing usually precedes significant structural (in this case phonetic) borrowing, we might anticipate that the Midwest should show greater convergence toward English: phonetically and otherwise.

7. Social Significance of Midwestern *Deitsch*

These dialect differences are both salient and socially diagnostic. In interviews conducted in Ohio and Iowa, when asked to identify a place where *Deitsch* is spoken differently, speakers will nearly always name Pennsylvania. In a dialect perception study, when Midwesterners are given a map of the United States and asked to circle the areas where *Deitsch* is spoken different from them, they overwhelmingly circle Pennsylvania. Speakers readily acknowledge that, just by listening, one can easily identify a *Deitsch* speaker from Pennsylvania, but one would be hardpressed to differentiate Iowa, Indiana, and Ohio speakers from each other (Keiser 2000, 2001).[20]

The features which attract the most overt commentary from Midwestern Amish are the presence of retroflex /r/ in Pennsylvania and lexical differences. Midwesterners have even crafted a stock phrase to illustrate the /r/ shibboleth: *Ich hab mei Ohre vefrore am faare* 'I froze my ears while driving.'

8. Paths of Continuity and Divergence in *Deitsch*

Having provided an inventory of salient dialect differences between the Midwest and Pennsylvania, we can now pursue the question of how these differences may have emerged and, in the case of the Midwest, spread to speech islands across such a vast region. First I will present results of a study on lexical variation in the Midwest and in Pennsylvania. The results indicate that, although lexical differences between the Midwest and Lancaster County exist and are salient to especially Midwesterners, the overwhelming pattern is one of *continuity* between the Amish in Lancaster and the Amish in the Midwest (as opposed to significant differences within Pennsylvania and even within Lancaster County). Second, I will discuss the phonetic change, specifically the monophthongization of /aɪ/ in Midwest speech islands and evaluate the possibility that it is the result of independent common innovations or dialect contact.

8.1. Lexical differences

I designed a study to test the possibility that the source of some of the lexical variants of Midwest *Deitsch* came from a historic connection of the Midwest Amish to *Deitsch* varieties in Pennsylvania other than Lancaster (that is, via their roots in Somerset and Berks Counties).[21]

I created a translation task of fifty lexical/morphological variants which according to the work of Reed and Seifert are diagnostic of regional variation within Pennsylvania and conducted interviews with speakers from Holmes County, Ohio , Madison County, Ohio, and Kalona, Iowa, in the Midwest, and Lancaster County and Montgomery/

Bucks Counties in Pennsylvania.[22] The Midwest speakers were Amish or of Amish-Mennonite background. The Montgomery/Bucks County speakers were Mennonite or Brethren. The Lancaster speakers were Amish or Old Order Mennonite or Mennonite or had descended from those groups. Results are seen in table 3.

Table 3. Patterning of Midwest Lexical Variants with Pennsylvania Regional Dialects

Pattern: Midwest same as...	example	Midwest	S. Lanc. PA	N. Lanc. PA	Bucks Co. PA
all Lanc. (n=24)	'lard'	fɛt	fɛt	fɛt	ʃmals
S. Lanc. (n=8)	'you (sg.) see'	senʃt	senʃt	seʃt	senʃt
Bucks Co. (n=6)	'bucket'	emɐ	kɪvl	kɪvl	emɐ

For 24 of the items—nearly half—the Midwestern speakers pattern after the general Lancaster variety. For an additional 8 items (16%) Midwestern usage matched that of southern Lancaster County—the historic hub of the Amish community—as opposed to northern Lancaster County. For this limited survey of the lexicon, Midwest Amish are linked more closely to the Lancaster Amish, than the Lancaster Amish are linked to their own neighbors within Lancaster County. For 6 items (12%)—Midwestern usage matched non-Lancaster forms. The remaining 12 items showed no definitive pattern.

The results confirm a strong historic connection between the Midwestern Amish and Lancaster County in general—Lancaster Amish in particular. They leave open the question of how the relatively small number of lexical differences might have appeared. Most probable is that lexical variation, which even today rarely shows categorical distribution in a given region, was simply leveled out in favor of different variants in the Midwest. Evidence for this is found in Bender's 1929 lexicon of *Deitsch* in Iowa in the early 20th century which lists both /emɐ/ and /kɪvl/ for 'bucket.' This suggests that in this Iowa community the leveling of these lexical variants in favor of /emɐ/ occurred only in the last few generations.

8.2. Monophthongization of /aɪ/

In contrast to the relative continuity of the native lexicon between Pennsylvania and Midwestern Amish, there appears to be growing divergence in the phonetic systems of the two varieties.

Data gathered from seventy speakers in Holmes County, Ohio and in Kalona, Iowa confirm that a sound change, the monophthongization of /aɪ/, e.g., [daɪtʃ] 'German' realized as [dɛːtʃ], is spreading among both Ohio and Iowa *Deitsch* speakers (see figure 1).

Figure 1. Fronting and raising of diphthong /ai/ in two Midwestern communities

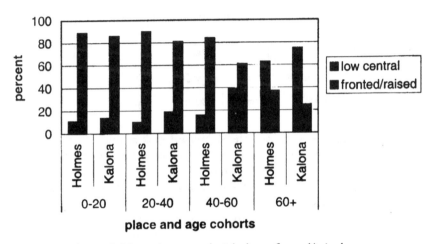

In each pair: left bar = low central, right bar = fronted/raised

Furthermore, I judge the change in question to be a recent one on the basis of apparent time evidence: older speakers in both communities retain a high percentage of unraised diphthongal tokens. In fact, the data in Figure 1 show a remarkable similarity in the distribution of variants across age cohorts in Holmes County and Kalona. This change is not taking place in Pennsylvania where speakers of all ages retain the diphthongal [aɪ] except in limited phonetic environments.[23]

Since this clearly is a recent change, taking place well after Holmes County and Kalona were founded in the early 1800s, how might we account for their nearly identical patterning—in opposition to Pennsylvania varieties?

There appear to be two possible explanations: parallel independent development due to chance (possibly "drift" as Sapir conceived of it) or dialect contact between distant speech islands

I believe that a review of the linguistic and sociohistorical facts points to a solution that combines both of the above explanations—provided we first reconceptualize the notion of "drift."

The term "drift," coined by Sapir (1949 [1921], 150), has often been used to account for changes that occur independently in related language varieties (e.g., umlaut in German and English). I prefer to think of drift in probabilistic terms: certain changes are cross-linguistically common—we might say "natural." The monophthongization of /aɪ/ is one of these as the examples in table 4 demonstrate.

Table 4. Cross-linguistic Examples of Monophthongization of /aɪ/.

language	example
French	Latin *lacte* 'milk' > [laɪt] (10th century) > [lɛt] (11th century)
Sanskrit	pre-Sanskrit *ai > e: (also *au > o:)
Slavic	pre-Slavic *ay > later Slavic e (thought to be phonetically [æ:])
Old Japanese	pre-Old Japanese *Cai > Ce(y)
dialectal Japanese	Tokyo vernacular: *zya nai* > *zya ne(e)* 'is not'
	Nagano region: *hai* > *hee* 'ash'
Old English	proto-Germanic *ai > a (e.g., *stainaz* > *stan* 'stone')
dialectal Am. Eng.	/aɪ/ > [a:]

In addition, both the Middle High German vowel shift and the Great Vowel Shift in Early Modern English involved the fronting and/or raising of long vowels (Labov 1994, 124, 145). There is no evidence yet to suggest that there is a chain shift underway in *Deitsch*. Still the change in question is compatible with Labov's Principal I of vowel shifting: long (tense) vowels rise (1994, 116, 176, 262). Labov offers an explanation based on physiology and articulatory overshoot (see 1994, 221, 261 which follows after Sievers 1850). Furthermore, cross-linguistic patterns of coalescence, the resolution of two adjacent vowels into a single vowel, show that the sequence /aɪ/ is most commonly resolved as [æ] or [ɛ]. (Parkinson 1996, 93-95).

Even so, this sound change is not occurring in all *Deitsch* speech islands. The diphthongal variant is vibrant in Ontario (Kate Burridge, p.c.) and in Lancaster, Pennsylvania (Louden 1997). The apparent limits of this "drift" lead us to search for clues to its origins and spread in the settlement histories and interactions of these communities.

Although at first glance Midwestern Deitsch speech islands appear geographically and socially isolated from each other, the earlier discussion of the settlement history of the Midwest clearly shows that, at least in the 19th century, these communities were far from insular. Families like the Keims moved frequently back and forth across the Midwest in the 19th century—possibly sowing monophthongal germ as they went. So it is possible that monophthongal variants were present in Midwestern communities by the beginning of the 20th century. Schlabach 1980 is the first to attest these variants, attributing them to Madison County, Ohio, usage in the mid-20th century. The ongoing contact between these communities, though now at a relatively low level of intensity, was enough to ensure that a "natural" sound change spread across speech islands throughout the Midwest.

8.3. Change as a Result of Contact

The other points of divergence between the Midwest and Lancaster can be attributed to different outcomes of contact with English. There is no clear explanation for why the Midwest more readily borrows English lexical items, but resists the American /r/ and /l/ variants common in Pennsylvania. Raith (1992, 161) suggests "ecological factors" for the adoption of American /r/ and /l/ by the Amish in Lancaster—specifically the fact that they apply English literacy skills in their readings of (Standard) German in worship services. This account seems unlikely since the same "ecology" holds for the Midwest.

9. Conclusions

In this essay I have established the existence of a regional dialect of *Deitsch* outside of Pennsylvania. Moreover, this Midwestern dialect is not limited to a small geographic region, but rather unifies *Deitsch* speech islands across a vast region. I have offered here a closer look at changes in two subsystems which contribute to both the perception and the reality of dialect divergence. One subsystem, the lexicon, shows itself to be a point of remarkable continuity across regions—a fact which runs contrary to popular perceptions. Accounting for the wide geographic spread of a sound change in progress, however, requires reference to both crosslinguistic markedness and an in-depth understanding of settlement history and current patterns of inter-island contact.

Today's Amish interact with each other in patterns that were established two centuries ago as the American Midwest was settled. The Amish settlements outside of Pennsylvania, stretching from the western foothills of the Appalachians to the Great Plains share a common linguistic and cultural identity apart from their eastern brethren and schwestern. In many ways this is similar to the American sensibility of "Midwest" vs. "east coast" culture—which also has its linguistic reflexes in, e.g., lexical items such as *soda* (East) v. *pop* (Midwest) and phonetic variation such as *carrot* pronounced as /kærət/ (East) v. /kɛrət/ (Midwest).

The linguistic features that differentiate the Midwest from the East are a relatively small number of lexical and phonetic contrasts which nonetheless carry significant weight as social evaluation criteria. This, too, is true of both English and *Deitsch*.

There are other differences in cultural practice and beliefs that tie together Midwestern Amish with their English neighbors such as the shared perception of "laidback" Midwesterners and "aggressive" Easterners.

Thus, the emergence of Midwestern *Deitsch* is tied into the geography, patterns of settlement and patterns of intraregional communication that have shaped the regional identity of the Midwest as a whole.

The existence of Midwestern *Deitsch* also raises questions about what is meant by a speech island. Is the Midwest a single, geographically noncontiguous ever-expanding speech island? Or is it a collection of speech islands united by a shared history and a set of linguistic features?

10. The Future of Midwestern *Deitsch*

Areas for future study include: a more complete documentation of variation within the Midwest. Are certain innovations, such as the use of non-feminine gender for females in Holmes County (described by Van Ness 1995) spreading? What is the possible impact of 19th century Amish immigrants on Midwestern varieties? What is the significance of differences within Lancaster County (e.g., between Amish and Old Order Mennonites)—particularly as they spread beyond their respective geographic hubs? Phonological incorporation—that is the degree to which English borrowings are "naturalized" into *Deitsch* phonology—is another potential point of divergence. Differences in phonological incorporation draw considerable overt commentary from speakers and are ripe ground for future investigation (e.g., Keiser 2000, Keiser 2002). It draws considerable overt commentary from speakers and is ripe ground for future investigation (e.g., Keiser 2000, Keiser 2001). As time passes and some of the newer far-flung Midwestern settlements become well established, is there evidence for nascent differences between them? What norms are being shaped in "mixed" (i.e., Pennsylvania and Midwest) settlements like Pinecraft, Florida? Finally, comparisons with research by Wolfram 2001 on "remnant" dialects of English, and by Trudgill et. al. 2000 on Southern Hemisphere English might be fruitful.

The study of regional variation in *Deitsch* can not help but be a growth area for future research. The number of Amish settlements doubled to over 220 between 1972 and 1992 alone (Luthy 1994, 243). The patterns of interaction that are established and maintained between these settlements and the linguistic reflexes of this interaction will shape the future of *Deitsch* in the 21st century.

Notes

[1] Seifert 1971, for example explicitly restricts his survey of the Word geography of PG to Pennsylvania settlements established prior to 1830—even though he acknowledges that Amish settlements in Ohio already existed at that point (and Indiana and Iowa Amish communities were soon to follow in the 1840s).

[2] There are, of course, other plain groups in the Midwest among whom *Deitsch* is a living language—most notably the Old Order Mennonites. But these groups are numerically much smaller than the Amish and I do not include them in this study. In addition, I will not consider here the so-called "Swiss" Amish of Allen and Adams Counties, Indiana whose Alemannic varieties are the result of direct migration from Europe in the mid-1800s. The "Swiss" Amish—a linguistic minority within a cultural minority—have had little or no impact on *Deitsch* in other communities (see Thompson 1994).

[3] The term "Midwest" eludes easy definition. The American Midwest has become as much a cultural idea as a geographical region: a place representing the average (Euro) American: simple, straightforward, with roots on the farm, the Heartland (Frazer 1993:ix-x).

[4] Northkill had perhaps 200 persons at its peak (Nolt 1992, 48, 56).

[5] Of course, some exceptions exist, for example Isaac Schmucker left Lancaster for Mifflin County, Pennsylvania and later Ohio and Indiana (Nolt 1992:99).

[6] Schlabach 23, 26 notes also the importance of the Big Valley settlement in Mifflin County (founded 1791). The Logan and Champaign Counties, Ohio settlement (now Mennonite) was almost entirely from Big Valley (Nolt 99, citing S. Duane Kauffman 1991), and the Fairfield County, Ohio settlement (founded c.1819, now extinct) may also have been from Mifflin County (Leroy Beachy, p.c., 3.15.00)

[7] Lancaster names King, Stoltzfus, Lapp are nonexistent among Amish in Holmes County, Ohio. Meanwhile, European Amish names of 19th century immigrants (e.g., Gingerich, Swartzentruber) are not represented among the Lancaster Amish (Hostetler 1993:245 and Leroy Beachy, p.c., 3.15.00)

[8] Leroy Beachy, p.c. 3.12.00, estimates the Holmes County settlement was 90% from Somerset County and 5% Europe and 5% Mifflin and Lancaster. European Amish names typical of Hesse-Kassel Amish, such as Gingerich and Swartzentruber are underrepresented in Holmes County (these two names account for only 31 and 26 families, respectively in the 1996 Ohio Amish Directory which includes some 5000 families.

[9] Beginning in 1817 a new wave of European Amish immigrants, many from the Hesse-Kassel region, came to the U.S. Most arrived in Baltimore and thus bypassed the old southeast Pennsylvania settlements, following the National Road west to Somerset where they remained for several years or perhaps a generation before continuing on to newer settlements in the Midwest.

[10] The 19th century Amish settlements in the Midwest also included (with founding dates): Nappanee, IN 1838; Elkhart-Lagrange Counties, IN 1841; Kokomo, IN 1848; Haven, KS 1883; Hutchison, KS 1883. There were also several settlements which eventually "failed" (either because Amish moved away or became Mennonites): Archbold, OH 1834; Tazewell/Woodford Counties, IL 1831; Tiskilwa, IL 1835; Lee County, IA 1840; Henry County, IA 1843; Butler County, OH 1819; Logan/Champaign Counties OH 1840; Fairfield County, OH 1823. The so-called "Swiss" Amish settled in Indiana in Adams County 1850,

Allen County 1852, and Daviess County 1868. Sources for these data are Luthy 1993:252-9, and Luthy 1986.

[11] Schlabach 1988, 211-12 notes a specific incident in 1820, in which Ohio Amish accepted as a member a Mennonite who had refused a request by Pennsylvania Amish that he be rebaptized as precondition to membership.

[12] Out of a total of sixty-one new Amish settlements founded during the 1800s forty-five (74%) failed.

[13] Roman Miller, p.c., 3.24.00. Other families have similar stories, e.g., Slabaugh, 72-74 notes that the Moses Slabaugh family moved from Holmes County to Madison County, OH in 1896, then to Michigan in 1904, then back to the Holmes County area in 1907.

[14] Luthy (1986:384) reports that Daniel D. and Anna Kaufman Miller lived in 8 states. Born in 1822, Anna lived in Somerset (20 yrs), Indiana (25 yrs), Illinois (4 yrs), Oregon (12 yrs), Mississippi (4 yrs), Texas (2 yrs), Kansas (1 yr), Oklahoma (3 yrs). Even in the early 20th century this pattern continued for some families: Floyd Beachy's mother was born in Hicksville, Ohio and his father in Farmerstown, Ohio. They lived in Kokomo, Indiana until 1941 when the family moved to Kalona, Iowa (p.c. 2000).

[15] The 108 Holmes County transplants in the survey account for only 5% of the adult children listed in the survey. The 5% figure is based on a detailed study of children born before 1975 in 7 districts. A random count of children born before 1975 in several of the remaining districts suggests that this figure is accurate in general: districts average a total of about 50 adult children of which only 2 or 3 have emigrated.

[16] The survey selected roughly every fourth church district listed in the Ohio Amish directory, revised 1996 edition, and counted those children who were listed as "Amish living in another community" (coded as "C" in the directory) as well as the "single and Amish" (code "E") individuals whose address indicated they lived outside the community. Of 108 adult Amish children from 43 different church districts who were no longer living in Holmes County in 1996, nearly half moved to other Amish communities in Ohio. Neighboring Indiana and northwest Pennsylvania (a settlement founded by Ohio Amish) each received over 10% of the outmigration. Only 4% moved to eastern Pennsylvania to settlements that were likely founded primarily by southeastern Pennsylvania Amish.

[17] I conducted a preliminary survey of Midwestern Amish correspondents' reports in the Sugarcreek (Ohio) Budget over a fifty-year period from 1950-2000. The survey included reports from the January editions (usually the first or second edition of the year in order to catch travel over the holidays) of 1950, 1955, 1960, 1990, and 2000, and one June edition of the Sugarcreek Budget National Edition. The focus was on travel to and from Iowa and to and from Ohio. Visitors to Iowa totaled 28; visitors to Ohio totaled 98. Travellers from Iowa totaled 31; travellers from Ohio totaled 67.

[18] Informal interviews were conducted at the Eastern States Draft Horse Sale, in Columbus, OH, February 1, 2000. Three Holmes County drivers and one Perry County, PA driver were interviewed.

[19] Beam also notes that "[s]ome [unspecified] native speakers of Pennsylvania German employ an American r in certain positions. Others use a slightly trilled r in an initial and medial position" (1994:x.). In addition, Beam notes *schteik* as Old Order Amish (OOA) pronunciation for more general *schtarick*. This is another example of the sound change in which /r/ and /g/ have been lost intervocalically where the

following vowel is /i/ (as in *darich/deich* in table 2), though Beam does not note the general process and the words it affects. Van Ness states that the future auxiliary tsɛl exists only in plain communities, but does not cite the source for this claim (1994, 432). This is not to deny the existence of any variation between plain and nonplain Deitsch. Certainly some lexical variation exists and Beam's dictionary 1994 (1991) notes a few examples of Old Order Amish (presumably Lancaster County) usage. Most are pronunciation variants:

gwunnerich 'curious' (OOA usage) v. *neigierich*

Oschder 'Easter season' (OOA usage) v. *Oschdere*

reiglesst 'let in' (OOA usage) v. *reiglosst*

daed, daadi 'daddy/grandpa' (OOA usage) v. 'dad/daddy'

schteik 'fast' (OOA pronunciation) v. *schtarick*

[20] There are also some lexical differences which appear between Midwestern speakers such as *dutt der butter druff* v. *schmerst der butter* 'spread the butter,' *tsaund* v. *laat* 'sound,' *lumbe* v. *duch* 'dish cloth', but it is not clear to what degree these differences are age-graded, individual differences, or in fact, nascent regional differences within the Midwest. One difference which does appear to be salient is the degree to which borrowed English words are "dutchified" that is, made to "sound German." Holmes County in particular is noted for the extent to which its speakers "dutchify" their English words, e.g. *call-e, tsaund* (Keiser 2000, 2002). Also Louden notes that Eastern Ohio speakers, as opposed to other Midwesterners, retain tapped [r] in syllable initial position (1997, 82).

[21] This is precisely the study that Glen Gilbert suggested in the course of a discussion of Seifert's presentation at the 10th Germanic Languages Symposium, though my focus is on what this can tell us about the Midwest, not Pennsylvania (Seifert 1971, 40).

[22] Not all speakers completed all of the survey. Some completed part and some responded as members of a group conversation. In Bucks/Montgomery 15 participated, 9 completely, 6 as part of two groups. In Lancaster 14 participated, 9 completely (1 was born in Indiana), 5 as part of two groups. In Holmes County 3 participated (1 born in Madison County), in Kalona 4 participated completely, 1 partially, and reference was also made to Ruth Bender's 1929 description of the language in Johnson County, Iowa.

[23] Louden 1997 describes the regional differences in the phonetic conditioning of monophthongal /aɪ/ as follows:

Lancaster rule:	Monophthongize only before liquids	
	/aɪ/ > [ɛ:]/___[ɹ, l]	e.g., [miɐ hɛːɹ] 'we marry'
	[aI] elsewhere	e.g., [daɪtʃ] 'German'
Midwestern rule:	Retain diphthong only before unstressed central vowels.	
	/aɪ/ > [aɪ]/___ [ə, ɐ]	e.g., [miɐ haɪərə] 'we marry'
	[ɛ:] elsewhere	e.g., [dɛ:tʃ] 'German'

References

Beachy, Thomas. 1999. *Pennsylvania Deitsh Dictionary.* Walnut Creek, OH: Carlisle Press.

Beam, C. Richard. 1991. *Revised Pennsylvania German Dictionary: English to Pennsylvania German.* Lancaster, PA: Brookshire Publications.

Bender, Ruth. 1929. "A study of the Pennsylvania-German Dialect as Spoken in Johnson County, Iowa." Thesis, State University of Iowa. Edited by C. R. Beam. June 11, 1991.

The Budget. Sugarcreek, Ohio.

Buffington, Albert F. 1939. "Pennsylvania German: Its Relation to Other German Dialects." *American Speech* 14:276-86.

Buffington, Albert F., and Preston Barba. 1954. *A Pennsylvania German Grammar.* Allentown: Schlechters.

Costello, John R. 1992. "The Periphrastic duh Construction in Anabaptist and Nonsectarian Pennsylvania German: Synchronic and Diachronic Perspectives." In *Diachronic Studies on the Languages of the Anabaptists*, ed. Burridge and Enninger, 242-63. Bochum: Brockmeyer.

Druckenbrod, Richard. 1994 (1981). *Mir Lanne Deitsch.* Allentown, PA.

Frazer, Timothy. 1993. *"Heartland" English: Variation and Transition in the American Midwest.* Tuscaloosa : University of Alabama Press.

Frey, J. William. 1985 (1942). *A Simple Grammar of Pennsylvania Dutch.* Lancaster, PA: Brookshire.

Gingerich, Melvin. 1939. *The Mennonites in Iowa.* Iowa City: State Historical Society of Iowa.

Hostetler, John A. 1992. *Amish Society*, 4th ed. Baltimore: The Johns Hopkins University Press.

Huffines, Marion Lois. 1989. "Case Usage among the Pennsylvania German Sectarians and Nonsectarians." In *Investigating Obsolescence: Studies in Language Contraction and Death*, ed. by Nancy Dorian, 211-26. Cambridge.

Kauffman, Stanley A., and Leroy Beachy. 1990. *Amish in Eastern Ohio.* Walnut Creek, OH: German Culture Museum.

Keiser, Steve Hartman. 1998. "From the Farm to the Factory: Variation in Pennsylvania German." Paper presented at New Ways of Analyzing Variation 27, October 2, 1998, Athens, Georgia.

Keiser, Steve Hartman. 1999a. "A Plain Difference: Variation in Case-Marking in a Pennsylvania German Speaking Community." Ohio State University *Working Papers in Linguistics* 52, ed. Brian D. Joseph. Columbus: The Ohio State University Department of Linguistics.

Keiser, Steve Hartman. 1999b. "Sound Change and Incipient Phonemic Merger: the Diphthong /aɪ/ in Midwestern Pennsylvania German." Paper presented at New Ways of Analyzing Variation 28, October 15, 1999, Toronto.

Keiser, Steve Hartman. 2000. "Who's the Most Dutchified of Them All?: The Perception and Evaluation of Dialectal Differences in Plain Pennsylvania German Communities." Paper presented at the American Dialect Society Annual Meeting, January 6, 2001.

Keiser, Steven Hartman. 2001. "Language Change Across Speech Islands: The Emergence of a Midwestern Dialect of Pennsylvania German." Diss., The Ohio State University.

Keiser, Steve Hartman. 2002."Pennsylvania German and the 'Lunch Pail Threat': Language Maintenance and Shift in an Amish Community." In *Perspectives on Language Conflict and Language Coexistence*, ed. J. Destefano, N. Jacobs, B. Joseph, and I. Lehiste. Columbus: The Ohio State University Press.

Labov, William. 1994. *Principles of Linguistic Change, Volume 1: Internal Factors*. Cambridge, MA: Blackwell.

Lind, Katie Yoder. 1994. *From Hazelbrush to Cornfields: The First One Hundred Years of the Amish Mennonites in Johnson, Washington and Iowa Counties of Iowa*. Kalona, IA: Mennonite Historical Society of Iowa.

Louden, Mark. 1993. Variation in Pennsylvania German Syntax: a Diachronic Perspective. *Proceedings of the International Congress of Dialectologists, Bamberg, July 29-August 4, 1990*, ed. Wolfgang Viereck, 169-79. Zeitschrift für Dialektologie und Linguistik, Beihefte 74/75. Stuttgart.

Louden, Mark. 1997. Linguistic Structure and Sociolinguistic Identity in Pennsylvania German Society. *Languages and Lives: Essays in Honor of Werner Enninger*, ed. James Dow and Michèle Wolff, 79-91. New York: Peter Lang.

Luthy, David. 1986. *The Amish in America: Settlements that Failed, 1840-1960*. Aylmer, ONT: Pathway Publishers.

Luthy, David. 1994. "Amish Migration Patterns: 1972-1992." *The Amish Struggle with Modernity*, ed. Donald Kraybill and Marc A. Olshan, 243-59. Hanover, NH: University Press of New England.

MacMaster, Richard K. 1985. *Land, Piety, Peoplehood: The Establishment of Mennonite Communities in America 1683-1790*. Scottdale, PA: Herald Press.

Nolt, Steven M. 1992. *A History of the Amish*. Intercourse, PA: Good Books.

Ohio Amish Directory: Holmes County and Vicinity, 1996 revised edition. 1997. Walnut Creek, OH: Carlisle Press.

Parkinson, Frederick. 1996. "The Representation of Vowel Height in Phonology." Diss., The Ohio State University.

Raith, Joachim. 1992. "Dialect Mixing and/or Code Convergence: Pennsylvania German?" In *Diachronic Studies on the Languages of the Anabaptists*, ed. Burridge and Enninger, 152-65. Bochum: Brockmeyer.

Reed, Carroll E., and Lester W. Seifert. 1954. *A Linguistic Atlas of Pennsylvania German*. Marburg.

Rosenberg, Peter. 1998. "Dialect Convergence and Divergence among Germans in Russia." Presentation at The Convergence and Divergence of Dialects in a Changing Europe, University of Reading, Sept. 17-19, 1998. To appear as "Speech Islands" in *Dialect Convergence and Divergence*, ed. P. Auer, F. Hinskens, and P. Kerswill.

Sapir, Edward. 1949 (1921). *Language: An Introduction to the Study of Speech*. New York: Harcourt Brace Jovanovich.

Schlabach, Raymond. 1980. Some Phonological Aspects of the Pennsylvania German of Ohio. M.A. Thesis. The Ohio State University.

Schlabach, Theron F. 1988. *Peace, Faith, Nation: Mennonites and Amish in Nineteenth-Century America*. Scottdale, PA: Herald Press.

Seifert, Lester W. J. 1971. "The Word Geography of Pennsylvania German: Extent and Causes." *The German Language in America: A Symposium*, ed. Glenn G. Gilbert, 14-42. Austin: University of Texas Press.

Seifert, Lester W. J. 2001. *A Word Atlas of Pennsylvania German*. Ed. Mark L. Louden, Howard Martin and Joseph C. Salmons. Madison, WI: Max Kade Institute for German-American Studies.

Slabaugh, John M. n.d. *Knit Together in Love: Moses Slabaugh and Lydia Yoder, Their Ancestry and Their Descendants*. Sugarcreek, OH: Schlabach Printers.

Stoltzfus, Grant M. 1969. *Mennonites of the Ohio and Eastern Conference*. Scottdale, PA: Herald Press.

Thompson, Chad. 1994. "The Languages of the Amish of Allen County, Indiana: Multilingualism and Convergence." *Anthropological Linguistics* 36:1.

Trudgill, Peter, Elizabeth Gordon, Gillian Lewis, and Margaret MacLagan. 2000. "The Role of Drift in the Formation of Native-Speaker Southern Hemisphere Englishes: Some New Zealand Evidence." *Diachronica* 17,1:111-38.

Van Ness, Silke. 1994. "Pennsylvania German." *The Germanic Languages*, ed. Ekkehard König and Johan van der Auwera, 420-38. London: Routledge.

Van Ness, Silke. 1995. Ohio Amish Women on the Vanguard of a Language Change: Pennsylvania German in Ohio. *American Speech* 70,1: 69-80.

Wolfram, Walt. 2000. "The Sociolinguistic Construction of Remnant Dialects." In *Methods in Sociolinguistics*, ed. Carmen Fought, et al.

Peter Wagener
Institut für Deutsche Sprache
Mannheim, Germany

Wozu noch Deutsch?:
Funktionen und Funktionsverluste des Deutschen in Wisconsin

1. Der Gegenstandsbereich

In einem Interview mit einem deutschstämmigen Amerikaner aus einem Dorf bei Cross Plains, Wisconsin, der im Laufe seines Lebens seine deutsche Sprachkompetenz eingebüßt hat, habe ich ihn gefragt, ob er die deutsche Sprache möge und ob er sie gerne beibehalten hätte. Die schlichte Antwort war: "If I had a need for it. . . . "[1]

Damit ist das Thema für diesen Beitrag umrissen, der eher den Charakter eines Werkstattberichts als einer Ergebnispräsentation hat, kein Expertenbericht ist, der nach Vollständigkeit strebt. Diese Übersicht über die Funktionsbereiche des Deutschen in Wisconsin ist eher ein Stück Selbstvergewisserung nach den ersten Feldforschungen in Wisconsin. Ich berichte über die Funktionen und Funktionsverluste des Deutschen in Wisconsin heute und damit über einen Aspekt unserer gegenwärtigen Forschung in Wisconsin, die sich insgesamt der Untersuchung verschiedener dialektaler und umgangssprachlicher Varietäten deutschsprachiger Migranten widmet—ihren sprachlichen Biographien, den Veränderungen des Gebrauchs und der sprachlichen Substanz in einer englischsprachigen Umgebung. Das Material für diese Analysen gründet auf der Basis eines dafür sehr wirkungsvollen methodischen Zugriffs, der vergleichenden Analyse historischer und aktueller Tonaufnahmen, d. h. die den Analysen zu Gunde liegenden Daten sind durch Re-Recording von Sprecherinnen und Sprechern aus früheren Tonaufnahme-Aktionen erhoben worden.

Wir verfolgen damit das Ziel, ausgewählte Sprachwandelphänomene bei verschiedenen Varietäten des gesprochenen Deutsch in realer Zeit zu untersuchen. Gegenstand der Untersuchung sind sowohl individuelle Veränderungen einzelner Sprecher als auch Phänomene sozialen Sprachwandels in den untersuchten Sprachgemeinschaften über einen Zeitraum von bis zu 55 Jahren. Grundlage sind Tonaufnahmen mit deutschsprachigen Immigranten aus Wisconsin aus den 1940er und 1960er Jahren. Vergleichend werden Tonaufnahmen der deutschen Basisdialekte und auch Tonaufnahmen von Dialektsprechern aus den ehemals deutschen Ostgebieten ("Flüchtlingen") herangezogen, die im Deutschen Spracharchiv im Institut für Deutsche Sprache, Mannheim, archiviert sind.[2] Im Mittelpunkt der Analysen soll ferner die Überprüfung einiger Hypothesen der Sprachwandelforschung stehen, z. B. ob untergehende Varietäten des Deutschen vor ihrem Verschwinden einen Verlust an Ausdrucksmöglichkeiten, eine Vereinfachung der grammatischen Struktur und regellose Variation aufweisen, wie in der Sprachwandelforschung postuliert wird.

Dazu ist es nötig, die Rahmenbedingungen kennen zu lernen, indem man z. B. versucht, die Funktionsbereiche der vielfältigen Varianten des Deutschen in Wisconsin zu beschreiben. Wisconsin gilt seit jeher als "deutscher" Staat der USA, vielleicht als der deutscheste. Noch heute liegt der Anteil der Wisconsinians, die sich als deutschstämmig bezeichnen, bei mehr als 50%. Es ist allerdings zu erwarten, dass die Ergebnisse des Zensus 2000, die für diese Detailfrage noch nicht vorliegen, eine deutliche Korrektur nach unten bringen werden. Die Herkunft der Einwohner hat es natürlich mit sich gebracht, dass lange Zeit die unterschiedlichen Sprachformen des Deutschen eine wichtige Rolle im privaten und öffentlichen Leben Wisconsins gespielt haben. Genauso klar ist, dass der Abbauprozess des Deutschen im Laufe des 20. Jahrhunderts rapide fortgeschritten ist. Er lässt sich im Ganzen beschreiben als Akkulturations- und Assimilationsprozess, forciert vermutlich auch durch feindselige Stimmungen in und nach den beiden Weltkriegen, vor allem des Ersten Weltkrieges.

2. Funktionsbereiche des Deutschen in Wisconsin

2.1. Deutsch als Mittel der alltäglichen Kommunikation: "Nahsprache"

Wisconsin ist vor allem in der Mitte und in der zweiten Hälfte des 19. Jahrhunderts in mehreren großen Wellen das Ziel von deutschsprachigen Einwanderern gewesen. Diese Einwanderer haben vielfach ihre mitgebrachten Dialekte für eine lange Zeit beibehalten. Vor allem in solchen Ortschaften, die ausschließlich oder überwiegend von Deutschen besiedelt wurden (und die z. T. bis heute auch einen deutschen Namen behalten haben, wie etwa Berlin oder New Holstein und Kiel im Nordwesten Wisconsins), ist der deutsche Dialekt auch von Generation zu Generation weitergegeben worden. Eher die Ausnahme ist es aber, dass diese Weitergabe bis in die vierte oder fünfte Generation bis heute erfolgt ist. Es gibt also längst keine Kontinuität der Erhaltung des Deutschen als Kommunikationsmittel des Alltags mehr. Die Sprecher deutscher Dialekte, die sich heute noch finden lassen, sind in der Regel ältere Sprecherinnen und Sprecher, deren Kommunikationsbedingungen in den letzten Jahrzehnten weitgehend unverändert geblieben sind. Wie dieser Prozess der Beibehaltung und der Aufgabe des Deutschen als Mittel der alltäglichen Kommunikation sich konkret vollzogen hat, werde ich an einigen Beispielen illustrieren. Über die tatsächliche Verbreitung des Deutschen in der Funktion einer "Nahsprache" (wie Heinz Kloss das so treffend benannt hat[3]) lässt sich übrigens auch deshalb so wenig Genaues, z. B. statistisch Relevantes sagen, weil sich diese Nahsprache oft der

Beobachtung entzieht. Deutsch ist durchaus auch heute noch ein Kommunikationsmittel zwischen gemeinsam alt gewordenen Ehepaaren oder in seit langem bestehenden Freundschaften und Nachbarschaften, das man mit diesem Partner und nur diesem teilt, das man aber Fremden—und eben auch den neugierigen Linguisten—vorenthält.[4]

Es ist deshalb keineswegs trivial, über den methodologischen Ansatz sorgfältig nachzudenken, wenn Deutsch in den USA, aber auch ein Dialekt in Deutschland in der Funktion einer Nahsprache zum Gegenstand linguistischen Bemühens werden soll. Ein Beispiel für den *undercover*-Status des Deutschen aus meinen Tonaufnahmen in Wisconsin: Die Tochter einer Sprecherin des Schweizerdeutschen in New Glarus im Süden Wisconsins hat mir im Interview erzählt, dass ihre Eltern in ihrer Kindheit das Schweizerdeutsche quasi als Geheimsprache benutzt haben, wenn sie von den Kindern nicht verstanden werden wollten, mit denen sie nur Englisch sprachen. Das hat bei dieser in den 1930er Jahren aufgewachsenen Sprecherin dazu geführt, dass sie auf Grund dessen eine Neugier entwickelt hat, die sie dazu geführt hat, in der Schule Deutsch zu lernen.

Es lässt sich generell feststellen, dass die Motive für die Beibehaltung oder Aufgabe des Deutschen sehr vielfältig sind. Eine Sprecherin des Niederdeutschen aus Manitowoc am Lake Michigan, im Nordwesten Wisconsins gelegen, teilt im Interview mit, dass in ihrer Kindheit der Wechsel vom Niederdeutschen zum Englischen mit der Schulreife der Kinder vollzogen wurde. Das ist eine häufig zu beobachtende Situation, die in der Regel dazu geführt hat, dass das Deutsche von den Kindern dann irgendwann völlig aufgegeben wird. In diesem Fall gab es die Besonderheit, dass in der Familie zwei Tanten dieser Sprecherin lebten, die taub waren und die gelernt hatten, Deutsch, aber nicht Englisch, von den Lippen zu lesen. Das war der Grund dafür, dass die Sprecherin das Deutsche—und zwar hier das Niederdeutsche—neben dem Englischen beibehalten hat, weil es ein notwendiges Kommunikationsmittel in der Familie war, so lange die Tanten lebten. Der folgende Transkriptausschnitt belegt, dass in der Familie ein interessanter Wechsel zwischen Niederdeutsch und Standarddeutsch stattfand. Das Interview ist weitgehend in Englisch geführt bis auf die erneute Abfrage und Übersetzung von Vergleichstexten (Testsätzen etc.). Es handelt sich um das Re-Recording einer Sprecherin, die 1968 von Jürgen Eichhoff schon einmal interviewt wurde, die ihre Niederdeutsch-Kompetenz aber inzwischen weitgehend verloren hat.

W = Interviewer Peter Wagener
A = Gewährsperson AH, weibl., Manitowoc, WI, März 2001

W: (. . .) let's äh try to * to switch to German * ähm wie ist das mit dem Hochdeutschen
A: okay

W: * bei Ihnen * ähm geht was geht eigentlich besser * Plattdeutsch oder Hochdeutsch

W: Plattdeutsch * und wenn ich jetz Hochdeutsch spreche * verstehn Sie
A:Plattdeutsch

W: das?   mhm
A: oh ja, ich verstehn das * Hochdeutsch * ja * my one aunt spoke High German

W: mhm mhm   mhm
A: * one spoke High German and the other one and my dad spoke Low German * but

W: mhm
A: see why my one aunt that lived with us spoke High German * because they were

W: oh
A: both deaf * and this one that spoke High German * when- they sent her to

W: mhm
A: Michigan * to school * so she could read lips*3*

A: and she learnt to speak High German up there (. . .)

W: (. . .) it was a normal situation what we are doing now * that I'm asking in High

W: German an you're answering in Low German *2* you knew that * äh * from your
A: mhm

W: childhood *and
A: mhm   see why she spoke High German because that's what she learnt when she

W: mh
A: went to school up in Michigan * but we converse back an forth * we would speak

```
W:                                    mhm
A:  Low German an she would repeat in HighGerman * and she would ask in High

W:                                    mhm   mhm it's interesting *3* mhm *
A:  German an we wou-  she would understand all Low Ger-        mhm

W:  an she could she could read Low German on the lips
A:                                    ya they kind of did * they

W: mhmhm                        mhm
A: both couldn't hear it  * read lips a lot *    ya that's they did * all both of 'em
```

Bevor ich genauer eingehe auf den Mechanismus des Verlustes des Deutschen als "Nahsprache," seien einige andere Funktionsbereiche des Deutschen erwähnt, die sich heute in Wisconsin finden lassen. Deutschstämmige verwenden in Gesprächen mit Leuten, von denen sie wissen, dass sie Deutsch sprechen oder Interesse am Deutschen haben, in der Englisch geführten Kommunikation Deutsch in Zitatfunktion, um ihren eigenen Bezug zur Sprache der Vorfahren zu belegen. Dazu weiter unten einige Beispiele. Zunächst sei erwähnt, dass in so einer Übersicht auch der Hinweis auf die öffentlichen Funktionsbereiche des Deutschen, die es noch gibt, nicht fehlen darf. Es handelt sich dabei vor allem um die Funktionen des religiösen Ritus, die z. T. ebenfalls der allgemeinen Tendenz des Abbaus unterliegen, z. T. aber auch unverändert beibehalten werden. Nur noch in einigen wenigen Beispielen lässt sich Deutsch als Sprache der Wirtschaft belegen. Hier hat es sicher den am deutlichsten ausgeprägten Abbau in den öffentlichen Funktionen gegeben, wenn man sich vor Augen hält, wie stark einige Branchen noch Anfang des 20. Jahrhunderts vom Deutschen dominiert waren.

2.2. Deutsch als Mittel der Identitätsstiftung

Es ist problematisch, generelle Aussagen über das historische Bewusstsein der deutschstämmigen Amerikaner und speziell über das Interesse an ihrer eigenen Geschichte zu treffen. Dieses Bewusstsein manifestiert sich z. B. in Anfragen, die an das Max Kade Institut in Madison gehen. Gerade solche Leute, die vom Verlust ihrer eigenen Kompetenz des Deutschen oder vom Sprachwechsel in der Familie betroffen sind, interessieren sich im Nachhinein gelegentlich für ihre Wurzeln. Dieses verstärkte Interesse in den letzten Jahrzehnten ist auch im Zusammenhang zu sehen mit den allgemeinen Tendenzen in der amerikanischen Gesellschaft unter dem Motto "back to the roots." Wie weit dieses Interesse unter Deutschstämmigen verbreitet ist, lässt sich nur schwer einschätzen, weil wir ja nur Kenntnis davon erhalten, wenn es etwa solche Anfragen an Institutionen wie das MKI gibt, die sich dann in konkreten Anliegen äußern müssen. Sehr häufig zeigt sich die Neugier, mehr über die eigene Identität wissen zu wollen, in den Bitten, bei genealogischen Recherchen zu helfen. Bei diesen durchaus verbreiteten Anfragen wird übrigens nach Auskunft der Mitarbeiter des Max Kade Instituts deutlich, dass sich die Leute ganz eindeutig als Amerikaner sehen, aber eben Amerikaner deutscher Abstammung, was als wichtiges Element der persönlichen Identitätssicherung empfunden wird.

Bei anderen deutschstämmigen Amerikanern kann man das Interesse an der deutschen Herkunft eher als nostalgisch bezeichnen. Das geht oft einher mit einem als Reise in die Vergangenheit empfundenen "trip to good ol' Germany," bei dem nach Möglichkeit der Ort oder die Region, aus der die Familie stammt, besichtigt wird (so weit das überhaupt bekannt ist) und daneben natürlich auch die als wichtig angesehenen deutschen Sehenswürdigkeiten (wie Heidelberg, München, Neuschwanstein etc.).

In einer Reihe von sehr interessanten Tonaufnahmen, die Steve Geiger mit Darmstädtern in Sheboygan am Lake Michigan durchgeführt hat, wird deutlich, welche zentrale Rolle diese Form des nostalgischen Interesses an Deutschland einnehmen kann. Diese Darmstädter (unter diese Bezeichnung werden hier generell Einwanderer aus Hessen-Darmstadt subsumiert) unterhalten sich in einer größeren Runde über Deutsch, ihr "Deutschsein," ihre Reisen nach Deutschland und ihre Verwandtenbesuche. Das Gespräch wird in Englisch geführt, aber fast jeder in der Runde nutzt einmal die Gelegenheit, die eigene, oft nur relikthaft vorhandene Deutschkompetenz in Geschichten, Phrasen oder auch nur einzelnen erinnerten Wörtern zu demonstrieren. Hier wird Authentizität durch Zitate hergestellt.

Ein anderes Phänomen, das sich des Deutschen als Mittel der Identitätsstiftung bedient, möchte ich als kulturelle Selbstvergewisserung der Intellektuellen bezeichnen. Ich meine hier solche Amerikaner, die das deutsche kulturelle Erbe bewusst rezipieren, also klassische Musik hören und klassische und moderne deutsche Literatur lesen und die, um das tun zu können, ihre deutsche Sprachkompetenz erhalten, reaktiviert oder neu erworben haben. Ich habe ein Interview mit einem Journalisten geführt, der aus einer jüdischen Familie aus Böhmen stammt und der mir als Motiv, wieder deutsch zu lernen, angab, dass er in der Lage sein wollte, Kafka und Kisch im Original zu lesen.

Schließlich möchte ich in diese Kategorie der Funktionen des Deutschen solche *Wisconsinians* einordnen, die ihr Interesse am Deutschen mit der "Spaß an der Freud" motivieren. Diese Formulierung fiel in einem Gespräch mit einem Mitglied des "Männerchors" in Madison, der schon seit dem 19. Jahrhundert "Männerchor" heißt und sich die Erhaltung "deutschen Liedguts" auf die Fahnen geschrieben hat, obwohl nur noch ganz wenige Mitglieder über die Liedtexte hinausgehende deutsche Sprachkenntnisse haben und die Sprache auf den Treffen Englisch ist. Einen ähnlichen eher folkloristisch motivierten Zugang zu deutscher Kultur haben auch die Besucher der durchaus noch zahlreichen "deutschen" Sommerfeste, deren größtes das *Germanfest* in Milwaukee ist. Hier manifestiert sich das klischeehaft erstarrte deutsche Erbe in Trachten und Lederhosen, in Polka, Bier und Bratwurst. Daraus resultieren typisch amerikanische Superlative wie diese: Madison feiert jedes Jahr im September das weltgrößte "Bratwurstfest"; die Welt-Bratwurst-Hauptstadt (das ist, zumindest nach Auffassung der Amerikaner, ein offizieller Titel) ist Sheboygan und das beste Bier, so heißt es, komme natürlich auch aus Wisconsin.

2.3. Deutsch als Sprache der Wirtschaft

Gerade im Brauereiwesen hat das Deutsche in der Tat eine sehr wichtige Rolle gespielt. Jahrzehntelang und z. T. bis heute waren große Teile der Beschäftigten von Brauereien Deutsche, vor allem in den Positionen, die einschlägiges Know-how verlangten, und werden amerikanische Mitarbeiter nach Deutschland zur Aus- und Weiterbildung geschickt. Die Rolle der deutschen Sprache reduziert sich aber heute in den Brauereien mehr und mehr auf eine bloße Beibehaltung eingeführter Begriffe, für die alltägliche Kommunikation spielt sie in den Betrieben fast keine Rolle mehr. Ich habe einen deutschen Braumeister interviewt, der vor knapp dreißig Jahren, in den 1970er Jahren, aus Ansbach nach Wisconsin gekommen ist. Seine einzigen Kommunikationspartner, mit denen er Deutsch spricht, sind ein Facharbeiter in seinem Betrieb, seine Frau und (gelegentlich) sein Sohn, während seine Tochter für sich und ihre Familie Wert darauf legt, nur noch Englisch zu sprechen—auch mit den Eltern.

Ähnlich scheint es in anderen Wirtschaftszweigen zu sein, in denen deutsches Know-how und die deutsche Sprache in der Vergangenheit eine große Rolle spielten. Auf vielen Wurstfabrikaten in den Supermärkten finden sich nach wie vor deutsche Namen, aber darauf scheint es sich zu beschränken. Unter den noch immer sehr zahlreichen kleinen *cheese factories* im Lande dagegen gibt es auch welche, wo nicht nur die Rezeptur des Käses, sondern auch die deutsche bzw. schweizerdeutsche Sprache weitergegeben wurde. Vor allem in der Gegend südlich von Madison, die sich "America's little Switzerland" nennt, wird Schweizerdeutsch durchaus im Arbeitsalltag noch verwendet. Die "German bakery," eine von zwei Brüdern aus Köln gegründete Bäckerei in Middleton bei Madison, führt ihren Namen hauptsächlich aus Gründen des Marketings weiter. Die jetzt für die Geschäftsführung verantwortliche zweite Generation zeigt schon deutliche Zeichen von Akkulturation.

2.4. Deutsch als Sprache des religiösen Ritus

Ich beschränke mich auf wenige Bemerkungen, weil hier natürlich vor allem die Sprache des religiösen Ritus bei Mennoniten und Amischen zu behandeln wäre, und das ist ein eigenes Thema. Der religiös motivierte Gebrauch des Deutschen bei Amischen und Mennoniten ist der einzige Bereich, wo eine Erhaltung der Funktionen des Deutschen konstatiert werden kann und wo trotz der Verluste durch die Mitglieder, die sich von den Gemeinschaften abwenden, insgesamt aufgrund der hohen Geburtenrate unter Amischen und Mennoniten ein Zuwachs an Sprecherinnen und Sprechern verzeichnet werden kann. Damit ist auch eine räumliche Ausdehnung verbunden: Es gibt ganz aktuell eine neue Ansiedlung von Amischen im Westen von Wisconsin.

Auch in anderen Religionsgemeinschaften, bei verschiedenen protestantischen und bei den Katholiken, wird der sonntägliche *service* (Gottesdienst oder Messe) in einigen wenigen Gemeinden auch heute noch in Deutsch angeboten, immer neben einem englischsprachigen *service*.[5]

3. Zum Vollzug von Sprachwandel, Sprachwechsel und Sprachverlust

Das häufigste Muster des Verlusts des Deutschen in Nordamerika ist der Sprachwechsel von Generation zu Generation. Das gilt in der Gegenwart z. B. für Leute wie den oben erwähnten Ansbacher Braumeister Hans. Hans ist bilingual; er spricht mit seiner Frau deutsch, ansonsten meist englisch. Von seinen Kindern ist der Sohn ebenfalls bilingual, seine Tochter hingegen bewusst monolingual. Und deren Kinder wiederum sind auch von der Kompetenz her monolingual. Solche Beispiele aus der Gegenwart lassen sich sehr oft finden, im Bereich der Universitäten und großen Firmen etwa, bei den Berufstätigen, die in den 1960er oder 1970er Jahren eingewandert sind.

Das geht meist einher mit einem entsprechenden Wechsel der Staatsangehörigkeit über die Generationen:

deutsch, deutscher Pass in der 1. Generation
beide Staatsangehörigkeiten häufig in der 2. Generation
amerikanische Staatsangehörigkeit in der 3. Generation.

Für die Vergangenheit galt lange Zeit das Modell, dass die erste Generation noch komplett deutschsprachig war, während Bilingualität in der Regel die zweite Generation kennzeichnet und der eigentliche Sprachwechsel sich in der dritten Generation vollzieht.[6]

Weit weniger wissen wir über den Wandel und ggf. auch den Verlust einer Sprachform während der Lebenszeit eines Sprechers—wie schon eingangs erwähnt. Ich habe deshalb seit einigen Jahren in Deutschland Tonaufnahmen mit Sprecherinnen und Sprechern gemacht, die längere Zeit vorher schon einmal interviewt worden waren. Solche Langzeitstudien mit zwei weit auseinanderliegenden Zeitschnitten lassen sich sehr gut am Material des Deutschen Spracharchivs (Institut für Deutsche Sprache, Mannheim) machen, weil dort ungefähr 9000 Tonaufnahmen mit deutschen Dialekten aus den 1950er und 1960er Jahren archiviert sind.

Auch in Madison gibt es ein Tonarchiv mit Tonaufnahmen deutscher Dialekte in den USA, u. a. eine Reihe von Aufnahmen, die Lester Seifert 1946 und 1947 in Wisconsin angefertigt hat, mit einem sogenannten *Sound Scriber*, einem Gerät, das kleine grüne Plastik-Schallplatten beschreibt, die man glücklicherweise noch auf einem Plattenspieler abspielen kann und die im Max Kade Institut in Madison im letzten Jahr digitalisiert worden sind. Einen Sprecher aus einem kleinen Ort bei Cross Plains, nordwestlich von Madison, der 1947 von Seifert aufgenommen worden ist, haben wir jetzt erneut aufgesucht. Nennen wir ihn Bill. Bill ist in zweiter Generation in Wisconsin. Sein Vater, 1880 in Frixheim bei Köln geboren, ist Anfang des Jahrhunderts nach Wisconsin gekommen und Bill ist 1918 geboren, war also zum Zeitpunkt der Seifert-Aufnahme 29 und war zum Zeitpunkt des Re-Recordings 83 Jahre alt. 1947 übersetzt er die Sätze des von Seifert entworfenen *Wisconsin Questionaires* fließend in eine Kölsch gefärbte rheinische Umgangssprache. In unserem erneuten Interview hat er große Mühe, einzelne Wörter zu erinnern und korrekt zusammenzufügen. Das gelingt meist nur sehr zögerlich und oft nur für einige Bruchstücke der Sätze.

Das folgende Transkript präsentiert einen Ausschnitt, in dem thematisiert wird, dass Bill schon lange Zeit kein Deutsch mehr gesprochen hat. Lange Sprechpausen und langsames, zögerliches Sprechen machen deutlich, wie schwer es ihm fällt, seine Deutschkompetenz zu erinnern. Anwesend sind auch Bills Frau (Sigle FM) und eine Mitarbeiterin des Max Kade Instituts Madison, die gelegentlich Kommentare einstreuen.

W = Interviewer Peter Wagener
MD = Interviewerin Mary Devitt (MKI Madison)
M = Gewährsperson "Bill," Cross Plains, WI, Dez. 2000
FM = "Bills" Frau

W: (...) ja, ich versuch das mal ich sprech einfach mal deutsch, * ja? *3* und. . .
M: sach das

W: ich, ich fange jetzt an deutsch zu reden. Ich wechsel in deutsch * und
M: nochemol

W:ich glaube Sie verstehen das. Ja? gut. * ähm *2,5* können Sie sich erinnern *1,5*
M: ja

W: wann Sie * das letzte Mal deutsch gesprochen haben? Ist das schon sehr lange her?
M: * das letzte

W: mmh.
M: Mal... *3* oh *5* (RASCHELN) vielleicht dreißich J—, dreißich Jahr zerück

W: *2* und mit wem haben Sie zuletzt regelmäßich deutsch gesprochen?
M: ah mm das, das weiß ich,

W: * mmh * mmh * mit - mit welchem, ist es Joe? Nein.
M: well, *4,5* mit mei Bruder

W: *2,5* mit welchem Bruder ist es   ist er - oh ja, es gibt so viele
MD: Joe, Joe ist, äh, nicht da

W: Müllers *   mmh * mmh *mmh*
M: well, ich weiß net * net for sure wer's war

W: aber danach haben Sie lange kein Deutsch mehr gesprochen.   Äh, was würden
M: no

W: Sie sagen, warum nicht? Warum hat das aufgehört?
M: *2* äääh *3* die * Leit * wo ich mit gesprochen han

W: mmh * mmh*
M: *2* sprechen * all englisch.   die han auch vleich *3* ähm *2* in-in-in

W: mmh * mmh* und wie war das in Ihrer Kindheit? * Sie
M: des *2* Englische geheirat.

W: haben - als Kind haben Sie zuerst deutsch gesprochen. Ja? Ist das richtich, oder

W: gleich englisch?　　　　　　　deutsch, ja, und wie lange?
M:　　　　　　　　no, deitsch　　　　　　　　Wie *2* wie ich nach de Schul

W:　　　　　　　　　　　　　　　　　　　　　　　mmh. In der Schule?
M: bin gegange * das isch des erschte Englisch was ich gesprochen hab.

W:　　　　　mmh Und mit Ihren Eltern und in der Familie wurde nur deutsch
M:　　　　Ja.

W: gesprochen?　　　　　　　　　ja. mmh, mmh *3,5* und wie ging das dann
M:　　　　　daheim immer deitsch.　　　　ja

W: weiter, öhm, Sie waren dann in der Schule und dann haben Sie in der Schule

W:englisch gesprochen und zu Hause deutsch.
M:　　　　　　　　　　　　*1,5* äh * mir han *2* englisch unn

W:　　　　　　　zu Hause auch? * Daheem?
M: deutsch gesprochen.　　　　　*2* oh daheim　　　daheim
MD:　　　　　　　　　　　　　　　　　　später?

W:　　　　　　　　　　　　mmh　　　　　　　　mmh
M: wars immer noch deitsch　　　*2* bis ich * elder * war　　you
MD:　　　　　　　　　　　　　　　That's alright,

W:　　　　ham Sie - es ist wunderbar
M: don't . . .　　　　　　. . . deitsch, wie ich nich gesprochen han die
MD: and you can . . .
(LACHEN, DURCHEINANDER)

W:　　　　　　ähm
M: letzten dreissich jahr
(DURCHEINANDER)

W: Haben Sie mit Ihren Eltern jemals englisch gesprochen oder immer deutsch?
M:　　　　　　　　　　　　　　　　　　　　*5*

W: mmh
M: immer deitsch. Wie mer geheirat han * in nine - nineteenfortysix   bis dann

W: mmh, mmh und mit Ihrer Frau, haben
M: hanwe immer deitsch gesproche daheim.
FM: mmh

W: Sie da mal, haben Sie im Anfang mit ihr deutsch gesprochen
M: mir han deitsch, am

W: mmh   ja, ah ja,
M: Disch han mir deitsch gesproche.   unn dann konnt sies net verstehe

W: aha, aha   und dann ham Sie gewechselt?
M: unn dann   ja
FM: it's all my fault
(LACHEN)

(. . .)

W: Ich würd Sie gern was fragen. Hätten Sie gerne weiterhin deutsch gesprochen?

W: Mögen Sie deutsch? Oder sind Sie froh, dass das vorbei is?
M: *3,5* ich hab des net richtich

W: ja ähm, Sie ham ja dann gewechselt, ins Englische.
M: verstehe

W: Würden Sie sagen Deutsch war eine schöne Sprache? Hätten Sie gerne Deutsch

W: weiter gesprochen? * Aber es ging nich mehr?
M: well *3* äh *1,5* wie ich vor-,* wie

M: ich gesagt hab,*2* zimmlich dreißich Jahr zerück, we married unn so, bei andre

W: mmh, mmh,
M: Leit gange* hingange * dann han die auch all englisch gesprochen.

W: mmh, aber, fanden Sie das schade? Oder war Ihnen das egal? * War das schlecht,

148

W: dass Sie aufgehört ham deutsch zu sprechen, oder würden Sie sagen egal, das macht

W: nichts?
               ja. Do you like to
M: *6* ich kann des, ich hab (. . .) net richtich verstanne.

W: speak German? Would you like to speak—to continue to speak German or did

W: you just say it doesn't matter, German is gone
M: ja. If I had a need for it, I suppose

W: ja, ja   Ja, aha. (. . .)
M: it would be nice.
FM: There's just nobody here around that speaks it any more.

Trotz aller Erinnerungslücken und seines besonders anfänglich dominierenden Bewusstseins der Unzulänglichkeit seiner Kompetenz des Deutschen ist dieses Gespräch von einer sehr positiven Einstellung gegenüber den Interviewern (der Verf. und eine Mitarbeiterin des MKI, Madison), einer Attitüde der Hilfsbereitschaft (und wohl auch insgesamt einer positiven Sicht der eigenen Wurzeln) geprägt, die dazu führt, dass Bill sich viel Zeit nimmt und Mühe macht, sein Deutsch zu revitalisieren. Im Laufe des Gesprächs wird sein Erinnerungsvermögen mehr und mehr aktiviert und gibt ihm auch selbst das Gefühl eines Erfolgserlebnisses.[7]

Notes

[1] Vgl. den Transkriptausschnitt im letzten Abschnitt dieses Beitrags.

[2] Zu den Beständen des Deutschen Spracharchivs vgl. Haas/Wagener 1992 oder die virtuelle Version des Archivs im Internet (http://www.ids-mannheim.de/DSAv).

[3] Vgl. Kloss 1978.

[4] Dieses Phänomen ist auch in Deutschland zu beobachten, z. B. in Norddeutschland, wo es geradezu gegen die kommunikativen Gesetzmäßigkeiten verstößt, mit Fremden Platt zu sprechen. Dieter Stellmacher hat das als „verdeckte Zweisprachigkeit" beschrieben (vgl. Stellmacher 1987, 42).

[5] Diese Übersicht über die Funktionsbereiche des Deutschen in Wisconsin lässt sich sicher ergänzen, weil meine Erfahrungen in der bisherigen Feldarbeit in Wisconsin und meine Recherchen nicht in alle Winkel der deutschen "Szene" vorgedrungen sind.

[6] Vgl. dazu den Beitrag von Klaus Mattheier in diesem Band.

[7] Auf der Basis solcher Tonaufnahmen lassen sich insbesondere im Vergleich zu den Aufnahmen des ersten Zeitschnitts detaillierte linguistische Analysen der Mechanismen von Wandel und Verlust anschließen, die ich an anderer Stelle weiterführen werde.

Literatur

Haas, Walter, und Peter Wagener. 1992. *Gesamtkatalog der Tonaufnahmen des Deutschen Spracharchivs.* Tübingen.

Kloss, Heinz. 1978. *Entwicklung neuer germanischer Kultursprachen seit 1800*, 2. erw. Aufl. Düsseldorf.

Stellmacher, Dieter. 1987. *Wer spricht Platt?: Zur Lage des Niederdeutschen heute.* Leer.

Renate Born
University of Georgia
Athens, Georgia

Regression, Convergence, Internal Development: The Loss of the Dative Case in German-American Dialects

1. Introduction

The loss of the dative case, a common morphological development in German-American language enclave dialects, has been the subject of extensive research in recent years most notably by Huffines (1991), Louden (1994), and Meister-Ferre (1994) on Pennsylvania German, by Gilbert (1965), Guion (1996), and Salmons (1994) on Texas German, and by Keel (1994) on Kansas Volga German. Case syncretism appears to be a relatively recent phenomenon since older informants (or earlier generations of dialect speakers) generally retain dative case markings whereas younger informants (or the present generation of speakers) exhibit merged oblique case forms which are morphologically identical with the accusative case. The cause of dative case loss is attributed either to a process of convergence with English or to internal development resulting from the general Germanic drift toward two-case systems. The convergence hypothesis is based on the observation that the dative case remains viable in non-sectarian Pennsylvania German, but has merged with the accusative case in the sectarian vernacular of the Order Amish and Old Order Mennonites (Huffines 1991, Louden 1994). Convergence is attributed to the common practice among sectarian speakers of translating from English into Pennsylvania German, which must fulfill all communicative needs of the speech community, thus opening their linguistic system to transfer from American English. The non-sectarian dialect, on the other hand, is considered to be less susceptible to English interference since speakers either translate from Pennsylvania German into English or, more commonly, shift entirely to English when the linguistic domain can no longer be covered adequately by the dialect. The fact that loss of the dative case is also common in colonial German dialects which are in contact with fully developed case languages such as Russian is the most convincing argument against the convergence hypothesis. Rosenberg (1994,152) states unequivocally "die . . . Zerfallsprozesse der Kasuskategorie werden vom voll ausgebildeten russischen Kasussystem in keiner Weise gehemmt." If the loss of the dative case in sectarian Pennsylvania German is indeed the result of convergence toward the case system of American English, it appears that this process can take place only if the contact languages are closely related and the dominant language is morphologically less complex that the minority language, so that convergence results in a morphological simplification rather than a complication of the affected dialect.

There is general agreement that the loss of the dative case is a gradual process extending over several generations. This has been documented especially well for Texas German in Salmons's (1994) diachronic study which relates increased rates of dative loss to the removal of standard German as the language of instruction in Texas schools. Taking into account data collected by other investigators, the author traces the beginning of dative case loss to the passage of two laws regulating language use: the first, in 1909, made illegal any language other than English as the language of instruction, the second, in 1918, banned all foreign language instruction from elementary and middle schools. Given the strident anti-German political climate during the First World War and the large German population in Texas, it is reasonable to assume that the second legal action was directed specifically at the rural German-speaking population less likely to pursue higher education while ensuring continued educational opportunities for the children of the middle and upper class anglophone mainstream. Since informants born between 1900 and 1912, who attended school after the passage of these laws, used fewer dative case markings than their elders, Salmons argues that the Standard German three-case system buttressed the dialectal case system, and that the removal of this supportive function led to a progressive decline in dative case markings, until they were restricted to the small repertoire of lexicalized relic forms Guion (1996) found in modern Texas German. Supported by evidence from Michigan German (Born 1994), this paper confirms Salmons's thesis that the loss of the standard German roof (*Dachsprache*) can contribute to the unraveling of a dialectal case system. The sequencing of dative case loss in Michigan German also corroborates the "regression hypothesis," the thesis that linguistic features are lost in the inverse order in which they are acquired by children.

2. Michigan German in Frankenmuth

The majority of dialect speakers in the language enclave of Frankenmuth are members of a congregation affiliated with the Lutheran Missouri Synod, formerly the German Lutheran Missouri Synod of Ohio and other States. Throughout the nineteenth century the church leadership discouraged linguistic and cultural accommodation to the anglophone mainstream by mandating that religious instruction be conducted entirely in German. The pervasive belief that the use of Standard German would insulate the religious community from the "corrupting" influence of mainstream American culture resulted in the establishment of a parochial school system where adherence to Standard German linguistic norms was an important part of the curriculum. Children were required to speak Standard German with teachers and pastors who were themselves trained in Lutheran seminaries where standard German was the primary language of instruction. As the writers of the original church charter had envisioned half a century before, at the beginning of the twentieth century the population of

Frankenmuth was composed entirely of German Lutherans. Since all children attended the parochial school from the first to the seventh grade, the public school, where according to a decree issued by the State Superintendent of Schools in 1901, no language other than English could be used, consisted merely of the eighth grade. In the private school the mornings were devoted to instruction in religion and German language, the afternoons to secular subjects taught in English. The strict enforcement of standard German linguistic norms appears to have had a similar effect on Michigan German as on Texas German as long as the dialect was roofed by Standard German rather than English. In contrast to Texas German, Michigan German lost its Standard German roof later and gradually, rather than abruptly, in the two decades between the World Wars. In general, the dialect retains the three case system of the East Franconian source dialect, but the tendency toward more extensive use of accusative case forms is stronger in the speech of informants who were educated entirely in English, less pronounced if a substantial part of an individual's education was conducted in German. Informants who were educated when the dialect was still fully roofed by standard German, those born between approximately 1910 and 1920, exhibit more consistent dative case markings than younger speakers educated primarily, or entirely in English.

Because of the extensive documentation of the earlier stages of Pennsylvania German and Texas German, it is certain that the simplified case marking structures in these dialects were developed in America rather than having been brought to America by the immigrants. In the case of enclave dialects for which no earlier studies exist, the vast majority, it is more difficult to determine whether case syncretism occurred before or after emigration. As Herman Paul has documented (1919, 215ff.), even in the literary language of the eighteenth century the assignment of the dative and accusative cases could still diverge considerably from modern Standard German norms, e.g,. *Gottschalk hilft das Kätchen in den Steigbügel* (Kleist); *Wenn diese Drohung mich gelten soll* (Frau Gottsched); *Das Büchlein wird sie noch lange im Bauche grimmen* (Goethe); *Ich verstund ihnen nichts* (Frau Gottsched). If this occurred in the most formal register of highly educated individuals, it is probable that the dialects of German immigrants departed from modern Standard German rules of case assignment to a greater degree.

Most colonial German dialects emerged when immigrants from two or more dialect regions in Germany settled in the same area and formed a language enclave. When dialects with varying degrees of grammatical complexity came into contact in this manner, it can be assumed that the resulting colonial vernacular (*Ausgleichssprache*) exhibited the grammatical features of the morphologically least complex of the source dialects. For a study attempting to distinguish inherited linguistic structures from those resulting from independent development after emigration, such mixed dialects with their amalgam of linguistic features are not suitable. To answer this question convincingly, an enclave dialect must be descended from a single German source and show no apparent signs of dialect admixture. Michigan German fulfills these requirements. Extensive church documents list the localities of origin in Germany for all but a handful of families and individuals who arrived in the first half century after the establishment of the rural language island in 1845. The vast majority of early settlers, those who founded the town of Frankenmuth and the surrounding villages of Frankenhilf, Frankenlust, and Frankentrost between 1845 and 1865, emigrated from an area no more than fifty kilometers distant from the city of Nuremberg. When settlers from other areas of Germany began to arrive in larger numbers during the final decades of the nineteenth century, they accommodated themselves linguistically to what by then had become the local prestige variety. Hence Michigan German exhibits no trace of non-East Franconian dialect admixture. For a century after settlement the community was sociologically comparable to that of the Old Order Amish today. All residents adhered to a single faith, marriage patterns were largely endogamous and education beyond the eighth grade rare. Rural isolation, deliberate separation from the anglophone mainstream combined with economic self-sufficiency permitted continued dialect maintenance and the teaching of Standard German in the parochial school until the beginning of the Second World War. After 1945 instruction in Standard German was provided for another decade on a voluntary basis for the ever decreasing number of children whose parents wanted them to become proficient enough to sing and understand German hymns. In this final stage Standard German had changed from a roofing language to a religious classical with a similar function as modern Amish High German.

3. Case Assignment in East Franconian and Michigan German

East Franconian case assignment diverges considerably from Standard German norms since prepositions and verbs requiring accusative objects in Standard German may require dative objects in the dialect and vice versa. The occurrence of final nasal consonants is phonologically conditioned, so that suffixes ending in /-m/ occur before lexemes with initial bilabial consonants, suffixes ending in /-n/ in all other environments. Therefore, the masculine dative and accusative case forms are not distinguished morphologically, e.g., *Morgen muß ich zun Doktor* 'tomorrow I have to go to the doctor.' Since the neuter singular dative case form is frequently replaced with that of the nominative/accusative as well, the dative case is marked distinctly only in the feminine singular, e.g., *mit den Karl is nigs ouzefonge aber mit dera Lies aa ned* 'you can't do anything with Karl and with Lies either' (Wagner 1987, 80). In the plural a common case form *die* has emerged. Differences in case assignment between Standard German and East Franconian are especially pronounced in the prepositional category. Many prepositions governing the accusative case in Standard German require the dative case in East Franconian, although the reverse may also occur, e.g., *ohne ihr* 'without her,' *fir meiner Frau* 'for my wife,' *mit mei Erwet* 'with my work,' *geecha dir spiel I ned*

'I won't play against you' (Russ 1990, 401, Wagner 1987, 84-86). The occurrence of a plural common case form also erases the distinction between the prepositional stative dative and dynamic accusative in the plural, e.g., *mir sin in die Berch gewesen* 'we were in the mountains,' *er is vor die Hund ganga* 'he went to the dogs.' Children transfer these vernacular rules of case assignment to Standard German. When Koller (1991, 130-32) analyzed the compositions of fourth and fifth graders he found 255 instances where the accusative case was used instead of the dative, 70 errors where the dative replaced the accusative. The obligatory choice between the prepositional stative dative and dynamic accusative was particularly problematic.

If the rules of case assignment in the modern source dialect differ to such an extent from the Standard German norm, it should not be surprising that this is also characteristic of Michigan German, the colonial off-shoot. After a century and a half of separation the case system remains essentially East Franconian although some differences have emerged. As in other colonial German dialects, the personal pronouns which carry more sentence stress have been most resistant to case syncretism whereas the possessive pronouns which are generally unstressed have lost all case markers:

> *ich muß mein Garten butzen* 'I have to clean up my garden'
> *des stirbt mit mei Generation aus* 'it (the dialect) will die out with my generation'
> *der woar bei sei Leit* 'he visited his people'

Case markings on personal pronouns, which are frequently formally identical with the demonstrative pronouns, do not diverge from those of East Franconian. The dative and accusative are distinguished in the first and second person singular, the feminine third person singular, and the third person plural:

> *Ich du mir boden* 'I am taking a bath'
> *Telefon fir dir* 'telephone for you'
> *Ich hob mit den gesprochen und mit dera a* 'I talked with him and with her too'
> *Ma muß mit dena deitsch sprechen* 'one has to speak German with them'

Michigan German case assignment in the verbal category appears to differ to some extent from East Franconian norms and may reflect nineteenth century usage rather than independent development. Verbs governing the accusative case in the modern source dialect may require dative objects, and, conversely, verbs governing the dative case in East Franconian may occur with accusative objects:

> *ich frog ira wo der Platz is* 'I'll ask her were that place is'
> *do hems ira ausgelacht in Schul* 'they laughed at her in school'
> *ich hob ira geheirat* 'I married her'

du zahlst mich ka Geld 'you aren't paying me'
der hot mi geholfen 'he helped me'
na hems di vergeem 'then they forgave you'

Prepositional case government in Michigan German seems to be a combination of inheritance and innovation. East Franconian *für, gegen* and *ohne* sometimes, but not always, require the accusative objects whereas *mit* appears to govern the dative case exclusively in the masculine and neuter singular, but not in the feminine singular where there is free variation between the accusative and dative cases, e.g. *mit die Erwet verdirbt ma si'n ganzen Dooch* 'with work one can spoil a whole day' as opposed to *mit den Karl is nigs ouzefonge aber mit dera Lies a ned* 'you can't do anything with Karl but not with Lies either' (Wagner 1987, 83-86). In Michigan German *bis, durch, in, um,* and *von* consistently govern the accusative, whereas *aus, bei, für, gegen, über, nach, neben, seit, wegen, während, zu,* and *mit (ohne)* generally, but not always, require the dative case markings on stressed personal pronouns, and accusative case markings on definite articles:

wie ma ham sin von die Kirch 'when we went home from church'
des war in die Mitten vo die Scheier 'it was in the middle of the barn'
mir hem zu die Kinder deitsch gesprochen 'talked German to her'
des is schwer fir dena 'that is for them'
ana von die Tomaten 'one of the tomatoes'
wenn ich mid dera sprechen tu 'when I talk to her'
ich hob mit des Madla gwaft 'I chatted with the girl'

In contrast to east Franconian, the semantic distinction between the prepositional stative dative and the dynamic accusative is not marked morphologically in Michigan German, although the oldest informants retain the contrast in a few lexicalized expressions:

mir ham a weng Englisch gelernt in der Schul
'we learned a little English in school'
wie ich in die Schul ganga bin 'when I went to school'

In general, however, informants no longer make the distinction:
mir woarn in die Kirch 'we were in church'
mir genna in die Kirch 'we go to church'
des woar in die lutherischen Schul 'that was in the Lutheran school'

mir genna in Haus 'we go into the house'
der woar in Haus 'he was in the house'

Since the static/dynamic distinction survives in lexicalized forms, it must have been productive at earlier stages of Michigan German for which no written documentation exists. The loss of this rule, which was probably already unstable in the East Franconian dialect the settlers brought with them because of the common case plural form and phonologically conditioned alternation between the bilabial and alveolar nasal consonants, is confirmed by a wire recording produced in 1945 and preserved by the local historical society. On the occasion of Frankenmuth's centennial celebration the Lutheran Men's Club invited the oldest male members of the community, those at least eighty years of age, to tell an assembled audience about life in their youth. In this relatively formal setting, these speakers, born in the first 20 years after the establishment of Frankenmuth, distinguish clearly between stative dative and dynamic accusative:

wann ma ins Bett ganga is 'when one went to bed'
da kimmt a frau unda der bricken raus
'then a woman came out from under the bridge'
der war schon hinda mir gstanna mitn Stecken
'he was standing behind me with a rod'

As in modern East Franonian, the plural common case form of the definite article erases the distinction between the stative dative and dynamic accusative cases: *do zwischen die Musikstend un des Gebeide woar a Stumpen* 'there between the music stands and the building was a tree stump.' The tapes suggest that the distinction between the static dative and dynamic accusative was maintained in Michigan German, at least in the most formal register used before a large audience, as long as Standard German functioned as the undisputed roofing language which was clearly the case when these men attended the parochial school in the nineteenth century. The gradual shift from the German roofing language to English at the parochial school in the two decades between the World Wars, which resulted in the establishment of the first (monthly) English church services in 1931, must have had an effect on German language instruction. It is probable that the linguistic norms were no longer enforced as strictly as had formerly been the case. When Standard German no longer buttressed the dialectal case system, linguistic change in Michigan German could proceed at a more rapid rate. Indeed, the only informants who retain lexicalized remnants of the stative/dynamic distinction in their dialect are fully literate in Standard German and entered school between 1918 and 1925 when German still functioned as the roofing language. The introduction of the English church service only a few years later indicates that English and German had become competing roofing languages for the older and younger generations of speakers.

Since loss of the dative case is such a frequent phenomenon in colonial German dialects the question arises why Michigan German should have retained a viable three-case system, even though most informants attended school when the dialect was clearly roofed by English, when Texas German lost dative case markings under similar circumstances. It is reasonable to assume that colonial dialects descended from a single source dialect with a strong dative case system are more resistant to case syncretism than mixed dialects which emerged when immigrants from two or more regions in Germany came together to form a linguistic enclave in roughly equal numbers at about the same time. If in such a setting a dialect with a strong three-case system came into contact with another making fewer case distinctions it is likely that the resulting colonial dialect (*Ausgleichsprache*) would have incorporated the features of the morphologically less complex dialect since marked features, such as the dative case, are more likely to be given up in language contact situations than those which are less marked. Mixed dialects such as Texas German, with a weaker three-case system than Michigan German, may have been more susceptible to dative case loss once the supporting function of the Standard German roof was removed.

4. Regression and Convergence

For colonial German dialects with the exception of sectarian Pennsylvania German, the loss of the Standard German roofing language marks the beginning of a period of decline, characterized by domain loss and frequent shifting to the dominant language, resulting in language death within the three-generational time frame typical of the general immigrant population. As the number of fluent dialect speakers decreases over time, the older members of the speech community cease enforcing dialectal grammatical norms, and the linguistic system of younger speakers becomes increasingly unstable as obligatory rules become variable, or are lost entirely. Grammatical distinctions, such as case markings, which do not fulfill an essential communicative function are particularly susceptible to leveling. The loss of case markings proceeds in the same manner in the vast majority of German enclave dialects regardless of the linguistic structure of the contact language: the dative case merges with the accusative which in turn may coalesce with the nominative, so that in the final stage before language death common case forms become more prevalent. Apparently, the loss of case distinctions occurs in the inverse order of the acquisition sequence exhibited by German children. Structures which are lost first in enclave dialects are acquired last and, conversely, structures which are retained longest in declining dialects emerge earliest in the child language acquisition process.

This parallelism between language acquisition and language attrition, the "regression hypothesis," was first proposed by Roman Jakobsen in his monograph *Kindersprache, Aphasie und allgemeine Lautgesetze* to account for language loss among individuals suffering from brain injuries. Only recently has regression been extended to language loss among individual emigrants (de Bot and Weltens 1991, 31, 46). However, the regression hypothesis also explains why in declining German enclave dialects the dative case tends to be replaced by the accusative rather than the reverse, and why certain word classes retain dative case markings longer than others. Children acquire the nominative case first, the accusative second, and the dative last. The nominative serves as a common case form until the accusative emerges, but errors in the subject-object distinction occur frequently until the age of four or beyond (Mills 1985, 157). According to Tracy (1986, 60), dative case forms of the personal pronouns emerge very early, even before the indefinite articles are clearly marked for the accusative case. Understandably, the first and second person pronominal forms *mir* and *dir* are acquired before the third person forms *ihm*, *ihr*, and *ihnen*. The definite and indefinite articles as well as the possessive pronouns appear first as common case forms with nominative markings, e.g., *jetzt hab ich der auch totgeschossen* 'now I shot him too,' *ich habe so ein grossen bösen Finger* 'I have such a big hurt finger.' Subsequently, the accusative forms are extended into dative contexts, e.g., *mach den Mann Beine* 'put legs on the man' (Mills 1985, 179-80). Verbs and prepositions governing the dative case initially appear with accusative objects as well, e.g., *ich werde dich helfen aufzustehen* 'I will help you get up,' *den Opa erzähl ich eine Geschichte* 'I will tell a story to grandfather,' *der Mann erzählt die Frau eine Geschichte* 'the man tells the woman a story,' *womit soll ich anfangen?— Mit den* 'with which (toy) should I start?—With that one' (Tracy 1986, 68,62, Mills 1985, 185). Mills (1985, 192) attributes the persistent extension of the masculine singular accusative case forms into dative contexts to the young child's difficulty with the distinction between bilabial and alveolar nasal consonants. Prepositional case government is particularly problematic for German children. Prepositions governing the dative case exclusively occur persistently with accusative case markings even after the age of five, and the obligatory distinction between the prepositional stative dative and dynamic accusative cases emerges last. Predictably, the accusative case initially covers both semantic contexts (Mills 1985, 188-92) and errors continue to occur frequently even after the rest of the case marking system has been fully acquired. For children speaking an East Franconian dialect the contrasting standard German and dialectal rules governing the alternation between stative dative and dynamic accusative cases cause frequent errors in compositions as late as the fifth grade (Koller 1991, 130).

If the regression hypothesis accounts not only for individual but also for communal language loss, dative case structures should be lost in declining colonial German dialects in the reverse order in which they are acquired by German children. Case markings which emerge earliest in child language should be retained best, while those which are acquired last should disappear first. Regression explains the retention of Michigan German dative case markings on personal/demonstrative pronouns, which German children acquire first, by all informants regardless of age, as well as the loss of the semantic distinction between the dynamic accusative and the stative dative which children acquire last. Dative case markings survive on feminine singular and plural personal pronouns. The masculine singular exhibits a merged oblique case form which is either phonologically conditioned in accordance with the east Franconian rule of nasal assimilation, or, as in child language, is marked with /-n/ exclusively, e.g., *ich hab zu dera/dena gesprochen* 'I talked to her/them' as opposed to *ich hab zu den gesprochen* 'I talked to him.' Even the youngest fluent speakers born in 1958 retain these pronominal dative case markings. In child language acquisition the oblique case form of the definite articles appears initially with accusative markings, e.g., *ich will bei die Lottel spielen* 'I want to play with Lottel' (Mills 1985, 189), *da kann man mit den Auto hinfar* 'you go there by car' (Clahsen 1984, 11). Older Michigan German informants frequently extend accusative case markers into dative contexts in the feminine singular and plural of unstressed definite articles, e.g., *ma muß mit die Kinder Englisch sprechen* 'one has to speak English with the children,' *zu die Zeit* 'at that time,' but retain dative case markings when the definite articles are stressed, in which case they are formally identical with the personal pronouns, e.g., *ma muß mit dena Kinder Englisch sprechen* 'one has to speak English with the children,' *zu dera Zeit* 'at that time.' Younger speakers, on the other hand, tend to employ accusative forms regardless of stress. Apparently, Michigan German is in the process of losing dative case markings on definite articles in accordance with the regression hypothesis as well.

German children produce an unmarked common case form of possessive pronouns and indefinite articles until about the age of four when the accusative case form emerges, e.g., *es gibt ein Turm* 'there is a tower,' *mit sein Schießgewehr* 'with his gun,' *das ist der Schornstein von mein brauner Baukasten* 'that is the chimney of my brown erector set' (Clahsen 1984, 9; Mills: 1985, 186). In accordance with the regression hypothesis, Michigan German has lost all case markings on the possessive pronouns, e.g., *ich woar bei mei Nichte/Leid* 'I was with my nice/people.' In the case of indefinite articles, an archaic masculine singular oblique case form inherited from East Franconian is produced occasionally by older individuals, e.g., *Wasser kannst ned aferan Haufen do* 'you can't put water in a pile,' *die had ana vo die erschten kriecht* 'she got one of the first,' but in most instances an unmarked common case form is used, e.g. *des schneidst mit a Sensen* 'you cut that with a scythe,' *mit a Messer schneidst des* 'you cut it with a knife.' Since these forms mirror the child language acquisition sequence, the loss of case markings on Michigan German possessive pronouns and indefinite articles also confirms the regression hypothesis.

Prepositional and verbal objects in the dative case, which emerge late in first-language acquisition, are produced by Michigan Germans regardless of age and thus appear to contradict the regression hypothesis. However, the dative case is marked only if the objects are personal pronouns, the word class where dative case markings emerge first in child language acquisition, e.g., *do hems ihra/dena ausgelacht* 'they laughed at her/them.' Since many verbs and prepositions which govern the accusative case in Standard German require dative objects in Michigan German and East Franconian, it is probable that first-language acquisition data from children speaking an East Franconian dialect would reveal significantly earlier occurrences of dative case markings on prepositional and verbal pronoun objects than was the case in the studies cited above. In general, the evidence from Michigan German corroborates the regression hypothesis since dative case markings have been lost in categories which children acquire last, and are retained in those which emerge first in child language acquisition.

5. Conclusion

The loss of the dative case in German-American language enclave dialects has been attributed either to convergence toward the English two-case system, or to independent development. Convergence, which appears to be restricted to sectarian Pennsylvania German, does not account for the fact that the reduction in dative case markings is also common in Russian-German dialects where the contact language has a fully developed case system. Evidently, convergence occurs only when the languages in questions are closely related and when the dominant language has a less complex case system than the German dialect. Dative case loss has also been related to the shift in roofing languages from Standard German to English. In Texas German, the dative case survived as long as Standard German buttressed the dialectal case system, but declined progressively thereafter until dative case markings were restricted to the handful of lexicalized expressions which survive in the modern dialect. In Michigan German where the dative case remains viable, informants who attended school when the dialect was roofed by Standard German produce more consistent dative case markings than informants who were educated entirely in English. Although the shift in roofing languages appears to have contributed significantly to the loss of dative case markings in both Michigan German and Texas German, it does not explain why the rate of dative case loss has also accelerated in many Russian-German dialects since the Second World War. These have been roofed by Russian since the late nineteenth century, and should have lost dative case markings much earlier. The regression hypothesis, the thesis that grammatical features are lost in inverse proportion in which they are acquired in childhood, explains why dative case markings are replaced with those of the accusative in the vast majority of German enclave dialects regardless of the contact language, and why, in the final stage before language death, common case forms with nominative case markers become more frequent: German children acquire the nominative case first, the accusative case second, and the dative case last. After the accusative emerges it functions as an oblique case form until the dative case markers appear relatively late in the acquisition process. It is interesting to note that regression is compatible with the process of convergence toward English posited for sectarian Pennsylvania German. As Raith (1992, 162) has pointed out, convergence also occurs in the reverse order of the first-language acquisition sequence.

While it is certain that the reduced case systems of Pennsylvania German and Texas German developed after immigration, this cannot be determined for the majority of German enclaves dialects which emerged when speakers from two or more dialect regions in Germany settled in the same area. The question of inheritance versus independent development cannot be answered unless the enclave dialect under investigation is descended from a single German source dialect. A comparison of the Michigan German case system with that of the German source dialects reveals that both dialects diverge considerably from Standard German norms of case assignment. What at first glance appear to be signs of instability in the case system of a declining language are inherited East Franconian features instead. In general, the replacement of dative case markers with those of the accusative has occurred in contexts which were already unstable in the dialect the immigrants brought with them. Compared to East Franconian, the changes in Michigan German can be summarized as follows: the possessive pronouns have lost all case markings and the distinction between the prepositional stative dative and dynamic accusative is no longer maintained. The retention rate of dative case markings also differs by lexical category. The personal/ demonstrative pronouns retain them best, definite articles to a lesser degree, whereas indefinite articles and possessive pronouns are unmarked for case. The changes in the Michigan German case system confirm the regressions hypothesis since the dative case remains strongly marked in categories which children acquire early, for example the personal pronouns, but has been lost entirely in those categories or contexts which emerge late in first-language acquisition, the possessive pronouns and the distinction between the prepositional stative dative and dynamic accusative cases.

References

Berend, Nina. 1998. *Sprachliche Anpassung: Eine soziolinguistisch-dialektologische Untersuchung zum Russlanddeutschen.* Tübingen: Narr.

Berend, Nina, and Hugo Jedig. 1991. *Deutsche Mundarten in der Sowjetunion.* Marburg: N.G. Elwert.

Berend Nina, and Klaus Mattheier, eds. 1994. *Sprachinselforschung: Eine Gedenkschrift für Hugo Jedig.* Frankfurt: Peter Lang.

Born, Renate. 1994. *Michigan German in Frankenmuth: Variation and Change in an East Franconian Dialect.* Columbia: Camden House.

Burridge, Kate, and Werner Enninger, eds. 1992. *Diachronic Studies on the Languages of the Anabaptists.* Bochum: Brockmeyer.

Clahson, Harald. 1984. "Der Erwerb von Kasusmarkierungen in der deutschen Kindersprache." *Linguistische Berichte* 8:1-42.

de Bot, Kees, and Bert Weltens. 1991. Recapitulation, Regression, and Language Loss. In Seliger/Vargo, 31-52.

de Bot, Kees. 1996. "Language Loss." In *Kontaktlinguistik: Ein internationales Handbuch zeitgenössischer Forschung* I, ed. Hans Goebel et al., 579-85. Berlin: de Gruyter.

Eikel, Fred. 1949. "The Use of Case in New Braunfels (Texas) German." *American Speech* 24: 278--81.

Gilbert, Glenn G. 1965. "Dative versus: Accusative in the German Dialects of Texas." *Zeitschrift für Mundartforschung* 32: 288-96.

Guion, Susan G. 1996. "The Death of Texas German in Gillespie County." In *Language Contact Across the North Atlantic*, ed. P. Sture Ureland and Ian Clarkson, 441-63. Tübingen: Niemeyer.

Herman, Paul. 1919 (1968). *Deutsche Grammatik*, vol. 3. Tübingen: Niemeyer.

Huffines, Marion. 1989. "Case Usage among the Pennsylvania German Sectarians and Nonsectarians." In *Investigating Obsolescence*, ed. Nancy Dorian, 227-42. Cambridge: Cambridge University Press.

Huffines, Marion. 1991. "Pennsylvania German: Convergence and Change as Strategies of Discourse." In Seliger/Vargo, 125-38.

Huffines, Marion. 1992. "Language Change and Enabling Strategies of Pennsylvania Anabaptists." In Burridge/Enninger, 166-81.

Jordens, Peter, et al. 1989. "Linguistic Aspects of Regression in German Case Marking." In *Studies in Second Language Acquisition* I, 179-204.

Keel, William D. 1994. "Reduction and Loss of Case Marking in the Noun Phrase in German-American Speech Islands: Internal Development or External Interference?" In Berend/Mattheier, 93-104.

Koller, Erwin, 1991. *Fränggisch geschriim?: Eine fehleranalytische Untersuchung unterfränkischer Schüleraufsätze.* Tübingen: Niemeyer.

Louden, Mark L. 1989. "Syntactic Variation and Change in Pennsylvania German." In *Studies on the Language and the Verbal Behavior of the Pennsylvania Germans II*, ed. Werner Enninger et al., 29-40. ZDL Beiheft 64. Stuttgart: Franz Steiner.

Loudon, Mark. 1994. "Syntactic Change in Multilingual Speech Islands." In Berend/ Mattheier, 73-91.

Meisel, Jürgen M. 1986. "Word Order and Case Marking in Early Child Language. Evidence from Simultaneous Acquisition of Two First Languages: French and German." *Linguistics* 24:123-83.

Meister Ferre, Barbara. 1994. *Stability and Change in the Pennsylvania German Dialect of an Old Order Amish Community in Lancaster County.* ZDL Beiheft 82. Stuttgart: Franz Steiner

Mills, Anne E. 1985. "The Acquisition of German." In The *Crosslinguistic Study of Language Acquisition I*, ed. Dan Slobin, 141-254. Hilsdale, NJ: Erlbaum.

Raith, Joachim. 1992. "Dialect Mixing and/or Code Convergence: Pennsylvania German." In Burridge/ Enninger, 152-65.

Rosenberg, Peter. 1994. "Varietätenkontakt and Varietätenausgleich bei den Rußlanddeutschen: Orientierungen für eine moderne Sprachinselforschung." In Behrend/ Mattheier, 123-64.

Russ, Charles V. J. 1990. *The Dialects of Modern German.* London: Routledge.

Salmons, Joseph. 1994. "Naturalness and Morphological Change in Texas German." In Berend/Mattheier, 59-72.

Seliger, Herbert W., and Robert M. Vargo, eds. 1991. *First Language Attrition*. Cambridge: Cambridge University Press.

Tracy, Rosemary. 1984. "Fallstudien: Überlegungen zum Erwerb von Kasuskategorie und Kasusmarkierung." In Syntaktische Struktur und Kasusrelation, ed. Hartmut Czepluch and Hero Jansen, 271-313. Tübingen: Narr.

Tracy, Rosemary. 1986. "The Acquisition of Case Morphology in German." *Linguistics* 24,1: 47-78.

Wagner, Eberhard. 1987. *Das Fränkische Dialektbuch*. München: C. Beck.

Janet Fuller and Glenn Gilbert
Southern Illinois University
Carbondale, Illinois

The Linguistic Atlas of Texas German Revisited

Introduction

The German language in Texas was introduced by immigrants from Germany, starting during the time of the Lone Star Republic and accelerating during the first years of statehood. Despite the initial shock of climatic and language differences, and later the active suppression of the German language and culture in the 20th century, German has survived in Texas for an exceptionally long time in cohesive *Sprachinseln*. This is due largely to three factors: vast distances between isolated ranches and farmsteads for a century or more, relatively poor schooling with less pressure toward language conformity to English monolingualism, and the proximity of Latin America which had the effect of increasing tolerance toward people who spoke more than one language, be it Spanish or German.

The published *Linguistic Atlas of Texas German*, which appeared in 1972, reports on data gathered from personal interviews with 186 bilingual language consultants in a 30-county area in the east central part of the state, roughly the region bounded by San Antonio, Austin, and Houston. To supplement the personal interviews, approximately 1000 questionnaires were mailed in the spring and summer of 1965 throughout the state to clergymen in churches known to have a substantial number of parishioners of German ancestry, and also to *Gesangvereine* and *Turnvereine*, which have remained active in Texas as glee clubs and Turner physical fitness associations. Following a procedure somewhat like Georg Wenker's famous *vierzig Sätze*, sent to over 40,000 Prussian schoolmasters in the 1870s—which became the basis of the *Sprachatlas des deutschen Reiches*—Gilbert asked the respondents in Texas to translate 128 items from English into local German, if they spoke it, and otherwise to collaborate with a local speaker in doing the translations. By Christmas of 1965, replies were received from 255 respondents in 62 counties, an area rivaling that of entire western European countries such as Germany and France.

Despite all the problems inherent in data gathered by means of a mail/translation procedure, the tabulated results surprised us by being very much like those of the published atlas. The Texas German dialect, if it can be called that, represents an interesting colonial koiné language, derived from central/northern Germany, flourishing in semi-isolation for 75 years in a relatively dry subtropic/temperate zone, with many changes in life style, agricultural practices, house architecture, cuisine, and so forth.

Although there are many features of this language worth further investigation, our report focuses on one of the most debated aspects of its grammar: case morphology.

No one doubts that the overt marking of case distinctions in noun phrases is rapidly changing in Texas German, as has been amply demonstrated in other American German dialects as well (e.g., Huffines 1989; Louden 1988). Texas German gender distinctions in nouns and the retention of the major features of German word order, especially where it differs from English, remain remarkably conservative, but not the morphological marking of cases.

Why Is Case Being Lost in Texas German?

There are two main options when considering the motivation for case loss in Texas German dialects: the changes could be internally or externally motivated. Each of these options contains a number of possibilities. Claims of internally motivated change include the possibility that the root of change was brought from Germany, or that simplification and reduction has occurred as part of language death. The external motivation we are concerned with in the case of Texas German is language contact. It has been claimed that English, as a language which does not have case morphology (except in personal pronouns), has exerted a strong influence on German dialects spoken over a number of generations in the United States, and that this is the catalyst for the loss of case in American German varieties. Each of the above-listed possible motivations for case loss will be briefly addressed below, beginning with the second.

As suggested by Keel (1994), in order to claim influence from English, there must be clear evidence for at least one, if not all, of the following points: a) the patterns in Texas German match the patterns in American English varieties spoken in that area, b) German dialects in Germany, which have developed from similar origins, do not show case mergers, and c) German dialects spoken by minority populations in countries where the majority language marks nominative, accusative, and dative case have not lost case distinctions. Broadly speaking, none of these claims can be convincingly supported.

First, as discussed in Fuller (1996) in an analysis of the loss of the dative case in Pennsylvania German, the surface structure of English does not provide a pattern of case loss in the way that American German dialects are developing. That is, the surface structure of English does not match the surface structures of German dialects which have lost the dative case. English, as we all know, with the exception of the s-genitive, does not mark case at all on nouns, and pronouns have subject and object forms, except for the second person pronoun *you*, which has the same form for the subject and object. (This is also true in Southern American dialects which employ *ya' ll* for the second person plural pronoun.)

Standard German has a case marking system which is considerably more complex, marking nominative, accusative, dative, and genitive cases on proper nouns and pronouns with different morphology depending on noun classes (which are partially determined by grammatical gender). Texas German, as outlined in Gilbert (1963), maintains some of this complexity. In particular, differences from English which are maintained include a subject-object distinction for nouns and pronouns, including the second person pronouns (e.g., *du* and *dich*) but excluding the third person pronoun *sie*, which is the same in both nominative and accusative cases. If English were indeed exerting influence on Texas German dialects, we would expect somewhat different patterns to develop. First, we would expect a leveling of all case marking on nouns (which clearly is not the case since there remain some distinctions). Second, we would expect that the subject-object distinction would be eliminated for the second person pronoun—with either *du* or *dich* serving in both contexts (this, however is not occurring). Third, we would expect that a distinction would be maintained between the subject and object forms for the third person singular feminine and third person plural pronouns *sie* and *ihr/ihnen*—but when leveling occurs, it appears to generally eliminate the dative pronouns and leave only the accusative for the object case, which is the same as the nominative (subject) pronoun. Although we do find some slight evidence for the retention of *ihr* (the most common of such pronouns), overall this has not been found in studies of case mergers in American German dialects.

The fact that the surface structure of English is not influencing Texas German case marking is doubly significant because Louden (1988) has shown that common English usages in utterances such as *me and Sally went home* have influenced Pennsylvania German case use. As can be seen in example (1), the accusative (object) pronoun is used in a nominative (subject) position by Louden's Pennsylvania German speaker. It would, therefore, be reasonable to expect parallel surface structures in the second and third person pronoun use if English was indeed the catalyst for the case merger in Texas German, or other American German dialects; but there is little evidence for this.

(1) Mich un die Sally sin heemgange. (Louden 1988, 153)
     'Me and Sally went home.'

A further nail in the coffin of the language contact argument for case mergers in Texas German is a comparison with other German dialects. Keel (1994), citing work done on the case systems of European German dialects by Shrier (1965) and Russ (1989), notes that there are many case mergers in many dialects that take on many different forms. Common versus dative case systems (similar to the system found in earlier stages of Pennsylvania German) are found in a number of High German dialects, and nominative versus oblique systems (similar to what has developed in Texas German) are commonly found in northern and eastern German dialects. Thus, similar case mergers can be found in German dialects which do and do not have intensive contact with English, suggesting that English contact is not a major influence in this linguistic change. A final piece of evidence provided by Keel is that case mergers are common in German dialects spoken in Russia, where there is no linguistic model for case coalescence.

Thus, we are forced to conclude—as Gilbert argued in 1963—that case loss in Texas German, and indeed in American German dialects as a whole, cannot be shown to be caused by English influence. What, then, is the motivation for case mergers? One explanation which suits the Texas German data is that reduction in case marking is part of overall simplification that occurs in languages which are undergoing attrition. This is the claim put forth by Guion (1996), who noted that while older fluent speakers of German do use the dative case, both semi-speakers and younger fluent speakers of German in Gillespie County (Fredericksburg and vicinity) show a reduced system with generalization of the nominative forms for all cases. A trend away from the Standard, although not necessarily in the direction of language death, is also supported by Salmons (1994, 62), who provides evidence that around the time that case marking in Texas German began to show variation, access to Standard German ended in the schools as a result of educational policy.

There is somewhat of a contradiction in these last two points—that case mergers are happening everywhere, and that they are part of language death. Obviously, not all dialects of German—especially not those spoken in Germany—are dying. If the vernaculars in Germany were dying out, we would expect them to be replaced by more Standard varieties of German, not less Standard ones. Thus, the issue of motivation for case mergers remains a puzzle that can only be explained in general terms. Loss of case marking has been documented in many languages, such as English, as part of a largely internally motivated change. In the Germanic languages, however, this process appears to have accelerated in cases where there was language contact and restriction, as seems to have happened with the speakers of Old English in contact with Old Norse and Norman French. Likewise, it has been claimed that even the extreme changes in morphology in Afrikaans vis-à-vis Dutch can be at least partially explained as internally motivated (Raidt 1995). In the case of Texas German, language shift does play a role in the loss of case, but not the role of providing a model for language change.

The exact path of the loss of the dative case—that is, what linguistic contexts appear to be best suited to retention or loss of case marking—has been studied by Salmons (1994), with the conclusion that pronouns are vastly preferred for case marking; this finding is supported by our data as well. In addition, Salmons shows that contexts that are consistently marked for the dative case—such as objects of prepositions that always require the dative, or in straightforward indirect object positions—retain case marking longer than contexts in which dative case marking is less prototypical. That is, constituents following verbs such as *helfen*, for example, which requires dative case to mark its object in Standard German, and objects of prepositions which take both dative and accusative case-marked objects, depending on whether motion or change of state is involved, are more quickly treated as accusative contexts. These generalizations are also supported in our research.

Examples of Case Coalescence in Texas German

Early observers of the Texas German dialect such as Eikel (1949) and Gilbert (1963, 1965, 1972) reported that the dative and accusative were merging in many locations in Texas into a common object case, generally with the morphological marking of the former accusative. To the extent that German is still spoken in Texas, this merger appears to be slowly generalizing to all syntactic positions where Standard German would require the dative marking. The following examples, all of which are attested, represent the end point of that merger, namely categorical accusative markings for a common oblique case. Case marking nevertheless remains variable; most speakers still use dative forms variably. Non-accusative usage seems to vary by geographic location, age, and contact with Standard German.

(2) NP in indirect object position: Er gibt/gebt **mich** das Geld.
    'He gives me the money.'

(3) Personal pronoun in indirect object position: Gib/Geb **sie** zwei Stick(e).
'Give her two pieces.'

(4) Personal pronoun as the object of a verb subcategorized for the dative:
    (a) Er hilft/helft **mich** jetz.
    'He's helping me now.'
    (b) Das Bild gehert (zu) **sie**.
    'The picture belongs to them.'

(5) Personal Pronoun after preposition subcategorized for the dative:
    (a) Lieber Gott, ich bidde Dich / Mach ein gudes Kind aus **mich**.
    'Dear God, I pray Thee / Make a good child of me.'
    [child's prayer in Fredericksburg common at least as early as the 1930s]
    (b) Mir/Wir sind mit **sie** gegangen.
    'We went with her.'

(6) NP after preposition subcategorized for both dative and accusative, depending
    upon location and movement:

(a) Das Bild hängt iber **das** [or ibers] Bett.
'The picture is hanging over the bed.'
(b) Da is was in dein linkes Aug.
'There's something in your left eye.'
(c) Koch das Ei in heißes Wasser.
'Boil that egg in hot water.'

Results

The data analyzed in this paper comes from 255 speakers from 62 counties who responded to the mail survey. (Because not every respondent answered every question, some of the questions have less than 255 responses.)

The questionnaire gave English sentences and asked for translations of all or part of the sentence; multiple choice answers and a blank for "other" were provided. We categorized answers according to whether they indicated dative or accusative marking on the noun in question. (Although most of this categorization was straightforward, there were some answers—both given in the questionnaire and written in—which indicated *den* as an article for a noun that was clearly neuter in gender. These answers were coded as dative answers, assuming a merger between the nasal [n] and [m].) Responses that indicated that both dative and accusative responses were acceptable were categorized as "other," as were answers which did not include overt case marking where it would be required in Standard German.

Overall, there is a clear loss of dative case marking in the varieties spoken by these respondents, and evidence of general lack of clarity in distinguishing the accusative and dative cases. In contexts which require the accusative case in Standard German, accusative case marking was used 73% of the time. In contexts in which the dative case is required, however, dative marking was chosen for only 41% of the nouns.

Dative/Accusative Contrast Following Prepositions: Location Versus Motion or Change of State

There are five pairs of sentences in our data which contrast objects of prepositions depending on whether the verb denotes location or motion or change of state. The accusative case is required in Standard German when motion or change of state is depicted, such as in sentences like 'He's putting the chair under the tree' *(Er stellt den Stuhl unter den Baum)*. Dative case is required in Standard German when the object is in repose, for example, 'He's sitting over there under the tree' *(Er sitzt unter dem Baum)*. The five pairs of sentences are given in table 1; in all cases, the first sentence in the pair would require accusative, and the second dative, in Standard German.

As shown in table 1, in the five pairs of sentences, the sentence which would require the dative case in the noun phrase which is the object of the preposition is assigned dative case at most by only 40% of the respondents (for the translation of 'It's lying down there on the floor'). The other sentences were markedly less likely to be assigned dative case, with the next two highest dative case marking rates being 26% (for 'He's sitting under the tree') and 23% ('He's sitting over there beside the tree'). The remaining two sentences were given dative case marking still less often, with 'He is already in the room' receiving dative marking by only 16% of the respondents, and 'The picture hangs over the bed' by only 9% of the respondents.

Table 1. Dative/Accusative Contrast Following Prepositions: Location Versus Motion or Change of State

Q #	sentence	use of accusative	use of dative
44	Hang the picture <u>over the bed</u>	**95%**	2%
45	The picture hangs <u>over the bed</u>	85%	**9%**
48	He's putting the chair <u>under the tree</u>	**77%**	17%
49	He's sitting <u>under the tree</u>	68%	**26%**
51	He's putting the chair beside <u>the tree</u>	**71%**	23%
52	He's sitting over there <u>beside the tree</u>	66%	**23%**
66	He is already in <u>the room</u>	66%	**16%**
67	He goes into <u>the room</u>	**82%**	7%
98	It's lying down there <u>on the floor</u>	47%	**40%**
99	Put it <u>on the floor</u>	**69%**	25%

Note. Bold numbers indicate the case that is required in Standard German.

In the sentences which require use of the accusative case in Standard German, the percentages of answers assigning accusative case were much higher than those which required dative case, ranging from 95% to 69%. In every case, accusative case marking was the majority pattern. This is in sharp contrast with dative case marking, which is never the pattern used by the majority in this set of sentences, regardless of whether the dative case is required in Standard German. As can be seen in table 1, the sentences asking for translations of 'Hang the picture over the bed' and 'The picture hangs over the bed' elicited the most accusative answers not only for the sentence which requires accusative in Standard German, 'Hang the picture over the bed' but for both sentences in the pair. The sentence 'Put it on the floor' received the fewest accusative responses, with only 69% of the answers indicating accusative usage, but this is still much higher than any rate of dative marking for sentences of this type.

These responses indicate that roughly three-quarters of the respondents do not consistently distinguish between dative and accusative case marking after prepositions which, in Standard German, can take either case depending on whether motion/change of state or location is indicated.

Case Marking on Pronouns

There are six questions in our data which involve pronouns, as shown in table 2. Overall, there is evidence that the dative case is being replaced by the accusative, but to a lesser extent than with the nouns.

Table 2. Case Marking on Pronoun

Q #	sentence	use of accusative	use of dative
46	The picture <u>belongs to them.</u>	**35%**	<u>**60%**</u>
62	The little children <u>see her</u>.	<u>**44%**</u>	51%
63	He came <u>with me</u>.	57%	<u>**35%**</u>
65	We went <u>with her</u>.	66%	<u>**17%**</u>
71	Give <u>her</u> two (pieces).	33%	<u>**58%**</u>
93	<u>He's helping me now</u>.	65%	<u>**25%**</u>

Note. Bold numbers indicate the case that is required in Standard German.

One of the sentences containing a pronoun (question 71) involves a straightforward use of a dative pronoun as the indirect object of 'give' *geben*, (i.e., 'Give her two pieces'). This is a context in which we would predict more consistent marking of the dative case, as there is a potential contrast between the direct and indirect objects of *geben*. In addition, this sentence contains the pronoun *her* in the translation model and for that reason it may reinforce the use of the phonetically similar *ihr* instead of *sie*. In keeping with these expectations, 58% of the respondents marked this pronoun as dative. This is a higher rate than any of the nouns were marked, and the second highest rate of dative marking for pronouns (and overall).

Two of the sentences containing pronouns involved verbs which, in Standard German, would require dative objects: *gehören* 'belong' and *helfen* 'help' (i.e., questions 46 and 93). Because the requirement of dative for these verbs is somewhat idiosyncratic, it would be predicted that the case marking of their objects would be more likely to be in accusative. These data only partially support that prediction. The translation of 'help me,' as would be predicted, receives relatively low rates of dative marking at only 25%. The translation of 'belongs to them,' however, receives the highest rate of dative marking at 60%. This may in part be due to the fact that the answers given in the multiple choice format involved use of the *zu* 'to,' a calque from English which is part of Texas German. What this indicates, then, is not that the verb 'belong' takes the dative case, but that the preposition *zu* remains a trigger for dative case marking, as it is in Standard German.

This cannot be said of all prepositions requiring the dative in Standard Germany, however, There are two sentences involving the pronouns 'me' and 'her' following the preposition 'with' in our data which yielded quite different translation results, namely questions 63 and 65. In Standard German, the preposition *mit* 'with' requires dative case in all contexts. In our data, however, there were very low rates of dative case marking. For the sentence 'He came with me,' 35% of the respondents chose the dative preposition *mir*, but for 'We went with her,' only 17% of the respondents selected the dative pronoun *ihr*.

Finally, the last sentence involving pronouns in the data had 'her' as a direct object, i.e., 'The little children see her.' This sentence, unlike the others, would require accusative case marking in Standard German. Interestingly enough, only 44% of the respondents provided an accusative response, and over half (51%) assigned dative case marking to this direct object pronoun.

Part of the explanation for this may lie in the pronoun itself, 'her,' which is translated into German as *sie*. Because the dative pronoun *ihr* has more phonetic similarity to 'her,' we could hypothesize that the similarity may cause this third person singular feminine dative pronoun to survive in some contexts. The results from the sentence 'Give her two pieces' also show a high use of the dative pronoun translation (in this case, also required by the Standard). Unfortunately, this hypothesis is not supported by the results from the translation of the sentence 'We went with her,' which elicited dative case pronouns from only 17% of the respondents, even less than was elicited for the other sentence involving a pronoun object of 'with.' Thus, there is not strong support for the hypothesis that phonetic similarity might favor retention of the pronoun *ihr* in Texas German.

Case Marking in Noun Phrases Containing Adjectives

Two questions in our data also address the issue of overt case assignment in constructions including an adjective in the noun phrase. The sentences are 'There is something in your left eye' and 'Boil that egg in hot water'. Both the German word for 'eye,' *Auge*, and the German word for 'water,' *Wasser*, are neuter gender. In Standard German, the adjective would be marked for dative case; accusative case marking would include an *-es* morpheme on the adjectives, e.g. *linkes Auge* 'left eye,' *heißes Wasser* 'hot water.' In both cases, the dative case is called for in Standard German.

In the former sentence 'There is something in your left eye,' accusative and dative case marking are used about evenly (47% and 46% respectively), as seen in table 3. In translation of the sentence 'Boil that egg in hot water,' however, there is very little use of the dative, at a rate of only 8%. Although the accusative case marking is chosen quite frequently—76%—there are also an unusually high number of "other" choices and write-ins for this question. Overall, those two questions indicate that more complex patterns of case marking—such as those involving adjectival endings—are even more unstable across speakers and communities than other case marking patterns.

Table 3. Case Marking in Adjectival Endings

Q#	sentence	use of accusative	use of dative	Other
47	There=s something in your left eye	47%	46%	7%
74	Boil that egg in hot water	76%	8%	16%

Conclusion

The overall picture in these data is clearly one of the loss of the dative case, with dative pronouns being used more frequently than dative case marked nouns. We have argued that this case merger is primarily an internally motivated development in Texas. There is no evidence that transfer from English is occurring, but there is some reason to believe that language contact may accelerate processes of language change, particularly if they favor simplification and reduction.

Whatever the exact causes of this case merger, in our data there is much variation between speakers, and within the speech of individuals. This suggests that the end result might well be, or has been, a dialect with *no* dative case marking—provided the case merger moves, or has moved, faster than language shift. Our data shows an optional dative case marking, though it does not seem to be systematically distinct in meaning from accusative case marking (for instance, it no longer indicates fixed location when following the prepositions *in* or *über*).

The picture of Texas German we are left with is that of a highly variable dialect that is being used by a last generation of speakers. It is our hope that future research can put detail in this picture in terms of specific language features and the patterns of discourse in localized varieties.

References

Eikel, F. 1949. "The Use of Cases in New Braunfels German."*American Speech* 24: 278-81.

Fuller, J. M. 1996. "When Cultural Maintenance Means Linguistic Convergence: Pennsylvania German Evidence for the Matrix Language Turnover Hypothesis." *Language in Society* 25: 493-514.

Gilbert, G. 1963. "The German Dialect Spoken in Kendall and Gillespie Counties, Texas." Diss., Harvard University. *Dissertation Abstracts International* 25 (11): 65-4785.

Gilbert, G. 1965. "Dative vs. Accusative in the German Dialects of Central Texas." *Zeitschrift für Mundartforschung* 32: 288-96 [re-keyed and placed on Gilbert's website, http://www.siu.edu/departments/cola/ling/glen_hpg/glen_h-1.htm January and February 2001].

Gilbert, G. 1972. *Linguistic Atlas of Texas German*. Marburg: Elwert Verlag, and Austin:University of Texas Press.

Guion, S. 1996. "The Death of Texas German in Gillespie County. " In *Language Contact across the North Atlantic*, eds. P. S. Ureland and I. Clarkson, 443-63. Tübingen: Max Niemeyer.

Huffines, M. L. 1989. "Case Use Among the Pennsylvania German Sectarians and Nonsectarians."In *Investigating Obsolescence: Studies in Language Contraction and Death*, ed. N. C. Dorian, 211-26. Cambridge, UK: Cambridge University Press.

Keel, W. D. 1994. "Reduction and Loss of Case Marking in the Noun Phrase in German-American Speech Islands: Internal Development or External Interference?" In *Sprachinselforschung: Eine Gedenkschrift für Hugo Jedig*, ed. N. Berend and K. J. Mattheier, 93-103. Frankfurt am Main: Peter Lang.

Louden, M. L. 1988."Bilingualism and Syntactic Change in Pennsylvania German." Diss., Cornell University.

Raidt, E. H. 1995. *Historiese taalkunde: Studies oor de geskiedenis van Afrikaans*. Johannesburg: Witwatersrand University Press.

Russ, C. 1989. *The Dialects of Modern German: A Linguistic Survey*. Stanford, CA: Stanford University Press.

Salmons, J. 1994. "Naturalness and Morphological Change in Texas German." In *Sprachinselforschung: Eine Gedenkschrift für Hugo Jedig*, ed. N. Berend and K. J. Mattheier, 59-72. Frankfurt: Lang.

Shreier, M. 1965. "Case Systems in German Dialects." *Language* 41,3: 420-38.

Göz Kaufmann
Universidade Federal do Rio Grande do Sul
Porto Alegre, Brazil

The Verb Cluster in Mennonite Low German[1]

1. Origins of this research

During the field work for my Ph.D. thesis which dealt with the maintenance of Low German in Mennonite communities in Texas (USA) and Chihuahua (Mexico), I realized that there existed a lot of variation with regard to the ordering of two or more verbal elements within verb clusters. Due to this, the informants were asked to translate a couple of sentences from English or Spanish into Low German. The data not only confirmed the impression about the existence of syntactic variation but showed a significant difference between the variants preferred in Texas and in Chihuahua. This came as a surprise because the former group had left Chihuahua (Kaufmann 1997, chapter 6.3.1.6) only twenty years before, and they probably did not leave because of syntactic differences. The change, therefore, must have occurred in Texas probably as a consequence of the new linguistic situation. Since then I have planned to obtain more and more structured data on this phenomenon.

2. The Sample Groups

All Low German-speaking Mennonite communities in the Americas immigrated from Russia where their ancestors had lived since the end of the 18th century. The Mennonites originally came from east Holland, Frisia, and what is today northwest Germany where they formed Anabaptist communities during the time of Reformation. Due to religious persecution most of them emigrated to West Prussia during the 16th century where they adopted first the local variety of Low German[2] and later a variety of High German for religious purposes and more formal contexts. When the Prussian government started to impose stricter rules on the Mennonites in the 18th century, they started to look for other places to live and gladly accepted an invitation by Catherine II of Russia to settle in the Ukraine. There they lived for a century in almost complete isolation, but at the end of the 19th century, the Russian officials started to change their policies towards the Mennonites by introducing laws to ensure a certain measure of integration. This caused the more conservative Mennonites to emigrate to Canada around 1870. The Mennonites who stayed in Russia accepted the new situation and introduced a more elaborate school system sending future teachers to Germany to study there and sometimes even inviting teachers from Germany to teach in their colonies. When the situation for German-speaking immigrants in Canada became more and more difficult during and after World War I, it was again the more conservative Mennonites who decided to move to Mexico where most of them settled in the state of Chihuahua. Others found a new home in Paraguay setting up the colony Menno. Mennonites from Mexico founded several daughter settlements, namely Santa Cruz de la Sierra in Bolivia—there are also Mennonites living in Santa Cruz who immigrated from Menno, Paraguay—various communities in Belize, and one in Seminole, Texas. The Mennonites who had stayed in Russia in 1870 faced new problems after the foundation of the Soviet Union and especially when Stalin came to power. Around 1930, many of them left the Ukraine, emigrating to Paraguay, setting up the colony Fernheim, and Brazil, where they lived first in the state of Santa Catarina and later in Paraná and Rio Grande do Sul.

All these Mennonite communities stem from colonies whose members emigrated from West Prussia, where their ancestors had stayed for more than two centuries, to the Ukraine, where they stayed for at least another century. This offers the linguist the rare opportunity to compare different paths of language change of an originally rather homogenous language. It may be granted that two different dialects existed in Russia, named after the colonies of Chortitza and Molotschna, but the differences between them do not seem to be very big. Therefore, if one wants to explain linguistic differences between the existing daughter colonies, one has to look for explanations in their different migration histories. This is probably the closest a linguist can get to a laboratory situation.

3. The Syntactic Phenomenon

The most researched area in West Germanic syntax seems to be the so-called verb second phenomenon in main clauses. Nevertheless, the verb cluster in West Germanic languages—another syntactic topic dealing with the position of verbal elements—has grown in importance during the last decades. Table 1 illustrates the pertinent facts in Standard Dutch and Standard German.

Table 1: Neutral sequences of clause final verb clusters in Standard Dutch and Standard German

	STANDARD GERMAN		STANDARD DUTCH	
verb cluster	VI in second position	VI not in second position	VI in second position	VI not in second position
2 verbal elements	V3-V2	V2-VI	V2-V3	VI-V2 / V2-VI
3 verbal elements	V4-V3-V2	V3-V2-VI / VI-V3-V2	V2-V3-V4	VI-V2-V3

VI is the finite verb, V2 the nonfinite verb depending on VI, V3 the nonfinite verb depending on V2, etc.

178

The only exception to the otherwise rigidly descending sequence of Standard German is the front position of the finite verb in clusters of three verbal elements. This position is obligatory in the case of modal verbs in the perfect tense with the finite auxiliary *haben* and the modal verb appearing in the form of an infinitive instead of the expected past participle (*infinitivum-pro-participio* effect; cf. examples in [1]),

(1a) (. . .) daß er ihn hat_{V_1} $sehen_{V_3}$ $können_{V_2}$
(1b) *(. . .) daß er ihn $sehen_{V_3}$ $können_{V_2}$ hat_{V_1}
   (. . .) that he has been able to see him

and optional with two true infinitives depending on finite *werden* (cf. examples in [2]):

(2a) (. . .) daß er ihn $wird_{V_1}$ $sehen_{V_3}$ $können_{V_2}$
(2b) (. . .) daß er ihn $sehen_{V_3}$ $können_{V_2}$ $wird_{V_1}$
   (. . .) that he will be able to see him

In Standard German it is not possible, though, to put a modal verb in front of two true infinitives (cf. examples in [3]) or in front of an infinitive perfect,[3] or to put the auxiliary *haben* into this position when a true past participle governing an infinitive depends on it (cf. examples in [4]):

(3a) *(. . .) daß er ihn $will_{V_1}$ $leiden_{V_3}$ $sehen_{V_2}$
(3b) (. . .) daß er ihn $leiden_{V_3}$ $sehen_{V_2}$ $will_{V_1}$
   (. . .) that he wants to see him suffer

(4a) *(. . .) daß er ihn hat_{V_1} $schwimmen_{V_3}$ $gelehrt_{V_2}$
(4b) (. . .) daß er ihn $schwimmen_{V_3}$ $gelehrt_{V_2}$ hat_{V_1}
   (. . .) that he has taught him to swim

In Standard Dutch the ordering of two verbal elements—one of them being the finite verb—is optional. The V1-V2 seems to be preferred for modal verbs while the V2-V1 ordering is more frequent for the perfect tense (cf. the examples in [5] and [6], and Zwart 1996, 233):

(5a) (. . .) dat hij kan_{V_1} $komen_{V_2}$
(5b) (. . .) dat hij $komen_{V_2}$ kan_{V_1}
   (. . .) that he can come

(6a) (. . .) wat hij $\mathbf{had}_{V1}$ gezegd$_{V2}$
(6b) (. . .) wat hij gezegd$_{V2}$ $\mathbf{had}_{V1}$
(. . .) what he has said

With three elements the Standard Dutch verb cluster is the mirror image of the default Standard German sequence (cf. Zwart 1996, 233). The exceptional sequence in Standard German verb clusters (V1-V3-V2) and the Standard Dutch V1-V2 and V1-V2-V3 sequences are generally agreed upon to be the result of Verb Raising (VR), i.e., the infinitive(s) move(s) to the right of the finite verb by way of adjunction.[4] The difference between Standard German and Standard Dutch is that VR in Standard Dutch is almost a rule whereas it is a strictly limited phenomenon in Standard German.

This does not mean, however, that VR is unknown in historic or modern German varieties. As early as 1978, Lötscher published an article dealing with verb clusters in the Zurich German dialect. After describing the different variants in the dialect, Lötscher develops an implicational ranking of six systems with regard to the sequence within verb clusters covering several southern German dialects (1978, 18-24). A higher system includes all VR variants of the lower system and adds new ones or transforms optional variants into obligatory ones. Standard German falls into Lötscher's System II; System I is a system with no VR whatsoever. Besides VR, many of the analyzed dialects show a slightly different phenomenon which is commonly known as Verb Projection Raising (VPR). In VPR it is not only the nonfinite verb which is being moved but the nonfinite verb with its complement(s). This rightward movement causes the disruption of the verb cluster. An example from Lötscher's data is:

(7) (. . .) wil de Joggel $\mathbf{wott}_{V1}$ es gottlett $\mathbf{\ddot{a}sse}_{V2}$ (Lötscher 1978, 4)
(. . .) because Joggel wanted to eat the pork chop

With regard to historic German varieties, Ebert (1981, 1998) analyzed a corpus of letters written by individuals from Nuremberg between 1300 and 1600. In his 1981 article he analyzes embedded clauses with two verbal elements (*haben/sein* + past participle, *werden* + past participle, and modal verbs (including *werden*) + infinitive) but only if the verbal elements are contiguous. He thus excludes occurrences of VPR (1981, 204-5). He also excludes clusters with more than two verbal elements writing: "Syntagms consisting of three or more verbal elements pattern quite differently at this time than do these two-part constructions and consequently are not considered here" (1981, 204), an observation which coincides with Lötscher's rule for VR (R2) whose application increases with the complexity of the verbal group (1978, 17). Ebert finds two linguistic factors to have an important influence on the ordering of the two verbal elements: the type of syntagm, i.e. whether the finite verb is the temporal auxiliary *haben* or *sein*, the passive auxiliary *werden*, or a modal verb (1981, 206), and the grammatical category of the word which precedes the verbal group or more precisely the question whether this word bears stress or not (206-7). Of minor importance is the question whether the embedded clause occurs before or after the main clause (205-6), the rhythmical patterns formed by the two verbal elements (207-9), and the position of the two verbal elements within the embedded clause (209; clause final vs. non-clause final). Curiously, Ebert does not discuss the type of embedded clause as an independent variable.

4. The Research Data

The aim of this research is to gather syntactic data from at least six Mennonite communities in order to analyze and compare the structure of the verb cluster in Mennonite Low German. So far field work has been carried out in Texas, USA (40 informants—about 1800 sentences), Chihuahua, Mexico (55 informants—about 2500 sentences), Rio Grande do Sul, Brazil (41 informants—about 1850 sentences), two colonies in the Paraguayan Chaco, namely Menno (42 informants—about 1900 sentences) and Fernheim (36 informants—about 1600 sentences), and on a smaller scale in a colony of originally Paraguayan Mennonites in Bolivia (8 informants—about 350 sentences). In this article the results of the data from Texas and Rio Grande do Sul will be presented, these two colonies representing the longest time of separation one can find for Mennonite colonies in the Americas. The ancestors of the Texan Mennonites separated from the ancestors of the Brazilian Mennonites about 130 years ago. In 1976-77 the Texas Mennonites arrived in the USA coming from Mexico. Today, there are roughly 4000 Mennonites living in Seminole, Texas. The Mennonites who live in Brazil arrived there in 1930, settling first in the state of Santa Catarina. In 1950 some of these Mennonites moved to Rio Grande do Sul where they settled close to the city of Bagé, the colony today having about 1000 inhabitants.

The data consists of the translation of 46 sentences from the respective majority languages, i.e., English, Spanish, or Portuguese, into the Mennonite Low German variety. The sentences were chosen in order to cover most of the independent variables which might influence the internal sequence of verb clusters. The goal was to obtain Low German clauses with one, two, and three verbal elements but the actual data also includes a fair number of clauses with four verbal elements. Different kinds of clusters of two verbal elements were elicited: the temporal auxiliary *habe(n)* + past participle, modal verbs + infinitives, and verbs with separable prefixes. The translations produced two more kinds, *woare(n)* (Standard German *werden*) + infinitive and the so-called do-support typical for many German dialects (*doon(e)* + infinitive). Different from Ebert's work, the analysis is not restricted to contiguous occurrences of the verbal elements thus not excluding VPR. Another difference is that this research distinguishes four types of embedded clauses: relative clauses (with the relative pronoun functioning either as subject or object), conditional clauses, causative clauses, and object clauses. In total, there are four clause types and five types of verb clusters (one verbal element, which is not a cluster, two elements with the three subdivisions mentioned above, and three elements) which adds up to twenty sentences. To improve the reliability of the data, two sentences for each type were created. The last six sentences were main clauses which were chosen according to the same rules. However, only one example of each type was included because main clauses were not the principal interest of the research. Two examples of main clauses were only elicited for the clauses with three verbal elements where the two nonfinite elements normally form a clause final cluster. All main verbs governed either a direct or an indirect object in order to be able to distinguish clearly between VR and VPR. To give the reader an idea of the sentences used for elicitation, the following list shows five of the ten object clauses:

one verb:
> (8) It's not good that he's buying the car

two verbs (verb with separable prefix):
> (9) Don't you see that I'm turning on the light

two verbs (modal verb + infinitive):
> (10) Henry doesn't know that he can leave the country

two verbs (auxiliary + past participle):
> (11) Peter is convinced that he's understood the book

three verbs:
> (12) He didn't know that he should have fed the dogs this morning

Many readers will rightly object that such a method is unable to elicit natural language data. One should not forget, though, that the amount of free speech necessary to elicit comparable syntactic data of hundreds of speakers would be hard to get. In contrast to phonetics, in syntactic empirical research it is not enough to analyze twenty minutes of recorded speech to extract enough material to do valid statistical analyses. This does not mean that no free speech was recorded in the communities in order to be able to verify the results of the translation exercise, but such material cannot be the base of a thorough statistical analysis. After all, translating is widely used for eliciting data in minority language studies (cf. Hill and Hill 1977; Dorian 1981; Huffines 1991). Nevertheless, there exist some problems connected with this elicitation method. Mennonites who have almost completed the shift from Low German to the majority language had to be excluded from the study because of their low competence in Low

German. This was a minor problem, though, because few Mennonites in the studied communities have reached this stage. A bigger problem was caused by the Mennonites whose competence in Spanish, Portuguese, or English was too low to take part in the research. This problem refers especially to women and members of the more conservative groups, a substantial group in Mexico and Bolivia. One has to admit that this problem has not been solved so far and may skew the results. It was not possible to resolve this problem by using Standard German instead of the majority language because the Standard German syntax is too close to Low German and would have influenced the outcome. Nevertheless, it is an astonishing fact how fast and how well most of the informants did the translation, which shows that the use of two languages is a common routine for many Mennonites. The fact that three different majority languages served as medium of elicitation probably does not pose a threat to the validity of the results. There are no major differences between Spanish, Portuguese, and English with regard to the position of verbal elements—all three languages have a basic SVO order, do not show a difference between embedded and main clauses, and do not exhibit the so-called verbal frame typical of German and Dutch varieties.[5] The informants were chosen in order to obtain an even distribution between the sexes and three age groups. The affiliation to a specific Mennonite church—an important social characteristic for the Mennonites in Mexico and the USA—in Brazil the whole community belongs to one progressive Mennonite Church, was included in the planning, but due to the fact that many members of the more conservative groups do not speak the majority language well enough, few of them could take part in the study. Therefore, these churches are underrepresented.

5.1. Linguistic Factors

Due to limitation of space, this article can be no more than a first presentation of the results. In particular, the possibility of gaining important theoretical insights into the working of syntactic change will only be touched upon and left for further publications. Also, this article will only deal with embedded clauses with two verbal elements. Examples for the three major variants in the translations of sentences (10) and (11) from the Texan sample are given below:

Standard German variant:
    (13a) Henrik weet daut nich, daut hee daut Laund **verloten**$_{V2}$ **kaun**$_{V1}$
    (10) Henry doesn't know that he can leave the country
    (14a) Peter es seck secher, daut hee daut Bük **verstonen**$_{V2}$ **haft**$_{V1}$
    (11) Peter is convinced that he's understood the book

Verb Raising variant:

(13b) Henrik weet daut nich, daut hee daut Laund **kaun**$_{V1}$ **verloten**$_{V2}$

(14b) Peter es seck secher, daut hee daut Bük **haft**$_{V1}$ **verstonen**$_{V2}$

Verb Projection Raising variant:

(13c) Henrik weet daut nich, daut hee **kaun**$_{V1}$ daut Laund **verloten**$_{V2}$

(14c) Peter es seck secher, daut hee **haft**$_{V1}$ daut Bük **verstonen**$_{V2}$

Table 2 shows the results for the variants and its distribution with regard to the type of finite verb.[6]

Table 2: Frequency of three major variants for the sequence of two verbal elements in embedded clauses and their distribution with regard to the type of finite verb in the USA and Brazil

| finite verb | U S A | | | B R A Z I L | | |
| | verb sequence | | | verb sequence | | |
(n for USA) (n for Brazil)	**Stand**	**VR**	**VPR**	**Stand**	**VR**	**VPR**
total (for these verbs)	332	187	415	706	78	159
(934) (943)	36%	20%	44%	75%	8%	17%
verb (with separable prefix)	69	1	15	121	0	6
(85) (127)	81%	1%	18%	95%	0%	5%
doon(e) (with infinitive)	144	12	84	99	2	19
(240) (120)	60%	5%	35%	83%	2%	16%
habe(n) (with past participle)	83	41	118	279	9	38
(242) (326)	34%	17%	49%	86%	3%	12%
modal verb (with infinitive)	30	101	177	170	45	87
(308) (302)	10%	33%	58%	56%	15%	29%
woare(n) (with infinitive)	6	32	21	37	22	9
(59) (68)	10%	54%	36%	54%	32%	13%

Explanation: Stand = Standard German variant (Comp NP$_{Subject}$ NP$_{Object}$ V2 V1); VR = Verb Raising variant (Comp NP$_{Subject}$ NP$_{Object}$ V1 V2); VPR = Verb Projection Raising variant (Comp NP$_{Subject}$ V1 NP$_{Object}$ V2)

It is important to mention at this point that the variation shown in table 2 is not just an artificial result of averaging individual data but a reflection of the individual variation of most informants[7] (cf. Lightfoot 1999, chapter 4). A detailed analysis of the individual variation will be carried out in further publications.

The most striking result is the fact that the Low German syntax in Brazil proves to be much closer to Standard German than the one in the USA. In 75% of the analyzed clauses, the Brazilian Mennonites prefer the standard variant, while this number drops to 36% in the USA. One explanation for the big difference between the syntax in Brazil and the USA could be the fact that the ancestors of the Brazilian Mennonites stayed sixty years longer in the Ukraine, and it was in these years that schooling was much improved which brought them into closer contact with Standard German. There are two possible scenarios with regard to this: The first scenario assumes that the closer contact with Standard German, which only the ancestors of the Brazilian Mennonites had, inhibited an ongoing syntactic change in Low German. This would mean that the Brazilian pattern, which is marked by less variation, represents the linguistic situation in 1870 more closely than that of the Mennonites in the USA. In the second scenario, the Texan variation pattern is assumed to be closer to the linguistic situation of 1870, which would mean that closer contact with Standard German caused the Mennonites who stayed in Russia (i.e., the ancestors of those who are now in Brazil) to reverse their syntactic behavior. This scenario seems to be less probable, though, because in order for syntactic change to take place as a result of language contact such contact must be very strong, and the Mennonites who stayed in the Ukraine after 1870 did not have that much contact with speakers of Standard German—nor does Standard German today play such a central role in the Mennonite communities studied here. Granted, in this respect there are differences between the Mennonite communities but even in the Brazilian community, where Standard German is much more important than in the USA, it is obvious that the influence of Low German linguistic patterns in Standard German by far outdoes the influence in the opposite direction. Therefore, it is more probable that the increased contact with Standard German in the Ukraine was strong enough to slow down syntactic change but was too weak to eliminate already existing variants. Also, there exists a statistically significant difference between the syntactic variation in the USA and in Mexico. In Kaufmann (1997, table 6.3.1.6a, 187) it was demonstrated that the Mexican Mennonites prefer the Standard German variant more than the Mennonites in the USA, who had left the Mexican community only twenty years before. This shows that a lot of syntactic change has taken place during these twenty years, probably a consequence of the stronger language contact in the USA (189-92).[8] Finally, Low German, at least as spoken today in northern Germany, seems to be one of the few West Germanic varieties which strictly place all finite verbs in embedded clauses behind the nonfinite verb(s): cf. Broekman (1995, 120) for the auxiliary *haben* in the perfect tense without the *infinitivum-pro-participio* effect of the modal verb (*dat he dat book lesen*$_{V3}$ *kunnt*$_{V2}$ *hett*$_{V1}$) and Haan (1996, 171) for clusters with two verbal elements. For the latter case one can find important confirmation in seven letters to the editor published in a weekly newspaper which appeared between 1741 and 1743 in the city of Gdansk (cf. Mitzka 1969). In these letters there is not a single case of V(P)R in 61 clusters with two verbal elements in embedded clauses.[9] Although Mitzka (1969, 81) comments that there is some influence of written High German in these letters, one should not forget that this reflects the linguistic reality in northern Germany at this time. Low German lost most of its written domains in the 17th century (Hartweg/Wegera 1989, 32-3). Nevertheless, the fact that there is not a single example for V(P)R in these letters is striking even compared to written High German at the time. In the 17th century written High German texts still showed 8% of VR, a number which had already dropped significantly from 28% in the 14th century (Hartweg/Wegera 1989, 136).

Because of the facts mentioned above, this article assumes that the Low German variety spoken by the Mennonites at the time when they left their West Prussian home showed no or little variation with regard to the sequence of two verbal elements in clause final clusters. V(P)R is considered a Mennonite innovation which took place in the Ukraine where the Mennonites had for at least 100 years little or no contact with other Low or High German-speaking people.

If one continues to analyze the occurrence of the Standard German variant, one sees that the ordering of the finite verbs is almost identical for both communities. It seems that the clause final position of the finite verb is preferred for verbs with little or no semantic content.[10] *Doon(e)* is probably semantically empty[11] and *habe(n)* as a temporal auxiliary has less semantic content than modal verbs. In Brazil it behaves almost identically to *doon(e)*.[12] The fact that *woare(n)* patterns like the modal verbs can be explained by the fact that it shares some morphological and semantic features with these verbs. It is, for example, well known that *werden* in present-day German expresses more frequently a supposition than a temporal meaning like *haben*.

The only exception to this semantic ranking are the verbs with separable prefixes where the semantically heavy verbal part strongly prefers the finite position in both countries. The VR variant is virtually absent (only one out of 213 cases in both countries) and the VPR variant is not very frequent either. Perhaps these verbs should not be considered as verb clusters but rather as single verbal elements, because although the position of the prefix in Standard German coincides with the position of nonfinite verbal elements like infinitives, their semantic nature is quite a different one, and the analysis shows that they behave very differently from the other types of finite verbs analyzed here. In the USA finite single verbal elements (300 tokens) appear in the final position in 71% of the cases and before the object NP in 29% of the cases, showing a pretty similar distribution to the prefixed verbs (81% vs. 18%). In Brazil the fit is perfect: In 95% of the cases the finite main verb (397 tokens) occurs in the final position and in only 5% of the cases before the object NP.

Comparing the frequency of the two non-standard variants one can detect an interesting similarity in the two communities, i.e., VPR occurs roughly twice as much as VR. Again the *doon(e)* and *habe(n)* pattern is similar in Brazil in that both clusters hardly appear with VR. The only verb which causes more VR than VPR in both countries is *woare(n)*. This exceptional distribution seems to be caused by the position of conditional clauses. *Woare(n)* almost exclusively appeared in conditional clauses which tend to occupy the position before the main clause in German—all ten conditional clauses used in this study obeyed this tendency different from all other clause types analyzed here. A confirmation of this hypothesis may be the fact that also the modal verbs and *habe(n)* show more VR variants than VPR variants in conditional clauses in both countries, although their overall distribution shows a massive preference of VPR. There might be a connection with a syntactic fact in colloquial German. In causal clauses appearing before the main clause, the otherwise allowed main clause syntax with epistemic *weil* is not possible (cf. Küper 1991, 136). Although epistemic *weil* functions as a coordinating conjunction in the case of main clause syntax which is not the case of conditional *wann* in Mennonite Low German, one should not forget that, at least on the surface, the verb second position of main clauses very often cannot be distinguished from the result of VPR.

Table 3 examines the distribution of different types of embedded clauses more closely.

Table 3: Frequency of three major variants for the sequence of two verbal elements in embedded clauses and their distribution with regard to the introductory word in the USA and Brazil

	U S A			B R A Z I L		
introductory word	verb sequence			verb sequence		
(n for USA) (n for Brazil)	**Stand**	**VR**	**VPR**	**Stand**	**VR**	**VPR**
total for these introductory words (832) (864)	280 34%	177 21%	375 45%	636 74%	74 9%	154 18%
wann (conditional) (261) (272)	118 45%	101 39%	42 16%	209 77%	36 13%	27 10%
waut (relative pronoun, subject) (73) (76)	34 47%	28 38%	11 15%	58 76%	11 15%	7 9%
waut (relative pronoun, object) (80) (68)	38 48%	17 21%	25 31%	49 72%	11 16%	8 12%
daut (object complementizer) (216) (241)	82 38%	30 14%	104 48%	188 78%	9 4%	44 18%
weil(s), wegen(s) (causal) (202) (207)	8 4%	1 0,5%	193 96%	132 64%	7 3%	68 33%

Explanation: Stand = Standard German variant (Comp NP$_{Subject}$ NP$_{Object}$ V2 V1); VR = Verb Raising variant (Comp NP$_{Subject}$ NP$_{Object}$ V1 V2); VPR = Verb Projection Raising variant (Comp NP$_{Subject}$ V1 NP$_{Object}$ V2)

The first interesting result from table 3 is the fact that the clauses introduced by wh-words (*wann* and *waut*) have a very similar distribution pattern in both countries. The only deviation is the behavior of *waut* in object function in the USA which shows a preference of VPR over VR.[13] But the frequency of the standard variant is again very similar. The object clauses with the complementizer *daut* show a marked increase in VPR and an equally dramatic drop in VR in both countries. In the USA there is also a drop in the frequency of the standard variant which does not occur in Brazil. Causal clauses show the biggest difference in both countries. In Brazil the standard variant drops to 64%, and in the USA both the standard variant and especially the VR variant are virtually inexistent. This leads to an interesting question: If, as has been said above, on the surface VPR is often not distinguishable from main clause syntax with the finite verb in second position, could it be that causal clauses display main clause syntax in the Low German of the Mennonites in the USA? To answer this question, one has to look for unambiguous cases of VPR. These are the cases where it is clear that the finite verb cannot possibly occupy the second position, i.e., where there are at least two positions before the finite verb, normally the subject NP and another category.[14] Ambiguous cases are those where the finite verb occupies the position after the subject NP which not necessarily has to be the second position. In the analyzed data one finds several adverbs, adverbial phrases, and the negation word *nich* which appear either before the finite verb or after it. Examples for this can be found in the slightly erroneous translations of sentence (10):

unambiguous VPR case:

(15a) Henrik weet daut nich, daut hee$_{(1st\ position)}$ **nich**$_{(2nd\ or\ later)}$ **kaun**$_{V1\ (3rd\ or\ later)}$ daut Laund **verloten**$_{V2}$

(10*) Henry doesn't know that he can(not) leave the country

ambiguous case:

(15b) Henrik weet daut nich, daut hee$_{(1st\ position)}$ **kaun**$_{V1\ (2nd\ or\ later)}$ **nich**$_{(3rd\ or\ later)}$ daut Laund **verloten**$_{V2}$

For all cases where the verb cluster is separated by an object NP, the data shows the following distribution of these elements.

Table 4: Position of adverbial phrases, adverbs, and the negation word *nich* in reference to the finite verb in embedded clauses with two separated verbal elements in the USA and Brazil

position of the adverbial element	U S A		B R A Z I L	
	in front of the finite verb (clearly VPR)	behind the finite verb (ambiguous)	in front of the finite verb (clearly VPR)	behind the finite verb (ambiguous)
causal clauses	1 (1%)	104 (99%)	12 (29%)	30 (71%)
other clauses	23 (17%)	109 (83 %)	21 (37%)	36 (63%)

Table 4 shows that in only one out of 105 cases (1%), one is able to say beyond any doubt that the Texan Mennonites really employ VPR in causal clauses with two verbal elements. With regard to the other clause types there are 17% of unambiguous cases. Interestingly, the situation in Brazil in absolute terms is less ambiguous, but the

188

difference between the clause types is similar. For causal clauses one has 29% of unambiguous cases, and for the other clause types this number rises to 37%. It seems that what happens with causal clauses in the USA is that the originally subordinating conjunction has turned into a coordinating one. If one accepts the hypothesis that the Mennonites in the USA changed the original Low German syntactic structure more than the Mennonites who live today in Brazil, there is only one possible explanation for these results. At a certain point the children of the Mennonites in the USA could no longer detect the effect of VPR on the surface and reclassified causal conjunctions as coordinating conjunctions.[15] Due to the fact that also in the other clauses the proportion of verb clusters interrupted by an object NP is larger in the USA than in Brazil and that the proportion of unambiguous cases of VPR is smaller in the USA than in Brazil, one could even hypothesize that the Texan Mennonites are losing the distinctive German phenomenon of a different position of the finite verb in embedded and main clauses. Besides this, it is interesting that the proportion of unambiguous cases in Brazil is smaller for causal clauses than for the other clause types and that the number of cases with a separated verb cluster is bigger for causal clauses. Perhaps causal clauses in Brazil are also leading a reorganization of the Mennonite Low German word order. If that were true, VPR could be an intermediate stage between embedded clauses with the finite verb in the final position and embedded clauses with the finite verb in second position.[16] A first confirmation of this hypothesis can be gained from the results of the Mexican data. There are 13 (10%) unambiguous cases of VPR in causal clauses and 120 (90%) ambiguous ones. For the other clause types, there are 28 (36%) unambiguous cases and 50 (64%) ambiguous ones. These results lie between the ones in the USA and the ones in Brazil. The reclassification of the causal conjunction in the grammar of younger Mennonites seems to have happened somewhere between Mexico and the United States. More detailed analysis is needed to strengthen this hypothesis. Especially, the results for embedded clauses with one verbal element and with more than two verbal elements will provide further clarification in this matter.

5.2. Sociolinguistic Factors

Besides the linguistic factors whose distribution is significantly different on the 0%-level (Pearson's χ^2) for both independent variables in both countries, it proved to be worthwhile analyzing the classic sociolinguistic factors *age* and *sex*. The distributions in the two countries follow in table 5 and 6:

Table 5: Frequency of three major variants for the sequence of two verbal elements in embedded clauses and their distribution with regard to sex and age in the USA

U S A	total sample	men	women	young (< 26)	middle (26 - 40)	old (> 40)	young women	non-young men
total number of informants	40	16	24	20	11	9	13	9
total number of clauses	937	368	569	495	236	206	321	194
Standard German variant (Comp NP$_{Subject}$ NP$_{Object}$ V2 V1)	332 35%	159 43%	173 30%	140 28%	111 47%	81 39%	80 25%	99 51%
Verb Raising variant (Comp NP$_{Subject}$ NP$_{Object}$ V1 V2)	189 20%	55 15%	134 24%	110 22%	35 15%	44 21%	76 24%	21 11%
Verb Projection Raising var. (Comp NP$_{Subject}$ V1 NP$_{Object}$ V2)	416 44%	154 42%	262 46%	245 50%	90 38%	81 39%	165 51%	74 38%

Table 6: Frequency of three major variants for the sequence of two verbal elements in embedded clauses and their distribution with regard to sex and age in Brazil

B R A Z I L	total sample	men	women	young (< 26)	middle (26 - 40)	old (> 40)	young women	old men
total number of informants	41	19	22	13	11	17	7	7
total number of clauses	949	454	495	300	261	388	153	165
Standard German variant (Comp NP$_{Subject}$ NP$_{Object}$ V2 V1)	710 75%	364 80%	346 70%	178 59%	193 74%	339 87%	74 48%	153 93%
Verb Raising variant (Comp NP$_{Subject}$ NP$_{Object}$ V1 V2)	79 8%	33 7%	46 9%	38 13%	21 8%	20 5%	17 11%	6 4%
Verb Projection Raising var. (Comp NP$_{Subject}$ V1 NP$_{Object}$ V2)	160 17%	57 13%	103 21%	84 28%	47 18%	29 8%	62 41%	6 4%

Again, the absolute numbers are very different in tables 5 and 6 but the distribution pattern is similar in both countries, with young people and women showing a higher degree of non-standard variants. This seems to be a clear case for syntactic change from below (cf. Labov 1990). If one compares the two extreme groups (younger women vs. older/non-young men), one may even speak of two completely different grammars which are being employed by different speakers of the same speech community. Before interpreting the data further, one should take a look at the level of significance for these groupings.

Table 7: Level of significance (Pearson's χ^2) for the distribution of three major variants for the ordering of two verbal elements in embedded clauses with regard to sex and age in the USA and Brazil

country	Age	Sex	Age (men)	Age (women)	Sex (young)	Sex (middle)	Sex (old)
U S A rate of change	0.00001	0.00006	0.00509	0.01823	0.07479 women: rapid men: semi-rapid	0.00224 women: moderate men: slow	0.45799 women: moderate men: moderate
B R A Z I L rate of change	0	0.00088	0	0	0 women: rapid men: moderate	0.03435 women: moderate men: moderate	0.01941 women: moderate men: slow

In Brazil it seems that the change is more recent and more vigorous because all groupings in table 7 show significant results, and these results are mostly clearer than in the USA. Trying to explain the different levels of significance and the direction of the differences, one might speculate that the change in Brazil started strongly with the young women leading women of other age groups. The younger and middle-aged men started the change later whereas the older men are almost untouched by this syntactic innovation. The gender difference for the middle-aged group results from a stronger preference of women for VR and of men for VPR. The standard variant shows the same frequency for both groups. In the USA the situation is different. There is also a change but it started from a linguistic level where there already existed more variation and the frequency of the standard variant was already lower. Perhaps the recent emigration from Mexico and the stronger language contact with US-Americans in the USA caused this renewed change. For two gender groups there is no significant difference at the 5%-level which may indicate that the change is older than in Brazil because most men seem to have already caught up, the only exception being middle-aged men who show a marked resistance towards this change, something which might have to do with their age. In Kaufmann (1997, 282-83) it was shown that Mennonite men in roughly the same age group (from 26 to 35 years in 1994) showed a strong initial rejection to learning English which was explained by the fact that most of them arrived in the USA after puberty, i.e. with an already established linguistic and sexual identity (cf. Bourdieu 1991, 88, 95, 97). In contrast to this, the youngest men who had arrived as children or were born in the USA, as well as all women up to the age of 35, learned English very fast. One could hypothesize that, for the group of middle-aged men, competence in English is a basically female characteristic whereas the Spanish they had used in Mexico represented their male identity better. Maybe the group of middle-aged men analyzed here (from 26 to 40 years in 1999) rejects the new syntactic change out of the same reason; it is led by women.

In Kaufmann (1997, 189-90) it was also demonstrated that the distribution of the variants depends on the competence in English. Therefore, the new informants were grouped according to their bilingual status: dominant in Low German, equal bilinguals, or dominant in English/Portuguese.

Table 8: Frequency of three major variants for the sequence of two verbal elements in embedded clauses and their distribution with regard to the informant's bilingual status in the USA and Brazil

linguistic dominance	U S A			B R A Z I L		
	Low German	equal	English	Low German	equal	Portuguese
total number of informants	13	7	17	13	15	13
young / women / young women	3 / 10 / 3	4 / 5 / 2	13 / 9 / 8	2 / 7 / 1	4 / 9 / 3	7 / 6 / 3
total number of clauses	297	162	416	295	342	312
Standard German variant (Comp NP$_{Subject}$ NP$_{Object}$ V2 V1)	125 / 42%	51 / 32%	120 / 29%	244 / 83%	259 / 76%	207 / 66%
Verb Raising variant (Comp NP$_{Subject}$ NP$_{Object}$ V1 V2)	62 / 21%	41 / 25%	82 / 20%	21 / 7%	25 / 7%	33 / 11%
Verb Projection Raising var. (Comp NP$_{Subject}$ V1 NP$_{Object}$ V2)	110 / 37%	70 / 43%	214 / 51%	30 / 10%	58 / 17%	72 / 23%

Both distributions in table 8 are highly significant (0.00072 in the United States, 0.00011 in Brazil) and support the findings in Kaufmann (1997). The higher the competence in the majority language the more non-standard variants are being employed. The question whether there is an interaction between this variable and other variables like age and sex is an important one. Young Mennonites and young Mennonite women are clearly more present in the groups of the equal bilinguals and of the informants more dominant in the majority language. For Mennonite women in general this is not true. The relationship between the informant's type of bilingualism and the distribution of the syntactic variants needs further investigation. One might consider the postposing of the nonfinite verb(s) a simplification strategy (cf. Lötscher 1978, 12; Bach et al. 1987; Louden 1990, 476; and Haan 1996, 175) which taken to the extreme can eliminate the syntactic difference between embedded and main clauses as mentioned above.[17] One should also not forget the possible influence of Standard German as a factor slowing down the rise of V(P)R. In both countries the competence in Standard German of the younger Mennonites is significantly lower than that of the older ones, and the competence of Standard German is lower in the USA than in Brazil (for the USA, cf. Kaufmann 1997, table 6.3.1.1c, 142).

6. Conclusions

This article presents the initial findings of a research project which started in 1999. There is still much to be done, both with regard to gathering more data (in Bolivia and Canada) and with regard to analyzing the data more thoroughly. Nevertheless, this data might offer a deeper insight into several fields of linguistics, i.e., variation studies, language contact, and syntactic change. The following problems and questions should be considered at the end of this article:

Firstly, this article suggests that the innovative variants are the non-standard ones, i.e., VR and VPR. To prove this, it is indispensable to examine Low German texts written in the Ukraine around 1870, if they exist at all, which would be the only authentic source for the variation pattern at this point. It is also important to analyze contemporary written Mennonite Low German texts in order to see whether style plays an important role in the distribution of the variants.

Secondly, the article did not discuss main clauses or embedded clauses with one, three or four verbal elements which also form part of the data set. This comparison is important because it seems that the more complex the verb cluster the more V(P)R takes place (cf. table 1 for Standard Dutch and Standard German, and also Lötscher 1978, 18-24). Besides this, linguistic factors like stress and rhythm have not been mentioned in the analysis although they seem to play an important role in this kind of variation (van de Velde 1981, 229-30 and Ebert 1981, 206-10; but cf. also Patocka 1999, 136-37, who is of a different opinion). The question whether or not there is a semantic difference between the three variants cannot be answered by this data set because the sentences are not embedded in a bigger context. There is, however, no indication for such a semantic difference in the literature, and the Mennonites do not sense such a difference either.

Thirdly, it would be useful to develop a system of quantification to measure the deviation of every clause from a fixed point of reference, regardless of the properties of the clause, namely the number of verbal elements, the kind of finite verb, and the introductory word of embedded clauses. Due to the fact that it will be difficult, if not impossible, to make final statements about the syntactic variation of Mennonite Low German verb clusters in the 19th century, it might be a good idea to take the strictly descending West Germanic deep structure sequence as such a reference system, which coincides with Lötscher's surface structure System I (1978, 19). It would then be possible to compare the deviation from this reference system of clauses with two or three verbal elements, of embedded and main clauses, of object and conditional clauses, etc. This would be an important advance because, especially for clauses with three and four verbal elements, there exists a confusing number of variants. Such a measure of deviation would also enable researchers to compare different speakers more easily, allotting a single value to each of them instead of comparing dozens of single clauses. One could, then, also use stronger and more versatile statistical tools such as regression analysis and analysis of variance. In order to develop such a measure one would need a highly developed theory of V(P)R capable of answering a question such as whether there is a relationship between VR and VPR, and what form this relationship takes (cf. the discussion in Kroch/Santorini 1991; Haegeman 1994; and Zwart 1996). Is VPR a more drastic transformation than VR because more material is involved? A detailed analysis of the individual variation of the informants might address this question if, for example, clear patterns could be found showing that more conservative speakers prefer VR and more progressive speakers prefer VPR.

Forthly, a more detailed analysis of the verb cluster in Mennonite Low German should aim to restrict itself to clear cases of verb clusters. If causal clauses frequently display main clause syntax, and if prefixed verbs do not form verb clusters like a modal and an infinitive, one should not include them in a final analysis. However, there arise certain problems: For example, how can one decide whether a causal clause with the finite verb at its end is a performance error of the informant, the proof for variation in one grammar or for two competing grammars in the individual's mind (cf. the methods used by Pintzuk 1991 and chapter 4 in Lightfoot 1999).

Fifthly, besides the results in the Mexican colony, the results from Paraguay should contribute to the overall picture of this syntactic change. There, one has two colonies which show the same time depth with regard to the separation of their ancestors as the Brazilian Mennonites and the Mennonites in the USA. The difference is that the Mennonites who arrived in Paraguay after emigrating first from the Ukraine to Canada and the Mennonites who emigrated directly from the Ukraine to Paraguay sixty years later live today only about fifteen miles from each other. It will be interesting to see whether the Mennonites who arrived directly in Paraguay, i.e., the ones who are comparable to the Brazilian Mennonites, are also closer to the Standard German syntax than the Paraguayan Mennonites who left Canada at roughly the same time as the ancestors of the Texan Mennonites.

Notes

[1] I would like to thank Sabrina Pereira de Abreu and Mark L. Louden for their helpful comments.

[2] How this happened is not completely clear. It probably was not a complete language shift because there are still many Dutch words in the Low German variety of the Mennonites and its pronunciation reminds many current Low German speakers in Germany more of Dutch than of Low German. One should also not forget that a process of convergence or koineization must have taken place between the different languages and varieties of the Mennonites who came to the Vistula Delta.

[3] However, this does not mean that this kind of variation does not exist, even in literary written German. A writer like Theodor Storm, who comes from northern Germany, exhibits exactly this phenomenon quite frequently: "*Hauke fiel es aufs Herz, daß er die Alte mit ihren jungen Enten den Ratten sollte*$_{V1}$ *preisgegeben*$_{V3}$ *haben*$_{V2}$" (without year: 906). Besides this, van de Velde mentions various authors who consider this construction as possible in Standard German (1981, 224). Takada, who analyzes clusters with three or four verbal elements for six German dialect regions in the 17th century, shows that the postposition of finite modal verbs in this construction (his type 3) became dominant in the High German regions after 1620 (1994, 206-8). Also, in Low German spoken in the northern regions of Germany a marked increase in the

postposition of the modal verbs took place during the 17th century but the variant was not dominant yet. This fact could be the reason for Storm's linguistic behavior.

[4] Zwart (1995 and 1996), based on Kayne's assumption that movement to the right does not exist, claims that V(P)R (Verb (Projection) Raising) is the consequence of adjunction of the infinitive(s) to the left of the finite verb or raising of a participle to a specifier position (1995, 216; 1996: 250). He, like Lattewitz (1997), argues that all Germanic languages are VO-languages (Zwart 1996, 230), and that the basic sequence in verb clusters is the ascending order V1-V2 (1996, 232). My study will not pursue this theoretical discussion.

[5] It seems that there was actually no direct English or Portuguese influence on the Low German syntax. In the data analyzed in this article which consists of more than 1900 sentences with two verbal elements there is only one case which on the surface appears to be a direct influence from English, i.e., the object NP appears after the two verbal elements forming a cluster.

[6] All percentages in all tables are rounded. Embedded clauses in which the last position was occupied by an adverb, an adverbial phrase, or the object NP (cf. n. 5) and not by the verb cluster or an nonfinite verb were disregarded because of the possibility of an interaction of different kinds of movements. Likewise all cases in which the verb cluster was disrupted by just an adverb or an adverbial phrase but in which the object NP occurred before the two verbal elements were disregarded as unclear cases of either VR or VPR. The position of adverbs and adverbial phrases in German is much less restricted than that of object NPs. Due to this procedure 23 sentences in the United States and 17 in Brazil were excluded from the analysis.

[7] In the United States only one informant shows no variation at all, generalizing the VPR variant. All other informants use all three variants, and with the exception of five informants, all of them use all variants more than once. In Brazil, where there is much less variation, seven informants use only the Standard German variant, but still 28 out of the 41 informants use the VR variant more than once (seven use it just once) and 32 informants use the VPR variant more than once (three use it only once).

[8] Obviously these hypotheses have to be checked first with regard to the new and much expanded database from Mexico and—if possible—with data about the linguistic situation in the Ukraine around 1870. The problem is that this can only mean written data in Low German which might be hard to get.

[9] Among the 61 cases there are twenty cases of modal verbs with infinitives, thirteen verbs in the perfect tense with the auxiliary *haben*, nine cases of verbs with separable prefixes, and four cases of *werden* plus infinitive. There are 23 object clauses, six conditional clauses, five relative clauses with *wat* and four causal clauses. The four types of embedded clauses and the different kinds of verb clusters chosen in this research are thus well attested in these letters. An interesting counter-example to the Low German represented by the letters might be the language of Ida Jungmann in the *Buddenbrooks*. She is born in 1815 and is a native of Marienwerder, a city close to the West Prussian home of the Mennonites. The narrator of the novel mentions several times a marked influence of her native dialect in her Standard German pronunciation (Mann 1953, 10 and 464). Her syntax shows likewise many nonstandard V(P)R variants, as for example: "*Ach wo, Tonychen! wenn ihn nicht wirst$_{v1}$ wollen$_{v2}$, und wenn er dich nicht wird$_{v1}$ glücklich machen$_{v2}$* . . . ." (Mann 1953, 302; cf. Kaufmann 2000).

[10] Interestingly, it seems that for clusters with three verbal elements the semantic weight of the finite verb works the other way round. More semantic content increases the probability for the finite verb to

195

occupy the last position (Takada 1994, 198-199), as can be seen from the fact that in modern German modal verbs have to occupy the last position in these cases (cf. sentences (1) through (4)).

[11] However, there exist different opinions. Louden categorizes the Pennsylvania German cognate *due* as a marker of iterative/habitual aspect, but also mentions the mere syntactic function of maintaining the OV structure in main clauses by its insertion (1992, 220-21). Langer sees in the Early New High German *tun* a polyfunctional auxiliary but mentions the widespread opinion that *tun* is semantically redundant (2000, 295). The Mennonite use of the Low German *doon(e)* is also another indication of the fact that the Mennonites in the USA are further away from Standard German than the Brazilian Mennonites. Finite *doon(e)* with the infinitive of the main verb is a frequent construction in German dialects but almost completely banned from Standard German. The number of occurrences of *doon(e)* in the United States is twice as high as in Brazil.

[12] The ranking of *habe(n)* and the modal verbs coincides with the VR variation of Modern Dutch (cf. Zwart 1996, 233) and the results of Ebert (1981, 228). This does not depend on the morphological form of the main verb because *doon(e)*, which behaves completely differently to the modal verbs, also takes an infinitive.

[13] The status of *wann* is not completely clear. Unlike Standard German and English, Mennonite Low German does not have a different word for the conditional complementizer *wenn/if* and the wh-word *wann/when*. Both functions are expressed by *wann*, which is here interpreted as a wh-word. The distribution of the variants in relative and conditional clauses might mean that the preference of VR over VPR depends not on the position of the embedded clause, as was mentioned in connection with finite *woare(n)*, but on the fact that the introductory word is a wh-word.

[14] Such unambiguous cases do exist in Standard German VPR as well: "*Meiner christlichen Überzeugung nach, liebe Tochter, ist es des Menschen Pflicht, die Gefühle eines anderen zu achten, und wir wissen nicht, ob Du(1st position) nicht einst(2nd or later position) würdest$_{V1}$ (3rd or later position) von einem höchsten Richter dafür haftbar gemacht$_{V3}$ werden$_{V2}$ [...]*" (Mann 1953, 129).

[15] To a certain extent this contradicts Lightfoot, because it is the ambiguous position of the finite verb in embedded clauses which seems to cause children to reanalyze the status of the causal conjunctions. Lightfoot claims that children use unembedded clauses in language learning, i.e., he assumes that they are degree-0 learners (1991, chapter 3).

[16] The process is obviously different from that observed in colloquial German, where epistemic *weil* is frequently followed by main clause syntax. Firstly, the causal conjunctions used here are not of an epistemic nature and secondly, there is no VPR with two verbal elements in colloquial German which could serve as an intermediate stage.

[17] Similar processes seem to take place in other German dialects spoken as minority languages. Wild (1997, 146-49) writes that there are many cases of embedded clauses—as with Mennonite Low German most frequently but not exclusively with causal clauses—with the finite verb in second position in German dialects spoken in Hungary.

References

Bach, Emmon, Colin Brown, and William Marslen-Wilson. 1987. "Gekreuzte und geschachtelte Abhängigkeiten im Deutschen und Niederländischen." In *Grammatik und Kognition*, ed. Josef Bayer, 7- 23. Obladen.

Bourdieu, Pierre. 1991. *Language and Symbolic Power*. Cambridge.

Broekman, Henry W. 1995. "Verb Clusters in Germanic: The Non-Existence of the Third Construction." In *The Berkeley Conference on Dutch Linguistics*, ed. Thomas F. Shannon and Johan P. Snapper, 117-30. Lanham, MD.

Dorian, Nancy C. 1981. *Language Death: The Life Cycle of a Scottish Gaelic Dialect*. Philadelphia, PA.

Ebert, Robert Peter. 1981. "Social and Stylistic Variation in the Order of Auxiliary and Nonfinite Verb in Dependent Clauses in Early New High German." *Beiträge zur Geschichte der Deutschen Sprache und Literatur* 103,2: 204-37.

Ebert, Robert Peter. 1998. *Verbstellungswandel bei Jugendlichen, Frauen und Männern im 16. Jahrhundert.* Tübingen.

de Haan, Germen J. 1996. "Recent Changes in the Verbal Complex of Frisian." *North-Western European Language Evolution* 28/29: 171-84.

Haegeman, Liliane. 1994. "Verb Raising as Verb Projection Raising: Some Empirical Problems." *Linguistic Inquiry* 25,3: 509-22.

Hartweg, Frédéric, and Klaus-Peter Wegera. 1989. *Frühneuhochdeutsch: Eine Einführung in die deutsche Sprache des Spätmittelalters und der frühen Neuzeit.* Tübingen.

Hill, Jane, and Kenneth Hill. 1977. "Language Death and Relexification in Tlaxcalan Nahuatl." *Linguistics* 191: 55-68.

Huffines, Marion Lois. 1991. "Acquisition Strategies in Language Death." *Studies in Second Language Acquisition* 13: 43-55.

Kaufmann, Göz. 1997. *Varietätendynamik in Sprachkontaktsituationen: Attitüden und Sprachverhalten rußlanddeutscher Mennoniten in Mexiko und den USA.* Frankfurt/Main.

Kaufmann, Göz. 2000. "Verbstellungsvarianten im Niederdeutschen der Mennoniten in Brasilien, Mexiko und den USA." *Actas del X Congreso Latinoamericano de Estudios Germanísticos.* Caracas. 11 pages (CD-Rom).

Kroch, Anthony S., and Beatrice Santorini. 1991. "The Derived Constituent Structure of the West Germanic Verb--Raising Construction." In *Principles and Parameters in Comparative Grammar*, ed. Freidin, Robert, 269-338. Cambridge, MA.

Küper, Christoph. 1991. "Geht die Nebensatzstellung im Deutschen verloren: Zur pragmatischen Funktion der Wortstellung in Haupt- und Nebensätzen." *Deutsche Sprache* 19,2: 133-58.

Labov, William. 1990. "The intersection of sex and social class in the course of linguistic change." *Language Variation and Change* 2: 205-54.

Langer, Nils. 2000. "Zur Verbreitung der Tun-Periphrase im Frühneuhochdeutschen." *Zeitschrift für Dialektologie und Linguistik* 67,3: 287-316.

Lattewitz, Karen. 1997. "Movement of Verbal Complements." In *Clitics, Pronouns, and Movement*, ed. James R. Black and Virginia Motapanyane. Amsterdam.

Lightfoot, David. 1991. *How to Set Parameters: Arguments from Language Change*. Cambridge, MA.

Lightfoot, David. 1999. *The Development of Language: Acquisition, Change, and Evolution*. Malden, MA.

Lötscher, Andreas. 1978. "Zur Verbstellung im Zürichdeutschen und in anderen Varianten des Deutschen." *Zeitschrift für Dialektologie und Linguistik* 65,1: 1-29.

Louden, Mark L. 1990. "Verb Raising and the Position of the Finite Verb in Pennsylvania German." *Linguistic Inquiry* 21,3: 470-77.

Louden, Mark L. 1992. "German as an Object-Verb Language: A Unification of Generative and Typological Approaches." In *On Germanic Linguistics: Issues and Methods*, ed. Irmengard Rauch, Gerald F. Carr and Robert L. Kyes, 217-31. Berlin.

Mann, Thomas. 1953. *Buddenbrooks: Verfall einer Familie*. Berlin.

Mitzka, Walther. 1969. "Danziger Niederdeutsch in Moralischer Wochenschrift 1741-1743." *Jahrbuch des Vereins für niederdeutsche Sprachforschung* 92: 81-93.

Patocka, Franz. 1999. "Zur Verbstellung in Nebensätzen mittelhochdeutscher Prosatexte."In *Vielfalt der Sprachen: Festschrift für Aleksander Szulc zum 75 Geburtstag*, ed. Maria Klanska and Peter Wiesinger, 131-44. Wien.

Pintzuk, Susan. 1991. "Phrase Structures in Competition: Variation and Change in Old English Word Order." Diss., University of Pennsylvania.

Storm, Theodor. n.d. *Werke - Der Schimmelreiter*, 889-973. München.

Takada, Hiroyuki. 1994. "Zur Wortstellung des mehrgliedrigen Verbalkomplexes im Nebensatz im 17. Jahrhundert." *Zeitschrift für Germanistische Linguistik* 22,2: 190-219.

van de Velde, Marc. 1981. "Zur Reihenfolge von Verbalen Elementen." In *Sprache: Formen und Strukturen*, ed. Manfred Kohrt and Jürgen Lenerz, 223-35. Münster.

Wild, Katharina. 1997. "Zur Verbstellung in den schwäbischen Mundarten Südungarns." In *Syntax und Stilistik der Alltagssprache: Beiträge der 12. Arbeitstagung zur alemannischen Dialektologie*, ed. Arno Ruoff, 145-54. Tübingen.

Zwart, Jan-Wouter. 1995. "A Note on Verb Clusters in the Stellingwerf Dialect." In *Linguistics in the Netherlands*, ed. Marcel den Dikken and Kees Hengeveld, 215-26. Amsterdam.

Zwart, Jan-Wouter. 1996. "Verb Clusters in Continental West Germanic Dialects." In *Microparametric Syntax and Dialect Variation*, ed. James R. Black and Virginia Motapanyane, 229-58. Amsterdam.

Peter Rosenberg
Europa-Universität Viadrina
Frankfurt an der Oder, Germany

Comparative Speech Island Research: Some Results from Studies in Russia and Brazil

1. Pivots of Speech Island Research

What are the reasons of language change? Of course, this might be considered a useless question: Following Eugenio Coseriu (1974) we could argue that language in general has to change because it has to serve as a means of communication. Addressing this question, however, in a historical way, we would have to account for the communicative needs and circumstances which cause a linguistic change in a given set of time, space and internal as well as external conditions.[1]

Some years ago Wayne O'Neil raised this question distinguishing between "grammatical change in which there is neutralization of the point(s) of difference between two languages in contact and grammatical change involving simplification of a feature of a language, change which is evidently not the result of one language working on another" (O'Neil 1978, 248). While neutralization may be explained as to be induced by language contact causing a need "to ease understanding" (O'Neil 1978, 275), simplification could be described as "a language-internal move to ease learning" (O'Neil 1978, 282). And he addresses the unsolved problem: "We cannot, however, explain this simplification" (O'Neil 1978, 248).[2]

Today, German speech islands are linguistic communities exposed to intense linguistic contact in different ways. And they dispose of language varieties sometimes displaying a rapid change including simplification of grammatical structure. Linguistic change and linguistic convergence are crossing their ways, and sometimes it may be difficult to draw the line between internally and externally induced linguistic developments. But in these times of accelerating external influence, change and decay, the demand for explanations is even more pressing.

Speech islands are more or less distinct linguistic communities on a limited area. These "restricted" circumstances make it easier to "control" converging and changing variables. Comparing some results of speech island studies in different language contact settings we will set out to shed a light on the relation of linguistic change and linguistic convergence and to discuss the link between so called internal and external phenomena.

Of course, speech islands are not a unique German phenomenon. Speech islands are existing all over the world: enclaves of the Portuguese language in West Africa, of

French in Southern Africa, numerous speech islands as a heritage of colonialism, the complex sociolinguistic situation in South Africa, the Finland-Swedes in the area around Åbo/Turku, Yiddish-speaking Jews in Vilnius/Lithuania before WW II, Dutch varieties in northwestern France or in the USA, Quechua speakers in Spanish-speaking towns in Peru, Urdu-speaking communities among the Hindi-speaking majority in North India, etc.

However, while research elsewhere has mostly been devoted to language contact the perspective of German speech island research has widely been focussed on language change:

For a long time research on German language enclaves, traditionally called German "speech islands" ("Sprachinseln"[3]), was a major subject of German dialectology.[4] Since German dialectology—after Indo-European studies the second main field of research in German linguistics of the late 19th and early 20th century—was prominent in international linguistics for some time, speech island research has been a methodological touchstone of the paradigms involved: Dialect geography[5] tried to prove the areal linguistics' framework by speech island research as well as the Neogrammarians[6] took up this subject by means of numerous "Local Grammars" and also the later "Kulturraumforschung"[7] was involved in the dialectological description of the linguistic heritage of the so called German East Colonization.

To a great extent speech island studies have been motivated by the researchers' interest in the description of language change, particularly in the reconstruction of former stages of linguistic processes. Most of the linguistic communities examined by speech island researchers were rather small units with restricted communicational activities outside, easily observable in time and space, explorable as a whole. Since these "conservative" communities had frequently preserved old features of the German language, speech islands were supposed to offer a unique observability of former linguistic elements which have been died out in the German language inland area.

The description of internal change or external interference requires patterns of "unaffected" purity. The myth of purity and homogeneity was perhaps the most attractive feature of speech islands. Thus, language variation and language contact were considered to be rather a contamination than a focal subject of speech island research.

Investigations of the first period were done by German dialectologists (not by researchers from the speech islands), as for example Johann Andreas Schmeller who included the German dialects of the South Tyrol and Venetia into his famous work on the Bavarian dictionary.[8] Jakob Grimm influenced and triggered the collection of speech island vocabulary. In the beginning, the main interest was directed to the old speech islands close to the German language area, as Transylvania, the Zips, and Venetia.[9] In the later 19th century Gottschee (Slovenia), Temesvar, Banat (Hungary/Romania), and even speech islands in Pennsylvania[10] and Australia were included. Since the turn of the century also the younger speech islands were subject to dialectological studies, more and more by researchers of these communities themselves. After World War I attention was paid to the German-speaking population in Russia, at first in the great cities, then in the rural colonies of the Black Sea region and around Petersburg (Schirmunski, Ström) as well as of the Volga region (Dinges, Dulson). Between World War I and II speech island research increased remarkably. In part, this was related to language shift processes which all German speech islands were confronted with, and it was motivated by the preservation of speech island dialects which were supposed to be inevitably condemned to perish.

In times of modernization, unification and nation building these colonies got into more intense contact with the host societies causing at first an "external" diglossia in the colonies: The majority language has been introduced into administrative affairs, external trade and (higher) education. Since the 19th century these colonies got under pressure of the national and local authorities—at first in Hungary, at the end of the century also in Russia, in Poland and Czechoslovakia at latest after WW I, at this time also in North America and in the 1940s in South America. With increasing contact and mobility diglossia became "internal," the autonomy of the German settlements was diminished and the local élites began to assimilate. After World War II most of the speech islands' inhabitants in East and Middle East Europe emigrated to Germany.

Related to a more intense contact it became obvious, that speech island research is bound to deal with linguistic convergence or divergence: In a sociolinguistic view, it has to answer the question if, why and how a more or less distinct linguistic community on a limited area keeps its distinctness from the different speaking surrounding[11]—or if, why and how linguistic convergence leads to the subsequent loss of this distinctness and to the "inundation" of the speech island.

At first glance this is, of course, connected to interlinguistic convergence. But since speech islands are to a certain extent "closed" communities, they have also been attracting researcher's interest as a "fast breeder" of small scale, but high speed intralinguistic convergence.[12]

Speech islands present a vast variety of internally structured linguistic communities under extremely differing contact settings, and speech island research is by all means a heterogeneous subject:

Speech islands have been founded through very different times and under very different conditions. As common traits, most of them share a limited area, enclosing a linguistically different community linked by a dense communicative network (in the sense of Milroy 1980 and Gumperz 1968) which is to a certain extent more introvert than extrovert, and connected by attitudinal distinctness.

None the less, speech islands are linguistically and socially structured. They often are inhabited by settlers of different origins, of different dialects and of different migration periods.

201

Some speech islands are communities with restricted social and linguistic structure: communities under a protective "hood." But if the development was uninterrupted, some speech islands reached the stage of social and linguistic complexity. Depending on the duration and separateness of settlement and the heterogeneity of linguistic varieties they display different stages of language variation systems: from (sometimes coexisting) local vernaculars (Siberia; Kazakhstan) to more or less mixed, leveled or merged dialects (Mennonite colonies, Chaco/Paraguay; Volga region/Russia), koines or regiolects ("Hunsrück" variety in South Brazil; Volhynian German) up to urban vernaculars with superregional usage (Hermannstadt/Sibiu, Romania).

Speech islands display very different settings of external language contact as Mattheier (1996) discusses. As Mattheier concludes, the most important sociolinguistic output of all intervening factors is an attitudinal structure of distinctness as the crucial basis of nonassimilation.

Obviously, homogeneity and purity of speech islands turn out to be a rare phenomenon which is rather a temporary exception than prototypical. Thus, speech island research has to take into account the interdependence of language change, language variation and language contact. But what is the nature of this interdependence and how does it affect linguistic convergence?

2. Linguistic Convergence in German Speech Islands

Speech island research might serve as a fruitful field for investigating convergence because of four reasons:

1) These communities frequently consist of several dialects gradually merging.
2) A roofing standard language of its own diasystem rarely exists and therefore does not slow down linguistic change.
3) Intensive language contact gives evidence of whether linguistic change is internally or externally induced (or both) if contact settings are compared.
4) Since community boundaries are a matter of minority survival speech island research is bound to work interdisciplinary including sociolinguistic, historical, ethnological and other methods.

Dealing with convergence, however, requires some distinctions concerning the notion of "convergence."

First of all, there have to be raised some questions: What is converging with what? Is a dialect variety converging with another variety of the same diasystem (another dialect, a standard language, a regiolect)? Or is it converging with a foreign language? And what are the results of convergence: one single variety as a result of dialect leveling or converging structures of still distinct varieties, or a kind of "koiné," a higher stratum within the variational system of a linguistic community. If there are intralinguistic or even interlinguistic convergence phenomena, do they also occur in other German varieties? If so, is this evidence for the assumption of a purely intralinguistic, maybe typological, change which all German varieties are subject to, sooner or later, wherever in the world they exist: a kind of polycentric "convergence" in the sense of a parallel development from different diachronic stages coming closer to each other?[13] Thus, if we try to answer the questions mentioned above in a systematical way we will have to break it down into three elementary problems: intralinguistic convergence, interlinguistic convergence, and polycentric "convergence."

2.1. Convergence as a Variety Contact Phenomenon

Dialect convergence is the classical topic of research on German speech islands in Russia. The German settlements founded more than 200 years ago near the river Volga, in the Black Sea region, in the Caucasus mountains and later on in Siberia and Central Asia display a unique diversity of dialect varieties brought from numerous German regions into these colonies. This was an exceptional trait of these speech islands which rarely could be found elsewhere in the world. In some villages several dozens of dialect varieties of German coexisted and some of them persisted for a long time due to the isolation of the settlements and their social, economical, cultural and even religious distance from the surrounding population. This has set in motion several waves of convergence starting from the very first moment of their existence.

The linguistic convergence during the first 100 years reduced the extreme heterogeneity of dialects to a still remarkable number of more or less integrated local varieties spoken as the everyday language. A common Russian-German variety or even regional colloquial varieties did not emerge. The High German Standard only existed among the elites within the colonies.

The deportations since 1938/1941 and the subsequent migrations after the abolishment of settlement restrictions 1956 reinforced linguistic heterogeneity. Migrations into mixed settlements in Siberia and Central Asia triggered a second wave of variety contact and dialect convergence, restricted, however, by the entirely new conditions of linguistic subordination and uprooting.

The construction of "central villages" out of closed-down small hamlets in the 1970s and the 1980s has led to a third period of linguistic discontinuity, of variety convergence and, now, of language shift. These recent processes concerning convergence phenomena are observable "in vivo" today.

Viktor Schirmunski (1930) called the convergence and new mixture of Russian German varieties a "large-scale experiment on language history" and a "linguistic laboratory," which was the origin of his theory of "primary" and "secondary" dialect features.

One of the linguistically well distinguished groups of the Germans in Russia are the Mennonites in West Siberia and in the Orenburg region close to the Ural mountains. Among the Mennonites in Russia there are existing at least two major varieties, which have been brought along from their pre-war settlements in the Ukraine: the oldest Chortica variety and the more prestigious Molotchna variety.

Most of the well-known dialectologists investigating Russian German varieties have studied the Mennonite varieties (see Schirmunski 1930, Jedig 1966). According to some studies there seemed to exist an upward convergence which has replaced Chortica features by those of the Molotchna variety: for example the Chortica rounded front vowel [y:] by the Molotchna long back vowel [u:] as in [fry:]—[fru:] (High German standard *Frau* 'woman').

Viktor Schirmunski discussed the convergence phenomena among Russian German varieties under the notion of "primary" and "secondary" dialect features: Variety contact induces linguistic shift in the direction of High German standard features (or variety features which are closest to these). Since in the Russian German colonies High German standard is rarely available as a criterion of dialect leveling this has always been somewhat doubtful. But there has been some evidence in Ukrainian German varieties (of Hessian and Swabian origins).

In a recent study of variety convergence among Mennonites in the Orenburg region Nyman (1997) describes a more complex structure of leveling. He has tested the direction of convergence in the still existing 22 Mennonite villages of the Orenburg region (by tape-recording interviews and collecting "distinction words"). Some features follow the Molotchna pattern, some others the Chortica pattern, and some do not converge at all:

Concerning the [u:]—[y:] distinction in [u:t]—[y:t] (High German standard *aus* 'out (of)'), the Chortica feature [y:] has spread over all villages which had been linguistically clearly separated since the colonization at the turn of the century. This is hardly compatible to the old assumptions, and neither to Schirmunski's "primary" and "secondary" dialect feature theory, because the Chortica feature [y:] is much more distant from the High German standard [au] than the Molotchna feature [u:] is. And this is true for other Mennonite settlements, too (cf. Berend/Jedig 1991, 177). At the time of colonization this feature was certainly a "primary" one. Either it has turned into a secondary (less distinctive) one or the speakers have adopted it due to the numerical superiority of Chortica settlements. Since the Chortica variety is less prestigious than the Molotchna variety, it looks like a downward convergence, but it may be also functioning as an attitudinal group symbol with the highest degree of traditionality, as a counter-movement against the strong assimilating pressure from the Russian outer world.

The lexical distribution of the words Molotchna *knout* and Chortica *strank* for 'rope' displays on the other hand a strict separation of the varieties as it is the case with some other items, too.

Concerning the [-n]-apocope typical for the Molotchna variety convergence occurs towards the Molotchna variety: the apocope has been spreading, but only reaching most of the surrounding villages, which are called the "Unjadarpa" ('lower villages') in contrast to the "Bowadarpa" ('upper villages'), apparently forming subregional communities.

Dania Asfandiarova (1999) has detected some interesting convergence phenomena among Russian Germans living in German settlements in the area of Ufa, Bashkortostan. She is describing dialect leveling in a representative three-generation study in the Prishib/ Alekseevka colony consisting of four central villages which have been constructed out of eleven settlements founded at the turn of the century. Each village had had its own variety, but after having been merged into central villages in the early 1980s convergence has got under way. The study of convergence in the vowel system of the speakers exhibits a complex and sometimes confusing structure. In the three "Lutheran" villages Rhinefranconian features are prevailing, the fourth one, a "Catholic" village, is different. But no one is homogeneous at all. The results of the study are impressive. What is striking is that dialect convergence seems to be highly selective: While the front vowel system and the closed back vowels are apparently leveled to a very high degree, this is not the case for the (MHG) long and short vowel *a* and the diphthong system. Here a considerable number of speakers are systematically using a back *a*-vowel, a half-open or even closed [o] as in [gro:s] 'gras' or [vo:re] 'waren' ('we were') which refers to the "Catholic" variety spoken in the "Catholic" village and among "Catholics" in the "Lutheran" villages. These speakers are presumably retaining some emblematic elements as markers of their variety which they call "Achterisch" (the number of their old village at the beginning of colonization), in contrast to "Sechserisch," the variety of the "Lutheran" majority even if the varieties have converged to a great extent.

Convergence seems to be a complex subject, with all directions of shifts, sometimes feature by feature. As Andreas Dulson in the 1930s has shown by dialectological studies in extremely heterogeneous Volga German villages the Schirmunski criterion of "primary" and "secondary" dialect features is only one of several possibilities, but as an internal guideline underlying the effects of other intervening factors. Dulson (1941, 85) proposed to consider seven factors: the norms of the standard and of a regional variety (if available), the nature of the original dialects, the social prestige of their speakers, the speakers' attitudes towards variety features, the degree of heterogeneity in the speakers' community and the internal developmental tendencies of linguistic change in the German varieties.

Primarity of dialect features in the sense of Schirmunski depends on their salience in the linguistic evaluation system of the speakers. What is salient or not does not generally depend on distance criteria established by linguists (such as systematicity, phoneme status or difference to the standard), but on listeners monitoring of this. It is paradigmatic, structured by markedness and affected by linguistic attitudes.

Thus, if compact groups of variety speakers are confronted with one another, varieties may persist over a long time, and markers are consciously applied to draw the line of the subgroup boundaries. Whether groups are assumed to be "compact" is a matter of the number of speakers and of their separation, of the stability of group norms (in a wider range of linguistic and cultural features), of attitudes concerning the in- and the outgroup (and the world outside as well) and of the inclination to speech accommodation (in the sense of Niedzielski/Giles 1996). The higher the degree of heterogeneity within the linguistic community the lower is the effect of group norms and the faster linguistic change occurs—up to the point, that "pure" inherent linguistic mechanisms are at work. Then, as Dulson (1941, 93) stated, it is no longer a matter of convergence or divergence of varieties, but a struggle "feature by feature."

2.2. Convergence as a Language Contact Phenomenon

Speech islands are linguistic communities under strange circumstances: They go their own ways, sometimes in accordance with the varieties they have been derived from, and sometimes not. If not, what are the reasons of different development?

As far as external influence of the contact language is concerned, we would like to plead for a comparative method of speech island research. It seems to be fruitful to compare the linguistic change of German speech islands in different countries. If we can observe different linguistic processes of German varieties under the roofing of the Russian language, of the American English (as a Germanic language) and of the Brazilian Portuguese (as a Romance language in some aspects closer related to German than Russian), we will be able to draw some conclusions on the evidence of external induced change.

This will be illustrated by the following examples: Among German settlers in the State of Rio Grande do Sul, South Brazil, the historical conditions of colonization have had much in common with those of the Russian Germans. Brazil is inhabited by about one million German-speaking people, this is the second place among all German minorities in the world (the former Soviet Union ranks first with about two million). Settlers have been living separated in small isolated colonies just like in Russia. Predominantly, they used their dialect varieties for communication, and since these varieties were quite different, dialect convergence was an inherent trait of their development. Dialect varieties cover a wide range from the prevailing (Rhine Franconian and Moselle Franconian) Hunsrück varieties to Swabian and Volga German to Low German Westphalian and Pomeranian varieties. The High German standard language was taught at school, but with the political restrictions under the nationalist government (of Getulio Vargas) in the 1940s all educational and political minority rights were suspended. Therefore, a redialectalization took place. In contrast to Russia, however, a superregional (Hunsrück) variety emerged which was never the case in Russia. Obviously the numerical dominance of the Hunsrück speakers (about 50% of the first settlers) and the closer network of communication which was not as limited as in Russia have led to this important difference. But dialect convergence in Brazil does not mean the complete integration of local basic varieties which still exist as so called "familetos" (varieties of family settlements). The superregional Hunsrück variety is not homogeneous at all but a dialect continuum.[14] It includes for example Rhine Franconian features with greater and Moselle Franconian features (e.g., *dat/wat*) with smaller acceptance.

Interestingly some elements emerging in Brazil and in Russia are quite similar, others are not although the dialect features partly were the same: The sonorization has spread in both groups (voicing of consonants in intervocalic position and between vowel and sonant, following the stress: *drogge* High German standard *trocken* 'dry'[15]).

On the other hand nasalization and rhotacism have developed different: Nasalization ([tsã:] High German standard *Zahn* 'tooth') is a common feature among Volga Germans,[16] but not among Hunsrück speakers even if the dialect bases were similar and even if Brazilian Portuguese has several nasalized vowels. Rhotacism ([sore], High German standard *sagten* '(we) said'[17]) is in some elements very common in Brazil, but in Russia only among some Upper Hessian speakers. There it has been replaced by standard forms, perhaps due to the fact that Volga Germans emigrated at least 60 years earlier than Brazil Germans, when rhotacism in Germany was just spreading.[18]

As we can see external linguistic influence plays a minor role in these differences. Of course, other elements exhibit much more interference: The loss of the definite article among younger Russian Germans is certainly due to Russian influence.[19] Brazilian Germans, on the other hand, velarize the lateral /l/ which is due to Portuguese interference.

A development which has been investigated very frequently is the reduction of case morphology among German speakers in Russia,[20] in Brazil,[21] among Texas Germans,[22] Pennsylvania Germans[23] and Kansas Volga Germans[24] in the United States and in other countries.[25] External effects might be possible in contact with Germanic and Romance languages, of course (cf. Louden 1994, 90). On the other hand it is just among some sectarian Mennonite and Amish groups widely using German varieties in every day conversation where case reduction maximally appears, but less among non-sectarians with intensive language contact.

For case reduction among Russian Germans Russian influence is rather unlikely. The Russian language possesses six cases, which are consistently used, in the noun, pronoun and adjective system. Russian interference should rather support the inflectional system of the German varieties and diminish or at least decelerate case reduction, but it does not.

2.3. Typological "Convergence"

Obviously, a typological change takes place which is observable in German varieties in general. Case reduction and loss of the preterite are part of a long term development from synthetic to analytic language structures. Of course, the German linguistic diasystem is still a "mixed type" with respect to the synthetic-analytic dimension.[26] Today typology compares structures not languages.[27] Consistently, some researchers argue that the German language does not display any uniform typological direction of development. But the main direction is the reduction of synthetic (or "fusionizing"[28]) elements and the "externalization" of syntactic features, i.e., the distribution of functional features to different markers each one carrying only little grammatical information.

Since the Germanic shift of stress from the inflection morphemes to the (first) stem vowel the case marking system in nominal declension has been reduced. Today High German noun inflection is for the most part restricted to the marking of the genitive singular and the plural,[29] only the strong declension paradigm marks also the dative plural. Dative singular markers are optional. Case marking in noun phrases is based on a principle of least "effort": "The adjective marks the noun phrase for case, number and gender ... , if no other constituent of the noun phrase does so" (Eisenberg 1994, 367). Case, number and gender are generally marked by determiners. Thus, grammatical information has been moved more and more leftward, away from the head of the noun phrase to the adjective or further to the determiner, into a predeterminative position.

The reduction of nominal declension in German dialect varieties, however, goes deeper and faster. In general, the noun system has two cases (three cases in some Swabian varieties). The genitive in most functions is substituted by prepositional or dative constructions (plus possessive pronouns). Dative and accusative have usually merged into one oblique case (with altering forms, in the south and west some more datives, in the other parts accusative).

In noun inflection the genitive case is the first to disappear, only resisting in possessive functions (mainly with proper nouns); the dative is the next bastion to be demolished, only a few dialect varieties maintaining dative noun marking (e.g., some Westphalian varieties). The last outpost of noun case inflection is the accusative. It is mostly the accusative which gives its shape to the oblique case.[30]

Pronoun inflection exhibits more case distinctions than the noun inflection, the masculine more than the feminine and neuter, the singular more than the plural. Since the definite and indefinite determiners often represented by enclitics are also reduced to a two-case system (especially masculine forms) or lose case marking totally (particularly feminine and neuter), the grammatical information is frequently given neither by noun nor by adjective nor by determiner inflection. This is or becomes true for German speech island varieties, too, even if they are strictly isolated from the German language mainland area for a long time.

In the German standard language the "rich inflectional morphology . . . fulfils in part purely semantic functions; on the other hand, it is in part clearly motivated syntactically" (Eisenberg 1994, 374). If case is marked in dialect varieties at all, syntactical or semantic information is morphologically expressed only to the extent of realizing the nominative (or common case)-oblique case distinction. Syntactic functions (e.g., noun-adjective-agreement) or semantic information (e.g., direct-indirect object relation) are more and more only a matter of word order, not of morphology. In prepositional phrases the information is moved one step further leftward to the lexical element, the preposition.

When reviewing morphological processes in German-speaking speech islands we can observe another striking fact which is again suggesting internal typological processes more or less common to all German varieties or even to all Germanic and other Indo-European languages: While reduction of noun declension is intensive, this is not the same in personal pronoun inflection which is more "conservative" and only in the last place subject to convergence. While in general dialect varieties exhibit a two-case system in noun, adjective and determiner inflection, personal pronouns frequently have a three-case system which includes the possibility to mark the direct-indirect object relation (by common case vs. dative) or retain at least the dative.

The case system in Pennsylvania German personal pronouns (attached at the end of this article) may serve as an example which holds for many other German varieties: This system applies for the linguistically more traditional nonsectarian speakers. Marion Lois Huffines investigated nonsectarian and sectarian speakers of Pennsylvania German. She stated: "The pronoun system has three cases: the nominative, accusative, and dative. Distinctively marked dative pronoun forms occur in the 1st, 2nd, and 3rd persons singular, and in the 3rd person plural. The interrogative personal pronoun also has two case forms, the common and the dative" (Huffines 1989, 216). But as Pennsylvania German is not transmitted to the nonsectarian children any longer this system is on the verge of being lost with the younger generations which is reflected by the results of her study:

> The nonsectarian native speakers with few exceptions use dative forms to express dative functions. . . . The speech of the nonsectarian native speakers reflects a firmly established norm for PG dative usage. The two youngest nonsectarian native speakers diverge from that norm in ways which are consonant with the linguistic performance of the first-native-English speakers. . . . The first-in-the-family native English speakers use fewer datives and

more accusative and common case forms to express dative functions than do the nonsectarian native speakers. . . . The second-in-the-family native English speakers use still fewer datives and more accusative and common case forms to express dative functions. . . . The norm established by the native speakers and aspired by the first-native-English speakers has not been acquired by Group 2 (the second-native-English speakers, P.R.); the second-native-English speakers simply do not know the PG norm. The sectarians use accusative and common case forms to express dative functions almost exclusively." (Huffines 1989, 222f.)

Sectarians tend to reduce case marking.[31] Other German varieties also exhibit a partial shift from dative to accusative, for example in Texas German: *Spricht er zu mich?* 'Is he talking to me?'.[32] But here, too, dative marking is remarkably higher on personal pronouns than on determiners (four times as much).[33]

This, however, occurs also in the most other Germanic and in some Romance languages, as is shown by the following synopsis:[34]

The case system in Danish personal pronouns has a three-term distinction (subjective or "non-oblique," oblique, and possessive), while the only case distinction in noun inflection is the one between the common case and the genitive.[35] The oblique forms in the third person singular and plural represent an Old Scandinavian dative.

The case system in Old English personal pronouns displays a three-term system in most personal pronouns.[36] In contemporary English pronouns of the third person singular (masculine and feminine) and plural in the oblique case refer to Old English dative forms (the accusative-dative distinction having been lost in Middle English), while noun inflection differentiates only between common case and possessive (old genitives).

French has lost almost all inflection, as Charles Bally (1965, 193) states:

Le français s'est débarrassé de la plupart des flexions héritées du Latin: elles ont presque disparu du substantif, végètent dans l'adjectif (distinction sporadique du genre et du nombre) et ne subsistent à l'état de demi-système que dans le verbe, où d'ailleurs les destinances sont constamment battues en brèche (remplacement de *nous* par *on*, abandon du passé défini, de l'imparfait du subjonctif . . .).

But the case system in French "pronoms personnels conjoints," the system of bound (or enclitic) personal pronouns, exhibits a two-term case marking, in the third person singular and plural ("reference" in the words of Weinrich 1982) even a three-term distinction which is similar to the German dative ("partner").[37]

So, what might be the supporting factors of case marking retention in pronoun inflection, and especially of retaining former or present dative forms? We can account for seven factors:[38]

1) The high frequency of pronouns makes them more resistant to change.

2) Pronouns are more likely to have animate referents which demands more morphological distinctions of syntactic roles.

3) Pronouns are closed classes which are differently lexicalised than open classes.

4) Pronouns function as the head of a noun phrase, and heads are supposed to carry more morphological marking.

5) Pronouns are highly suppletive forms, and therefore individually lexicalised. Loss of case marking on nouns seems to be less disruptive than the replacement of entire lexical items.

6) The syntactic serialization in the middle field of the German verbal frame exhibits (in contrast to noun phrases) the unmarked order: subject—direct object (accusative)—indirect object (dative). This corresponds to an unmarked order: known before *new*, unstressed before stressed. This might support dative retention, too.[39]

7) In neurolinguistics researchers are recently discussing, whether words are represented in the lexicon as entire units ("full listing") or in decomposition. New research gives evidence for a full listing representation of monomorphematic words and polymorphematic words with irregular word formation (as well as less productive morphological paradigms and semantically less transparent words).[40] That is exactly true for personal pronouns. According to Kiparsky (1982) these full listed items are represented on the deepest lexicon level. This might protect them from change.

Thus, we have good reasons to assume that the dynamic and even the structure of case reduction in German dialect varieties is to a great extent a typological change, not directly caused by intralinguistic or interlinguistic convergence. On the other hand we may ask what the conditions of a "typological" change might be. Sometimes we do not exactly know what we mean by a "typological" change. Do we attribute a certain kind of a linguistic process to something we can label as a clear-cut linguistic "type," or is this labeling of a typological "family" rather the result of the occurrence of special kinds of linguistic processes? The reduction of complex information attached to a single formal unit and the externalization of syntactic features may lead us to neurolinguistic explanations which could perhaps be paralleled with processes underlying pidginization and creolization.

3. Sociolinguistics of Convergence

If we have differentiated between the three processes of intralinguistic convergence, interlinguistic convergence and linguistic change this has been due to analytic correctness. We did not yet answer the question: Why do these processes take place in that moment? Due to which conditions occurs an acceleration of convergence or of change? Why are some features at a time salient to linguistic change and others not? What is the sociolinguistic environment that makes some features survive and others be lost? Describing the structure of linguistic developments includes shedding a light on the relation between all these factors mentioned above.

In order to have a more concrete linguistic phenomenon at hand, we will give an example which will show the complex nature of the convergence problem:

Fora couple of years even the Russian German Mennonites have displayed remarkable changes in the morphological system of their variety: the reduction of cases mentioned above as well as a gradual loss of the preterite.[41] Actually, the loss of the preterite is not typical for Low German varieties, but for Middle and Upper German varieties. What might be the conditions of this rapid change?

Of course, Mennonites have been establishing linguistic contact with other German-speaking groups. The construction of "central villages" has also transformed the former Mennonite settlements into heterogeneous villages. This caused intensive dialect contact.

But, on the other hand, Mennonites have maintained their variety and use it for intragroup communication, whereas the German standard language or Russian serves for intergroup communication. The tight Mennonite network functioned as a stronghold of the Low German variety which rarely can be used for intergroup contacts, because only some older non-Mennonite people understand it, but not the younger generation (which has lost the German Standard, too). For intergroup communication Russian has replaced German, but not for intragroup conversation. This is well attested by an investigation in a village in the Altai region, West Siberia, a major German settlement area in Russia: For intragroup communication Mennonites use exclusively German to a degree of about 60%, for intergroup communication only 20%.[42]

As we can see, even young Mennonites partly have their own linguistic network. This protects the Mennonite variety more or less from interferences induced by other German varieties. Thus, linguistic change directly related to dialect convergence is not very likely.

The loss of preterite might rely on Russian influence. The replacement of the German preterite by the present perfect could be motivated by an intended "simulation" of the Russian perfective verbal aspect. But, on the other hand, the Mennonites are the group with the most separated use of bilingualism, and therefore borrowing and interference of Russian elements are less than among other groups. Separateness, however, does not protect from structural changes as we know from the sectarians in the United States. Transmitted by the intergroup communication the Russian language pervades into the peer group and more and more into the family.

Of course, all factors mentioned above have an impact on the change process. The direction of change is not surprising: It fits the common patterns of change occurring in most German varieties.

But change is very rapid. All German speech island varieties are subject to this kind of change, and since some time also the Mennonite varieties. How could this be explained?

As we have stated above, systematic or typological change depends on the stability or instability of norms. Norms are affected by the distinctness of linguistic communities, by the discreteness of marking group boundaries. Norm stability is first of all norm certainty and norm loyalty. In our case norm certainty is lowered by the heterogeneity of the mixed settlements. Loyalty as an attitudinal matter tends to decline if cultural and linguistic group boundaries become doubtful. In fact, this is even true for the Mennonites because religious and cultural values are weakened, intermarriages are spreading, and mobility is increasing.

Similarly, in her conclusions Marion Huffines (1989) stresses case reduction depending on norm instability:

For the nonsectarians, native speakers use Pennsylvania German among themselves and with their linguistic peers, and they switch languages as is socially appropriate. . . . Among the nonsectarians there is a sharp discontinuity in the transmission of Pennsylvania German: the present generation of native speakers chose to speak English to their children. . . . The PG norm was effectively removed from the acquisitional potential for the next generation. As Pennsylvania German dies out among the nonsectarians, one finds the loss of the PG norm reflected in faulty linguistic formulations, such as unsuccessful attempts to employ the dative case. Convergence to English is minimal. . . . Among the sectarians, Pennsylvania German continues a forced existence where sociolinguistic norms prescribe its use but not its form. Convergence toward an English model is readily apparent. (Huffines 1989, 225)

In our view this could be interpreted as follows: Nonsectarian (older) native speakers clearly display stable norms in terms of norm certainty but somehow lowered norm loyalty (concerning the transmission to the next generation): A speaker who switches languages, reestablishes distinct linguistic norms, and linguistic group boundaries are clear-cut. Thus, convergence is minimal. Consequently, case reduction in the personal pronoun is low (retaining the dative with about 80%).[43]

Nonsectarian younger speakers are losing PG norms in terms of norm certainty, but particularly of norm loyalty. They converge only to some extent, but switch to English. Case reduction in personal pronoun inflection increases (retaining the dative in the first-native-English generation with about 50 % and in the second with about 40%). Sectarians display high norm loyalty, but low norm certainty. Since they do not dispose of a distinct code switching model, linguistic norms get perforated. Convergence is maximal. Case reduction is high (the dative case almost lost).

The interdependence of a change in linguistic behavior and the erosion of group norms has been proved by Göz Kaufmann (1997): Kaufmann investigated Mennonites in Mexico and Texas. In his conclusions he emphasizes the fact that a strong correlation between attitudinal and linguistic data points to an extreme heterogeneity of the groups affecting their disposition to linguistic behavior.[44] Kaufmann discusses this in terms of Weinreich et al. (1968: 185f.): "in the earliest and latest stages of a change, there may be very little correlation with social factors." Strong correlations are related to behavior guided by attitudes, weak correlations to normative behavior.

This corresponds to recent sociological approaches concerning the general "framing" of the situation of interaction. Esser (1996a, 1996b) discusses the "logic of situation" in a so called rc+ ("rational choice plus") framework: The perception and interpretation of a given set of situational features depends on utility and probability of "frames" and "habits." Chronic and easy accessible attitudes (as well as "typical" and marked situations) have an impact on the probability of a shift of frames and habits: Non-normative attitudes, a mismatch of cultural knowledge and situational markers and a somehow "untypical" situational setting will tend to weaken group-guided perceptions of the situation as well as to disturb an automatic processing of habitual routines of behavior.[45]

Thus, the obfuscation or obsolescence of cultural and linguistic knowledge or the blurring of group boundaries may cause a decay of normative frames as well as the automatic obedience to normative patterns of behavior. In such times of cultural crisis linguistic norms fade away giving way to unhindered change.

This may be the very basis of Howard Giles's recent emphasis on "subjective vitality"[46] as the key of interethnic group behavior, instead of given prerequisites of group vitality (such as status, demography, institutional support, cf. Giles et al. 1977): It may be more important what ethnolinguistic groups perceive of an interethnic situation than the real features of the situation.

Since perception is by no means autonomous but interactional, this is related to what Le Page and Tabouret-Keller call the "focussing" or "diffusion" of social and linguistic border lines by symbolic interaction, labeled as "acts of identity" (cf. Le Page/Tabouret-Keller 1985).

As Eugenio Coseriu states, linguistic (and cultural) norms are the front line of linguistic change: "A linguistic change starts and develops always as a 'shift' of the norm" (Coseriu 1974, 119; transl. P.R.). As the norm is the linguistic amount of what is usually done in a language, while the system contains what is possible in a language, the norm will always be the gateway for linguistic change within the limits of the system (and in the same way the system for typological change).[47] Thus, systematical changes "are very frequent and widely spreading in times of weak tradition and of cultural decay or in communities with limited linguistic culture" (Coseriu 1974: 117; transl. P.R.). Among the Russian German Mennonites, this decline of linguistic and cultural norms clears the way for an accelerated systematical and typological change which is not linear due to convergence, but contact-related: "The most important force supporting the development of the latent intralinguistic tendencies just turns out to be the external influence of 'extralinguistic,' mainly sociological effects" (Hutterer 1987, 453; transl. P.R.).

4. Language Contact and Language Change

Considering internal and external causation of change, let us come back to the question addressed by Wayne O'Neil mentioned initially. Concerning the reduction of the inflectional system of Old English O'Neil distinguishes between "neutralization" induced by language contact and "simplification" caused by language-internal processes. This is just addressing the problem we are dealing with. Therefore it may be worthwhile to discuss this distinction in the following section:

O'Neil (1978) characterizes the reduction of the Old English inflectional system as a neutralization since "the complex inflectional system of Old English was largely and rapidly neutralized in the northern parts of England on contact with the complex inflectional system of Old Norse" (O'Neil 1978, 249).[48]

On the other hand, in the southern Middle English a simplification has taken place which was not induced by language contact (Old French contributing at best to favoring its extension), "a continuation of the inflectional change that had been going on for centuries in the Germanic languages, this change itself a result of a balancing off of the learnability of inflections against their perceptibility" (O'Neil 1978, 256).

O'Neil compares these processes with other examples of neutralization and simplification[49] and concludes with the generalizing hypotheses:

If there is significant and more-or-less permanent contact between two closely related languages differing for the most part only in superficial aspects of their grammars (inflections, accent, tone, etc.) these superficial differences will be rapidly neutralized or erased. . . . Without language contact, inflectional systems will simplify only so far as there is room for easing learning without greatly decreasing perceptibility. (O'Neil 1978, 283)

Neutralization is considered to be a sociolinguistic phenomenon, a "sudden response (in a generation or two) to a pressing problem of communication," the problem "to ease understanding" (O'Neil 1978, 275). Simplification is regarded as an psycholinguistic phenomenon, "a function of a language-internal move to ease learning, to rebalance an imbalanced learnability-perceptibility state" (O'Neil 1978, 282). Neutralization is done by adults "forming a new language community," simplification is done by children "learning the language of their community" (O'Neil 1978, 283).

O'Neil's hypotheses are attractive mainly because of making a breach into the barrier between grammatical change (of the inflectional structure) and language contact phenomena (which do not merely consist of borrowing).

Of course, the assumption of a contact-induced reduction of Old English inflections, however due to French influence (which declension of nouns was already partly reduced), is not new. But the striking argument of O'Neil is the collapse of the rich inflectional system of Old English on contact with the rich, but different inflectional system of Old Norse.

On the other hand drawing a strict line between neutralization and simplification causes some difficulties and leaves some problems unsolved: Language contact may have accelerated the processes of change in Old English but probably they were already on the way, like the reduction of the verb inflection, e.g., the uniform plural (for first, second and third person) in present and past tense, in strong and weak conjugation.

Furthermore, the Scandinavian languages (except of Icelandic) have also been subject to a radical erosion of inflections. O'Neil (1978, 267) argues that these languages got into intense contact with Middle Low German. These contacts, however, were certainly of different nature than those between Old English and Old Norse speakers. Intense contact with Middle Low German was limited to the centers of trade (of the Hanseatic League); it was expanding throughout the countryside only in Denmark.[50]

The world of linguistic change divided into two parts—neutralization with language contact, simplification without—may be too simple, of course. This admits O'Neil himself when he mentions "middle state" cases like Faroese.[51] His explanation is that Faroese had been "subject to contact with closely related languages of two extreme inflectional persuasions" (O'Neil 1978, 280). The demands of contact to both languages had been limiting changes in the one or the other direction respectively. This, however, is somehow unsatisfactory, because Faroese is by far much more closely related to Icelandic than to continental Scandinavian languages, in terms of the inflectional system:[52] Its noun inflection is Icelandic without the genitive (but it exists in proper nouns); its verbal inflection is Icelandic with a common plural.[53]

The main problem left unsolved, however, is the demand to explain simplification—or in the words of O'Neil 1978, 284): "what triggers off simplification is not at all clear." He suggests a "language-internal move" to ease the "learning burden" (within the limits of the perceptibility of deep structure distinctions)[54] as mentioned above.

But do the languages of the world in fact become easier and easier? Do they follow a sort of economical principle? New distinctions emerged, systems which became more simple in terms of morphology substituted these lost means of grammatical information by lexical items or word order; determiners (definite, indefinite and zero-determiner) came into being as well as prepositions (encoding complex semantic conceptions),[55] auxiliaries developed and sometimes merged, creating an even more confusing subsystem of stem allomorphy and suppletive forms. The assumption of a language-internal simplification move unaffected by language contact tends to be a waste basket category: suitable for all processes of change without reliable explanation.

Why (and when) do speakers or learners of a language feel a need to ease the "learning burden"? And what are the reasons, why processes of change are accelerating from time to time, processes which are not different by nature from those of "slow motion" change?

Is the merger of the second and third person singular in the verb inflection (indicative present) of the Icelandic (*sit—situr—situr*) differing by nature from the Norwegian merger of all persons (*sitter—sitter—sitter*) or are they just different stages?

And, the other way round, are the limits of change in "simplification" and "neutralization" completely differing? Consider the borrowing of the Old Norse third person plural pronoun π*eim*—leading to π*aim* in (northern) Middle English ('them')— which replaced the third pers. plur. (dative) *him* in Old English (identical with third pers. sing. dat. *him*) thus reestablishing the distinction of singular and plural. Obviously, neutralization, too, was restricted to maintaining "deep structure" distinctions (like number). Thus, neutralization turns out to be a special case of simplification: a high-speed simplification, but not differing fundamentally from simplification processes.

As we have argued above linguistic convergence and linguistic change (like simplification) may be tightly connected: In times of tremendously destabilizing norms (in terms of norm certainty and norm loyalty) language change may be speeded up. Norm loyalty as an attitudinal matter tends to decline if cultural and linguistic group boundaries become doubtful. Norm certainty may dramatically decrease as a result of intense contact including the emergence of mixed varieties or mixed languages or of code mixing—up to the point where ingroup and outgroup distinctions are fading away or become shapeless.

This is not very far from processes well known from pidgin or creole language studies. Thus, we have to take a look into these similarities of speech islands in dissolution and pidgin and creole languages.

5. Convergence, Change, and Pidginization

As we have seen, morphological reduction, particularly case syncretism, is one of the most important features displayed in almost all German speech islands regardless if they are exposed to contact languages which are case marking or not. The radical reduction of the morphological system in German speech island varieties is obviously not simply the result of interference from contact languages but in many cases of a receding of the grammatical system. "Case syncretism or case merger . . . characterizes terminal stages of receding languages" (Huffines 1989, 212).

In fact, language "contraction" in German speech islands can be regarded as a kind of language obsolescence or even language death. Dying languages may be compared with processes of pidginization, because they obviously exhibit some structural similarities as well as common sociolinguistic restrictions of use.[56] "Pidgins can be recognized as a special or limiting case of reduction in form resulting from restriction in use" (Romaine 1989, 370).

Dressler and Wodak-Leodolter (1977) were among the first to point to an analogy of language death and pidginization. Peter Trudgill (1978) called language death a "creolization in reverse." In creole linguistics some authors refer to processes which are the same in creolization and in ordinary language change.[57]

What is in the focus of this analogy? Suzanne Romaine (1989, 379) emphasizes the "loss of productivity of morphological processes in language death" and draws attention to case syncretism and to a "tendency to eliminate allomorphy":[58] Pidgins typically lack word-≠formation rules (but acquire them as part of their expansion). "A preference for analytical, as opposed to synthetic, syntax is a hallmark of both pidgins and dying languages" (Romaine 1989, 379). If we accept this analogy, is there more in it than just a similar output of morphological "simplification" growing on a perhaps completely differing ground?

There are at least some underlying similarities we ought to pay attention to: Campbell/Muntzel (1989, 185) stress the "proficiency continuum" of the speakers of a subordinate language which resembles a creole continuum.[59] This continuum is mainly determined by age and attitudes.

In dying languages or languages undergoing functional restrictions it is sometimes even difficult to decide "who is a speaker of the language or a member of the community which speaks a particular language" (Romaine 1989, 371). And this is not a problem of linguists alone but of the speakers themselves which is evidently affecting linguistically marked group boundaries.

The children are considered to be introducing changes into the subordinate language due to little corrective pressure imposed by the adults in times of lowered normativity.[60] Lowered normativity is apparently a gateway of these innovations in receding languages as well as in pidgins or creoles: "Some of the similarities which exist between dying languages and creoles may be due . . . to the relaxing of the norms" (Romaine, 382). Characterizing this diffusion of the norms Campbell/Muntzel (1989, 189) state that "obligatory rules may come to apply optionally."

What they precisely describe by this assumption is perfectly fitting the structure of changes in German speech islands mentioned above: They observe an "overgeneralization of unmarked features," i.e., a "tendency for marked forms to be replaced by less marked ones . . . , when distinctions are lost it is the marked member of opposition which is lost" (Campbell/Muntzel 1989, 187). Some other authors, too, tend to assume that "contact involves a progressive unmarking" (Romaine 1989, 382).

Of course, change may be often regarded as externally motivated by the dominance of the contact language. But frequently the susceptibility for change and the ways of change are determined by "the nature (marked or unmarked) of the linguistic phenomena in the structure of the dying language which leads to loss (i.e. 'internal factors')" (Campbell/Muntzel 1989, 188).

From a different vantage point, viewing language contraction from a second language perspective,[61] Andersen (1989, 386) claims that "'simplification' is the surface result of a process whereby each linguistic form is uniquely linked to one and only one intended meaning (or function) and that language transfer (or interference) operates only in conjunction with this and related cognitive principles."[62]

The "One-to-One Principle" and the markedness argument may be paralleled to a certain extent in that the "greater functional load" of preserved features mentioned by Andersen (1982, 95) fits the unmarked features addressed by Campbell/Muntzel (1989). With respect to the reduction of noun inflection in German speech islands this seems to be the accusative case.[63]

Apparently, in pidgin or creole languages as well as in receding languages, simplification is guided by "internal" regularities. In times of norm erosion due to intense language contact, the gate is open for what may be called "internal" change. Mostly and first of all, marked features of "surface structure" phenomena seem to be involved. However, what is marked or unmarked is not always clear, and, the distinction is of course a gradual one.

If we want to explain these processes more precisely we have to observe which structures are simplified and which are not: As we have shown with reference to personal pronouns reduction is most effective related to less "disruptive" replacements, less individually represented items of higher level. These items are subject to simplification of the inflectional structure, others are not.

Thus, we still have to come to grips with the "internal" processes of simplification which may be induced by language contact, but obviously under widely differing conditions.

Again: What is "simplification"? And which language structures are "sensitive" to language contact in which way? To get a notion of this we will add some remarks concerning the cognitive representation of language structures exposed to simplification.

6. Cognitive Structures of Linguistic Simplification

As Steven Pinker (2000, 256ff.) states, simplification frequently consists of transformations into "default rules": The expansion of the weak verb inflection paradigm (e.g., German past tense marking of the preterite by *–te*, English by *-ed* instead of the strong verb inflection by stem allomorphy) or of the plural marker *–s* are considered to be default rules. In this view, irregular forms are lexically represented. Default rules are regularities based on the principle to act upon the mere category (of a "noun" or a "verb" for example). Pinker concludes: where memory fails, rules apply.[64]

If we observe an almost complete reduction of inflection in the noun system as well as in the system of possessive or determiners, but not in the same way in the personal pronoun system, we have to account for the difference in the cognitive representation of these forms. As we have stated above, personal pronouns, especially third person singular and plural pronouns, are highly suppletive forms, individually lexicalized and as entire units represented on the deepest lexicon level. But what means the metaphor of the "deepest" lexicon level?

We could argue with Roman Jakobson's "regression hypothesis" predicting that language dissolution is language acquisition in reverse: linguistic structures that appear first in language acquisition are retained last in language attrition; structures that are acquired last are lost first (cf. Jakobson 1969; cf. Renate Born in this volume).

The sequence of language acquisition may partly explain the specific way of case reduction in the noun and in the personal pronoun inflection: The accusative is usually acquired before the dative; prepositions with accusative objects before those with datives; the distinction between stative dative and directional accusative is acquired late. But the dative form of personal pronouns and demonstratives is the first acquired by children. Except of the demonstrative this succession matches perfectly our observations related to case syncretism in German speech islands: All items acquired early are retained last in speech island varieties.

On the other hand, accusative is subject to case reduction, too; and even the demonstrative loses the dative. Apparently, case marking inflectional morphemes are more susceptible to reduction than "full listed" pronouns. Obviously, nouns as well as possessive pronouns and demonstratives are exposed to simplification due to the fact that they are represented in decomposition.

This may explain some processes of reduction, e.g., the subsequent loss of inflections in nouns, possessive pronouns or determiners, step by step transforming the case marker for dative *–em* into *–en* (thus merging into the accusative marker), both into a ("long")

−*n* and then becoming optional or getting lost. This is true for a lot of German dialect varieties (including speech island varieties).[65] Since personal pronouns are probably not lexically represented in decomposition they are not in the same way accessible to an overgeneralization of grammatical default rules.[66]

Of course, "deeply" lexicalized representations are not protected from change. But frequently they undergo at first a transformation into a default rule, and then they become a subject to simplification and (over)generalization of rules.

In a similar way, Caroline Smits (1996, 47ff.) discusses internal changes in Iowa Dutch concerning rules and surface forms (i.e., "non-systematic properties of word forms") related to language contact. "Contact situations . . . are claimed to create favorable circumstances for these changes to take place." The main condition for these radical changes is supposed to be the disappearing of linguistic norms.[67]

She distinguishes three types of changes based on the rule system: regularization, simplification, loss of inflectional distinctions (and their compensation). In some cases mentioned above there is evidence to assume that these types of changes can be interpreted as stages of chronological succession.

Pinker (2000, 363) accounts for some conditions of "regularization" in the sense of a transformation to defaults: Regular forms are constructed (or irregular forms turn into regular ones) if a word is new, rare or unusual, if it does not possess a normal root or if its information cannot be transferred to the whole word.[69]

As we can see, new words, borrowing, obsolescence of linguistic knowledge, and a mismatch concerning linguistic norms can affect these processes of construction or reconstruction. The historical spreading of the past tense inflective −*ed* and that of the plural marker −*s* is mentioned by Pinker (2000, 270) himself emphasizing the interplay of the destabilizing French influence and the usage of the default attached to all new words.[70]

In times of cultural "crisis" the loss of cultural knowledge or the blurring of group boundaries can affect norm stability. If norm stability is decreasing, linguistic knowledge will not be transmitted in a sufficient way. Then language structures may become obsolescent, learners of the language may feel a "learning burden": Processes of change will be set in motion to simplify uncertain structures by expanding default rules leading to the dissolution or the collapse of the morphological system.

Obviously there are two different processes of grammatical change: Irregular forms are transformed to regular forms (by means of defaults); and regular forms are exposed to reduction (like case syncretism) sometimes leading to the complete loss of distinctions. The first device is to apply the system of combinatory procedures subsequently attaching formal elements one after the other, each one carrying only little (semantic or grammatical) information. The second device is to simplify these elements by (over)generalizing one of the formal representations of each element or sometimes, in case of inflectives, by dropping them at all. These changes might be regarded as a single process of simplification, and they may occur at the same time, but they are different by nature.[71] They do not always co-occur. The application of the second device must be preceded by the first device: regularization is a prerequisite of the simplification of rules. Simplification may follow regularization but this is not necessarily the case. On the other hand, regularization once emerging may lead to an expanded use of "defaults" if linguistic norms get obsolescing or eroding due to language contact.

What, however, may be the line which links regularization and loss of morphology? The "externalization" of marking external relations could be regarded as a redistribution of functional features to different markers each one carrying only little grammatical information. Given the successive simplification of noun inflection, the replacement of morphological markers by determiners, then by prepositions and finally by word order may be interpreted as further steps of transformation into default rules: a determiner (without morphological marking), a preposition as well as the combinatory rules of word order act upon the mere category.

7. Conclusion

Dealing with convergence in German speech islands we have discussed the linguistic phenomena related to this notion from different vantage points including processes of intralinguistic convergence, interlinguistic convergence, typological "convergence" (or intralinguistic change), pidginization, and "regularization" (i.e., the expanding of rules due to cognitive "defaults").

As stated above, we would suggest to use the notion of convergence with caution. Some attention will need to be given to the relationship between the different processes labeled under the heading of "convergence." The linguistic description of these interrelated processes requires an integrated approach providing methodology from sociolinguistics, dialectology and research on language change, including the attempt to highlight the cognitive structures which furrow the line for internal simplifications under external pressure. A theory of the intermesh of these processes may be the main subject of a sociolinguistic speech island research. Comparative speech island research seems to be a promising field of application:

Most of the German speech islands are considered to be contracting—if not dying— varieties with respect to the reduction of their grammatical systems. Evidently, for a long time language contact (and sometimes variety contact) have severely increased. Linguistic norms have been weakened in terms of both norm certainty and norm loyalty thus giving way to processes similar to those common to pidgin languages. To be sure, external induced changes have been emerging in all German speech islands. But the susceptibility for change and the ways of change are structured by systematical and typological constraints which probably turn out to be cognitive processes underlying quite "normal" linguistic change:

Suzanne Romaine (1989, 380) remarks rather laconically that perhaps "the kinds of changes which take place in language death are just ordinary changes speeded up." With all that caution recommended above we may now come into the position to rethink this in a more revealing way. And it might be more than a truism stating that "in a way all linguistic developments are 'internal'" (Coseriu 1975, 146, transl. P.R.).

Notes

[1] According to Coseriu (1974) linguistic change is to be addressed as a threefold problem (Coseriu 1974, 56): as a "rational" problem (why languages change), as a "general" problem (which conditions cause language change), and as a "historical" problem (of a specific change): While on the rational level language change is the very condition of communication, on the general level it is a matter of the varying balance of the linguistic system, and especially of the interplay of language system and norm. As a historical problem we have to analyze this interplay in a specific historical situation: Language change will be supported by regional or social variability of linguistic knowledge and by its susceptibility to variation in times of cultural decay or of social divergence (cf. Coseriu 1974, 100).

[2] We will come back to this issue in section 4.

[3] "Sprachinseln sind räumlich abgrenzbare und intern strukturierte Siedlungsräume einer sprachlichen Minderheit inmitten einer anderssprachigen Mehrheit" (Hutterer 1982, 178).

"Sprachinseln sind punktuell oder areal auftretende, relativ kleine geschlossene Sprach- und Siedlungsgemeinschaften in einem anderssprachigen, relativ größeren Gebiet" (Wiesinger 1983, 901).

[4] For more details concerning the development of speech island research cf. Rosenberg (in press), Mattheier (1996), Kuhn (1934).

[5] Georg Wenker and his successors of the Marburg school, after 1876 up to the 1920s.

[6] Several researchers (and numerous philologists) in the tradition of the Leipzig school, following the prototypical "Ortsgrammatik" of Jost Winteler 1876, mainly around the turn of the century. Until WW I a series of similar works was published, concerning almost all of the German speech islands in Hungary and also several studies on the Alpine region.

[7] An interdisciplinary framework consisting of linguistic, historical, ethnological research, following Theodor Frings, mainly between World War I and II.

[8] The Bavarian dialect of the "Sette Communi" speech island in Northern Italy, for example, is considered to be the oldest German dialect, a "first class linguistic monument" (Hornung 1994, 20, transl. P.R.). It has preserved a remarkable amount of Old and Middle High German features, e.g., a very old consonantism; the preterite is still existing which has vanished in the Bavarian dialects elsewhere 400 years ago as well as the genitive case and some other features.

[9] The first reports on speech islands trace back to the 16th (Transylvania/Romania) and 17th (Zips/Slovakia) century (cf. Kuhn 1934, 76f.). For the first time, the term "Sprachinsel" was used in 1847 applied to a Slavic community surrounded by a German-speaking population close to Königsberg, East Prussia (now Kaliningrad/Russia; cf. Mattheier 1996, 812).

[10] Pennsylvania Dutch was the first subject of interest concerning speech islands far away from the German language area. Very early German-American researchers carried out several studies on Pennsylvania Dutch (S. S. Haldemann in 1872 or the dictionaries of A. R. Horne in 1875 and J. C. Lins in 1887).

[11] Mattheier (1996, 817) argues for this subject as the very task of sociolinguistic speech island research.

[12] To put it with Schirmunski (1930), speech islands have been regarded as a kind of a "language laboratory" bringing about linguistic processes in short time which emerged over centuries on the way to our contemporary standard languages. Even if this might be a myth, overestimating the output of koineization in the Black Sea colonies, Schirmunski's focussing on dialect leveling, its forces and resources rather than on the linguistic origins of the settlers was paradigmatic.

[13] Eugenio Coseiu (1975) calls these phenomena "convergence": "sprachliche Konvergenzen, d.h. voneinander unabhängige Parallelentwicklungen, die in historisch verwandten Sprachen offenbar auftreten" (Coseriu 1975: 134). As "typological" convergence he addresses the "functional coherence" of all Romance languages (except of French and Occitan) based on a common principle: "internal" (paradigmatic) expression of "internal," non-relational functions (like gender and number); "external" (syntagmatic) expression of "external," relational functions (like case or adjective comparative) (cf. Coseriu 1975, 142).

[14] Cf. Altenhofen (1996, 27).

[15] Cf. Altenhofen (1996, map 29).

[16] Cf. *Wolgadeutscher Sprachatlas* (1997, map 143).

[17] Cf. Altenhofen (1996, map 56).

[18] C.f. Schirmunski (1962, 317ff.); Dulson (1941, 96).

[19] As Nöth (1994, 127) found out, Russian Germans who had any even rudimentary competence of German varieties performed significantly better than those who had not.

[20] Cf. Jedig (1966).

[21] Cf. Altenhofen (1996, 254ff.).

[22] Cf. Salmons (1994, 60).

[23] Cf. Louden (1994, 84); Huffines (1989, 216ff.; 1994, 50f.).

[24] Cf. Keel (1994, 98).

[25] Huffines (1989, 212ff.) reports on case syncretism research in the United States, particularly concerning the loss or maintenance of the dative case.

[26] Cf. Lang (1996, 12).

[27] Cf. Comrie (1996, 16).

[28] Cf. Wurzel (1996, 522).

[29] Cf. Eisenberg (1994, 362).

[30] Some authors propose a case hierarchy in terms of the markedness theory (or naturalness theory): Nominative is considered less marked (i.e., more "natural") than accusative, accusative less marked than dative, dative less marked than genitive (cf. Mayerthaler et al. 1998, 167). "Natural" change then means: marked elements turn into less marked elements. While perfectly fitting the general direction of case syncretism, the criteria of "naturalness" are somehow unclear. Other authors emphasize the syntactic flexibility of the accusative in terms of communicative or discourse grammatical motivation: The accusative is supposed to be more resistant due to its functional "load" (e.g., usable for passive transformation, topicalization,

fronting and transfer outside of the verbal frame, reflexive constructions, connection of relative clauses etc.). Of course, the accusative is frequently supported by the uniformity of nominative and accusative. And furthermore, there are certainly some phonological processes promoting the accusative form, e.g. the replacement of *–m* by *–n* (a process which in several German varieties applies also to the neuter: *in dem/im Haus* > *in den/in Haus* ('in the house'); cf. Rosenberg 1986, 341ff., with 300 examples taken from class room dictations and essays in Berlin).

[31] Cf. Louden (1994, 84).

[32] Cf. Salmons (1994, 66); Keel (1994, 96).

[33] Cf. Salmons (1994, 64).

[34] Tables are attached at the end of this article. Please note the shadings.

[35] Cf. Haberland (1994).

[36] Cf. van Kemenade (1994).

[37] Cf. Weinrich (1982).

[38] Cf. Salmons (1994, 64f.).

[39] Cf. Eisenberg (1994, 383f.).

[40] Cf. Cholewa (1993), see table at the end of this article.

[41] Cf. Grinjowa (1990).

[42] Cf. Rosenberg (1994, 294); the study covered about 750 queries, including the whole school youth and every fifth adult of the village. Additionally, we compiled a sociogram of an eleventh school class illustrating this effect. The pupils were asked: Who are your friends in this class, and which language do you predominantly use for communication with him/her? The sociogram displays friendship clusters within the class: Multiplex patterns mainly link Mennonite-Mennonite-clusters (with differences between boys and girls). The communicational activities are conducted in Russian and German. Russian is used in all types of clusters, but mainly with non-Mennonites. The striking result is the fact that communication in German is (with two exceptions) only taking place with Mennonites.

[43] Cf. Huffines (1989, 217).

[44] The young "progressive" males among the Mexican Mennonites display many and strong correlations, the conservative ones few and weak correlations. This may explain the remarkable change of linguistic behavior among the young progressive males who are converging to the Spanish language (replacing the Mennonite High variety Hüagdietsch), whereas the conservative Mennonites do not. The Texas Mennonite group displays only few and weak correlations, because their process of change is largely completed (shift to English) (cf. Kaufmann (1997, 320).

[45] The inclination to use a minority or majority language, for example, depends on calculating advantages or disadvantages of different strategies as well as on competence and status of the addressee, on topic, place, and other features of the interaction. But the definition of a "minority (or majority) language" frame will also be related to the *perception* of the validity of that frame as matching situational patterns. This is subject to normative or nonnormative attitudes. (For details concerning the rc+ framework and its applicability to ethnolinguistic conflicts cf. Lapinski/Rosenberg 2001).

[46] Harwood/Giles/Bourhis (1994, 175) emphasize "subjective vitality as a predictor of ethnolinguistic behavior;" cf. also Niedzielski/Giles (1996).

225

[47] "Die sprachlichen Konvergenzen (in the sense of parallel developments of historically related languages, cf. n. 13, P.R.) haben nichts Geheimnisvolles an sich . . . : es handelt sich dabei einfach um die Anwendung systematisch und typologisch analoger Muster in verschiedenen Sprachen, . . . was in der Norm als Wandel erscheint, ist vom System her gesehen nichts weiter als seine Anwendung; und Wandel im System ist dementsprechend Funktionieren des Sprachtyps" (Coseriu 1975, 145).

[48] As O'Neil (1978, 262) argues Old English and Old Norse had been closely related displaying a "basic underlying sameness": "Imagine . . . a situation and an area in which there are two groups of people speaking languages which because of their common origin are remarkably similar in their phonology, syntax (deep and surface), and semantics, but which for historical reasons contrast sharply in their inflections, in those markers of superficial relationships, surface structure clues on the basis of which deep structure guesses are made. In such a situation, granting that the two groups are reasonably at peace and willing to mix and trade back and forth, how could communication be improved—indeed, made possible? Easy: radically and quickly simplify the inflectional noise" (O'Neil 1978, 257).

[49] Processes of *neutralization* are seen in the collapse of inflections in Afrikaans related to the contact of mixed Dutch dialects and Low German in Capetown as well as in the inflectional reduction in the Continental Scandinavian languages due to contact with Middle Low German; *simplification* is found in Icelandic because of its isolation, and in High German due to its general motion away from the Germanic area (cf. O'Neil 1978, 275ff.).

[50] Of course, in the Middle Ages Danish was the dominant language among the Scandinavian languages and it might have played a role as a mediator of (contact-induced) change. It is true that for a long time the Norwegian language has been influenced by Danish, and the Swedish language by Norwegian and Danish. But changes of the inflectional system were already going on in early Old Danish when contacts with Middle Low German just increased, long before the Low German variety of Luebeck became the most important language of the Baltic Sea region. Related to the early Old Danish period Hutterer (1987, 174, transl. P.R.) explicitly states: "The decay of noun inflection was already going on." He mentions the merger of nominative and accusative. (Old Swedish moved into this direction at about the same time.) In the Seeland dialect only a non-genitive versus genitive distinction remained, in the dialect of the Jutland peninsula, close to the Low German speaking area, the noun inflection system was almost completely collapsing. This is it, what we mean by the objection of a merely *accelerated* simplification due to language contact.

[51] Faroese, the language of the islands half-way from Scandinavia to Iceland, is regarded as a "middle state" inflectional system "between the complexity of Icelandic and the simplicity of the continental Scandinavian languages" (O'Neil 1978, 277). O'Neil (1978, 280) points to the main problem: "although it is interesting to contemplate the hypothetical state of half-isolation, half-contact, it finally makes little sense: there is either isolation or contact, and then their attendant consequences—simplification or neutralization."

[52] Its phonological system is closely related to South Norwegian dialects; cf. Hutterer (1987, 160).

[53] Of course, the Faroe islands were subject to colonization by Norwegians and Danes since the Middle Ages (being part of the Norwegian kingdom and then—with Norway—of Denmark), but this was the fate of Iceland, too. May be, the absence of a written language and the prevailing use of several different dialects is a better way to account for simplifications in the inflectional system of Faroese.

[54] Number and tense, for example, are regarded as deep structure distinctions. (cf. O'Neil 1978, 261).

[55] Figure-ground or "trajector-landmark" conceptions in terms of Langacker (1999) which underlay other— syntactical or compositional—structures as well.

[56] Suzanne Romaine (1989) sets out to compare "the similarities and differences between dying languages, pidgins, creoles, and immigrant languages," with respect to the sociolinguistic context and to structural features common to these varieties of language. She mentions similar language contact settings due to "basic inequalities which may exist between the users of languages with differing prestiges, utility, and recognized legitimacy in situations of contact . . . : encroaching diglossia, failure of children to acquire the mother tongue, schooling in a second language, resettlement, dispersion and intermarriage. . . . Among the linguistic effects common to situations of language contact are the following: convergence, loss of morphological and syntactic complexity, and an overall increase in semantic transparency" (Romaine 1989, 371, 375).

It was the merit of Nancy Dorian to establish a research field of "language obsolescence" linking the scattered investigations on language contraction, death, attrition, shrinkage and so on (cf. Dorian 1989).

[57] Mufwene (1998, 316ff.) raises the question: "If the origins of creoles are so special, we would indeed like to know how special they are. . . . To be sure, there are differences between the ecologies in which creoles developed and those in which languages putatively changed normally. . . . I contend that the ecological factors and selective restructuring which produced creoles are of the same kind as those which produced 'normal' language change. Contact, I argue, is a critical factor in almost any case of language change. . . . Creolization is a social, not a structural, process."

[58] Allomorphy is substituted by "fixed and invariable word order": Rabaul Creole German, for example, has exclusively SVO word order in main as well as in subordinate clauses (Romaine 1989, 376).

[59] Cf. also Romaine (1989, 371).

[60] "It may be that in a community of expanded-pidgin or dying-language speakers the innovations of children have a better chance of catching on than in 'normal' communities. . . . In normal communities the expectation is that adults act as brakes in the innovations produced by children. . . . In the case of dying and pidgin languages it may be that the children have greater scope to act as norm-makers due to the fact that a great deal of variability exists among the adult community. . . . Simplified forms can persist in the speech of children [. . .] because there is little corrective pressure or model" (Romaine 1989, 372f.). Therefore the domain of the home seems to be decisive for language shift and death (cf. Haugen 1989).

[61] "Language contraction is typically a phenomenon of second language development in that the weaker, contracting language is almost always a secondary language for the speaker, even though it may be the speaker's original mother tongue" (Andersen 1989, 386).

[62] These two principles are called the *One-to-One Principle* and the *Transfer to Somewhere Principle* (Andersen 1989, 386). Examples for the *One-to-One Principle* applied by second language learners are: SVO word order (even in subordinate clauses) in German, postverbal position of the object (even of pronouns) in French and Spanish, placement of the negator directly before the entity to be negated in German or English, reduction of agreement markers (being redundant). The *Transfer to Somewhere Principle* entails that transfer occurs if and only if these (and other) principles are consistent with the L1 structure or if the L2 input has a model for generalization. In transfer preference is given to *free, invariant,* functionally *simple* and *frequently*

occurring forms congruent with L1 and L2. An example for this principle is the postverbal placement of noun phrase objects in French serving as a model for English learners of French to place even pronoun objects postverbally. French Learners of English have no model for preverbal placement of objects in English and therefore do not use French rules in their English interlanguage (cf. Andersen 1989, 388ff.).

[63] Cf. n. 30. Andersen (1989, 392) argues that case reduction by PG speakers departing from the nonsectarian norm "can easily be interpreted as evidence for the operation of the 1:1 Principle."

[64] The preterite inflective *–te* (English *–ed*) as well as the plural marker *–s* (in both languages) are regarded as "defaults" which are used in cases of "emergency" where memory and strategies of analogy are not applicable: "in all den 'Notfällen,' in denen Gedächtnis und Analogie die Segel streichen—bei ungewöhnlichen Wurzeln, nicht assimilierbaren Lehnwörtern, Namen, Akronymen, Kurzwörtern, Phrasen und Zitaten. . . . Die Regularität beruht . . . auf der Fähigkeit des menschlichen Geistes, symbolische Regeln zu erwerben—Operationen, die vorbehaltlos auf jedes Exemplar einer Kategorie anwendbar sind" (Pinker 2000, 269). According to Pinker language contains "words and rules," the former connected to our associative memory representing a "knowing what" system, the latter related to procedures of symbolic combination, to a "knowing how" system (Pinker 2000, 342).

[65] Rosenberg (1986, 348-75) contains about 1.000 examples of this kind collected from class room dictations and essays in. O'Neil (1978, 254ff.) describes the same process of simplification of the noun inflection in the Middle English of the south of England.

[66] Certainly, they are also subject to simplifications like the replacement of *–m* by *–n* (e.g. *ihm* by *ihn* 'him'). This— if not phonologically motivated—could be a default rule to serve as the general common case or oblique case marker.

[67] "Iowa Dutch is not developing into a newly crystallized language. . . . Instead, the language is disintegrating, meaning that the grammatical system is collapsing—slowly but steadily—while language norms are disappearing" (Smits 1996, 58). In Smits (1998, 383) she discusses Iowa Dutch as a case of "imposition" in terms of van Coetsem (1995) due to changes in phonology and grammar (not vocabulary) being the most prominent and to "imperfect proficiency."

[68] "a.) The extended use of the rule system of the recipient language (regularization). This means that the rule system remains intact, but that the domain in which it is applied is extended at the expense of irregular forms. . . . b.) The original inflectional system of the recipient language is changed in such a way that it becomes simpler (simplification), while meaning distinctions are preserved. . . . c.) The inflectional devices for the expression of a distinction have been lost—or are avoided—because speakers are insecure about their application. This is compensated for by means of the use of other devices offered by the recipient language itself, often in the form of periphrastic constructions" (Smits 1996, 47f.).

[69] According to Pinker (2000, 274f.) regular forms are constructed (or irregular forms turn into regular ones) if:

- a new word does not sound like a known (irregular) one (e.g. *snarfed, abgezockt*)
- an irregular form is rarely used (e.g. *chide – chid, pflegen – gepflogen*)
- a word has been invented without a root: onomatopoetics (*pinged, gequietscht*); proper nouns (*the Childs, die Manns*); borrowings (*succumbed, geoutet; talismans, Mokassins*)
- a word has been derived from another word class (*braked, gewachst*)

- a complex word appears without a "head" thus lacking semantic information (*grandstanded, gehaushaltet*).

Of course, irregular words come also into being, mainly by way of analogy, merger or as a remainder of former regularity.

[70] "Das Suffix –*s* übernahm die Vorherrschaft, weil es hörbar war, sich hinter Vokalen wie auch hinter Konsonanten sprechen ließ und, vor allem, in großer Zahl an Pluralnomen aus dem normannischen Französisch importiert wurde, das zufällig ebenso ein Pluralsuffix mit –*s* besaß, und weil sie es an all jenen fremd klingenden Wörtern hörten, reanalysierten sie es als allmächtiges reguläres Suffix, das ganz allgemein an Nichtwurzeln treten konnte" (Pinker 2000, 272).

[71] Contact-induced *norm* instability causes the extended application of *systematical* rules (like "defaults"). The simplification of these rules reduces the system, according to *typological* patterns (like "externalization"). (Cf. n. 47).

References

Altenhofen, Cléo Vilson. 1996. *Hunsrückisch in Rio Grande do Sul: Ein Beitrag zur Beschreibung einer deutschbrasilianischen Dialektvarietät im Kontakt mit dem Portugiesischen*. Mainzer Studien zur Sprach- und Volksforschung, 21. Stuttgart.

Andersen, Roger W. 1989. "The 'up' and 'down' Staircase in Secondary Language Development." In *Investigating Obsolescence: Studies in Language Contraction and Death*, ed. Nancy Dorian, 385--94. Cambridge.

Asfandiarova, Dania. 1999. "'Mir verzehle doch Lutherisch und die Katholisch': Dialektmischung im Vokalismus in der deutschen Sprachinsel Prisib/Alekjevka (Baschkortostan, Russische Föderation)." In *Historische Soziolinguistik des Deutschen IV: Soziofunktionale Gruppe—Kommunikative Anforderungen—Sprachgebrauch. Intern. Fachtagung, Rostock, 13.-16.09.1998*, ed. Gisela Brandt, 241-62. Stuttgarter Arbeiten zur Germanistik, 372. Stuttgart.

Askedal, John Ole. 1996. "Überlegungen zum Deutschen als sprachtypologischem 'Mischtyp.'" In *Deutsch—typologisch*, ed. Ewald Lang and Gisela Zifonun, 369-83. Institut für deutsche Sprache. Jahrbuch 1995. Berlin.

Auer, Peter, and Frans Hinskens. 1996. "The Convergence and Divergence of Dialects in Europe: New and Not So New Developments in an Old Area." In *Sociolinguistica: Internationales Jahrbuch für Europäische Soziolinguistik / International Yearbook of European Sociolinguistics / Annuaire International de la Sociolinguistique Européenne*, ed. Ulrich Ammon, Klaus J. Mattheier and Peter H. Nelde, 10: Konvergenz und Divergenz von Dialekten in Europa / Convergence and divergence of dialects in Europe / Convergence et divergence des dialectes en Europe, 1-30. Tübingen.

Berend, Nina, and Hugo Jedig. 1991. *Deutsche Mundarten in der Sowjetunion: Geschichte der Forschung und Bibliographie*. Marburg.

Campbell, Lyle, and Martha C. Muntzel. 1989. "The Structural Consequences of Language Death." In *Investigating Obsolescence: Studies in Language Contraction and Death*, ed. Nancy Dorian, 181-96. Cambridge.

Cholewa, Jürgen. 1993. "Störungen der lexikalisch-morphologischen Wortverarbeitung bei Aphasie: Ein Literaturüberblick." *Neurolinguistik* 7,2: 105-26.

Comrie, Bernard. 1996. "Sprache und Sprachen: Universalien und Typologie." In *Deutsch typologisch*, ed. Ewald Lang and Gisela Zifonun, 16-29. Institut für deutsche Sprache, Jahrbuch 1995. Berlin.

Coseriu, Eugenio. 1974. *Synchronie, Diachronie und Geschichte: Das Problem des Sprachwandels*, transl. Helga Sohre. München.

Coseriu, Eugenio. 1975. "Synchronie, Diachronie und Typologie." In *Sprachwandel: Reader zur diachronischen Sprachwissenschaft*, ed. Dieter Cherubim, 135-49. Berlin.

Deutscher Sprachatlas auf Grund des von Georg Wenker begründeten Sprachatlas des Deutschen Reichs und mit Einschluß von Luxemburg, der deutschen Sprachteile Österreichs, der Tschechoslowakei, der Schweiz, der Sprachinsel Gottschee, Liechtenstein in vereinfachter Form bearbeitet beim Deutschen Sprachatlas, begonnen von Ferdinand Wrede, fortgesetzt von Walther Mitzka und Bernhard Martin, 8th vol. 1935. Marburg.

Dinges, Georg. 1925. "Zur Erforschung der wolgadeutschen Mundarten: Ergebnisse und Aufgaben." *Teuthonista* 1,4: 299-313.

Dorian, Nancy. 1989. "Introduction." In *Investigating Obsolescence: Studies in Language Contraction and Death*, ed. Nancy Dorian, 1-10. Cambridge.

Dressler, Wolfgang U., and Ruth Wodak-Leodolter. 1977. "Language Preservation and Language Death in Brittany." *International Journal of the Sociology of Language* 12: 33-44.

Dulson, Andreas. 1941. "Problema skreschtschenija dialektow po materialam jasyka nemzew Powolshja. In *Iswestija Akademii nauk Sojusa SSR, Otdelenie literatury i jasyka* 3: 82-96.

Eisenberg, Peter. 1994. "German." In *The Germanic Languages*, ed. Ekkehard König and Johan van der Auwera, 349-87. London.

Esser, Hartmut. 1996a. "Die Definition der Situation." *Kölner Zeitschrift für Soziologie und Sozialpsychologie* 48: 1-34.

Esser, Hartmut. 1996b. "Ethnische Konflikte als Auseinandersetzung um den Wert von kulturellem Kapital." In *Die bedrängte Toleranz: Ethnisch-kulturelle Konflikte, religiöse Differenzen und die Gefahren politisierter Gewalt*, ed. Wilhelm Heitmeyer and Rainer Dollase, 64-99. Frankfurt.

Giles, Howard, and Nikolas Coupland. 1991. *Language: Contexts and Consequences*. Milton Keynes: Pacific Grove, CA.

Grinjowa, Nelly M. 1990. "Interferenzerscheinungen im grammatischen System einer niederdeutschen Mundart in der Sowjetunion infolge intensiver Sprachkontakte." Unpublished typescript.

Gumperz, John J. 1968. "The Speech community." In *Language and Social Context*, ed. P. P. Grignioli, 219-31. Harmondsworth.

Haberland, Hartmut. 1994. "Danish." In *The Germanic Languages*, ed. Ekkehard König and Johan van der Auwera, 313-48. London.

Harwood, Jake, Howard Giles and Richard Y. Bourhis. 1994. "The Genesis of Vitality Theory: Historical Patterns and Discoursal Dimensions." *International Journal of the Sociology of Language* 108: 167-206.

Haugen, Einar. 1989. "The Rise and Fall of an Immigrant Language: Norwegian in America." In *Investigating Obsolescence: Studies in Language Contraction and Death*, ed. Nancy Dorian, 61-73. Cambridge.

Hinskens, Frans, Jeffrey L. Kallen and Johan Taeldeman. 2000. "Merging and Drifting Apart: Convergence and Divergence of Dialects across Political Borders." *International Journal of the Sociology of Language* 145: *Convergence and Divergence of Dialects across European Borders*, ed. Frans Hinskens, Jeffrey L. Kallen, and Johan Taeldeman, 1-28. Berlin.

Hornung, Maria. 1994. "Die sogenannten zimbrischen Mundarten der Sieben und Dreizehn Gemeinden in Oberitalien." In *Die deutschen Sprachinseln in den Südalpen: Mundarten und Volkstum*, ed. Maria Hornung, 19-43. Studien zur Dialektologie, 3. Hildesheim.

Huffines, Marion L. 1989. "Case Usage among the Pennsylvania German Sectarians and Nonsectarians." In *Investigating Obsolescence: Studies in Language Contraction and Death*, ed. Nancy Dorian, 211-26. Cambridge.

Huffines, Marion L. 1994. "Directionality of Language Influence: The Case of Pennsylvania German and English." In *Sprachinselforschung: Eine Gedenkschrift für Hugo Jedig*, ed. Nina Berend and Klaus J. Mattheier, 47-58. Frankfurt.

Hunnius, Klaus. 1990. "Französische Flexionslehre." In *Lexikon der Romanistischen Linguistik (LRL)*, ed. Günter Holtus, Michael Metzeltin and Christian Schmitt, 5,1: 59-71. Tübingen.

Hutterer, Claus J. 1987. *Die germanischen Sprachen: Ihre Geschichte in Grundzügen*, 2d ed. (1st ed. 1975). Budapest.

Hutterer, Claus J. 1982. "Sprachinselforschung als Prüfstand für dialektologische Arbeitsprinzipien." In *Dialektologie: Ein Handbuch zur deutschen und allgemeinen Dialektforschung*, vol. 2, ed. Werner Besch, Ulrich Knoop, Wolfgang Putschke and Herbert Ernst Wiegand. Berlin.

Jakobson, Roman. 1969. *Kindersprache, Aphasie und allgemeine Lautgesetze*. Frankfurt.

Jedig, Hugo H. 1966. *Laut- und Formenbestand der niederdeutschen Mundart des Altai-Gebietes*. Sitzungsberichte der Sächsischen Akademie der Wissenschaften zu Leipzig: Philologisch historische Klasse. 112/5. Berlin.

Kaufmann, Göz. 1997. *Varietätendynamik in Sprachkontaktsituationen. Attitüden und Sprachverhalten rußlanddeutscher Mennoniten in Mexiko und den USA*. VarioLingua, 3. Frankfurt.

Keel, William D. 1994. "Reduction and Loss of Case Marking in the Noun Phrase in German-American Speech Islands: Internal Development or External Interference?" In *Sprachinselforschung: Eine Gedenkschrift für Hugo Jedig*, ed. Nina Berend and Klaus J. Mattheier, 94-104. Frankfurt.

König, Ekkehard. 1996. "Kontrastive Grammatik und Typologie." In *Deutsch—typologisch*, ed. Ewald Lang and Gisela Zifonun, 31-54. Institut für deutsche Sprache, Jahrbuch 1995. Berlin.

König, Ekkehard, and Johan van der Auwera , eds. 1994. *The Germanic Languages*. London.

Kuhn, Walter. 1934. *Deutsche Sprachinsel-Forschung: Geschichte, Aufgaben, Verfahren*. Ostdeutsche Forschungen, 2. Plauen i. Vogtl.

Lang, Ewald. 1996. "Das Deutsche im typologischen Spektrum: Einführung in den Band." In *Deutsch—typologisch*, ed. Ewald Lang and Gisela Zifonun, 7-15. Institut für deutsche Sprache, Jahrbuch 1995. Berlin.

Langacker, Ronald. 1999. *Grammar and Conceptualization*. Cognitive Linguistics Research, 14. Berlin.

Lapinski, Dariusz, and Peter Rosenberg. 2001. "Sprachnationalismus und die 'Logik' ethnosprachlicher Konflikte." Paper presented at the 2001 Annual Conference of the Society of Applied Linguistics (GAL), Passau, 27-29 Sept. 2001.

Le Page, Robert B., and Andrée Tabouret-Keller. 1985. *Acts of Identity: Creole-based Approaches to Language and Ethnicity.* Cambridge.

Louden, Mark L. 1994. "Syntactic Change in Multilingual Speech Islands." In *Sprachinselforschung: Eine Gedenkschrift für Hugo Jedig,* ed. Nina Berend and Klaus J.Mattheier, 73-91. Frankfurt.

Mattheier, Klaus J. 1996. "Methoden der Sprachinselforschung." In *Kontaktlinguistik /Contact linguistics / Linguistique de contact: Ein internationales Handbuch zeitgenössischer Forschung /An international handbook of contemporary research /Manuel international des recherches contemporaines,* ed. Hans Goebl, Peter H. Nelde, Zdenek Star and Wolfgang Wölck, 1: 812-19. Berlin.

Mayerthaler, Willi, Günther Fliedl and Christian Winkler. 1998. *Lexikon der Natürlichkeitstheoretischen Syntax und Morphosyntax.* Tübingen.

Milroy, Lesley. 1980. *Language and Social Networks.* Oxford.

Mufwene, Salikoko S. 1998. "What Research on Creole Genesis Can Contribute to Historical Linguistics." In *Historical Linguistics: Selected Papers from the 13th International Conference on Historical Linguistics, Düsseldorf, 10-17 August 1997,* ed. Monika S. Schmid, Jennifer R. Austin and Dieter Stein, 315-38. Amsterdam.

Niedzielski, Nancy, and Howard Giles. 1996. "Linguistic Accommodation." In *Kontaktlinguistik /Contact linguistics /Linguistique de contact: Ein internationales Handbuch zeitgenössischer Forschung /An international handbook of contemporary research /Manuel international des recherches contemporaines,* ed. Hans Goebl, Peter H. Nelde, Zdenek Star and Wolfgang Wölck, 1: 332-42. Berlin.

Nöth, Dorothea. 1994. "Spuren der verlernten Muttersprache?: Beobachtungen zum Artikelgebrauch beim Sprachwiedererwerb von Rußlanddeutschen." Unpublished typescript. Berlin.

Nyman, Lennart. 1997. "Einige Beobachtungen zu Varietäten und Varietätenausgleich im Niederdeutsch der Orenburger Rußland-Mennoniten." In *Historische Soziolinguistik des Deutschen III: Sprachgebrauch und sprachliche Leistung in sozialen Schichten und soziofunktionalen Gruppen: Internationale Fachtagung Rostock/Kühlungsborn 15.-18.9.1996,* ed. Gisela Brandt, 261-76. Stuttgart.

O'Neil, Wayne. 1978. "The Evolution of the Germanic Inflectional Systems: A Study in the Causes of Language Change." *Orbis* 27: 248-86.

Pinker, Steven. 2000. *Wörter und Regeln: Die Natur der Sprache,* transl. Martina Wiese. Heidelberg.

Romaine, Suzanne. 1989. "Pidgins, Creoles, Immigrant, and Dying Languages." In *Investigating Obsolescence: Studies in Language Contraction and Death,* ed. Nancy Dorian, 369-83. Cambridge.

Rosenberg, Peter. 1986. *Der Berliner Dialekt und seine Folgen für die Schüler.* Tübingen.

Rosenberg, Peter. 1994. "Sprachgebrauchsstrukturen und Heterogenität der Kommunikationsgemein-schaft bei den Deutschen in der GUS: Eine empirische Studie." In *Satz—Text—Diskurs: Akten des 27. Linguistischen Kolloquiums, Münster 1992,* ed. Peter-Paul König and Helmut Wiegers, 2: 287-98. Tübingen.

Rosenberg, Peter. 1998. "Deutsche Minderheiten in Lateinamerika." In *Particulae particularum: Festschrift zum 60. Geburtstag von Harald Weydt,* ed. Theo Harden and Elke Hentschel, 261-91. Tübingen.

Rosenberg, Peter. In press. "Dialect Convergence in German Speech Islands." In *Dialect Convergence and Divergence in Europe*, ed. Peter Auer, Frans Hinsken and Paul E. Kerswill.

Salmons, Joseph. 1994. "Naturalness and Morphological Change in Texas German." In *Sprachinselforschung: Eine Gedenkschrift für Hugo Jedig*, ed. Nina Berend and Klaus J. Mattheier, 59 72. Frankfurt.

Schmeller, Johann Andreas. 1855. *Sogenanntes Cimbrisches Wörterbuch, das ist deutsches Idioticon der VII und XIII communi in den venetianischen Alpen: Mit Einleitung und Zusammenfassung im Auftrag der Kaiserlichen Akademie der Wissenschaften*, ed. J. Bergmann. Wien.

Schirmunski, Viktor M. 1930. "Sprachgeschichte und Siedelungsmundarten." *Germanisch-Romanische Monatsschrift* 18,3/4: 113-22; 18,5/6: 171-88.

Schirmunski, Viktor M. 1962. *Deutsche Mundartkunde: Vergleichende Laut- und Formenlehre der deutschen Mundarten*. Berlin.

Smits, Caroline. 1996. *Disintegration of Inflection: The Case of Iowa Dutch*. Amsterdam.

Smits, Caroline. 1998. "Two Models for the Study of Language Contact: A Psycho-Linguistic Perspective Versus a Socio-Cultural Perspective." In *Historical Linguistics: Selected Papers from the 13th International Conference on Historical Linguistics, Düsseldorf, 10-17 August 1997*, ed. Monika S. Schmid, Jennifer R. Austin and Dieter Stein, 377-90. Amsterdam.

Trudgill, Peter. 1978. "Creolization in Reverse." *Transactions of the Philological Society 1976/77*: 32-50.

van Coetsem, F. 1995. "Outlining a Model of the Transmission Phenomenon in Language Contact." *Leuvense Bijdragen* 84, 1: 63-85.

van Kemenade, Ans. 1994. "Old and Middle English." In *The Germanic Languages*, ed. Ekkehard König and Johan van der Auwera, 110-41. London.

van Ness, Silke. 1994. "Pennsylvania German." In *The Germanic Languages*, ed. Ekkehard König and Johan van der Auwera, 420-38. London.

Weinreich, Uriel, William Labov, and Marvin I. Herzog. 1968. "Empirical Foundations for a Theory of Language Change." In *Directions for Historical Linguistics: A Symposium*, ed. W. P. Lehmann and Yakov Malkiel, 95-188. Austin.

Weinrich, Harald. 1985. *Textgrammatik der französischen Sprache*. 1st ed. 1982, reprint. Stuttgart.

Wiesinger, Peter. 1983. "Deutsche Dialektgebiete außerhalb des deutschen Sprachgebiets: Mittel-, Südost- und Osteuropa." In *Dialektologie: Ein Handbuch zur deutschen und allgemeinen Dialektforschung*, ed. Werner Besch, Ulrich Knoop, Wolfgang Putschke and Herbert Ernst Wiegand, 2: 900-29. Berlin.

Wolgadeutscher Sprachatlas (WDSA), aufgrund der von Georg Dinges 1925-1929 gesammelten Materialien, ed. Nina Berend and Rudolf Post. 1997. Tübingen.

Wurzel, Wolfgang U. 1996. "Morphologischer Strukturwandel: Typologische Entwicklungen im Deutschen." In *Deutschtypologisch*, ed. Ewald Lang and Gisela Zifonun, 492-524. Institut für deutsche Sprache, Jahrbuch 1995. Berlin.

Case system in Pennsylvania German personal pronouns
(cf. van Ness 1994, 430; Huffines 1989, 216)

Person	Nominative	Accusative	Dative
1st sing.	iç	miç	mir mer (unstressed)
	'I'	'me'	'me'
2nd sing.	du	diç	dir der (unstressed)
	'you'	'you'	'you'
3rd sing. masc.	ar	in en (unstressed)	im em (unstressed)
	'he'	'him'	'him'
3rd sing. fem.	si	si	ire/ir re (unstressed)
	'she'	'her'	'her'
3rd sing. neut.	es	es	im em (unstressed)
	'it'	'it'	'it'
1st plur.	mir mer (unstressed)	uns	uns
	'we'	'us'	'us'
2nd plur.	dir/ir der/er/ner/nir (unstressed)	aiç	aiç
	'you'	'you'	'you'
3rd plur.	si	si	ine ne (unstressed)
	'they'	'them'	'them'

Case system in Old English personal pronouns
(van Kemenade 1994, 121)

Person	Nominative	Accusative	Dative	Genitive
1ˢᵗ sing.	ic	me:	me:	mi:n
	'I'	'me'	'me'	'my/of me'
2ⁿᵈ sing.	_u	_e:	_e:	_i:n
	'you'	'you'	'you'	'your/of you'
3ʳᵈ sing. masc.	he:	hine	him	his
	'he'	'him'	'him'	'his/of him'
3ʳᵈ sing. fem.	he:o	hi:	hire	hire
	'she'	'her'	'her'	'her/of her'
3ʳᵈ sing. neut.	hit	hit	him	his
	'it'	'it'	'it'	'its/of it'
1ˢᵗ plur.	we:	u:s	u:s	u:re
	'we'	'us'	'us'	'our/of us'
2ⁿᵈ plur.	ge:	e:ow	e:ow	e:ower
	'you'	'you'	'you'	'your/of you'
3ʳᵈ plur.	hi:	hi:	him	hira
	'they'	'them'	'them'	'their/of them'

Case system in Danish personal pronouns
(Haberland 1994, 328)

Person	Non-oblique	Oblique	Possessive
1st sing.	jeg	mig	min
	'I'	'me'	'my'
2nd sing.	du	dig	din
	'you'	'you'	'your'
3rd sing. masc.	han	ham Old Scand. dative: honum	hans
[+ human]	'he'	'him'	'his'
3rd sing. fem.	hun	hende [hinne] Old Scand. dative: henni	hendes
[+ human]	'she'	'her'	'her'
3rd sing. neut.	det	det	dets
[- human]	'it'	'it'	'its'
3rd sing. non neut.	den	den	dens
[- human]	'it'	'it'	'its'
1st plur.	vi	os	vores/vor
	'we'	'us'	'our'
2nd plur.	I	jer	jeres/(eder)
	'you'	'you'	'your'
3rd plur.	de [di]	dem Old Scand. dative: _eim (distal demonstrative)	deres
	'they'	'them'	'their'

Case system in French "pronoms personnels conjoints"
(cf. Weinrich 1982, 82)

	Subject	Object	Partner
Speaker	je	me/m'	me/m'
(sing.)	'I' ('ich')	'me' ('mich')	'me' ('mir')
Addressee	tu	te/t'	te/t'
(sing.)	'you' ('du')	'you' ('dich')	'you' ('dir')
Reference (masc.)	il	le/l'	lui
(sing.)	'he' ('er')	'him' ('ihn')	'him' ('ihm')
Reference (femin.)	elle	la/l'	lui
(sing.)	'she' ('sie')	'her' ('sie')	'her' ('ihr')
Speaker	nous (on)	nous	nous
(plur.)	'we' ('wir')	'us' ('uns')	'us' ('uns')
Addressee	vous	vous	vous
(plur.)	'you' ('ihr, Sie')	'you' ('euch, Sie')	'you' ('euch, Ihnen')
Reference (masc.)	ils	les	leur
(plur.)	'they' ('sie')	'them' ('sie')	'them' (ihnen)
Reference (femin.)	elles	les	leur
(plur.)	'they' ('sie')	'them' ('sie')	'them' (ihnen)

Lexical representation of words: "decomposition" versus "full listing" (cf. Cholewa 1993)

DECOMPOSITION	FULL LISTING
	monomorphematic words
polymorphematic words:	polymorphematic words:
regular word formation	irregular word formation
productive morphological paradigms	less productive morphological paradigms
semantically transparent word structure	semantically less transparent word structure
morphemes of high frequency	morphemes of low frequency

Nina Berend
Institut für Deutsche Sprache
Mannheim, Germany

Zur Vergleichbarkeit von Sprachkontakten: Erfahrungen aus wolgadeutschen Sprachinseln in den USA und Russland

In diesem Beitrag werden Sprachinselvarietäten beschrieben, die in den amerikanischen wolgadeutschen Sprachinseln in Ellis County, Kansas existieren. Zwar liegen verschiedene Untersuchungen dieser Sprachinseln von dialektgeographischen und strukturellen Gesichtspunkten vor, nicht beschrieben wurden diese Sprachinseln aber bisher aus der Sicht der russlanddeutschen Dialekt- und Varietätenforschung. Dieser Gesichtspunkt scheint aber bezüglich der vergleichenden Sprachinselforschung besonders interessant und vielversprechend zu sein, da es sich um Sprachinseldialekte handelt, die einen Teil gemeinsamer russlanddeutscher Entwicklung aufweisen—die wolgadeutsch-russische Geschichtsphase. Es wird versucht, auf dieser Grundlage Gemeinsamkeiten und Unterschiede in der gegenwärtigen Sprachinselkonstellation, struktureller Beschaffenheit und Spracheinstellungslage in den Sprachinseln darzustellen. Nach einer kurzen Einleitung über die Geschichte und einige Anmerkungen zur gegenwärtigen Lage der Wolgadeutschen in Russland und in den USA im ersten Abschnitt wird dann ein typisch kansasdeutscher Beispieltext präsentiert (2). Danach erfolgt eine skizzenhafte Darstellung der Gemeinsamkeiten und Unterschiede der Kontaktvarietäten nach den einzelnen Bestandteilen bzw. Komponenten: des Dialekts als eigentlicher Basisvarietät des Wolgadeutschen (3.1) und des Einflusses der Umgebungssprache (Englisch und Russisch) auf die entsprechenden Dialektvarietäten (3.2). Abschließend werden einige Anmerkungen zum russischen Bestandteil, bzw. zu den Sprachresten des Russischen im Kansasdeutschen gemacht (3.3).

1. Was ist Wolgadeutsch?

Unter Wolgadeutsch wird die Sprache der früheren deutschen Sprachinseln in der Region um den russischen Fluss Wolga in Zentralrussland verstanden. Diese Sprachinseln wurden von Auswanderern aus verschiedenen Teilen Deutschlands, insbesondere aus westmitteldeutschen Regionen, und aus anderen Gegenden von 1764 bis 1767 gegründet. Die Einwohner werden traditionell "Wolgadeutsche" genannt, auch in Abgrenzung zu anderen regionalen Sprachinselgruppen in Russland, z.B. zu

Kaukasus-, Wolhynien-, Schwarzmeer- oder Sibiriendeutschen. Entsprechend hat sich für die in diesen Sprachinseln gesprochenen Dialekte die Bezeichnung "Wolgadeutsch" eingebürgert, die sich bis heute gehalten hat. Sprachgeographisch gesehen handelte es sich bei der Gründung dieser Sprachinseln im 18. Jahrhundert vorwiegend um westmitteldeutsche Dialekte rheinfränkischer Prägung; vorhanden waren aber auch einige ostthüringische, obersächsische und niederpreußische Mundarten, wie von der Forschung am Anfang des 20. Jahrhunderts festgestellt wurde (Dinges 1923). Obwohl keine genaueren dialektgeographischen Untersuchungen zur Ausgangssituation vorliegen, kann man anhand vorhandener Informationen davon ausgehen, dass Hessisch und Pfälzisch die vorherrschenden Dialekttypen an der Wolga waren.

Die Region in Zentralrussland, in der Wolgadeutsch gesprochen wurde, war vergleichsweise groß und umfasste zu Beginn mehr als hundert Siedlungen. Die unten abgebildete Karte aus dem *Wolgadeutschen Sprachatlas* (vgl. WDSA 1997) vermittelt einen Eindruck über Größe, geographische Strukturierung und teilweise über die ethnische Zusammensetzung der gesamten wolgadeutschen Sprachinselregion am Anfang des 20. Jahrhunderts. (Zum Zeitpunkt der Entstehung des Atlasses war die wolgadeutsche Sprachinselregion bereits zu einer "Wolgadeutschen Republik" geworden.) Die ursprünglichen Erstsiedlungen, für die von Georg Dinges die Bezeichnung "Mutterkolonien" eingeführt wurde, befinden sich rechts und links des Wolgaflusses; die rechts und links weiter entfernten Siedlungen sind die sog. Tochterkolonien und wurden im Laufe des 19. Jahrhunderts von Umsiedlern aus den Mutterkolonien gegründet. Diese Neugründungen sind auch häufig durch "neu" markiert, wie Neu Mariental, Neu Obermonjou usw.

In allen ursprünglichen und in dieser Zeit neugegründeten Kolonien war das Wolgadeutsche die Hauptverkehrsvarietät in den Sprachinseln: Es wurde in allen Domänen, allen Sprachsituationen und zu verschiedenen Kommunikationszwecken eingesetzt. Die wolgadeutschen Dialekte waren zunächst keinem Einfluss von anderen russlanddeutschen— dialektgeographisch gesehen sehr unterschiedlichen—Dialekten ausgesetzt, z.B. dem Bairischen, Schwäbischen oder Wolhyniendeutschen, da diese Dialekte nicht an der Wolga, sondern in ganz anderen Regionen Russlands verbreitet waren. Typisch für spätere Phasen der Existenz des Wolgadeutschen (im 20. Jahrhundert) waren dann bestimmte Dialektmischungen, die sich aus den neuartigen Dialektkontakten in und zwischen den einzelnen Mutter- und Tochterkolonien ergaben (Dinges 1925, Dulson 1941). Außerdem ist für das ursprüngliche, Original-Wolgadeutsche, auch eine bestimmte "Russisch-Färbung" typisch, wie Untersuchungen aus dieser Zeit bezeugen (Dinges 1917, 1929; Schiller 1929). Die Existenz in anderssprachiger Umgebung ist nicht ohne sprachliche Folgen geblieben. Laut den Untersuchungen von Dinges haben die Wolgadeutschen bis 1876, also bereits bis zum Beginn der offiziellen Russifizierung der Kolonien, rund 800 Russizismen in ihren Sprachgebrauch integriert (Dinges 1929).

Am Anfang des 20. Jahrhunderts, mit der sog. stolypinschen Bodenreform, begann dann die Neugründung von wolgadeutschen Siedlungen auch in weiter entfernten Regionen Russlands, insbesondere in Westsibirien (Altai-Region, Omsker, Tomsker und Nowosibirsker Gebiete) und in Nordkasachstan. Auch hier entstanden zunächst einzelne geschlossene Siedlungen, die von Umsiedlern aus den wolgadeutschen Mutterkolonien gegründet wurden. Als 1941 der zweite Weltkrieg ausbrach, wurde die gesamte wolgadeutsche Sprachinselregion beseitigt, indem die deutsche Bevölkerung auf Befehl der Regierung komplett in den Osten des Landes umgesiedelt wurde. Damit wurde die fast zwei Jahrhunderte andauernde kontinuierliche Sprachentwicklung des Wolgadeutschen abrupt beendet und es begann die neue, sibirische (bzw. kasachische, mittelasiatische oder fernöstliche) Phase der Sprachentwicklung der Wolgadeutschen: die Zwei- oder Mehrsprachigkeitsphase, die den gesamten Nachkriegszeitraum prägte und auch in der Gegenwart noch andauert. Vielerorts kamen Wolgadeutsch-Sprecher durch diese Umsiedlung zum ersten Mal in unmittelbaren Kontakt nicht nur mit dem Russischen, sondern auch teilweise mit dem Kasachischen, Kirgisischen, Usbekischen oder verschiedenen Sprachen und Dialekten der einheimischen Völker im Norden und Osten des Landes.

Diese Umstrukturierungen führten dazu, dass im Laufe der Nachkriegszeit die Sprecher des Wolgadeutschen, insbesondere die jüngere Generation, allmählich zwei- bzw. auch dreisprachig geworden sind. Wolgadeutsch war nicht mehr die allein verwendete Sprache, sondern es bildete sich nach und nach eine wolgadeutsch-russische Diglossie heraus, die bis heute besteht. Ein bestimmter Teil der jungen Generation der Wolgadeutschen ist russisch-einsprachig geworden und ist mit dem Wolgadeutschen höchstens als "Erinnerungssprache" vertraut. In der Nachkriegsentwicklung ist außerdem eine starke Vermischung mit anderen russlanddeutschen Dialekten eingetreten, mit denen das Wolgadeutsche sich nun seit mehreren Jahrzehnten in unmittelbaren Kontakt befindet. Gegenwärtig existieren in Russland nur noch vereinzelt typisch wolgadeutsche Siedlungen, in denen die Nachfahren der ursprünglichen Wolgadeutschen leben, die noch das originelle Wolgadeutsch sprechen. Diese Siedlungen befinden sich in Westsibirien (Omsker und Altai-Gebiet) und wurden in den 1970er und 1980er Jahren von den Mitarbeitern der Omsker dialektologischen Schule unter der Leitung von Hugo Jedig erforscht (vgl. Berend/Jedig 1991).

In Kansas existiert das Wolgadeutsche seit 1875, seit eine intensive Auswanderungswelle aus dem Wolgagebiet nach Übersee begonnen hatte. Wolgadeutsche aus Russland siedelten nach Kansas um und gründeten zahlreiche Siedlungen in Ellis County (Keel 1982). Die neugegründeten Orte bekamen die "alten" Namen aus Russland, so dass wir die vermutlichen Auswanderungsorte auf der Karte der Wolgadeutschen Republik (Abb. 1) ausfindig machen können: Obermonjou, Herzog, Marxstadt (vorher Katharinenstadt), Liebental, Schönchen, Pfeiffer Eine sprachgeographische Klassifikation im Jahr 1982 hat ergeben, dass in den

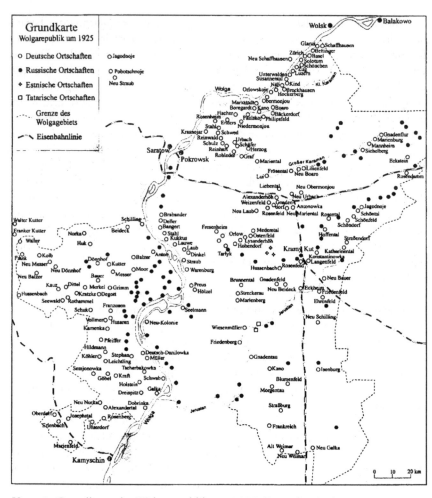

Karte 1. Grundkarte der Wolgarepublik um 1925 (Berend, 1997).

wolgadeutschen Siedlungen Obermonjou, Pfeifer, Schoenchen und Liebenthal südhessische Dialekte und in Herzog/Victoria westpfälzische Dialekte gesprochen wurden. In Catherine wurde eine westmitteldeutsche Stadtmundart festgestellt (Keel 1982, 108). Die Existenzbedingungen der mitgebrachten wolgadeutschen Dialekte haben sich in der neuen amerikanischen Umgebung nicht gravierend verändert: Auch hier war zunächst das Wolgadeutsche die einzige Verkehrsvarietät, die—ähnlich wie in Russland—in allen Funktionen und Domänen verwendet wurde und die nur zu anderen wolgadeutschen Dialekten im Kontakt stand. (Es gab in der näheren Umgebung zunächst keine anderen deutsch-amerikanischen Sprachinseln außer dem Wolgadeutschen.) Dank der kompakten Ansiedlung war auch hier am Anfang die Möglichkeit gegeben, über eine Zeitphase hinweg vorwiegend deutsch-einsprachig zu bleiben, ohne intensive Kontakte zum Englischen aufzunehmen. Dies hat sich aber im Zusammenhang mit politischen Ereignissen am Anfang des 20. Jahrhunderts rasch verändert. Das Deutsche wurde aus politischen Gründen als Unterrichtssprache aufgehoben, in den Verwendungsdomänen eingeengt und die Wolgadeutschen wurden von einer Generation zur anderen zweisprachig. Als Folge büßte das Wolgadeutsche seine Kommunikationsfunktionen ein und besitzt heute nur noch symbolisch identitätsstiftenden und –erhaltenden Wert bei der älteren Generation der Wolgadeutschen. Die Erforschung des Deutschen in Kansas wurde in den letzten Jahrzehnten vor allem am Deutschen Seminar der Universität Kansas in Lawrence intensiv geführt (Keel 1981, 1982, 1989, 1993, 1994 u.a.; Johnson 1993, 1994 u.a). Zur Zeit wird unter der Leitung von William Keel ein Atlas der deutschen Dialekte in Kansas vorbereitet, der auch *online* zur Verfügung gestellt werden soll. Die unten abgebildete Karte der deutschen Sprachinseln in Kansas ist die Grundkarte dieses Atlasunternehmens (vgl. dazu Keel 1989).

Trotz der um sich greifenden fast vollständigen englischen Einsprachigkeit ist das Deutsche in den Sprachinseln in Ellis County gegenwärtig noch relativ gut präsent. Durch die Doppelmigration in der Vergangenheit (Deutschland – Russland – USA) scheint die wolgadeutsche Sprachbevölkerung so etwas wie eine dreifache Identität entwickelt und bewahrt zu haben. Erstaunlich ist dabei das zum Vorschein kommende starke wolgadeutsche Selbstbewusstsein. Sie sind in erster Linie natürlich—und zwar bei direktem Nachfragen—*Amerikaner*, aber mit *deutschem background*, wobei auf die Angabe "deutsch" auch gleich unmittelbar die Präzisierung "wolgadeutsch" folgt. Zumindest in Gesprächen mit mir hat sich die wolgadeutsche Komponente der Identität als erstaunlich lebendig dargestellt. Auffällig war auch die äußerst positive Einstellung zur wolgadeutsch-russischen Vergangenheit. Zwar sei es in Russland *hart* gewesen, im allgemeinen herrscht jedoch die positive Erinnerungsattitüde. Diese überwiegend positive Einstellung sollte eigentlich auch nicht überraschend sein: Im Vergleich zu den "echten" Russlanddeutschen und Wolgadeutschen kennen die Kansasdeutschen aus eigener Geschichte weder die Periode der starken Russifizierung nach 1870, noch

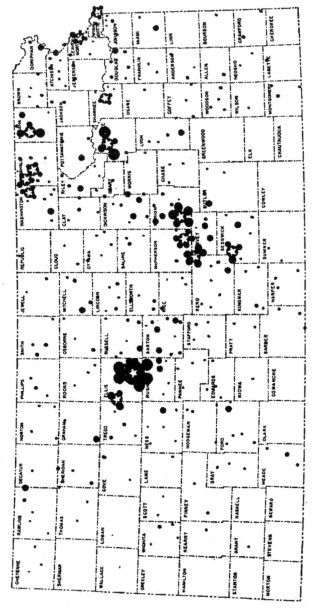

GERMAN
SETTLEMENTS IN KANSAS

• Unimportant   • Quite Important

• Of some importance   ✱ Of major importance

Karte 2. Kansasdeutsche Sprachinseln (Carman, 1962).

die russische Revolution 1917, die harten Jahre der stalinistischen Diktatur und den ersten und zweiten Weltkrieg. Diese politischen Ereignisse, die die Geschichte der Russlanddeutschen in Russland, wie bekannt, sehr negativ prägten, sind den kansasdeutschen Wolgadeutschen erspart geblieben. Äußerlich kommt die positive Einstellung—um nur ein Beispiel zu nennen—an den immer noch vorhandenen Straßennamen zum Ausdruck: Viele Straßen tragen Namen, die an Russland erinnern, z.B. Samara, Moskau, Petersburg, Kazan. Auch Namen nach den großen russischen Flüssen Volga, Karaman und Don existieren noch (vgl. Abb. 3).

Dieser Beitrag beruht auf Daten, die ich während einer Forschungsreise in die wolgadeutschen Siedlungen von Ellis County gesammelt habe. Es handelt sich um Interviews und Gruppengespräche mit Wolgadeutschen, die auf Band aufgenommen und anschließend inhaltlich und sprachlich ausgewertet wurden. Alle Interviews und Gespräche wurden auf Wolgadeutsch geführt.[1] Das Ziel dieses Beitrags ist, einen Überblick über die wolgadeutschen Sprachkontaktvarietäten zu bekommen, die gegenwärtig noch in Kansas existieren, und diese mit den wolgadeutschen Varietäten in Russland zu vergleichen. Bei dieser vergleichenden Analyse sollen zunächst einige auffällige Erscheinungen des Wolgadeutschen in den USA festgehalten und interpretiert werden, die während der separaten Entwicklung stattgefunden haben.

2. Beispieltext

Der Text "Hays Daily News" wird hier als ein typischer Auschnitt aus einem größeren Korpus von Sprachaufnahmen präsentiert und soll dem Leser eine allgemeine Vorstellung über die kansasdeutsche Sprechweise vermitteln. Er dokumentiert das gegenwärtig in den Sprachinseln verwendete Deutsch,[2] für dessen Bezeichnung im Folgenden der Ausdruck "kansasdeutsche Kontaktvarietät" verwendet wird. Es handelt sich bei dieser Sprechweise nicht mehr um "reine" Dialekte, wie das vermutlich zum Zeitpunkt der Auswanderung aus Deuschland im 18. Jahrhundert der Fall war, sondern um mit zwei Kontaktsprachen gemischte und aus verschiedenen Komponenten bestehende Varietät. Entsprechend der Entwicklungsgeschichte konstituiert sich die kansasdeutsche Kontaktvarietät aus drei verschiedenen Sprachteilen. Das ist erstens der deutsch-dialektale Bestandteil, also das eigentliche Deutsche, der zunächst aus Deutschland nach Russland und später in die USA "mitgenommen" wurde. Der zweite Bestandteil des Textes ist das Englische—das Ergebnis der deutsch-englischen Sprachkontakte während des letzten Jahrhunderts. Den dritten Sprachteil bilden die Russizismen—die aus Russland mitgebrachten Teile der früheren Kontaktsprache Russisch aus dem vorletzten Jahrhundert, die sich bis in die Gegenwart in der Sprache der Wolgadeutschen in Kansas gehalten haben.

Aus Gründen der Verständlichkeit für das Lesen der Originalvariante des Textes wurde auf eine enge Transkription verzichtet und eine sprech- und schriftnahe Form

Russische Straßennamen in Munjor, Ellis County, Kansas, USA

der Darstellung gewählt. In der linken Spalte ist die Originalvariante des Kansasdeutschen angeführt, in der rechten die Übersetzung ins Hochdeutsche. Die explizit englischen Teile sind in Originalform angeführt (ohne Markierung der eventuell deutsch beeinflussten Aussprache). In der rechten Spalte ist der Text ins Hochdeutsche übertragen; in den rechteckigen Klammern einige russische und Mischformen auf Hochdeutsch erklärt. Die russischen Teile im Text sind unterstrichen, die englischen Elemente und verschiedene Mischformen sind durch Kursivschrift hervorgehoben.[3]

"Hays Daily News"

S: Sprecherin des Catherine-Deutschen
I: Interviewerin

Kansasdeutsch   Übersetzung

S: Wie ich kleen war / han se so viel   S: Wie ich klein war, haben sie so viel
Dreckstorme gehat / *dust storms* han se se   Dreckstürme gehabt. Dust storms
geruuve / un *for* ein paar Jahr in eine Reihe   haben sie sie gerufen, und paar Jahre
han se gar keine / gar nix geernt *you know* /   in einer Reihe haben sie gar keine . . .,
and des ware die arme Zeide / wie ich kleen   gar nichts geerntet,you know. And . . .
war / drum wejs ich was arme Zeide sin /   Das waren die alten Zeiten, wie ich
because / weche des - ich kann mich des   klein war. Deswegen weiß ich, was
noch erinnre // s- war doch nicht so   arme Zeiten sind, because wegendas,
schlimm als wie in Russland *or sou you*   ich kann mich daran noch erinnern. Es
know / mir hääre viel von do driwwe was   war doch nicht so schlimm als wie in
driwwe vorgong / des war schlimm..-   Russland or so, you know. Wir hören
                                                  viel von da drüben, was drüben
                                                  vorging, das war schlimm.

I: A vun wem härt ihr was do driwwe   I: Und von wem hört ihr, was da
vorgeht?   drüben vorgeht?
S: *by* Daily News hört man da,you know   S: Von Daily News hört man das, you
wie arm das allweil is—in Russland seit das   know.
communism nicht mehr is / die arme Leit do   Wie arm das allweil [jetzt] ist in
driwwe / die / was ich denk / die sin-s nicht Russland,seit das communism nicht
gewejnt / *see* / do war *communism for*   mehr ist. Die armen Leute da drüben,
siebzig Jahr un die Leit wo ware /   die ... Was ich denke, die sind es nicht
die sin das gar nicht gewejnt / die / mich   gewöhnt, see, da war communism
kommts so vor als wenn sie / die wize gar   siebzig Jahre und die Leute, wo waren
nicht / mich bedauern se / aber mich kommts   . . . ,die sind das gar nicht gewöhnt,

vor als / die sin das gar nicht gewejnt / die hawwe immer mit *communism* gewohnt / un jetz haben sie ihr *freedom* / ihr fr..../ die wisse gar nicht wie sie-s zu *handle* hawwe *for* jetz / denkste nicht das das so is / Mich kommts so vor / *Am I saying this*—tu ich dir recht verzähle?

I: Ja ja
S: So kommts mich vor / Und die /

I: Tut ihr woll Zeidunge lese?
S: Tu ich . . . ? / oh ja
I: un was forche Zeidung lest ihr?
S: Die *Hays Daily News* / Ja ich les die *Hays Daily News* / Un ich hab <u>vor ne Rass</u> haw ich hier paar Jahr zurick haw ich kleine Kinner / ... lerne hier - *catechism* gelernt / *for* zwanzig Jahr / ich hab awer ufgehört, geb zu alt for des, die jungen tun das jetz /

I: Ihr seid doch noch ganz jung
S: Ich bin *sixty two* / zweiunsechzich
I: Ah, zweiunsechzich schon?
S: Ja zweiunsechtich / *Sou* no bin ich grad zahaus un schaff grad *for* die Phadesch / Ich hab/ mein Zwillingbruder der *teacht* noch drunne in A. / der *teacht* Deutsch heit un *Spanish* / sou dem seine Kinnr kenne ouch Deutsch un *Spanish* sprechen.

I: Awwe high-Daitsch, high German ja?

die . . . Mich kommt es so vor, als wenn sie . . . , die wissen gar nicht . . . Mich bedauern sie, aber mich kommt es vor als. . . Die sind das gar nicht gewöhnt, die haben immer mit communism gewohnt und jetzt haben sie ihr freedom, ihr . . . , die wissen gar nicht, wie sie es zu handle [bewerkstelligen] haben jetzt. Denkst du nicht, dass das so ist? Mich kommt es so vor. Am I saying this— tue ich dir recht erzählen?

I: Ja ja
S: So kommt es mich vor. Und die . . .

I: Tut ihr wohl Zeitungen lesen?
S: Tu ich . . . ? Oh ja!
I: Und was für Zeitung lest ihr?
S: Die Hays Daily News. Ja, ich lese die Hays Daily News. Und ich habe— vor einer Weile habe ich hier—paar Jahr zurück habe ich kleine Kinder (tue lernen hier) . . . catechism gelernt, zwanzig Jahre. Ich habe aber aufgehört, werde zu alt, die Jungen tun das jetzt.

I: Ihr seid doch noch ganz jung!
S: Ich bin sixty-two, zweiundsechzig
I: Ah, zweiundsechzig schon?
S: Ja, zweiundsechzig. So, nun bin ich gerade zu Hause und schaffe gerade für die Pfarrer. Ich habe . . . Mein Zwillingsbruder, der teacht noch da unten in A. Der teacht Deutsch heute, und Spanish, so, dem seine Kinder können auch Deutsch und Spanish sprechen.
I: Aber high-Deutsch, high German, ja?

248

S: Der kann se alle zwei, der kann all zwei Deutsch wege der - der war in Deutschland *for* paar Jahr..- hats *gegliche* driwwe.

I: Und mit eurem Bruder, der wo farmt, mit dem tut ihr Deutsch verzähle?

S: Oh ja, midm sprech ich Deutsch.

I: Wenn wir jetz hinkomme, kennt ihr e bisje verzähle?

S: Wenn er dorre is / der is am End ins Feld / der is am End ins Feld / awwr wenn er dorre is / nicht . . . / *see* wenn ich *talk* von die arme Zeit no krich ich bisje Träne in die ouche

S: Der kann sie alle zwei, der kann alle zwei Deutsch wegen der . . . der war in Deutschland) paar Jahr. Hat es geglichen[gefallen] drüben.

I: Und mit eurem Bruder, der wo farmt, mit dem tut ihr Deutsch erzählen?

S: Oh ja, mit ihm spreche ich Deutsch.

I: Wenn wir jetzt hinkommen, könnt ihr ein bisschen erzählen?

S: Wenn er dort ist, der ist am Ende ins Feld.

Der ist am Ende ins Feld, aber wenn er dort ist . . . Nicht . . .
Wir können bisschen sprechen mit ihm. See, wenn ich talk von die arme Zeit , dann kriege ich bisschen Tränen in die Augen.

3. Kansasdeutsche Sprachkontaktvarietäten: Ausgewählte Beispielanalyse

3.1. Was ist russlanddeutsch an dem Kansasdeutschen?

Betrachten wir nun als erstes die Grundkomponente der kansasdeutschen Sprachkontaktvarietät: den deutschen Dialekt. Zunächst stellten sich in unserem Zusammenhang Fragen nach dem wolgadeutsch- bzw. russlanddeutsch-dialektalen Bestandteil der kansasdeutschen Sprachkontaktvarietäten. Sind diese Varietäten an einigen Merkmalen als russlanddeutsche zu erkennen? Sind russlanddeutsche bzw. wolgadeutsche Marker in der Dialektstruktur vorhanden? Würden russlanddeutsche und kansasdeutsche Sprecher des Wolgadeutschen einander verstehen, wenn sie ausschließlich ihre wolgadeutsche Dialektvarietät sprechen würden (ohne englische und russische Kontakteinflüsse)? Eine erste Auswertung einiger in Kansas erhobenen Materialien weist darauf hin, dass eine Kontrastierung mit dem Wolgadeutschen in Russland einerseits viele Ähnlichkeiten der deutsch-dialektalen Struktur der verglichenen Varietäten ergibt, andererseits aber zeigen sich auch einige Unterschiede. Versucht man die einzelnen Phänomene zu systematisieren, so ergeben sich drei Gruppen von Spracherscheinungen, die Ähnlichkeiten und Kontraste repräsentieren und die im Folgenden an einigen ausgewählten Beispielen veranschaulicht werden sollen.

In der ersten Gruppe können solche Erscheinungen bzw. Sprach- oder Dialektmerkmale zusammengefasst werden, die an den russlanddeutschen Sprachgebrauch allgemein erinnern bzw. als allgemein-russlanddeutsche Erscheinungen zu erkennen sind.[4] Es sind zahlreiche Erscheinungen dieses Typs im Kansasdeutschen festgestellt worden. (1)-(4)—die Doppelnegation und die Umschreibungen für Genitiv[5]—sind z.B. typische Belege dieser ersten Gruppe:

(1) So hun mir unser Fleisch angemacht, weil mir hadde *ka* Eisbox *net*. [T8:4]

(2) *Mei Tade sei Wees*, die war von Russland "Mein(em) Vater seine Tante, die war von Russland." [T6:14]

(3) Un awr *den Jack sei Kinner* die kenne gar ka Daitsch. Der hot Daitsch in der University genomme, high German, but der kann nix, nix spreche. [T8:6].

(4) un *mei äschte Mann den sei Lait* des ware Pannestiel und den sei Lait hun bloß Daitsch geplaudert. [T8:2]

Ein besonderer Effekt der Ähnlichkeit entsteht aber vor allem durch die gemeinsame Lexik. Es handelt sich hier besonders z.B. um phonetisch eigenartig geformte Lexeme, die genau in derselben Form auch im Russlanddeutschen vorkommen, wie z.B. *ejndun* [eindu:n] "gleich"; *wurum* [vu:rum] "irgendwo" u.a. Zu den allgemein-russlanddeutschen Erscheinungen im lexikalischen Bereich zählen auch typische semantische Verschiebungen. So bedeutet *Fraind* z.B. immer "Verwandte" und niemals "Freunde." Genau in dieser Bedeutung sind die Lexeme auch im Kansasdeutschen belegt:

(5) do sain so viel—my Rohr family is net arich groß, der GR da oben ist net *Freind* mit mich. No ich denk wenn man noch weit zurick geht und na sin sie wahrscheinlich alle *Freind*—wenn sie zurick nach Daitschland gehe. [T8:8]

Das Wort *nejdiche* (eigentlich: *nötigen*) ist allgemein verbreitet in der Bedeutung "einladen"; die semantische Komponente *zwingen* (wie *nötigen*) ist in diesem Zusammenhang nicht bekannt. Eine ähnliche Verwendung wurde auch im Kansasdeutschen festgestellt:

(5) Oh ja die—wenn jemand heiratet, die werden bald alle *genötigt*. [T2:7].

Die angeführten Beispiele (1) bis (5), die als Phänomene der ersten Gruppe zusammengefasst wurden, zeigen die gemeinsamen Merkmale der dialektalen

Bestandteile der kansasdeutschen und russlanddeutschen Varietäten. Sprachliche Erscheinungen, die in einer zweiten Gruppe zusammengefasst werden können, konkretisieren die sprachliche Herkunft des Kansasdeutschen und bestimmen sie als Wolgadeutsch. Das sind in erster Linie auffällige typisch wolgadeutsche Wörter, die in Russland nur in wolgadeutschen Dialekten vorkommen (auch mit typischer phonetischer Realisierung), z.B. *Tade* (Vater, Papa), *Filzstiwwel* (Filzstiefel), *sachtig* (langsam, nicht schnell), *marodig* (müde), *bal* (bald, in der Bedeutung *fast*), *Hemm* (Hemd), *schamant* (ziemlich gut), *Schtigger* (Stück, in der Bedeutung *ungefähr*), *holle* (holen, immer statt *nehmen*), *nodr* (nachher, statt *dann*), *maaje* (zu Besuch sein, Zeit gemeinsam erholend verbringen). Einige Beispiele zu dem Gebrauch dieser Wörter im Kansasdeutschen (die typischen wolgadeutschen Wörter sind durch Kursivschrift hervorgehoben):

(6) Der *Tade* kunnd bissje englisch, awr die Mame net—so wie wir gelernt han in die Schul, dann haben wir die Mame gelernt drhem. [T6:2]

(7) well, ich misst halt denge—you know, des kommt mir grade so bissje *sachtich* in Kop nai, you know. [T5:14]

(8) Du gebst wohl *marodig*? . . . ich kann lang schlafe morje früh. [T3:3]

(9) Wie lang muss ich noch schawwe? *Schtigger* värzehn Johr. [T3:10]

(10) Mir winshe eich Glick   [Wir wünschen euch Glück
     Midm *Hemm* uwm Rick   mit dem Hemd auf dem Rücken
     Geld uwm Leib   Geld auf dem Leib
     Das die Hosse druff bleibt [T]   dass die Hose drauf bleibt]
     (wolgadeutscher Neujahrswunsch)

Neben den typisch russlanddeutschen Escheinungen der ersten Gruppe und den typisch wolgadeutschen Lexemen der zweiten Gruppe lassen sich im Kansasdeutschen auch andere Sprachphänomene beobachten, die zwar einerseits auch in das russlanddeutsch-wolgadeutsche Bild passen, andererseits aber den Eindruck eines übermäßig "konservativ" wirkenden Wolgadeutschen hervorrufen, zumindest auf dem Hintergrund des gegenwärtig in Russland existierenden Wolgadeutschen. Dieser Eindruck entsteht zu einem großen Teil auf der Grundlage der Häufigkeitsverschiebung bei der Verwendung von bestimmten Merkmalen, die zwar auch im Russlanddeutschen bekannt sind, aber bei weitem nicht so häufig vorkommen. Merkmale dieser Art können als kansasdeutsche Phänomene gelten und in einer dritten Gruppe von Sprachmerkmalen zusammengefasst werden. Dazu gehören z.B. Erscheinungen des

Rhotazismus wie *harre, guuri* in (11); verschiedene Phänomene der im Kansasdeutschen sehr häufigen Kasusmischung,[6] und viele andere Sprachmerkmale, die bei allen Sprechern in allen Erhebungsorten belegt wurden.

(11) Well I mean, for zwei Woche *harre* mir e *guuri* Zeit "Gut, ich meine, zwei Wochen lang hatten wir eine gute Zeit." [T7]

(12) (. . .) un die Lait früher hadde all en Platz do *ins Dorf*, un nachher ihr Land drauß, un Summers sain sie uf die Farm gange und hun die Farm gschafft un *in Winter* hun sie do *in Dorf* gewohnt. [T8:1]

Ein sehr typisches Beispiel aus dieser Klasse von Sprachmerkmalen soll hier etwas näher beleuchtet werden. Es handelt sich um die Verwendung des Verbs *geben* statt *werden* in der Funktion eines Hilfsverbs und in der Passivperiphrase (Bellmann 1998). Die Beispiele (13) bis (20) zeigen zunächst die typische Verwendungsweise[7] des Verbs *geben* im Kansasdeutschen:

(13) Des nemmt dene Russe noch värzich Johr, bis die besser *gebe* als wie sie jetz sin, see. [T5:7]

(14) See später naus, des *gebt* immer besser deng ich "Später hinaus, das wird immer besser denke ich." [T5:28]

(15) Was mache die do driwwe, wenn die Lait alt *gebe*? [T3:7]

(16) haw ich kleine Kinner / . . . lerne hier—*catechism* gelernt / *for* zwanzig Jahr / ich hab awer ufgehört, *geb* zu alt for des. [T2:3]

(17) well die Lait die schawwe net do driwwe—die sitze ufn Arsch you know un *gebe* faul, . . . you know—me muss schawwe we- me was will, gelle? [T5:17]

(18) . . . would like that, Rohr—ja, no täde die all widich *gebe*, gelle? . . . dann täten die alle wütig werden, gell? [T5:25]

(19) see wir han . . . in south west Kansas han mir viel Geld, auch unser Taxe sin hoch, . . . well unser Haiser *gebe* alle Johr tairer. [T3:6]

(20) Des is ach dohiwwe so, do *gebts* bezahlt. [T3:9].

Wie ist das Verhältnis in Bezug auf diese Spracherscheinung in Russland? In den wolgadeutschen Dialekten in Russland[8] ist die Passivperiphrase nur im Wolgadeutschen aus der ursprünglichen westpfälzischen Mutterkolonie Mariental belegt (vgl. Abb. 1). Das entspricht in etwa auch den sprachgeschichtlichen Überlegungen Bellmanns über die Verbreitungsareale der Passivperiphrase im Deutschen (Bellmann 1998). Es ist anzunehmen, dass das *geben*-Passiv im 18. Jahrhundert vermutlich in die Siedlungskolonien an die Wolga aus der Westpfalz mitgebracht wurde, wo es in den Nachfolge-Ansiedlungsgebieten teilweise bis heute erhalten geblieben ist. Das Beispiel (21) veranschaulicht die typische Verwendung der Passivperiphrase im gegenwärtigen Wolgadeutschen im Altai-Gebiet (Sibirien):

(21) un sive Krents—bis an die Fenschter hat mize *abgeriss kin*, hat mize *unerbaut kin*, ach ganz *gschmiert kin* "Und sieben Kränze bis an die Fenster hat müssen *abgerissen werden*, hat müssen *unterbaut werden*, auch ganz *geschmiert werden*." [RT 2/12]

Die Passivperiphrase wurde aber in Russland nur im Westpfälzischen, nicht jedoch in anderen, z.B. hessischen Dialekten belegt. Die häufige Verwendung im Kansasdeutschen ist daher auffällig und es stellt sich die Frage nach dem Ursprung dieser Erscheinung z.B. im hessisch-geprägten Dialekt von Munjor oder dem Katharinenstädter Dialekt von Catherine. Angesichts der dialektgeographischen Unterschiede zwischen den einzelnen Sprachinseln in Ellis County (Keel 1982, 108) ist das Erscheinen der Passivperiphrase in allen gegenwärtigen kansasdeutschen Varietäten nicht selbstverständlich. Zu erwarten wäre diese Konstruktion—in Anlehnung an die bisher für diesen Fall dokumentierten Sprachverhältnisse im Wolgadeutschen in Russland— allenfalls im westpfälzischen Victoria/Herzog. Die Tatsache, dass diese Erscheinung nicht nur im Rheinfränkischen, sondern auch im Hessischen und in der Ausgleichsmundart von Catherine vorkommt, kann meines Erachtens nur durch Konvergenzerscheinungen in den kontaktierenden kansasdeutschen Sprachinseldialekten erklärt werden, die in den letzten Jahrzehnten stattgefunden haben. Die Konvergenz sieht ja den Wandel des Grades der Variation vor. Auer / Di Luzio (1988, 4) schreiben "[. . .] it should be obvious at this point that convergence may diminish or increase variation in the individual's or the speech community's repertoire."

Es ist offensichtlich, dass in den kansasdeutschen Dialekten eine derartige Konvergenz im Sinne der Verminderung der Sprachvariation stattgefunden hat, indem die *geben*/*werden*-Variation sich zugunsten der *geben*-Variante gewandelt hat. Das Ergebnis ist die Expansion des Gebrauchs des Verbs *geben*, wie sie für die russlanddeutschen Sprachverhältnisse keineswegs typisch ist. In Russland lässt sich genau das Gegenteil beobachten: Die Verminderung der *geben*/*werden*-Variation zugunsten der *werden*-Variante. Die Konvergenz im Kansasdeutschen kann sowohl interne als auch externe Gründe haben. Eine mögliche Erklärung könnte vermutlich auch die formelle Ähnlichkeit der Verben dt. *geben* und engl. *get* sein, die zum Ersatz des englischen *get* durch *gebt* führt (to *get* older—ich *geb* zu alt), ohne dass das dt. *werden* überhaupt hier ins Spiel gebracht wird.

Als Schlussfolgerung aus den hier vorgeführten Beispielanalysen kann festgehalten werden, dass die kansasdeutschen Dialekte (bzw. der deutsch-dialektale Kern der Varietäten) den russlanddeutschen wolgadeutschen Dialekten strukturell gesehen insgesamt sehr ähnlich sind. Intensive Kontakte der Dialekte in Kansas untereinander (im Rahmen des überwiegend westmitteldeutschen Typs rheinfränkischer Prägung) haben jedoch zu verschiedenen Konvergenzerscheinungen geführt, die die lokale Variation vermindert haben. Die Variation gegenüber dem gegenwärtigen Wolgadeutschen in Russland wurde dadurch erhöht. Durch diese Konvergenzerscheinungen sind bestimmte typisch wolgadeutsche (im Sinne von Viktor Schirmunski: primäre) Merkmale in der Struktur des Kansasdeutschen verfestigt und im Gebrauch stabilisiert worden. Durch diese Merkmale vermittelt das Kansasdeutsche schließlich einen ursprünglicheren ("konservativen") Eindruck im Kontrast zu dem Wolgadeutschen in Russland, in dem diese primären Merkmale zum großen Teil bereits abgebaut wurden, und somit eine Angleichung an andere russlanddeutsche Dialekte erfolgt ist.

3.2. Deutsch-englisch und deutsch-russisch

In diesem Abschnitt geht es um die zweite Komponente der kansasdeutschen Kontaktvarietät: um den Einfluss der englischen Umgebungs- und Kontaktsprache auf das Deutsche in den wolgadeutschen Sprachinseln in Kansas. Auch hier wird, wie in der vorherigen Betrachtung, das Kansasdeutsche mit dem Russlanddeutschen kontrastiert. Es handelt sich um den Vergleich des englischen Bestandteils im kansasdeutschen Wolgadeutsch mit dem russischen Bestandteil im russlanddeutschen Wolgadeutsch. Diese Vergleichskonstellation ist deswegen besonders günstig, weil es sich beim Wolgadeutschen um eine konstante Komponente als Ausgangsbasis des Vergleichs zweier Sprachenpaare handelt: des wolgadeutsch-russischen und des wolgadeutsch-englischen Sprachenpaars. Selbstverständlich kann im Folgenden keine ausführliche Analyse der deutsch-englischen Sprachkontakte in Kansas erfolgen.[9] Es sollen lediglich einige wichtige Gemeinsamkeiten und Unterschiede mit dem Russlanddeutschen skizziert und vom kommunikativen Gesichtspunkt aus und aus der Sicht der Sprecher interpretiert werden. Eine vollständige linguistische Analyse und Interpretation muss einer detaillierten Untersuchung vorbehalten bleiben.

Bei der Analyse des englischen Einflusses im Kansasdeutschen konnten, wie erwartet, zahlreiche Parallelen zu dem russischen Einfluss in den wolgadeutschen Dialekten in Russland festgestellt werden. Zumindest in einigen zentralen Bereichen scheint das Deutsche strukturell genauso auf das Englische wie auf das Russische als Kontaktsprache zu "reagieren." Wie im Russlanddeutschen (Berend 1998) konnten auch im Kansasdeutschen zwei Typen von englischen Merkmalen belegt werden. Das sind erstens die auffälligen, auf den ersten Blick "hörbaren" und "sehbaren" Sprachphänomene, für die bereits Uriel Weinreich den Begriff "direkter Transfer von Phonemfolgen" geprägt hat (Weinreich 1953), und zweitens die weniger auffälligen Sprachkontaktphänomene, die formal in der lexikalischen Form des Deutschen erscheinen und oft z.B. als "Lenübersetzungen" bezeichnet werden. Betrachten wir zunächst den ersten hier genannten Typ des direkten Transfers etwas näher. Vom Gesichtspunkt des formalen Repertoires aus gesehen handelt es sich um abwechselnde Verwendung von Elementen des deutschen Dialekts und der englischen Sprache. Der im zweiten Abschnitt angeführte Beispieltext des Kansasdeutschen "Hays Daily News" veranschaulicht diese typische Verwendungsweise der englischen Komponente im Kansasdeutschen sehr deutlich. Schon in diesem kurzen Abschnitt ihrer Rede hat die Sprecherin folgende Anglizismen im Sinne des direkten Transfers von Phonemfolgen verwendet, einige davon mehrmals:

(22) *Duststorms, you know, and, because, or, so, you know, Daily News, by, is, comunism, is, see, communism, for, communism, freedom, handle, for, am I saying that, Hays Daily News, Hays Daily News, catechism, for, sixty, two, so, for, teacht, teacht, Spanish, so, Spanish, for, see, talk* [T2:3-4]

In allen vorliegenden Aufnahmen sind englische Lexeme auf eine ganz ähnliche Weise in das Deutsche "eingeflochten," ohne irgendwelche Veränderungen zu erfahren. Neben diesen "rein" englischen, dem Deutschen nicht angepassten Wörtern kommen aber auch Mischwörter, teilweise angepasste Wörter oder verschiedene Kompromissbildungen (Hybridbildungen) vor, wie z.B. *zweistorichi Bus* oder *Galooneimerchen*, und viele andere, die sich allmählich verfestigt haben und repräsentieren gegenwärtig den typisch kansasdeutschen Sprachgebrauch. Einige dieser Merkmale sind allerdings teilweise auch für andere amerikanisch-deutsche Sprachinseln belegt worden und sind dort anscheinend sehr typisch,[10] wie z.B. die eigenartige Umformung des Verbs *(to) like* zu dem deutschen Äquivalent *gleichen* wie in (23) (und im Beispieltext, Abschnitt 2), oder die Verwendung von engl. *soon* in der Bedeutung von dt. *schon* wie in (24), vermutlich auf der Basis der Ähnlichkeit der Lautform der Wörter.

(23) [*gleichen* statt to *like*]
- ich *gleich's* mit die alde Lait zu schawwe [T2:23]

(24) [*soon* statt *schon*]
- Oh, ich hun *soon* hart gschafft [T5:4]
- ja die sin - ich sein do gebore un ich hun *soon* . . . andere Plätz gelebt, aber ich komme immer heim [T8:1]

Stellen wir uns nun die Frage: Welche Gemeinsamkeiten und Unterschiede sind für diesen ersten Typ des Einflusses der entsprechenden Kontaktsprache zwischen dem Russlanddeutschen und Kansasdeutschen zu beobachten? Ohne auf die Einzelheiten der aktuellen Diskussion über Sprachkontaktaspekte wie Entlehnungen, Code Switching u.a. einzugehen, sei hier nur auf einige wenige Punkte eingegangen, die für die Untersuchung der Gesamtsituation der Zweisprachigkeitsverhältnisse in den deutschen Sprachinseln von Bedeutung sein können.

Vergleicht man die Häufigkeits- bzw. Quantitätsverhältnisse des englischen Bestandteils im Kansasdeutschen, so können keine grundsätzlichen Unterschiede im Russlanddeutschen festgestellt werden. Ein in Berend (1998, 169) abgedruckter russlanddeutscher Text veranschaulicht sehr deutlich, dass es sich prinzipiell um dieselbe Strategie der Einbindung der Anglizismen und Russizismen in den deutsch-dialektalen Text handelt. Auch die Strategien der Bildung von Mischwörtern, z.B. russisch-deutsche Wortbildungen, sind durchaus vergleichbar. Vergleicht man jedoch die Struktur und Beschaffenheit der englischen Komponente im Kansasdeutschen und der russischen Komponente im Russlanddeutschen bezüglich der Angleichung an das Deutsche, so fällt auf, dass die Russizismen insgesamt häufiger in einer phonetisch-morphologisch dem Deutschen angepassten Sprachform vorkommen als die entsprechenden englischen Wörter. In dem vorliegenden Material sind englische Wörter meistens (nicht immer) mit englischer Phonetik ausgesprochen. Im Russlanddeutschen dagegen sind die Russizismen häufig in die deutsche Form integriert, d.h. dem Deutschen entsprechend strukturell angepasst (phonetisch, morphologisch). Es gibt eine ganze Schicht von russischen Wörtern, die in fester russlanddeutscher—also angepasster, akkommodierter—Form existieren. Einige Beispiele von integrierten und nicht integrierten Formen zum Russlanddeutschen und Kansasdeutschen werden in folgender Tabelle veranschaulicht. Aus der Tabelle ist ersichtlich, wie russische Wörter in Richtung deutsch verändert werden (feste Formen im Russlanddeutschen in der mittleren Spalte).

Tabelle 1: Beispiele von russischen und englischen
Entsprechungen im Wolgadeutschen

Deutsch	russisches Wolgadeutsch	kansasdeutsches Wolgadeutsch
Einmachglas	*Banke* von Banka [банка]	jar
Feier, Fest	*Guljanke* von Guljanka [гулянка]	party
Postsendung, Paket	*Posylke* von Posylka [посылка]	box
Laden, Geschäft	*Lafke* von Lawka [лавка]	shop, aber: *schtor*

Im Russlanddeutschen werden Russizismen außerdem häufig spontan integriert. Jedes russische Wort kann praktisch im deutschen Satz als "deutsches" verwendet werden, indem entsprechende strukturelle Veränderungen vorgenommen werden. Die Sprecher des Russlanddeutschen besitzen die Fähigkeit, spontan—aber nach bestimmten Mustern und in Abhängigkeit von kommunikativem Bedarf—jedes russische Wort auf die entsprechende Weise phonetisch und/oder morphologisch zu verändern und dem Deutschen anzupassen. Bei den von mir interviewten Sprechern des Kansasdeutschen scheint dies nicht (mehr) der Fall zu sein: Fast alle Anglizismen werden mit englischer Phonetik verwendet und dem Deutschen nicht angepasst. Zu demselben Schluss kommt auch Chris Johnson bezüglich des englischen Einflusses in Schoenchen. Er schrieb (1993, 172):

The number of borrowings show the relative amount of influence Russian and English have had on the Schoenchen dialect in its 224 year history English borrowings   being more numerous. Most borrowings from both languages have in the past been adapted to the native phonology and morphology of the dialect. This could be analyzed as a sign of resistance to the advances of the intruding languages. However, many English expressions occur today without modifikation, which shows how much English has encroached into the Schoenchen dialect in recent years, particularly in adverbs, conjunctions and interjectons.

Hier lässt sich ein Unterschied im gegenwärtigen Integrationspotential der beiden Varietäten—dem Russlanddeutschen und Kansasdeutschen—feststellen. Die phonetische Integrationsfähigkeit des Kansasdeutschen scheint nachgelassen zu haben, wie das auch von Ch. Johnson bestätigt wird über die wolgadeutsche Varietät von Schoenchen, Kansas. In diesem Zusammenhang wäre es sinnvoll, empirisch nachzuprüfen, wie sich das Kansasdeutsche vor fünfzig Jahren (um die Mitte des vorigen Jahrhunderts) bezüglich der Integration der englischen Wörter verhalten hat. Das könnte die immer noch wenig erforschte Frage beleuchten, wie eigentlich die einzelnen Sprachentwicklungsphasen und konkrete Sprachveränderungen in einzelnen Sprachinseln aufeinander abgestimmt sind und ob solche Sprachveränderungen zu bestimmten Phasen in den deutschen Sprachinseln parallel bzw. zeitverschoben ablaufen. Nach einer These von Mattheier (1996, 817), die im Zusammenhang mit theoretisch-methodischen Überlegungen zur Sprachinselforschung aufgestellt wurde, entsprechen die Konstellationen in den heutigen russlanddeutschen Sprachinseln denen der amerikanischen Sprachinseln der Zwischenkriegszeit. Die vorliegenden Daten bestätigen diese Annahme.

Neben diesem generell festzustellenden Unterschied zwischen dem Russlanddeutschen und dem Kansasdeutschen gibt es gerade in diesem Sprachkontaktbereich aber auch eine erstaunliche Ähnlichkeit, die hier nicht unerwähnt bleiben soll. Es geht um die Veränderung der verbalen Formen der Kontaktsprachen nach den strukturellen Gesetzmäßigkeiten des Deutschen, also um die formale Anpassung der englischen und russischen Verben, eine Anpassungsveränderung, die in beiden Varietäten noch funktioniert. So erhalten Verben bei der Anpassung ein deutsches Partizip-II-Präfix ge-, das Suffix -t oder die entsprechenden Personalendungen: *gewatcht, getalkt, gecallt, gebuggert, gemeet, gemixet, gechanget, gecleant, geownt, geregisted, gemoovt, ufgepickt, gerejst, gehomestead,* usw. Aber auch englische Verben in der deutschen Infinitivform (*use*), in anderen Personalformen (wir *use*) und in Kombination mit dem Verb tun (*tut neimixe*) sind in den untersuchten Sprachinseln häufig verwendet worden:[11] Diese Integrationsmuster sind in beiden Varietäten sehr produktiv (zahlreiche Beispiele zum Russlanddeutschen finden sich in Berend 1998).

Es sei angemerkt, dass aber auch in diesem Fall im Russlanddeutschen eine höhere Stufe der Improvisation mit dem Sprachmaterial zu beobachten ist als im Kansasdeutschen. Russlanddeutsch-Sprecher können—wie die Materialien aus den Sprachinseln zeigen—praktisch jedes russische Verb nach dem oben dargestellten Muster spontan in ihre deutsche Varietät integrieren. Im Kansasdeutschen dagegen scheint der Prozess der Integration der englischen Verben in die deutsche Struktur weniger spontan, sondern bereits mehr verfestigt und nicht auf das gesamte Lexikon, sondern auf bestimmte Schichten der Lexik beschränkt zu sein.

Schließlich ist noch eine weitere Gemeinsamkeit des Russlanddeutschen und Kansasdeutschen in Bezug auf den direkten Transfer zu erwähnen. Es ist auffällig, dass die Sprachinselvarietäten offensichtlich die gleichen oder sehr ähnlichen lexikalischen Lücken aufweisen, die entsprechend dann mit russischen oder englischen Wörtern gefüllt werden (Berend 1995). In den vorliegenden Materialien konnten zahlreiche englisch-russische Äquivalente festgestellt werden, die eine lexikalische Lücke im Deutschen ausfüllen. Liegt das an der Struktur der deutschen Dialektvarietäten in Sprachinseln überhaupt oder ist es die Folge der russischen Sprachgeschichtsphase des Kansasdeutschen bzw. wird es durch bestimmte universale Faktoren im Sprachkontakt hervorgerufen? Für die Beantwortung dieser Fragen sind weitere vergleichende Untersuchungen notwendig, insbesondere auch Vergleiche des Kansasdeutschen mit anderen amerikanischen Sprachinselvarietäten (z.b. dem Pennsylvaniadeutschen) und mit weiteren Sprachenpaaren in verschiedenen Sprachinselregionen. Bezüglich der Kontaktphänomene des "direkten Transfers" ist abschließend noch anzumerken, dass sie in bestimmten Konstellationen ein direktes Kommunikationshinderniss darstellen können, denn es handelt sich hier ja um Fragmente einer fremdem Sprache—genau wie dies auch z.b. im Falle von fehlenden Fremdsprachenkenntnissen zu erwarten wäre. Allenfalls würde die Kommunikation zwischen unseren Probanden—den Sprechern des kansasdeutschen Wolgadeutschen und den Sprechern des russlanddeutschen Wolgadeutschen—in erster Linie an diesen englischen und russischen "Zweisprachigkeits-Zusätzen" unbedingt scheitern. Denn russlanddeutsche Wolgadeutsche sind des englischen ganz bestimmt nicht mächtig, und wie es mit dem Russischen bei den kansasdeutschen Wolgadeutschen besteht—diese Frage wird unten untersucht (vgl. Abschnitt 3.3).

Neben dem beschriebenen direkten Transfer existieren im Kansasdeutschen noch—wie schon erwähnt—die weniger auffälligen, verdeckten Sprachkontaktphänomene. Es handelt sich bei diesem Typ um verschiedene Spracherscheinungen, z.B. um die sog. "Lehnübersetzungen"—Phänomene, die dafür verantwortlich sind, dass das Sprachinseldeutsch in Kansas eine englische Struktur aufweist. Sie stellen zwar häufig kein direktes Hindernis für den Kommunikationsprozess dar, sind aber zum Teil nur auf dem Hintergrund von Englischkenntnissen verständlich. Es handelt sich hier nicht nur um Übersetzungen im engeren Sinne, sondern um zahlreiche und sehr unterschiedliche Erscheinungen. Im Folgenden werden einige Beispiele angeführt: die Beeinflussung von Wortstellungsregeln und die Füllung der syntaktischen Struktur des englischen mit deutschem lexikalischen Materials; die Verwendung von Ausdrücken und typischen Redewendungen im Deutschen nach englischem Muster; die Übernahme von sprachspezifischen Formulierungen aus dem Englischen u.a. Es gibt in dem vorliegenden Material zahlreiche andere Erscheinungen, die hier nicht weiter thematisiert werden können (vgl. auch Belege im Beispieltext, Abschnitt 2). All diese Phänomene gehören zu Spracherscheinungen, die im Russlanddeutschen nicht möglich sind, da sie auf englischem Einfluss basieren.

(25) der hat oft gsotze *mit sein Hut an*. [T8:2/7]
do war mol e meedje *wu ich gschafft hun mit*. [T8:2]

(26) mei ei Jung hat Daitsch gehol, der war in die seminary, Pader äscht wolld er lärne, mei zwede Sohn der hat German gehol in die Schul. [T6:2-3]

(27) but des *nemmt* noch ein Rassje—des *nemmt* dene Russe noch värzich Johr bis die besser gebe. [T5:7]

(28) wir *gucken* net so alt (Wir sehen nicht so alt aus). [T4:8]

(29) oh, so wie die Japps, ja? —no was tun die dort *for Lebe mache*? [T5:17]

(30) see um die zwanzich dreisich do *host du* Öl überall gfunne, jetzt is es vorbei. [T3:6]

Die Durchsicht der vorliegenden Materialien zeigt, dass auch bezüglich dieser verdeckten Sprachkontaktfolgen das Kansasdeutsche in viel größerem Ausmaß vom englischen infiziert ist als das Russlanddeutsche vom Russischen. Es ist offensichtlich, dass das Russlanddeutsche auf dem gegenwärtigen Entwicklungsstadium stabiler und näher an der ursprünglichen Struktur des Deutschen ist als das Kansasdeutsche. Auch diese Sprachzeugnisse bestätigen die oben angesprochene Annahme über die verschiedenen Entwicklungsphasen der amerikanischen und russischen Sprachinseln (Mattheier 1996, 817).

Abschließend zu diesem Teil der Analyse der kansasdeutschen Sprachkontaktvarietäten soll noch kurz auf die Einstellung der kansasdeutschen Sprecher zu ihrem Englisch eingegangen werden. Während der Interviews wurde deutlich, dass den Sprechern ihre besondere Gestaltung des Englischen bewusst ist, wie das Beispiel (31) verdeutlicht:

(31) Mir *talke* mehr Englisch jetzt, bissje broken, wie me sage tut - mir wisse des all, das mir so *sounde*. [T4:71]

Das folgende Beispiel (32) zeigt in besonders deutlicher Weise, wie kansasdeutsche Sprecher über ihr eigenes Englisch reflektieren:

(32) BL: Sprecherin des Kansasdeutsch
N: Interviewerin N. Berend

BL: Da sind noch viel Leute, wo so . . . deutsche Sprache haben, wenn sie auch Englisch spreche, da kann man, da kann man hören, dass sie deutsch sind.

N: Ja, kann man das hören noch?

BL: Ja, das kann man hören . . . da sind ihrer noch mehr, wo so deutsch . . . wenn sie auch englisch sprechen, das sound bisschen wie deutsch.

N: Ja und wie, wenn du jetzt jemand hörst, dass der englisch erzählt oder plaudert und wie tätst du das verstehen, dass das ein Deutscher ist?

BL: Oh, das kommt so bisschen deutsch raus. Alle Gebot tun sie so ein deutsches Wort use.

N: Ja?

BL: <u>Gelle</u> ist ein Wort, wo viel deutsche Leut use. Die sprechen so . . . Englisch und nun auf einmal sagen sie: <u>gelle</u>? Und man weiß, dass das deutsch ist. Und es ist alle Gebot, dass jemand was sagt in Englisch, aber die sagen es mehr wie deutsch, wie . . . Da war einmal ein Mädchen, wo ich geschafft habe mit. Und die sagte immer, die konnte kein Deutsch. Und der ihr Name war Brull und ich wusste ja, dass sie deutsch war und ihre Leute waren deutsch. Und na hat sie mal geplaudert von . . .—die waren in die post office gegangen, na hat sie so Briefe—wollte sie hinein schmeißen und hat sie—ist sie aus die car gegangen, und na war ein Brief, wo in des Glas—in den Door hinein ist gegangen und nachher—in Englisch sagt man: <u>You have to take it apart</u>. Und in Deutsch sagt man: <u>Man nimmt es auseinander</u>. Das musst alles auseinander nehmen. Und nachher sagt sie es in Englisch: <u>I had to take it out apart</u>. Und das ist nicht recht englisch, das ist deutsch. Und nachher—so kann man wissen, dass . . . noch mehr deutsch sind wie sie englisch sind. [T8:2-3]

3.3. Interessante russische Erscheinungen

Die russische Sprache beherrschen die Wolgadeutschen in Kansas nicht. Sie sind aber mit ganz bestimmten Elementen des Russischen vertraut, und zwar deswegen, weil diese Elemente Bestandteil ihres Kansasdeutschen sind. Dieses russische Sprachmaterial ist die Folge der deutsch-russischen Sprachkontaktphase, die die wolga-kansasdeutsche Kommunikationsgemeinschaft erlebt hat. Stellen wir zunächst die Frage: Was ist russisch an der Sprache der Kansasdeutschen? Was ist erhalten geblieben von der hundertjährigen deutschrussischen Sprachkontaktphase, trotz der darauffolgenden hundertjährigen deutsch-englischen Sprachkontaktphase? Die Ausgangshypothese bei der Untersuchung dieser Aspekte war, dass die russische Komponente in den deutschen Varietäten sehr gering ist und dass sie sich auf den sog. "Erinnerugswortschatz" beschränkt.

In Bezug auf den Erinnerungswortschatz hat sich die Hypothese bestätigt. Die meisten belegten Russizismen gehören zu der Kategorie des Erinnerungswortschatzes. Ihr Gebrauch während der Interviews erfolgte bei der Thematisierung der russischen Vergangenheit und betraf ausschließlich Realienbezeichnungen aus dieser russischen Sprachentwicklungsphase der Kansasdeutschen. Da es keine Fragebogenbefragungen, sondern freie Interviews waren, war der Gebrauch der Russizismen nicht durch Nachfragen und entsprechende Andeutungen hervorgerufen, sondern erfolgte "automatisch." Erst am Ende des Interviews wurde dann eine Befragungsstrategie eingesetzt, die zur gezielten Feststellung / Offenlegung des russischen Bestands in der passiven Sprachkompetenz der Wolgadeutschen führen sollte. Die gezielte Nachforschung hat dann noch eine Schicht von Russizismen offenbart, die eine Vorstellung geben über den Sprachgebrauch der älteren Generation (der Eltern und Großeltern der befragten Wolgadeutschen) und über die Existenzart des Erinnerungswortschatzes in der passiven Kompetenz der Sprecher. Einige Beispiele:

Tabelle 2: Beispiele von Russizismen im Kansasdeutschen

Russisch	Belege aus dem Kansasdeutschen	Deutsch
Амбар - Ambar	*Ambaar*	Korn-Vorratskammer
Нужник - Nushnjik	*Nuschnik*	Toilette im Freien
Фуфайка - Fufajka	*Kufajke*	warme Jacke
Пышки - Pyschki	*Pyschkis*	russische Küchlein (Pl.)
Котелок - Kotjelok	*Kotelok*	russischer Kochtopf
Арбузы - Arbusy	*Ärbuse*	Wassermelonen
Крыльцо - Kryljtzo	*Krilitz*	Vorhaustreppe

Die belegten Russizismen zeigen unter anderem folgendes. 1) Es ist anzunehmen, dass die ältere Generation der kansasdeutschen Wolgadeutschen den gesamten Kernwortschatz der russischen Entlehnungen in ihrem Gebrauch hatte, der von Dinges in seiner 1929 erschienenen Arbeit dokumentiert wurde (Dinges 1929). Es handelt sich um den russischen Wortschatz, der bis 1870 in die Sprache der Wolgadeutschen in Russland integriert wurde, also genau bis zum Zeitpunkt der Auswanderung der Vorfahren der kansasdeutschen Wolgadeutschen nach Amerika. 2) Die meisten Russizismen sind auch im Gebrauch noch korrekt, d.h. man kann davon ausgehen, dass sie in der früheren Sprachentwicklungsphase wohl noch intensiv verwendet wurden. 3) Einige Russizismen haben Gebrauchsveränderungen erfahren. Dazu ein Beispiel. Das Wort *Babuschka* wurde im Gespräch in der Bedeutung *Halstuch* verwendet, in Reflexion über den Sprachgebrauch der älteren Generation, (in diesem Fall der Schwiegermutter), vgl. Beispiel (32).[12] In diesem Beleg haben wir es mit einer Verschiebung im Gebrauch zu tun, die als anschauliches Beispiel für das Phänomen des Sprachverlusts dienen kann, wie das folgende Beispiel sehr deutlich veranschaulicht:.

(33) BL: Sprecherin des Kansasdeutsch
N: Interviewerin N. Berend

BL: Halstuch Ba'buschka sagt ihr in Russisch?
N: Was ist das Ba'buschka?
BL: Halstuch.
N: Halstuch?
BL: Halstuch. Wo man so über'n Kop tut.
N: Ja aber wie haben die gesagt? "Das ist meine Ba'buschka"?
BL: Ja, meine Mutter—Schwiegermutter hat Ba'buschka gesagt, aber wir haben immer Halstuch gesagt
N: Die Schwiegermutter hat Ba'buschka gesagt?
BL: ja.
N: Ja wie hat die gesagt?
BL: Ich muss meine Babuschka uftue.
N: ja?
BL: Wir haben Halstuch gesagt. Die hat wahrscheinlich mehr russische Wörter gesagt, als wie meine Leute, aber Ambar war einer . . . wo mein Großvater gesagt hat, und Ärbuse war noch eines. [T8:9]

Das Vorhandensein des Russischen Erinnerungswortschatzes im Kansasdeutschen ist, wie erwähnt, im Vorfeld der Studie angenommen worden und war somit nicht unerwartet. Es handelt sich jedoch bei dem russischen Einfluss im Kansasdeutschen nicht nur um den Erinnerungswortschatz, der im kollektiven Sprachbewusstsein der Wolgadeutschen verankert ist. Der zweite Typ der belegten Russizismen umfasst Spracherscheinungen, die entscheidend dazu beitragen, dass das Kansasdeutsche als "russlanddeutsch" charakterisiert wird, und die das Kansasdeutsche auch so unterschiedlich machen im Vergleich zu anderen amerikanischen Sprachinselvarietäten. Typisch für diese Erscheinungen der zweiten Gruppe ist, dass sie als "echte" Russizismen bezeichnet werden können. Unter "echt" wird verstanden, dass sie nicht nur in der Erinnerung der Sprecher, sondern auch im tatsächlichen Sprachgebrauch realistisch sind und häufig verwendet werden. Die Sprecher selbst erkennen diese Wörter nicht als russische und betrachten sie daher nicht als Russizismen. Diese Lexeme sind für die Sprecher ganz gewöhnliche, keine "exotischen," sondern gebräuchliche Wörter ihres deutschen Repertoires, und keiner der Sprecher ist sich dessen bewusst, das es sich eigentlich um Russizismen handelt. In Wirklichkeit handelt es sich tatsächlich teilweise um Übernahmen und Verwendungen aus dem Russischen, die bereits im russlanddeutschen Wolgadeutschen auffällig sind. Der Grund für die Verfestigung solcher Sprachelemente im Deutschen kann nur in der Prägnanz dieser russischen Ausdrücke liegen und in der Tatsache, dass im Deutschen an dieser Stelle kein entsprechend guter und prägnanter Ausdruck, also möglicherweise eine lexikalische Lücke vorliegt. Eines dieser Lexeme ist das kleine Wörtchen *ras*, von russ. das im Kansasdeutschen überraschenderweise genauso häufig wie im Russlanddeutschen verwendet wird. Einige Beispiele aus dem Kansasdeutschen:

(34) un ich hab *vor ne Rass* haw ich hier . . . paar Jahr zurick haw ich kleine Kinner / . . . lerne hier—*catechism* gelernt / *for* zwanzig Jahr.

(35) Mei Mann hat for e *Rass* do drunne gschafft, ein *Rassje* hiwwe "mein Mann hat eine Zeitlang da unten gearbeitet, eine kürzere Zeit hüben." [T8:13]

(36) Mir fahre mol nuf nouch e *Rassje* un-no weis ich's dir wie es ist (wir fahren mal hinauf nach einer Weile, und dann zeige ich es dir, wie es ist). [T5:28]

(37) des was die selle tun in Russland jetz you know—unter ihr eigenes gehe see, but des nemmt noch ein *Rassje*—die ware siebzich Johr in Russland. [T5:7]

Ras bedeutet "eins, einmal." In die Sprache der Wolgadeutschen ist dieses Wort in der Bedeutung *Weile, Zeitlang* integriert. Im Russischen wird auch oft die Diminutivform *Rasotchek* verwendet, die im Wolgadeutschen ein *Rassje* heisst und mit dem typisch wolgadeutschen Suffix *-chen* (*-je*) gebildet wird. Ein *Rassje* bedeutet also ein *Weilchen*, ein *Rass*—eine *Weile*, eine *Zeitlang*. Die Verwendungsweise im Kansasdeutschen wird sehr deutlich durch die Beispiele (34)—(37) veranschaulicht. Dieses und ähnliche so fest ins Kansasdeutsche integrierte russische Lehnwörter sind der eigentliche Grund, der das Kansasdeutsche eher als einen *russlanddeutschen*, und nicht als einen *deutschen* Dialekt erscheinen lässt. Die Existenz der russischen Bestandteile zeigt, dass der hundertjährige deutsch-russische Sprachkontakt und die Doppelmigration eine wichtige Rolle bei der Interpretation der modernen Struktur des kansasdeutschen Wolgadeutschen einnehmen müssen.

4. Schluss

Der vorliegende Beitrag bietet keine umfassende vergleichende Analyse des Wolgadeutschen in Kansas und Russland, sondern lediglich einen ersten Schritt in diese Richtung. Aber bereits diese skizzenhafte Darstellung zeigt, wie produktiv und vielversprechend eine solche vergleichende Analyse für die Beschreibung der Sprachentwicklung und des Sprachwandels in Sprachinseln sein kann. Es wird möglich sein, offene und viel diskutierte Fragen der Forschung aus der vergleichenden Perspektive neu anzugehen, wie z.B. die Frage nach den internen oder externen Ursachen des Sprachwandels in den Sprachinseln, die in vielen Arbeiten diskutiert wird.[13] Viele Jahrzehnte wurden in Kansas und in Russland zahlreiche Einzelsprachinsel-Untersuchungen durchgeführt, und es ist jetzt an der Zeit, die vorliegenden Ergebnisse der vor Ort durchgeführten empirischen Analysen aus einer vergleichenden Perspektive neu zu bewerten und die aufgestellten Hypothesen zu überprüfen. Insbesondere für die Theoriebildung der Sprachinseln ist die vergleichende Sprachinselanalyse unentbehrlich. So können die von Mattheier (1993, 39) aufgeworfenen theoretisch-methodischen Fragen nur unter der Vorrausetzung von vergleichender Forschungsperspektive beantwortet werden. Als eine Aufgabe formuliert er die "Erarbeitung einer soziolinguistischen Theorie der Sprachveränderung":

> Die einzelnen Verfallszustände, in denen sich die deutschen Dialekte in den verschiedenen Sprachinseln in der ganzen Welt befinden, stellen—unter diesem allgemeinen Gesichtspunkt vergleichend betrachtet—Phasen, Schritte in einem allgemeinen Varietätenveränderungsprozess dar. Durch einen systematischen Vergleich solcher Phasen müsste . . . in der Gegenwart ein Tableau von unterschiedlichen Entwicklungsstufen in diesem Prozess erkennbar werden.

Die hier durchgeführte Analyse in Bezug auf das Kansas—und Russlanddeutsche hat bereits einige solcher Phasen und Schritte offengelegt, die als Teil eines allgemeinen Veränderungsprozesses in Sprachinseln angesehen werden können. Angesichts der unterschiedlichen sprachgeschichtlichen Konstellationen und der verschiedenen Faktoren, die Einfluss auf die Gestaltung der Sprachverhältnisse innerhalb der kansasdeutschen und russlanddeutschen Sprachinseln nahmen, wird es eine schwierige Aufgabe der künftigen wolgadeutschen Sprachinsel- und Sprachkontaktforschung sein, die Vergleichbarkeit und die Ähnlichkeit von Sprachentwicklungen in diesen Inseln zu begründen.

Anmerkungen

[1] Es kam in diesem Fall der Forschungssituation sehr entgegen, dass ich als Interviewerin über Muttersprachkenntnisse des russischen Wolgadeutschen verfügte.

[2] In diesem Text handelt es sich um die Catherine-Variante des kansasdeutschen Wolgadeutschen. Zur dialektgeographischen Einordnung vgl. Keel 1982.

[3] Ein Beispieltext des Russlanddeutschen vgl. Berend 1998, 169ff.

[4] Es ist anzunehmen, dass diese Erscheinungen allgemein-dialektale sind, die auch in einheimischen Dialekten (in Deutschland) vorkommen können. Für die hier gewählte Perspektive der Darstellung wird diese Frage nicht weiter thematisiert.

[5] Vgl. Beispiele dazu auch in Schoenchen (Johnson 1993, 164).

[6] Die Kasusmischung ist ein im Kansasdeutschen häufig vorkommendes Phänomen, das auch im Russlanddeutschen um sich greift (vgl. Zusammenfassung bei Keel 1994). Sie ist im Russlanddeutschen aber bedeutend weniger verbreitet und auch nicht in allen Dialekten wie das im amerikanischen Deutschen der Fall zu sein scheint.

[7] Johnson (1993, 169) stellt ähnliche Verwendung in Schoenchen fest. "*Geben* can occur with a secondary meaning 'to become': / ɪç gɛb krank/ *Ich werde krank* 'I'm getting sick.' /du mʊst grezər gɛbə/ *Du mußt größer werden.* 'You must get older.'

[8] Die Frage der Passivperiphrase ist in Bezug auf die russlanddeutschen Dialekte noch nicht untersucht. Ich stütze mich bei der folgenden Analyse auf meine eigenen Aufnahmen und Beobachtungen, die ich bei der Durchführung der Omsker Forschungsprojekte in den Sprachinseln Sibiriens gemacht habe.

[9] Es existiert wie bekannt eine außerordentlich umfangreiche Forschung und Diskussion zu verschiedenen Aspekten der deutsch-englischen Sprachkontakte. In diesem Beitrag verzichte ich bewusst auf die bibliographischen u.a. Angaben dazu, da es in dieser Analysephase zunächst lediglich um den Vergleich mit dem Russlanddeutschen geht.

[10] Auch für andere amerikanische Sprachinseln des Deutschen häufig belegt, vgl. z.B. Huffines 1993, Louden 1994, Salmons 1990, 1993.

[11] Vgl. auch Beispiele von Schoenchen mit dem Verb *tun* (Johnson 1993, 167).

[12] Die Verschiebung besteht darin, dass das russ. *Babuschka* "Großmutter" bedeutet, die in der Vorstellung der Kansasdeutschen immer ein Halstuch (auf eine ganz bestimmte Weise gebunden) tragen, und daher wird das *Halstuch* allmählich "Babuschka" bezeichnet.

[13] Eine erste Untersuchung mit Einbezug des Wolgadeutschen in Kansas und Russland liegt bereits vor, vgl. Keel 1994.

Literatur

Auer, Peter, und Aldo Di Luzio. 1988. "Introduction: Variation and Convergence as a Topic in Dialectology and Sociolinguistics." In *Variation and Convergence: Studies in Social Dialectology*, hrsg. Peter Auer und Aldo Di Luzio, 1-10. Berlin / New York: de Gruyter.

Bellmann, Günter. 1998.Zur Passivperiphrase im Deutschen: Grammatikalisierung und Kontinuität. In *Deutsche Sprache in Raum und Zeit: Festschrift für Peter Wiesinger*, hrsg. Peter Ernst und Franz Patocka, 241-69. Wien: Edition Praesens.

Berend, Nina, und Hugo Jedig. 1991. *Deutsche Mundarten in der Sowjetunion: Geschichte der Forschung und Bibliographie*. Marburg: Elwert.

Berend, Nina. 1995. "Des is arich intresting . . .": Deutsch im Kontakt mit anderen Sprachen." In *Sprachreport* 2: 1-3.

Berend, Nina. 1998. *Sprachliche Anpassung: Eine soziolinguistisch-dialektologische Untersuchung zum Russlanddeutschen*. Tübingen: Narr.

Dinges, Georg. 1923. "Über unsere Mundarten." In *Beiträge zur Heimatkunde des deutschen Wolgagebietes*, 60-72. Pokrowsk.

Dinges, G. G. 1925. "K isutscheniju goworow Powolshskich nemzew." In *Utschonye sapiski Saratowskogo Uniwersiteta*, 12-20.

Dinges, G. G. 1929. "O russkich slowach, saimstwowannych powolshskimi nemzami do 1876 goda." In *Utschonye sapiski Saratowskogo Uniwersiteta* 7,3: 195-236.

Jedig, Hugo H. 1986. "Die deutschen Mundarten in der Sowjetunion." In *Das Wort: Germanistisches Jahrbuch DDR-UDSSR*, hrsg. G. Uhlisch, 74-80.

Jedig, Hugo. 1990. "Die deutsche Sprachkultur in der Sowjetunion." In *Die Deutschen in der UDSSR in Geschichte und Gegenwart*, hrsg. I. Fleischhauer Und H. Jedig, 203-24. Baden Baden: Nomos Verlagsgesellschaft.

Johnson, Chris D. 1993. "Structural Aspects of the Volga German Dialect of Schoenchen, Kansas." In *The German Language in America, 1683-1991*, hrsg. Joseph C. Salmons, 158-87. Madison, Wisconsin.

Johnson, Chris. 1994. "The Volga German Dialect of Schoenchen, Kansas." Diss., University of Kansas.

Huffines, Marion Lois. 1993."Dying by Convergence?: Pennsylvania German and Syntactic Change." In *The German Language in America, 1683-1991*, hrsg. Joseph C. Salmons, 250-63. Madison, Wisconsin.

Keel, William. 1981. "On Dialect Mixture: The Case of Ellis County (Kansas) Volga German." In *Proceedings of the Mid-America Linguistics Conference 1981*, hrsg. T. Bennett-Kastor, 320 35. Wichita: English Department/ Linguistics Program, Wichita State University.

Keel, William D. 1982. "On the Heimatbestimmung of the Ellis County (Kansas) Volga- German Dialects." *Yearbook of German-American Studies* 17: 99-109.

Keel, William. 1989. "Deutsche Mundarten in Kansas: Sprachatlas der wolgadeutschen Mundarten." In *Sprachatlanten des Deutschen: Laufende Projekte* (Studien zum kleinen deutschen Sprachatlas, Bd. 2), hrsg. Werner H. Veith und Wolfgang Putschke, 387--98. Tübingen: Niemeyer.

Keel, William D. 1994. "Reduction and Loss of Case Marking in the Noun Phrase in German-American Speech Islands: Internal Development or External Interference?" In *Sprachinselforschung*, hrsg. Nina Berend und Klaus J. Mattheier, 93-104. Frankfurt/Main: Lang.

Louden, Mark L. 1993. "Patterns of Sociolinguistic Variation in Pennsylvania German." In *The German Language in America, 1683-1991*, hrsg. Joseph C. Salmons, 284-306. Madison, Wisconsin.

Louden, Mark. 1994. "Syntactic Change in Multilingual Speech Islands." In *Sprachinselforschung*, hrsg. Nina Berend und Klaus J. Mattheier, 73-92. Frankfurt/Main: Lang.

Mattheier, Klaus J. 1993. "Sprachinselsoziolinguistik: Beobachtungen und Überlegungen an deutschsprachigen Sprachinseln." In *The German Language in America, 1683-1991*, hrsg. Joseph C. Salmons, 38-61. Madison, Wisconsin.

Mattheier, Klaus J. 1994. "Theorie der Sprachinsel. Voraussetzungen und Strukturierungen." In *Sprachinselforschung*, hrsg. Nina Berend und Klaus J. Mattheier, 333-48. Frankfurt/Main: Lang.

Mattheier, Klaus J. 1996. "Methoden der Sprachinselforschung." In *Kontaktlinguistik: Ein internationales Handbuch*, hrsg. Hans Goebl, Peter H. Nelde u.a., 812-19.

Salmons, J. 1990. "Bilingual Discourse Marking." *Linguistics* 28: 453-80.

Salmons, J., Hrsg. 1993. *The German Language in America, 1683-1991*. Madison, Wisconsin.

Schiller, F. P. 1929. "O wlijanii wojny i rewoljuzii na jasyk nemzew Powolshja." *Utschonyje sapiski Instituta jasyka i literatury* 2: 67-87. Moskau.

Wolgadeutscher Sprachatlas (WDSA). 1997. Aufgrund der von Georg Dinges 1925-1929 gesammelten Materialien hrsg. Nina Berend unter Mitarbeit von Rudolf Post. Tübingen und Basel: Francke.

Weinreich, Uriel. 1953. *Languages in Contact*. The Hague.

Elisabeth Knipf-Komlósi
Eötvös Loránd Tudományegyetem
Budapest, Hungary

Sprachwahl und kommunikative Handlungsformen der deutschen Minderheit in Ungarn

Als vergleichendes Beispiel zur Sprachinselsituation von Übersee möchte ich zu am Beispiel einer deutschen Sprachinsel in Mittelosteuropa einige Anmerkungen machen. Mein Aufsatz gliedert sich in drei Einheiten: zunächst wird der soziohistorische Hintergrund der deutschen Sprachinseln in Ungarn und der Region beschrieben, als zweites werden die in Folge der gesellschaftlich-historischen Entwicklung entstandenen Eigenheiten der Sprachkompetenz und Sprachwahl dieser Sprachgemeinschaft thematisiert und zuletzt werde ich über einige kommunikative Strategien, von denen die Ungarndeutschen in der Gegenwart häufig Gebrauch machen, sprechen.

1. Der soziohistorische Hintergrund

In den von Deutschland nach Osten liegenden sieben Ländern (Österreich, Tschechien, Polen, Slowakei, Kroatien, Ungarn) sowie in den dazu gehörenden—in diese inkorporierten—drei historischen Regionen (die Karpatukraine, Siebenbürgen und die Wojwodina) leben insgesamt 107 nationale und ethnische Gruppen. Ein zahlenmäßiger Überblick zeigt uns, dass eine Millionengrösse der Sprecher lediglich bei den Siebenbürger Ungarn und den Roma zu verzeichnen ist; eine Größenordnung von über 100 000 erreichen jedoch 16 der oben erwähnten ethnischen Gruppierungen und eine Größe von etwa 1000 erreichen etwa 61 der erwähnten Gruppen.

Die historisch gegebene und auch erlebte sprachlich-kulturelle Vielfalt dieses Gebietes von Europa kam im 20. Jahrhundert grundsätzlich ins Schwanken, wenn man berechnet, dass die einige Tausend zählenden Minderheitengruppen Mitteleuropas die ethnische Struktur und Zusammensetzung von höchstens 1-2 Siedlungen beeinflussen, so dass sich für das Fortbestehen dieser ethnisch-kulturellen Gruppen in diesem Teil Europas im 21. Jahrhundert eigentlich nur mehr wenig Chancen zeigen.

Die Gesamtzahl der erwähnten 107 ethnischen Gruppen liegt etwa bei 7 Millionen, was ein Anteil von 8,6 % der Gesamtbevölkerung von 81 Millionen dieses Gebietes ausmacht.[1] Global gerechnet sind es 12-13% der Gesamtbevölkerung dieser Region(en), die irgendeiner der oben erwähnten Minderheitengruppen angehören.

Von den oben erwähnten Ländern gibt es in sechs von ihnen eine deutschsprachige Minderheit. Trotz dieser—auf den ersten Blick—hohen Zahl kann im Leben dieser Minderheiten im 20. Jahrhundert über eine kontinuierliche Abnahme ihrer Zahl, über eine Zwangsassimilation, über Ethno- und Genocide, ethnische Säuberungen, über eine agressive Aus- und Umsiedlung dieser Menschengruppen und deren negative Auswirkungen berichtet werden. Ein Blick auf die ethnische Landkarte Mitteleuropas zu Beginn des 20. Jahrhunderts zeigt uns, dass in unseren Tagen die deutschen und jüdischen Minderheitengruppen dieser Regione(en) zum Großteil verschwunden sind. Es ist kein Zufall, dass man in intellektuell-politischen Diskursen, in soziologischen und ethnologischen Erhebungen in diesem Gebiet heutzutage immer öfter und öffentlicher, über das Syndrom der "letzten Minute vor 12" spricht, mit anderen Worten, von einer totalen Assimilation und einem vollkommenen Verschwinden der ursprünglich hier ansäßigen, die Region maßgebend prägenden ethnisch- kulturellen Minderheiten.

Während zu Beginn des 20. Jahrhunderts ein Großteil der Minderheiten durch die neuen Staatsgrenzen entstandene Zwangsminderheiten betrachtet werden, können die Minderheitengruppen der Gegenwart—ausgehendes 20. Jahrhundert, Jahrhundertwende—fast ausnahmslos als Restminderheiten charakterisiert werden, wobei zwischen den Zwangs- und den Restminderheiten ein enger Zusammenhang besteht und diese oft nicht exakt getrennt werden können.

Als Hauptursache der oben geschilderten (traurigen) Situation ist wohl anzugeben, dass die mittelosteuropäischen Nationalstaaten—abgesehen von kürzeren Perioden—nicht gerade eine Anerkennung, eine Gleichberechtigung ihrer Minderheiten anstrebten, sondern gewollt oder nicht gewollt, eher ihre Assimiliation förderten.

Die Entstehung der Minderheitengruppen in diesem Teil Europas kann in vier größeren Etappen zusammengefasst werden. Diese sind wie folgt:

1) Die Prozesse der Kolonisation und Migration im Mittelalter;

2) Die Neubesiedlung dieser Gebiete nach der Türkenherrschaft in einer Zeit, als die ethnische Raumstruktur Europas sich mosaikartig zu entfalten begann. Das zeigen die Beispiele der multiethnischen Regionen wie die Batschka mit ihrer Zusammensetzung von deutschen, slawischen und ungarischen Bevölkerungsanteilen, oder die Entstehung des Banats mit seiner charakteristischen deutsch-ungarisch-rumänischsprachigen Zusammensetzung.

3) Die interregionalen, internationalen und interkontinentalen Migrationswellen und auch die gewaltigen Assimilationsprozesse im 19. und 20. Jahrhundert—gleichzeitig auch die ersten Anzeichen der entstehenden Nationalstaaten.

4) Zuletzt betrachtet man als die 4. Etappe jene Zeit, als an Stelle der vielnationalen Reiche die nationalen Kleinstaaten entstanden, als dessen Folge die früher dominanten nationalen Gemeinschaften—sozusagen von heute auf morgen—in Minderheitenpositionen gedrängt wurden, wie z.B. das Deutsche und das Ungarische.

Hinsichtlich der historischen Umstände ihrer Entstehung stammen die Minderheitengruppen aus der Zeit des Mittelalters, in den darauf folgenden Jahrhunderten kamen die mehr oder minder freiwillig angesiedelten Minderheiten, die allesamt als historische Minderheiten bezeichnet werden. Die im 20. Jahrhundert durch politische Entscheidungen und Grenzziehungen, bzw. auf Grund externer Verfügungen und Rechtsregelungen entstandene Minderheitengruppen werden als Zwangsminderheiten bezeichnet.

Bei einer typologischen Charakterisierung der Minderheiten ist nicht die Zeit ihrer Ansiedlung der ausschlaggebende Aspekt, vielmehr das Moment ihres Entwicklungsstadiums, in dem sich die betreffende Minderheit befand, als sie sich von ihrer ursprünglichen nationalen Gemeinschaft, von ihrer Urheimat, getrennt hat. Es geht hierbei um die Trägereigenschaft des Nationalbewusstseins. Aus dieser Sicht sind die Mitte des 19. Jahrhunderts entstandenen, geographisch von der ursprünglichen nationalen Gemeinschaft weit entfernten Minderheitengruppen—wie die meisten deutschen Sprachinseln in Südosteuropa—nur durch ihre ganz dünne Intellektuellenschicht oder überhaupt nicht mehr an der weiteren Entwicklung ihrer ursprünglichen nationalen Gemeinschaft, an deren sprachlich-kultureller und politischwirtschaftlicher Entwicklung beteiligt gewesen.

Die Erhebungen zur Identität einiger Minderheitengruppen[2] zeigen, dass diese Minderheitengruppen in der Zeit nach ihrer Ansiedlung in Südosteuropa über die sprachlichkulturelle und politische Entwicklung ihrer alten Heimat verständlicherweise nur mittelbare, sehr vage oder gar keine Kenntnisse mehr hatten. Dominant bei der Entstehung und Entfaltung der historischen Identität dieser Minderheitengruppen ist ihre Identifikation mit der Geschichte des Aufnehmerlandes, der neuen Heimat.

In der aktuellen Zeitgeschichte sind wir Zeugen eines Prozesses, der die oben erwähnte sogenannte völlige Abkapselung vom Mutterland in gewisser Hinsicht in ein neues Blickfeld rückt. Infolge der im letzten Jahrzehnt des 20. Jahrhunderts erfolgten politisch-historischen Veränderungen und gesellschaftlichen Umstrukturierungen wurde diesen Minderheiten durch die Aufnahme von kulturell-politisch-wirtschaftlicher Beziehungen zu ihren Mutterländern neue Perspektiven und Möglichkeiten für ihre evtl. vorhandenen, oder gar erst jetzt entstandenen Revitalisierungsbestrebungen geboten. Die positiven Auswirkungen dieses Prozesses sind bei den deutschen, slowenischen, kroatischen, slowakischen, ukrainischen und teschechischen Minderheiten eindeutig wahrzunehmen. Hervorragende Beispiele dafür sind vor allem die deutschen Minderheitengruppen in Ungarn und Polen, aber auch die Slowenen in Ungarn und Kärnten.

Relevant ist hinsichtlich des Minderheitendaseins im weiteren auch die Raumstruktur, in der die Minderheiten eingebettet sind. Eine charakteristische Formation für die oben erwähnten ethnischen und sprachlichen Minderheiten sind die Streusiedlungen und die Sprachinseln. Gerade diese Raumstruktur beeinflusst auch die Gestaltung der sprachlichen Situation: ein Großteil der untersuchten Minderheiten ist im Laufe des 20. Jahrhunderts—gerade ducrh ihre gegebene räumliche Einbettung— zwei- oder mehrsprachig geworden, im Gegensatz zur strikten Einsprachigkeit der Mehrheitsnationen dieser Länder.

Nach dem Kompetenzgrad der Zweisprachigkeit der untersuchten Minderheitengruppen lassen sich zwei größere Gruppen aufstellen. Zur ersten Gruppe gehören die Muttersprachdominanten Minderheiten, wie z.B. die Ungarn in der Slowakei und in Siebenbürgen, die Litauer und die Weißrussen in Polen. Doch auch hier ist die Dominanz der Muttersprache keine Selbstverständlichkeit mehr, insbesondere wenn man die Erosionsprozesse der Gegenwart, wie die gesellschaftliche Mobilität von ganzen Bevölkerungsgruppen, die fortlaufenden Urbanisierungsprozesse, die Streulage der Minderheiten, die alltäglich und selbstverständlich gewordenen Mischehen, oder das jeweilige gesellschaftliche Prestige der Muttersprache der Minderheiten im Land, die juristischen und kommunikativen Hindernisse ihres muttersprachlichen Sprachgebrauchs berücksichtigt, gehen die Domänen des Minderheitensprachgebrauchs allmählich immer mehr zurück.

In die zweite Gruppe gehören die Minderheiten, bei denen die Landessprache die dominante ist und die Minderheiten-Muttersprache in ihrem Gebrauch, in ihrer Funktion und Einsetzbarkeit im alltäglichen Verkehr, ja selbst in der familiären Umgebung, weitgehend hinter der Sprache der Mehrheit zurücktritt und verschwindet. Hierher gehören fast alle in Ungarn lebenden Minderheiten, allen voran die deutsche Minderheit, aber auch die in anderen Ländern lebenden Deutschen, Slowenen, Tschechen etc.

Betrachtet man das Verhältnis der beiden Sprachen zueinander, so fällt ein chronologischer Unterschied ins Auge: Eine subtraktive Zweisprachigkeit, d.h. eine ungleiche, niedrigere gesellschaftliche Akzeptanz der deutschen Sprache, d.h. der deutschen Ortsdialekte[3] gegenüber der ungarischen Sprache ist bis in die 80er Jahre charakteristisch. Dieser externe Faktor hatte die Einstellung der Ungarndeutschen zu ihrer eigenen Sprache maßgebend beeinflusst. In der gegenwärtigen Sprachenkonstellation könnte wohl über eine additive Zweisprachigkeit auf Grund der wirtschaftlich-politischen Situation gesprochen werden. Es erfreuen sich alle Fremdsprachen einer hohen Akzeptanz in Ungarn,[4] was natürlich zu einem kognitiven Vorteil der bilingualen Sprecher führt.

Somit gelangte die deutsche Minderheit in Ungarn in die glückliche Lage, dass sie durch das Erlernen der deutschen Standardsprache ihren Ortsdialekt ersetzen oder gar retten kann. Auch jene Tatsache ist wichtig, dass für die deutsche Minderheit in diesem Teil Europas die deutsche Einigung, die wirtschaftlich-sozialen Erfolge Deutschlands einen Prestigezuwachs der deutschen Sprache und vielleicht auch eine Stärkung ihrer ethnischen Identität bewirken kann.

Zu einer allgemeinen Charakterisierung der deutschen Minderheit in Ungarn ist es unerlässlich, ihre Verbundenheit mit den übrigen mittelosteuropäischen Minderheiten auf verschiedenen Ebenen darzustellen. So müssen bei ihrer typologischen Einordnung die historischen Ursachen ihrer Entstehung, die territorialen und sprachlichen Verhältnisse ihres Daseins als objektive Kriterien angesetzt werden.

Selbstverständlich gehören hierher z.B. auch der juristische Status, wie auch eine Reihe von subjektiven Faktoren, wie z.B. die Hingezogenheit oder das Zusammengehörigkeitsgefühl mit einer muttersprachlichen oder lokalen Gemeinschaft.

2. Sprachliche Situation und Sprachwahl

Aus dem bisher Erörterten geht hervor, dass die sprachliche Situation dieser Minderheit ein ziemlich heterogenes Bild zeigt. Wir sind Augenzeugen von komplexen Prozessen, die auch bei den anderen Minderheiten dieser Region anzutreffen sind, zum anderen aber als typische Erscheinungen der ungarndeutschen Situation zu betrachten sind. Die Typizität ergibt sich aus der eigenartigen Entwicklung und der Konstellation der historischen, soziokulturellen und sprachsoziologischen Faktoren, die die sprachliche Situation dieser Minderheit mitbestimmen.[5]

Eine der wichtigsten Fragen bezüglich der Existenz einer Sprachminderheit ist die der Sprachkompetenz. Da es um eine Minderheit geht, erwartet man die Kenntnis, den Gebrauch der Minderheitensprache, hier einen deutschen Ortsdialekt. Doch dieser ist nur sehr eingeschränkt vorhanden: man beklagt einen Domänen- und damit parallel einen Funktionsverlust der lokalen Mundarten, dessen historische Wurzeln sich eigentlich schon um die Jahrhundertwende im Kreise der städtischen Bevölkerung sichtbar machten.

Nach dem zweiten Weltkrieg setzte sich der schon seit geraumer Zeit in der Schicht der Intellektuellen begonnene Assimilationsprozess, vor allem die sprachliche Assimilation, auch in der ländlichen Bevölkerung durch.[6] Von den zahlreichen Ursachen sollen hier nur einige relevante soziolinguistischer Art angeführt werden:

1) In der Nachkriegszeit (nach 1945) erfreute sich die deutsche Sprache in Ungarn keiner Beliebtheit. Selbst in dem dialektfesten südlichen Teil des Landes—in einer Region mit vielen deutschstämmigen Siedlungen— beschränkte sich der Ortsdialekt (früher die einzige Kommuikationssprache)

auf die vertraute private Sphäre. Das war die Zeit, wo man sich seines deutschen Dialektes schämte;

2) Die sozialen Aufstiegschancen in Ungarn waren schon immer an das vollkommene Beherrschen der ungarischen Sprache gebunden. Diese Tatsache hatte u.a. zur Folge, dass selbst in der primären Sozialisation häufig die deutsche Sprache verdrängt und die ungarische bewusst in den Vordergrund gestellt wurde. Leider ging man damals oft von der falschen Annahme aus, dass eine zweisprachige Sozialisation eine zusätzliche Belastung für das Kind sein könnte und seine schulischen Leistungen negativ beeinflussen könnte;

3) Bei den Ungarndeutschen fehlte in der oben erwähnten Zeit eine deutschsprachige Schriftlichkeit, es gab weder repräsentative, in der Öffentlichkeit auftretende deutschschreibende, sich zur deutschen Minderheit bekennende Autoren, noch sonstige Möglichkeiten der Etablierung des Deutschseins, der Anerkennung und Verbreitung der deutschen Sprache und Kultur;[7]

4) Die Ende der 1950er Jahren für die deutsche Minderheit ins Leben gerufenen Medien (Lokalrundfunk: Fünfkirchner Rundfunk und die *Neue Zeitung*, das Wochenblatt der Ungarndeutschen) übten schon seit ihrer Entstehung eine große Wirkung auf die Bevölkerung aus, doch eher auf lokaler Ebene. Zudem erschienen sie in einer Zeit, als die Dialekterosion schon eingesetzt hatte, also der Sprachverlust schon fortgeschritten war und Generationen ausschließlich in ungarischer Sprache sozialisiert worden sind.

Mit den genannten Ursachen ist auch der Wandel des Prestiges des Deutschen zu erklären. Während für die älteste Generation der Ortsdialekt die Identitätssprache ist, ist dies bei allen anderen Generationen heute nicht mehr der Fall. Interessant ist jedoch anzumerken, dass in all der Zeit ihres Daseins für die Ungarndeutschen die ungarische Sprache, die Landessprache einen Prestige besaß und für die Intellektuellen, auch für die städtische deutschsprechende Bevölkerung es die Identitäts- und Prestigesprache gelichzeitig war, war doch der soziale Aufstieg an diese Sprache gebunden.

Infolge der oben angeführten historisch bedingten und mehrere Jahrzehnte dauernden sprachverändernden Prozesse setzt sich das gegenwärtige Sprach-Mosaik zusammen. Grundsätzlich kann man heute noch von einem deutschen Sprachbewusstsein sprechen, das sich mehr auf den rezeptiven als auf den produktiven Gebrauch des Deutschen[8] beschränkt. Die Ungarndeutschen haben eine bewusste Kenntnis über den plurizentrischen Charakter des Deutschen, sie wissen wohl um die verschiedenen Erscheinungsformen des Deutschen: So differenzieren sie nicht nur zwischen den von älteren Menschen gesprochenen Ortsdialekten, einer ungarndeutschen Mischsprache und dem "noblen" Deutsch, sondern man erkennt auch schon die Unterschiede der deutschen Sprache in den deutschsprachigen TV-Sendungen, die schon überall zu empfangen sind.

So nimmt es auch nicht wunder, dass es Anzeichen einer Doppelidentität gibt, die u.a. auch dadurch zum Ausdruck kommt, dass von den Gewährspersonen in den meisten Fällen Ungarisch als Muttersprache, als Nationalität jedoch Deutsch angegeben wird.

Aus den Fragebogenuntersuchungen geht hervor, dass ein steigendes Interesse und die eindeutige Motivation bei der mittleren und jungen Generation der Ungarndeutschen vorhanden ist, die deutsche Standardsprache durch gesteuerten Schulunterricht oder auf privatem Weg, evtl. durch Deutschlandaufenthalte, durch Reisen, die Medien etc. zu erlernen.

Aufgrund der bisherigen Untersuchungsergebnisse lassen sich für die Ungarndeutschen folgende Sprachgenerationen aufstellen:

Generation A: Dialektgeneration (Vorkriegsgeneration, vor 1930 Geborene).
Ihre Muttersprache und erste Sprache ist der lokale Dialekt, den sie heute noch ungezwungen gebrauchen und über stabile Dialektstrukturen verfügen. Ihre Zweitsprache erlernten sie in der sekundären Sozialisation, in der Schule auf dem Arbeitsplatz und häufig merkt man ihnen einen Akzent an. Sie sind noch Mundart-dominante Zweisprachige, die meistens ortsansässig und wenig mobil sind.

Generation B: Stumme Generation (Kriegsgeneration, 1930-45).
Auch ihre primäre Sozialisation erfolgte im lokalen Dialekt, doch ihre funktional erste Sprache ist durch ihre sekundäre Sozialisation und Erwebstätigkeit Ungarisch geworden. Sie sind die sog. stumme Generation, die ihre Muttersprache zu Gunsten der Landessprache verdrängen musste und daher nicht mehr Vermittler dieser sein können.

Generation C: Die Generation der Passiv Zweisprachigen (Nachkriegsgeneration, 1946-60).
Im günstigen Fall hatten sie von zu Hause noch durch die Großeltern, evtl. Eltern den Ortsdialekt gehört, doch überwiegend wurden sie durch Schule, Ausbildung und Beruf ungarisch sozialisiert. Die Mischehen sind in dieser Generation nichts Auffälliges mehr. Die Mobilität ist in dieser Generation groß, auch gab für sie die Möglichkeit, schon in der Schule an einem gesteuerten Deutschunterricht (Minderheitenunterricht) teilzunehmen. Durch die bereits in den 1980er Jahren gestatteten Reisemöglichkeiten, die

Medien, durch persönliche Kontakte, evtl. ihren Beruf sprechen sie auch die deutsche Standardsprache. Oft haben sie noch eine Verstehenskompetenz der Mundart, auch ein Zugehörigkeitsgefühl zur deutschen Minderheit.

Generation D: Die Generation mit Deutsch als Fremd- oder Zweitsprache (1960-).

Ihre primäre wie sekundäre Sozialisation verlief in Ungarisch, meistens sind keine oder mit Ausnahmen nur Dialektkenntnisse vorhanden. Die deutsche Sprache (Standardvarietät, Umgangssprache, Jugendsprache, auch Fachsprachen) erlernten sie in der Schule, durch Medien, Reisen, Freundschaften. Durch die Jugendorgansiation der Ungarndeutschen gibt es Anzeichen einer Mundart-Revitalisierung, einer erwachenden Identität,die vor allem durch eine Intensiveierung des Kontaktes mit den Großeltern, durch das Konsumieren der ungarndeutschen und deutschsprachigen Medien, sowie durch Reisemöglichkeiten und Studienaufenthalte in Deutschland wichtige Impulse erhalten.

Das allgemeine Bild der gegenwärtigen Sprachkompetenz dieser Minderheit ist mit dem der übrigen in Sprachinselsituation lebenden Minderheiten ziemlich identisch, es kann höchstens zu einigen Verschiebungen im Assimilationsgrad kommen: wegen dem allgemeinen Funktionsverlust bzw. dem Verschwinden der ursprüng ichen Ortsdialekte sowie der kontinuierliche und wachsende Einfluss der Landessprache, der ungarischen Sprache auf den Sprachgebrauch dieser Gruppe, führte verständlicherweise zu einem erhöhten Codeswitching, zu einer sog. Mischsprache. Das sind bekannte Kommunikationsmechanismen in Kontaktsituationen, die früher oder später, zu einem völligen Sprach- und Identitätsverlust der Minderheit führen werden. Gleichzeitig sind es auch ernst zu nehmende Zeichen für das Setzen sprachpolitischer Maßnahmen.

Die oben erwähnte Mischform, der häufige Gebrauch ungarischer lexikalischer Elemente in deutschen Äußerungen (Mundart) ist charakteristisch auch für ältere Menschen im Gespräch über Alltagsthemen, in der mittleren Generation eher typisch für Sprecher und Sprecherinnen, die mangelhafte Dialekt- und Deutschkenntnisse haben. Atypisch ist das Codeswitchen im Sprachgebrauch von Jugendlichen. Letztere sprechen ein "schulisches Hochdeutsch" oder antworten nur ungarisch auf die in Deutsch gestellten Fragen.

In dieser Mischsprache haben wir es mit einem spezifischen Fall der CodeswitchingSituation zu tun.[9] Hierbei geht es nicht um das klassische Diglossie-Konzept, in dem zwischen zwei Varietäten ein und derselben Sprache der Codewechsel erfolgt, sondern es wird zwischen zwei dieser Sprachgemeinschaft am nächsten stehenden und die am häufigsten gebrauchten Sprachformen, dem funktional primären

Ungarisch und dem im Sprachgebrauch dieser Minderheit an der Peripherie angesiedelten deutschen Dialekt gewechselt.

Dieses durch die Nominationslücken entstandene Switchen hat sich insbesondere nach der Auflösung der deutschen Sprachgemeinschaften nach 1945, durch die kontinuierliche Kontaktsituation und den äußerst eingeschränkten Gebrauch der Mundart herausgebildet. Die Füllung der lexikalischen Lücken durch ungarische Lexeme hat sich im heutigen Sprachgebrauch dermaßen durchgesetzt, dass es den Sprechern gar nicht mehr bewusst und zudem auch ganz natürlich erscheint.

Grundsätzlich geht es um intersequentielle Codeswitching-Formen, die im Sprachgebrauch der Ungarndeutschen die wichtige Funktion haben, im Kommunikationsakt eine höhere referentielle Effizienz beim Gesprächspartner zu erzielen. Zu verstehen ist dies aufgrund der Überzeugung der Minderheitensprecher— dies belegen die Fragebogenergebnisse—dass gewisse, für die Situation relevante Gegenstände, Tatsachen, Begebenheiten oder für den aus dem gleichen Milieu kommenden Gesprächspartner gewisse Inhaltswörter, Lexeme in ihrer ungarischen Form aussagekräftiger, expressiver und transparenter sind, als die in der Mundart gebrauchten oder aus dem Ungarischen mühsam übersetzten lexikalischen Einheiten. Nebenbei ist es auch schneller, daher ökonomischer, parate ungarische Wörter einzusetzen, als lange nach dem entsprechenden deutschen Wort (auch Mundartwort) zu suchen.

Ausagekäftiger erscheinen die ungarischen Lexeme aus dem Grunde, weil die Begrifflichkeit der Alltagssprache dieser Menschen, ihre kognitive Erfahrung, aufgrund ihrer soziokulturellen Einbettung in die Gesellschaft, sich in ungarischer Sprache gestaltet. Infolge des ständigen inter- und intrasequentiellen Codeswitchens wird zwar die systemlinguistische Kohärenz ihrer Äußerungen verletzt, dass nämlich im Laufe der Interaktion durchgehend zwei Sprachen gesprochen werden, es wird jedoch gleichzeitig, in der Perzeption der Sprecher, die kommunikative Kohärenz der Äußerungen gestärkt. Diese kommunikative Kohärenz wird von einer kognitiven Kohärenz unterstützt, und diese basiert auf dem Wissen der Sprecher, dass nämlich die Gesprächspartner die ungarischen Wörter mitsamt ihren Konnotationen verstehen, kennen und situationsadäquat deuten können.

Somit ist der Kommuikationsradius dieser Mischsprache eingeschränkt auf die Interaktion mit den Ortsansässigen und den Ungarndeutschen, die beider Sprachen mächtig sind.

Die Sprachwahl stellt ein dynamisches System dar, das nach den soziolinguistischen Parametern, wie Alter, Bildung, Situation, Thema und Ort, variieren kann. Auf die gegenwärtige Sprachsituation und Sprachgenerationen bezogen entsteht folgendes Gefüge der Sprachen:

A-A Mundart
A-B Mundart
A-C Mundart/Ungarisch
A-D Mundart/Ungarisch

B-A Mundart
B-B Mundart, im Beisein von A, sonst Ungarisch
B-C Ungarisch
B-D Ungarisch

C-A Standarddeutsch/Ungarisch
C-B Ungarisch
C-C Ungarisch
C-D Ungarisch

D-A Ungarisch/Standarddeutsch/selten Dialekt
D-B Ungarisch
D-C Ungarisch
D-D Ungarisch/selten Standarddeutsch/Dialekt zur Ausgrenzung zu anderen

Eine Varietätenumschichtung setzt bei Generation C, der passiv Zweisprachigen ein, die mangels dialektaler Kenntnisse die deutsche Standardsprache als Kommunikationsmittel mit Ungrandeutschen einsetzen, bzw. einsetzen können. Bei Generation D, der Generation mit Deutsch als Fremdsprache sind—wie bereits erwähnt—Anzeichen einer bewussten Revitalisierung der Dialekte bzw. der ungarndeutschen Identität zu sehen. Diese Revitalisierungsversuche fallen mit dem Erkennen der wirtschaftlichen Rolle der deutschen Sprache zusammen und diese beide Tendenzen unterstützen einander gegenseitig.

3. Sprachhandlungsstrategien

Wie oben angeführt, hat das Feld der Sprachwahl zwischen den verschiedenen Generationen gezeigt, dass der deutschen Minderheit, überhaupt den Sprachinselminderheiten ein Repertoire an Sprachen und Varietäten zur Verfügung steht, mit Hilfe derer sie ihre Sprachhandlungen durchführen können. Bestimmend und charakteristisch für eine Minderheit ist ihre—aus welchen Gründen auch getroffene—Wahl vom gegebenen Repertoire, in einer gegebenen Situation, unter gegebenen soziokulturellen Umständen.

Die Sprachwahl erfolgt teilweise bewusst, wie das im Sprachgefüge der Generationen zu sehen war, teilweise jedoch erfolgt die Wahl der entsprechenden

Sprache oder Varietät in der gegebenen Situation unbewusst. Das kommunikative Handeln im Alltag wird bestimmt durch ihre kognitiv erlebte Welt, ihre Erfahrungswelt und durch ihren sprachlichen Alltag, der infolge der sehr eingeschränkten Domänen für die deutsche Sprache, bis zu 90% in ungarischer Sprache verläuft.

Mit anderen Worten, die Allgegenwärtigkeit der ungarischen Sprache, ihr Nutzbarkeitsgrad und kommunikativer Wert ist dermaßen hoch, dass es für die Minderheit—bis auf einige private Situationen in den Sprachhandlungen der ältesten Generation—kein Anlass, keine Notwendigkeit zu geben scheint, Sprachhandlungen in einer Varietät des Deutschen durchzuführen.

Die diese Minderheit umgebenden narrativen Welten sind durch das Ungarische geprägt. Lediglich bei Generation A lässt sich über mundartgebundene- und geprägte Narrativen sprechen, wie die Erzählungen über die Vergangenheit, ihre Erlebnisse aus der Kindheit, Familiengeschichten, Autobiographien, aber auch manche, mit den Bräuchen und Sitten zusammenhängende situationsgebundene Alltagsdialoge.[10]

Selbst diese Situationen werden nicht ausschließlich im Dialekt versprachlicht, sondern eher abwechselnd im Ortsdialekt und Ungarisch, bzw. in der erwähnten Mischsprache. Der Ortsdialekt ist in diesen Fällen nur eine komplementäre Form, manchmal eine Ausweichform mit Signalwert, zum Ungarischen. Es sei hier jedoch angemerkt, dass in Fällen, in denen der Ortsdialekt gebraucht wird, die Norm und die Regeln der Mundart dominieren, wenn auch eine Reihe von Interferenzphänomene sicherlich zum Vorschein kommen.[11]

Das erscheint für die Sprecher aller Generationen auch als selbstverständlich, denn Bestandteile der Narrativen, in die die Sprachinselminderheit eingebettet ist, sind auch jene Klischees, Idiome, Kollokationen, alle semiproduktiven Elemente, auch die gängigen Fachjargonismen, die im Alltagsgespräch vorkommen, die alle in ungarischer Sprache gespeichert und auch in dieser abrufbar sind. Zu diesen unser Bewusstsein prägenden Narrativen gehören auch bestimmte Textfragmente und Textteile, die während des Gesprächs aktiviert werden, wie z.B. der gesamte Dialog bei einem Arztbesuch, bei den Behörden, etc. Durch diese Textteile öffnet sich ein Script, jenes Drehbuch, das nicht übersetzt zu werden braucht, sondern in der erlebten und gebäuchlichen sprachlichen Form zum Vorschein kommt. Es kann zwar vorkommen, dass manche Matrix-Sätze im Dialekt gesprochen werden oder dass Textteile in einer anderssprachig erlebten Situation als Zitat oder als ein nonproduktives Element eingefügt werden, doch grundsätzlich bildet die ungarische Sprache das Grundgerüst der bewussten und unbewussten Sprachhandlungen.

4. Fazit

Die bewusste Sprachwahl der Sprachinselminderheiten in ihren täglichen Interaktionen hat, wie oben angeführt, zahlreiche linguistische und außerlinguistische Ursachen, die als ein komplexes Gefüge in der Sprachhandlung aktiviert werden. Hinzu kommt noch das jeweilige Sprachrepertoire des Gesprächspartners, das ebenfalls ein wichtiger Parameter bei der Sprachwahl darstellt. Aus dem Erörterten zur Sprachkompetenz und Sprachwahl deht eindeutig hervor, dass beim überwiegenden Teil der Sprachgenerationen der Ungarndeutschen die ungarische Sprache das wichtigste Kommunikationsmittel wurde und somit sich der Sprachwechsel bei dieser Minderheit vollzogen hatte. Allein gezielte und differenzeiert ausgearbeitete Fragebögen mitsamt der sozioökonomischen Hintergrundkenntnissen dierser Minerheit vermögen den bereits vollzogenen Prozess des Sprachwlchsels chronologisch einorden.

Der deutsche Ortsdialekt ist lediglich an der Peripherie ihres Kommunikationsrepertoires angesiedelt, wobei die deutsche Standardsprache immer mehr an Bedeutung gewinnt. Dadurch kann sie sich—unter bestimmten Voraussetzungen und gesellschaftlichen Bedingungen—auch zu einer Varietät mit hoher Gebrauchsfrequenz mindestens für einen Teil der Sprachgenerationen entwickeln.

Ob dadurch der Dialektverlust der Ungarndeutschen ausgeglichen werden kann, ist noch unbeantwortet. Offen ist auch die Frage, welche Funktionen diese Varietät des Deutschen übernehmen kann und wird, bzw. in welchen Domänen sie vorherrschen wird. Die Frage nach der sprachlichen und kulturellen Identität der Sprachinselminderheiten wird somit zu einer Existenzfrage schlechthin.

Anmerkungen

[1] Die Daten stammen von einem Vortrag von Laszlo Szarka, dem Leiter der Forschungsgruppe für ethnische Minderheiten an der Ungarischen Akademie der Wissenschaften, gehalten an einer Konferenz pber den Muttersprachunterricht der Minderheiten an der Akademie der Wissenschaften, am 8-10 April 1999, in Budapest.

[2] Es geht um Identitätserhebungen bei den deutschsprachigen Minderheiten im Komitat Pest, Veszprem, in den Streusiedlungen der Sathmarer Region und in der Zips, bei den Slowkane im Pilis Gebirge, durchgeführt von der Forschungsgruppe für Minderheiten der Akademie der Wissenschaften in Ungarn. Die hier benutzten Angaben stammen aus dem oben erwähnten Vortrag von L. Szarka.

[3] Man könnte ohne Übertreibung auch über eine Stigmatisierung der deutschen Mundarten sprechen, was selbstverständlich dazu führte, dass selbst die primäre Sozialisation in den Familien nicht in der stigmatisierten Sprache, sondern in der Landessprache erfolgte.

[4] Man spricht über einen sog. Fremdsprachenboom, in der Fremdsprachenwahl nimmt nach Englisch die deutsche Sprache den vornehmen zweiten Platz ein.

⁵ Die in diesem Aufsatz dargestellten Fakten basieren auf einer mit Dr. Maria Erb (Budapest) gemeinsam durchgeführten Fragebogenuntersuchung in der ungrandeutschen Erwachsenenbevölkerung im südlichen (Pecs, Baja und Umgebung) bzw. im nördlichen Teil (Budapest und Umgebung) in den Jahren 1996-99.

⁶ Wohlgemerkt, es geht hierbei um eine Minderheit, die seit ihrer Ansiedlung in Ungarn nie in geschlossenen Sprachgebieten lebte, sondern in einigen mehr oder weniger kompakten Gebieten und in Streusiedlungen. Auch waren die von Deutschstämmigen bewohnten Ortschaften hinsichtlich ihrer ethnischen Zusammensetzung nicht homogen. Besonderns im südlichen Teil des Landes (Batschka, Branau) gab es viele gemischte Dörfer mit einem beträchtlichen slawischen, später grossen ungarischen Bevölkerungsanteil. Heute sind es mehrheitlich Dörfer mit einer überwiegenden ungarischen Bevölkerung.

⁷ Eine Gruppe ungarndeutscher und deutschschreibender Autoren ist erst in den 70er Jahren entstanden. Ihre Akzeptanz und ihr Bekanntsheitsgrad bei der Bevölkerung ist bis heute noch nicht bedeutsam.

⁸ Unter Deutsch verstehe ich hiermit jede mögliche Varietät des Deutschen, die von Sprechern dieser Minderheit gebraucht wird.

⁹ Vgl. dazu die Ausführungen Bartha Cs.1999, 119-22; sowie Calderon,M.(1999, 76 ff.)

¹⁰ Z.B. Kochgewohnheiten, Schlachten, manche Handwerkertätigkeiten, Hochzeitsbräuche, etc.

¹¹ Diese Mundartsituationen liefern den Exploratoren das sprachliche Material, das linguistisch beschrieben werden kann. So sind die ungarndeutschen Dialekte besonders auf der phinetischen, morphologischen, teils lexikalischen Ebene gut erfasst, weniger gut erfasst auf der syntaktischen und der Ebene der Wortbildung. Ganz unbesprochen ist die pragmatische Ebene dieser Dialekte.

Literatur

Bartha, Csilla. 1999. *A kétnyelvıség alapkérdései (Fundamental Questions of Bilingualism)*. Budapest.

Calderon, Maria. 1999. "Codeswitching am Beispiel der spanischsprachigen israelischen Wochenzeitung AURORA." *Moderne Sprachen* 43,1: 35-45.

Erb, Maria, und Elisabeth Knipf. 1998. "Sprachgewohnheiten bei den Ungarndeutschen." In *Beiträge zur Dialektologie des ostoberdeutschen Raumes*, hrsg. Klaus J. Hutterer und Getrude Pauritsch, 253-67. Göppingen.

Huesmann, Anette. 1998. *Zwischen Dialekt und Standard: Empirische Untersuchung zur Soziolinguistik des Varietätenspektrums im Deutschen*. Tübingen.

Hutterer, Klaus J. 1991. "Hochsprache ünd Mundart bei den Deutschen in Ungarn." In *C. J. Hutterer: Aufsätze zur deutschen Dialektologie*, hrsg. Karl Manherz, 313-44. Budapest. Ungarndeutsche Studien 6.

Kiss, Jenö. 1995. *Társadalom és nyelvhasználat (Society and Language Use)*. Budapest

Knipf, Elisabeth, und Maria Erb. 2000. "Observations on the Proficiency of the German Minority in Hungary." In *Minorities Research* 2, hrsg. Cholnoky Gyözö, 99-112. Budapest.

Philip E. Webber
Central College
Pella, Iowa

Speel up't Plattdüütsch: . . . so ein Theater!

This is one of the success stories, albeit with its own fair share of ups and downs, in the history of insular speaker-pools in the American Midwest. It remains to be seen whether there will be further chapters in this narrative.

Iowa's oldest East Frisian settlement extends into the counties of Butler, Franklin, Grundy and Hardin.[1] Here a well-maintained sign proclaims local pride in the immigrant heritage, showing Ostfriesland (not Germany) as the land of origin, and a spot in north-central Iowa as the ultimate point of destination.

At the East Friesland Presbyterian Church and nearby, one can find gravestones documenting birthplaces in such communities of the fatherland as Simonswolde. Enviable genealogical resources (both published and unpublished) abound at the Wellsburg Public Library and at the Ackley Heritage Center, though many remain inaccessible to the majority of residents, for whom High German is a very foreign language. Nevertheless, one can still hear fourth-generation speakers, and fifth-generation semi-speakers, of the locally dominant variety of East Frisian Low German.

But . . . do not wait too long to capture and document this language. In early 2001, Albert Kruse passed on at the age of 101 years. The days of the fluent speakers are numbered, and the author of this paper does not claim any sort of proprietary or territorial claim to linguistic fieldwork in this community. Research by other investigators is welcome.

Although this area, on which the present paper focuses, is fairly well defined, the residents feel far from isolated. Other sizable speaker pools exist in the state, especially further west and north along the Minnesota border in the Iowa counties of Osceola, Emmet, Kossuth and Winnebago. Local residents travel to, and receive visits from, out-of-state communities of *Ostfriesen* (as they often call themselves). Invitations are regularly extended to, or received from, fellow-East Frisians in Illinois and Minnesota. Even those who cannot speak the ethnic language enjoy periodic festivals and special commemorative events. At the very least, one can enjoy a cup of strong tea with rock sugar and the much-admired decorative "blossom" of cream floating on the surface of the beverage.

Burdette Walters is unusual in several regards. He is one of only a few pre-retirement-age fluent speakers of the local East Frisian Platt. He is also one of the rare individuals in the area who is also fluent in High German, which he taught for some years before entering another line of work.

In the mind-1990s, two separate but related events took place. Although Iowa had been home to the now-defunct *Ostfriesische Nachrichten*, and continued to claim the Ostfriesen Genealogical Society, East Frisian-Americans in the Butler-Franklin-Grundy-Hardin County area came to the sad but correct realization that, though they had been active in researching the legacy of their past, some provision needed to be made for the future cultivation of the heritage and the language. The result of this was the founding of the now quite active Ostfriesen Heritage Society.[2] This initiative received a major infusion of interest when, in the autumn of 1995, the Ländliche Akademie Krummhörn toured the Midwest, giving three sellout performances at the Grundy Center high school auditorium of the Low German musical play *Achter de Sünn an*.[3]

The energy and enthusiasm of local residents expressed itself in the 1995 "Ostfriesland Days," a festive series of events encompassing not only the musical theater production of *Achter de Sünn an*, but also a display on immigration entitled "Van de een an de andere Kant" introduced by University of Oldenburg's Dr. Horst Rößler, a photo exhibition by Martin Stromann on contemporary Ostfriesland, and readings by Heye de Vries from his novel *Moyhut*.

No doubt, *Achter de Sünn an* owed much of its success to the fact that the Ländliche Akademie Krummhörn had provided for the transformation of Hamburg author Ingo Sax's Low German and Helga Joesten's libretto (set to music by Kai Leinweber) into the language of the Krummhörn, a variety of East Frisian readily understood by virtually all local (Iowa) speakers in attendance.

In this same general period, various informal efforts began to reflect an unmistakable increase in energy and sense of purpose. These included, among other things, periodic church services with the sermon in East Frisian (or in a variety easily understood by the local audience), the inimitable Ostfriesen Gab Fest, and wintertime language lessons. From time to time, poetess Ebalena Kruse shared her original East Frisian poetry, or adapted a short text for recitation in the local ethnic language.

Though High German lessons never enjoyed much popularity, those in Platt certainly did, with one section for beginners, and another for speakers wishing to resuscitate such language skills as might lie dormant. One speaker regularly traversed parts of three counties in order to participate in these "language revival" sessions.[4]

Language Class at Wellsburg Library

In 1998, the author of this paper devoted a one-term sabbatical leave from Central College to the collection of personal memories, sayings, anecdotes, and speech samples by speakers at varying levels of fluency. The resulting product, made possible by support from the Iowa Humanities Board (now Humanities Iowa), was a series of three videos entitled "Telling What's on Our Minds: Orally Transmitted Culture in Iowa's Oldest East Friesian [*sic*] Colony."[5] The taped material, close to eight hours after selective

285

editing and accompanied by a sixteen-page log of contents, consists primarily of individual and group interviews, usually with some material in both East Frisian Platt and English, on topics related to ethnicity and language in the local community. As frequently happens in such undertakings, modest local residents who barely dared at first to contribute to the project, began to sense that the intactness of their heritage was of unsuspected value to the outside research community.

It was also at this time that a handful of zealots launched an initiative to put on a stage production in the ethnic language. Two speakers of the local variety of East Frisian Low German "modified [and] translated" Hans Balzer's Low German play *Sien gefährliche Vittelstünn*, thereby creating *Sien gefohrl'ke Voertelstuenn*, a "Plaatdüüts Play" [*sic*] that enjoyed tremendous local popularity.[6]

A scene from the October, 1999 premier performance
of *Sien gefohrl'ke Voertelstuenn* before a packed house
in Wellsburg, Iowa

Two productions were staged in the autumn of 1999 and one in the summer of 2000. In the late spring of 2001, the troupe performed in Germany.

Because *Sien gefohrl'ke Voertelstuenn* manages to reach the local audience while maintaining remarkable fidelity to its model, it provides an excellent basis for a contrastive study of language varieties from Germany's not-so-very homogeneous "Low German" territory.[7] (Passages from Balzer's *Vittelstünn* and from the adaptation *Voertelstuenn* are cited by the scene number of the original version.)

One obvious change from Balzer's text is the fact that all stage directions are in English. The original High German would be totally incomprehensible to virtually all local speakers. Actors' lines appear in their "modified [and] translated" form with an idiomatic translation into English, the dominant language even of those local speakers who claim East Frisian Platt as their first language.

Another change lies in the unheralded yet important fact that the text of the adaptation appears in an ad hoc orthography created to reflect local speech realities (an accomplishment meriting its own study). Word-final syllabic sonorants, for example, are typically written without a preceding vowel, but separated by an apostrophe to indicate separation from the preceding syllable, e.g., *kom'n, Schloet'l*. The orthography is usually quite regular, occasional inconsistencies notwithstanding (e.g., *dit* alongside *ditt*).

Several changes in language result from the social milieu in which the adaptation evolved. For example, the question in Balzer's text "Wöllt wi nich du seggen?" has little meaning in the Iowa speaker pool where no distinction exists between informal and formal pronouns of address; the question becomes "Sull'n wi uns nu naet altied bi 't erst Naam'n anprot'n?" and "Broderschaft drinken" is rendered as "up Fruendschkupp drink'n" (18).

Still another adaptation lies in avoiding any appearance of taking God's name in vain. Earthy though the Iowa East Frisian may be, they generally take their faith seriously. Language classes, for instance, begin with recitation of the Lord's Prayer in a local translation. Hence, it is not surprising that (to cite but a few examples) "Och Gott!" becomes "Nee, sowat gift ja wall naet?" and "Gottsidank, dat alles nich wohr is" rolls off the Iowa tongue more easily as "Oh, Mann, wat bin ick blied dat dat all naet wohr is" (1, 7). In this same vein of thinking, mention of the devil undergoes a complete turnabout when "Dat mag de Düwel weeten!" is transformed into "Dat mag de Himmel waet'n!"(3)

These religious Iowans nevertheless have limited acquaintance with some expressions familiar to native Germans of their generation, including many sayings and maxims derived from (German) Scripture. Those who can recall services with readings from Luther's translation of the Bible, and preaching in an idiom that imitated it, readily confess that High German was a totally foreign language to be "tuned out" while waiting for the moment that "de kark was ut" and use of a familiar language might resume. The resultant situation is one in which a fair number will discuss matters of faith in the ethnic language, but virtually all cite the Bible in English. Hence, for purposes of the stage production, 'Hiobspost' becomes simply "mahl Boeskup" (10).

Obvious though it may be, we need to remember that the adaptation *Voertelstuenn* is, after all, an American production requiring a few cultural cues for better comprehension. The Iowans are neither ignorant nor disdainful of the virtues of good "echt Pils," but respond more readily to the designation "n'echte Pilsner Beer" (4). Until America embraces the metric system, it is perhaps inevitable that "dörtig Meter" will need to be rendered as "hunnert faut" (17).

Near the end of the play, Marquardt tells Elly "Deern, Deern, wat hebbt Se hier för'n Theater up de Been bröcht!" to which Elly replies "Un nu kummt de letzte Akt" (22). Because *Theater* does not have the pejorative meaning "fuss, fracas" for Iowa East Frisians, Marquardt simply says "Wicht, watt hesst Du hier doch watt up dae Baeh'n brocht!" to which Elly replies in a manner that cannot be ambiguous to speakers of English for whom "de letzte Akt" might have other meanings: "Ja, un nu kumt daeh laesde Akt van ditt Theater." (22)

The fact that the language of the original *Vittelstünn* is one variety of Low German does not guarantee a familiar vocabulary and idiom for Iowa speakers of East Frisian Low German. After all, Ingo Sax's Hamburg Low German required modification before the Ländliche Adakemie Krummhörn could produce *Achter de Sünn an* in Pilsum, and subsequently for the Iowa East Frisians.

Thus, we note that Balzer's colloquial lines "wi staht hier rüm en denkt uns allerhand appeldwatschen Kram ut" become "wi stahn hier al wat rum und denk'n uns 'n haelbuelt Kram ut" (9); "[he] hett...nich papp seggt" is now "[hae] hett...gaehn Woordje proot" (23). Among the more frequently recurring lexical substitutions from Balzer's Low German to Iowa East Frisian are: *bös > mal; Deern, Mäken > Wicht; froh > blied; gornich > haelnaet; hüt > vandaag; Klock > Uehr; mal > eb'n; Minschen > Keerl* (with the medial consonant usually pronounced as an alveolar flap); *rein > schkon; snacken > proot'n; schön > moej; Slaapstuw > Schlaapkamer; töwen > wachten.*

Even more substitutions come in the wake of what one might describe (with no pejorative intent) as the systematic elimination of any High German felt to be lingering in the original *Vittelstünn*. Examples of modification include: *Fetzen > Stueckje Tueg* (13); *eine Person weiblichen Geschlechts > 'n Frauminschke* (7); *Platz nehmen > hensett'n* (18); *Quatsch > dumm' Prootereiy* (4); *Schritt > Stappke* (10); *Unordnung > doernanner* (6); *ehr Wirtin > dae, wor sae bi wohnt* (10). Forms that strike the Iowa East Frisian ear as High German with a mere bit of a Low German veneer also undergo modification: *in Orrnung maken* appears as *up Stee mak'n; in Upregung* as *doerdreiht* (18), etc.

Though my investigation is not primarily one of phonology, I do wish to include a sampling of *Vittelstünn / Voertelstuenn* contrastive pairs illustrating some main differences between the probable intended pronunciation patterns of the two texts. The following list is intended to complement, rather than to repeat, examples already cited. In addition, I have selected items whose East Frisian forms reflect patterns that I have encountered with consistency among members of the speaker pool: *beten / bietje* (passim); *besapen / besoop'n* (2); *verdreegen / verdrag'n* (4); *schöllt / sullt* (4); *du lebe Tiet / du laewe Tied* (8); *Tasch / Taschke* (8); *Bost / Borst* (9); *Swien / Schwien* (16); *swümmen / schwemmen* (17); *nöger / nahder* (18); *Luf / Luecht* (19); *Husslötel / Husschloetel* (23); pronouns without and with initial [h], for example, *em / hem* (passim).

Differences in grammar and syntax are often less pronounced, though present. Balzer's text still has a marked subjunctive form, e.g., *wör* vs. *was* (2); it also has a pronoun of polite address, *Se /Ehr*, while the Iowa version uses *du* or, when situation calls for it, the plural *jie* with an initial palatalized alveolar glide. Verbs with a plural subject are marked in Balzer's text with a final [t], whereas in Iowa, the form is identical with the infinitive, and in most cases the morphemic element is pronounced (and represented in writing) as a syllabic sonorant, e.g., *proot'n*. The Iowa text also shows a propensity for noun plurals marked by an alveolar fricative. Finally, use of the verb *gehören* to indicate possession is not common in *Voertelstuenn* or among the Iowa East Frisians for whom the play was produced, e.g., "Gehört disse Kamm Frollein Klüth?" vs. "Is dit Elly hoer Kaam?" (13).

While there is a definite decline in the number of younger speakers of Iowa East Frisian, one needs to bear in mind the group's record of linguistic tenacity, and the fact that this play was produced to celebrate and cultivate the local vitality of the language. While I fear that the prognosis for the language is one of endangerment, and that scholars wishing to study this language island need to do so soon, I am far from ready to sound the death knell for Iowa East Frisian. Rather, I wish to rejoice in the fact that, while it was possible to do so, active speakers produced a play that will remain a significant linguistic monument well into the future.

Notes

[1] For a general sketch of (West, North, and East) Frisians in the United States, see Philip E. Webber, "Frisians," in *American Immigrant Cultures: Builders of a Nation*, ed. David Levinson and Melvin Ember (New York: Simon & Schuster Macmillan, 1997), 297-301. The specific cultural history of the East Frisians, including that of the area of Iowa that offers the focus for this study, appears in John A. Saathoff, "The Eastfriesians in the United States: A Study in the Process of Assimilation," Ph.D. diss., University of Iowa, 1930; George Schnucker, *The East Friesens in America: An Illustrated History of their Colonies to the Present Time*, transl. Kenneth De Wall (Topeka, Kansas: Jostens, 1986); Jürgen Hoogstraat, *Von Ostfriesland nach Amerika. Aus dem Leben ostfriesischer Auswandrer des 19. Jahrhunderts* (Norden: Soltau-Kurier-Norden, 1990); Robert H. Behrens, *We Will Go to a New Land: The Great East Frisian Migration to America 1845-1895* (Mahomet, Illinois: Behrens Publishing, 1998). I have found on many occasions that it pays to consult the literature on East Frisians in America with a copy nearby of W. Lüpkes, *Ostfriesische Volkskunde*, 2d ed. (Emden: Schwalbe, 1925).

[2] Many pertinent personal and organizational addresses appear in *The Ostfriesen Heritage Society Membership Directory*. Currently, individuals to contact for information are Rick Gersema, <rgersema@aol.com> or Nancy Hook, <ronahook@gcmuni.net>. The author is also willing to facilitate initial contacts. Gersema is working on an analysis of the *Nachrichten* necrologies; Matthew R. Lindaman, in the History Department at University of Kansas, is preparing a broad-based study of the *Nachrichten*, with analysis of material relating to language use, advertising, inter-colony networking, and other topics of interest to linguists as well as historians.

³ An article on the musical appeared as a special feature in *Ostfriesland Magazin* (June 1995): 15-22, and subsequently as an eight-page offprint. That same year, the Ländliche Akademie Krummhörn published an expanded, magazine-length program in both German and English: *Achter de Sünn an: Der Weg nach Iowa – Ein Plattdeutsches Musical* for the performance in Pilsum, and *Achter de Sünn an: Follow the Sun—The Way to Iowa—A Musical in LowGerman. Ostfriesland Days Sept. 29 – October 10, 1995 in Iowa* for performances in Buffalo Center and in Wellsburg/Grundy Center, Iowa. This expanded program in the English version also highlighted the other events of 1995 Ostfriesland Days.

⁴ Although Don De Neui conducted classes for beginners and Roger Hook offered a "language revival" section, a strong sense of community prevailed, with a refreshing emphasis on sharing whatever language survived in the community, rather than on teacher-focused instruction.

⁵ Project director was Dee Lindaman, in consultation with the Board of the Ostfriesen Heritage Society: Nancy Hook, Roger Hook, Warren Lindaman, and Lil Marks. The Project Scholar and chief investigator was the author of this paper. Copies of the videotapes "Telling What's on Our Minds" were produced and sold at cost by the Ostfriesen Heritage Society. Unfortunately, the supply on hand has been exhausted. Nevertheless, the tapes are available in a number of key Iowa libraries. For an example of statewide media coverage enjoyed by this project, see Kirsten Scharnberg, "Capturing history before it fades out," *The Des Moines Register*, March 4, 1998, 5M.

⁶ Hans Balzer, *Sien gefährliche Vittelstünn: En lustig Stück in een Akt*. Verden (Aller): Karl Mahnke, n.d.; *Sien gefohrl'keVoertelstuenn (His dangerous quarter-hour): En luestig Stueck in een Akt (A lively piece in one act)*, modified/translated by John A. Conrads and Bernie Conrads, with suggestions from the Eastfriesian Heritage Society, Grundy County, Iowa: 1999. Members of the original cast were Herman Emkes, Mary Schmidt, Mae Hinders, Roger Hook, Jessie Folkerts, and Calvin Wiltfang. With the passing of Wiltfang, Dennis Hippen has joined the cast. The director is Harold Heeren. The Ostfriesen Heritage Society owns tapings of the various productions and parts of productions.

⁷ After using various more comprehensive and/or more recent works, I found that the most practical standards against which to compare the language of the group in question are Wolfgang Lindow, *Plattdeutsch-Hochdeutsches Wörterbuch*, published by the Institut für niederdeutsche Sprache, 4th ed. (Leer: Schuster, 1993), with frequent references to specifically East Frisian forms; *Ostfriesisches Wörterbuch*, comp. and ed. Cirk Heinrich Stürenberg, repr. of the Aurich ed. of 1857 (Leer: Schuster, 1972). and Tjabe Wiesenhann, *Einführung in das ostfriesische Niederdeutsch* (Leer: Schuster, 1977).

Kurt L. Rein
Ludwig-Maximilians-Universität
Munich, Germany

The Dialect Identification Program (DIP)

0. Preliminary Remarks

I would have like to have provided an insight into a real linguistic island not very far from Lawrence, Kansas: The Bukovinians in the west of this state in Ellis County, a group of Germans who immigrated at the end of the nineteenth century from the Austro-Hungarian province of Bukovina, today divided between Rumania and Ukraine. Most of them were farmers and setteled on farmland around Ellis, at that time terminal of the western railway. These "Austrians," as they were called, fell into two groups: Protestant "Swabians," descendants of immigrants from southwest Germany who in southeast Europe were known as "Donauschwaben" and whose dialect comes closest to the speech of the Palatinate, and Catholics speaking a Bavarian dialect as it was spoken in the most southwestern parts of today's Czech Republic. Among its speakers the dialect is called *Deitsch-Behmisch*.

After three or four generations these Bukovinians now are changing from their German dialects to Midwestern English. I have had the opportunity to talk to the last speakers in our native dialect and was able to tape their speech. We thus have before us a linguistic island in its final stages. It is also a small and clearly defined population with a history that is well investigated. Thus these Bukovinians are an ideal subject for further studies concerning such "mobile speech islands" as I referred to them after my research on the Hutterites and other ethnic German immigrants from Eastern Europe, "Auslandsdeutsche" who came to North America during the new wave of immigration at the end of the nineteenth century (Rein 1977).

Whereas the history of this group is fairly well known and researched (Keel/Rein 1996), the linguistic aspects proper have only been superficially documented. The dialect of the "Deutschböhmen," which until recently had received little notice from linguists—in Bukovina or in Germany—has now been thoroughly investigated by Gabriele Lunte and explicitly documented for the first time in her dissertation "The Catholic Bohemian German Dialect of Ellis, Kansas" (1998). Both of the linguistic groups of the Bukovina Germans await more intensive investigations (cf. Rein/Keel 1996; Bücherl/Keel 1996).

1. The Dialect Identification Program (DIP)

One of the results of earlier conferences dedicated to German speech islands in the early 1990s was to invigorate further research in neglected parts of our field. From those meetings the concept of a manual or handbook for speech island research ("Handbuch Sprachinselforschung") was conceived that was to provide better—and easier—access to our rather specialized field of linguistics. It was especially targeted at American colleagues, eager to enter in this field of research without the detailed knowledge of the intricacies of German dialectology and dialect varieties. We, the participants from Munich (myself and my assistants Rainald Bücherl and Bernhard Stör) thought of an instrument for the investigation of any newly discovered speech island in Brazil or Uruguay, in Russia or for that matter in the American Midwest. Our device was to provide all those preliminary dialectological specifics that are necessary to understand and classify a "speech island" within the German dialects and thus contribute to its history.

Our Dialect Indentification Program (DIP; conceived by us in 1995-96 and digitized by one of the best experts for the computerization of German dialect research, Rudolf Post in Kaiserslautern), of course, reflects the "state of the art" of the 1990s—and that means the "Stone Age" in this rapidly growing field. But it is being modernized and prepared for a publication by the Gunter Narr Verlag in Tübingen—hopefully in the not-too-distant future. I therefore will introduce the underlying concepts of our project and invite comments on those concepts as well as on the applicability and usefulness of the DIP in German speech island research.

2. Basic Assumptions

2.1. Dialect Speech as a Relic of German Speech Islands

In these days we are witnessing the near end or disappearance of many, or even most speech islands—at least the German ones—all over the world. Thus seemingly confirming the opinion of some modern researchers, who—not including or not knowing the historical details— regard the very intricate phenomenon of preserving one's language as a minority language as a mere mishap based on the incapability of the speakers to assimilate (cf. Mattheier 1994). But when such linguistic minorities have lasted for centuries, as the Greeks in Southern Italy have for over a thousand years, one finds it worth studying these groups in a more detailed fashion. And, the history that can be reconstructed by their language or dialect is the first step that has to be taken before all the other research.

Whatever the theoretical discussion might be, there is no denying that even in dissolving speech communities, where the use of Standard German has been stopped or never in use, that even in these cases dialects are still known or in use. Often it is the last trace of the origin of the speakers. This normally is the first step of investigation. It therefore is this dialect—or the relics of it—that can give the first evidence about the origin of a newly discovered speech island. It can be traced back to its German origin if one knows something about the many varieties of dialect speech in Germany—or Central Europe.

Our program is nothing else but a systematization of all of the steps necessary if you want to localize a sample of vernacular (non-standardized) German within the net of regional/local speech varieties or dialects. By knowing and using the dialect maps of the "Deutscher Sprachatlas" it is possible to find short cuts and the right criteria, which normally are hard to find. For those who cannot rely on such highly specialized knowledge, our system of analysis and use of dialect criteria will provide an easy access to all further studies in this field.

In doing so, we doing nothing else than what the eighteenth-century philosopher J. G. Leibnitz proposed when asked for his advice in solving the riddle of existence of the Transsylvanian Saxons then being discussed vigorously among the historians at the University of Göttingen. He asked for a "Specimen iherer Sprache" as the best, if not only proof of their descent. Thus he became the father of *Sprachinselforschung*, and all of the subsequent research by Walter Kuhn (1934) and all of the others in the twentieth century used the same simple method–though with more linguistic knowledge und refined technical devices. Here we are doing the same more systematically, i.e., using language as an indicator to trace a speaker's language or that of a speech community back to the place or group, where it originally was spoken. Language has the same function as "Ariadne's thread," the yarn the Greek princess gave to her lover who by this device found his way out of a labyrinth and back to her.

2.2. Language as Ariadne's Thread: The Underlying Linguistic Materials

Our program makes systematic use of the well known and documented materials— of the *Deutscher Sprachatlas* (1927-56) and the *Deutscher Wortatlas* (1951-80). The maps published in these huge volumes are based on the famous 40 "Wenker Sentences" translated into local language varieties or dialects in over 50,000 locations with German-speaking populations before World War I. In addition, we used the 200 or so lexical items Walther Mitzka collected from almost as many places in the years prior to the end of World War II. These two atlases represent the widest distribution of German language in Central Europe and the potential motherland of all possible distributions of German language abroad. The evaluation of this huge collection of linguistic data has not yet been exhausted—despite all of the efforts undertaken at the Central Sprachatlas Institute in Marburg and elsewhere.

But the discoveries and "linguistic laws" found by Wenker and Wrede when drawing their maps on the basis of the answers of these 50,000 informants turned out to be the underlying principles of the dialectal makeup of the German language: e.g., the participation in the second sound shift (*zweite Lautverschiebung*) or the diphthongization of Middle High German long vowels—together with regionally restricted shibboleth words these principles define a network of small linguistic areas for the German-speaking part of Central Europe and characterize each speaker of a German dialect.

Following Leibnitz it should be possible to locate a (longer and characteristic) sample of German dialect within this net of "isoglosses" (lines separating the use of regionally distributed criteria). The prerequisite, however, is to determine those characteristic features of that "specimen," i.e., dialect sample. In order to do this effectively our DIP has integrated a minimal questionnaire that targets these characteristic features and determines a method of tracing them as directly as possible.

2.3. The German Dialects as a Binary System

With the help of the criteria extracted from their questionnaires and used as the basis for their maps, Wenker and Wrede made it possible to conceive of the German language as a system of rules based on the German dialects. These rules can be compared to Chomsky's concept of the grammar of a language as a set of hierarchical transformations. Without going into details, a German dialect can be defined by a series of binary decisions concerning largely phonological features. For example, the participation or non-participation in the second sound shift determines whether a dialect is Low German or High German. Other criteria discern whether it is part of the set of Middle German or Upper German dialects and so forth. These criteria can be systematically displayed as in our diagram (pp. 298-301) in accordance with most German dialect maps. They can also be transformed into the path of a program with simple "yes/no" decisions and lead us to a distinct German dialect area with the most obvious co-ocurrence — or at least greatest resemblance — of German dialect features. At the end of the path our program offers general and specialized literature on the dialect area for further research (with specific references to items in Wiesinger/Raffin 1982). This systematic tracking enables even the interested non-dialectologist to further investigate a particular dialect.and/or its speakers. We are well aware that this "tracing back" or "finding a home locale" is not the sole or ultimate aim of modern linguistic research. The *Heimatsuche* occupied a long, sometimes frustrating period for the (older)

Sprachinselforscher and led them at times astray. But the linguistic identification of the dialect in question remains an important first step as well as an indispensible element for all further research.

3. Problems of Practical Application

3.4. The Problem of Authentic Material

In earlier research in German dialects the key to substantive fieldwork was an effective way of eliciting authentic dialect speech; this was mostly done by translation of Wenker's "unspeakable" and therefore "antidialectal" sentences into genuine dialect. This methodology constituted a significant problem for the fieldwork of every German dialectologist, who wanted to use—and therefore follow—the methods and results of the huge amount of linguistic data that had already been accumulated. That difficulty, to get samples of the genuine dialect—and not merely socalled "echo-forms" of the written German standard—is even greater under speech island conditions with another, a "second" language ever present. But this also offers the opportunity to elicit dialect data without using standard German in the questionnaire by translating the Wenker sentences into the other languages. We therefore have provided English, Russian and Hungarian versions of the Wenker sentences and also the Mitzka word list; Spanish and Portugese ones are being prepared. And, we do not need the complete corpus of Wenker and Mitzka to identify a dialect. We have selected the relevant words or features and added others from other sources and put them into a system of word questions that create a path, which, if followed correctly, leads to a dialect region with the characteristic features.

3.2. The Application

Our DIP diagram displays our concept of the underlying system that constitutes the German dialects. By certain criteria the German dialects fall into Low or High German, the latter broken down into Upper German (divided into Alemannic and Bavarian) and Middle or Central German and so on—according to the participation in the criteria specified in our program.

Our program operates in the following fashion. By asking our informants for the equivalents of the standard German words in the local dialect, it obtains values for the criteria on the basis of the features represented in several items. To distinguish Low German and High German, equivalents for forms such as "Zeiten, zu, Salz, Herz, besser, isst, Wasser, groß, machen, gebrochen, kochen, Kuchen, Pfeffer, schlafen, Seife, Affe, Löffel—all referenced to their occurence in the Wenker sentences or the Mitzka word list are checked. The DIP then offers possible realizations of these forms in two alternative versions (e.g., "maken/machen"; "Salt/Salz"). By selecting the appropriate variant the user is led to the next stage of the program.

For instance, if the data indicate the Low German forms "maken" and "Salt," the user would be requested to make a further differentiation leading to a distinction between Western and Eastern Low German, marked for instance by distinguishing between "wi hebt/wi hebn" or "Saterdag/Sonnabend" (cf. DIP for Low German, p. 299). Dialect forms equivalent to "wir haben/gehen, sie fliegen/haben/beißen, ihr habt /wollt, Bruder, Schwester, hinter, Samstag" would provide the basis for the second selection. From the determination that the dialect is now associated with Eastern Low German, the user is ultimately led via östliches Ostniederdeutsch and Niederpreußisch to Weischselplatt (1.11 in the DIP on p. 299)—similar to the Low German dialects spoken by the Mennonites who at one time lived in the region of the Vistula Delta. Dialect forms for "zwei, zehn, zwölf, zwanzig, sich, Schwester, hinter, Stückchen, Ziege, Igel, Roggen" would have forced the user to select between Weichselplatt and Samländisch at the final stage of the DIP.

Another path might lead us—based on other criteria like "Peffer/Pfeffer"—via Hochdeutsch and Central German to the western part of Central German with the dialects of Hesse or the Palatinate (cf.. DIP for Central German, p. 300). With the help of additional criteria like the pronounciation of "heiß" as "hees" or "haas" we can even discern between the northwestern part of the Palatinate and the southeastern part (similar to the dialect of the Pennsylvania Germans). In this case, we would be looking at the realizations of dialect forms such as "gebrochen, Schäfchen, einschlafen, machen" to make our final determination.

In both cases we find at the end of these five to seven steps a list of dialect literature pertinent to that dialect area, with both general overviews and highly specific studies in that region. For instance, the user in the second example would be provided with references to pertinent entries in handbooks such as the *Lexikon der germanistischen Linguistik*, Russ (1989), Post (1992) as well as the material referenced in Wiesinger/ Raffin (1982). These examples make clear the usefulness and advantage of a systematic classification of the dialect as the first step in any investigation of a speech island.

References

Bücherl, Rainald, and William Keel. 1996. "The Catholic Bukovinans in Kansas and Their Bohemian-German Dialect." In *German Emigration from Bukovina to the Americas*, ed. William Keel and Kurt Rein, 277-84. Lawrence, KS: Max Kade Center for German-American Studies.

Deutscher Sprachatlas. 1927-56. Ed. Ferdinand Wrede and continued by Walther Mitzka and Bernhard Martin on the basis of the Sprachatlas des Deutschen Reiches founded by Georg Wenker. Marburg.

Deutscher Wortatlas, 22 vols. 1951-80. Ed. Walther Mitzka (vols. 1-20), Ludwig Erich Schmitt (vols. 5-20), Reiner Hildebrandt (vols. 18-22) and Klaus Gluth (vols. 21-22). Gießen.

Keel, William, and Kurt Rein, eds. 1996. *German Emigration from Bukovina to the Americas.* Lawrence, KS: Max Kade Center for German-American Studies.

Kuhn, Walter. 1934. *Deutsche Sprachinseln: Geschichte, Aufgaben, Verfahren.* Ostdeutsche Forschungen, 2. Plauen.

Lexikon der germanistischen Linguistik. 1980. 2d ed. Hans P. Althaus, Helmut Henne and Herbert E. Wiegand, eds. Tübingen.

Lunte, Gabriele. 1998. "The Catholic Bohemian German Dialect of Ellis, Kansas." Diss., University of Kansas.

Mattheier, Klaus J. 1994. "Theorie der Sprachinsel: Voraussetzungen und Strukturierungen." In *Sprachinselforschung: Eine Gedenkschrift für Hugo Jedig,* ed. Nina Berend and Klaus J. Mattheier, 333-48. Frankfurt: Peter Lang.

Post, Rudolf. 1992. *Pfälzisch: Einführung in eine Sprachlandschaft.* Landau.

Rein, Kurt L. 1977. *Religiöse Minderheiten als Sprachgemeinschaftsmodelle: Deutsche Sprachinseln täuferischen Ursprungs in den Vereinigten Staaten von Amerika.* Wiesbaden: Franz Steiner.

Rein, Kurt, and William Keel. 1996. "The 'Swabian' Dialect of the Protestant Bukovinians." In *German Emigration from Bukovina to the Americas,* ed. William Keel and Kurt Rein, 265-76. Lawrence, KS: Max Kade Center for German-American Studies.

Wiesinger, Peter, and Elisabeth Raffin. 1982. *Bibliographie zur Grammatik der deutschen Dialekte: Laut-, Formen-, Wortbildungs- und Satzlehre, 1800 bis 1980.* Bern: Peter Lang.

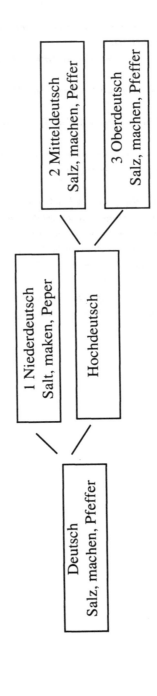

Dialect Identification Program (DIP): Primary Branches
The German Dialects as a binary system of morphophonemic markers.

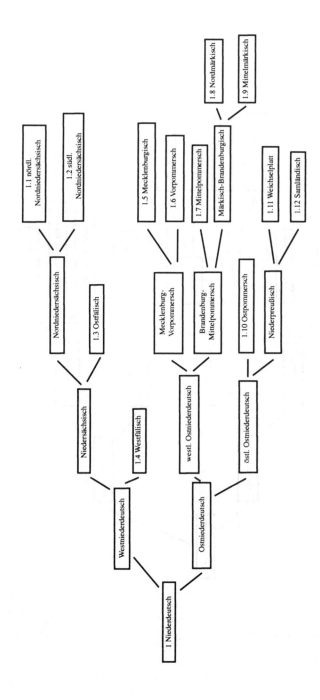

DIP: Low German Branches

299

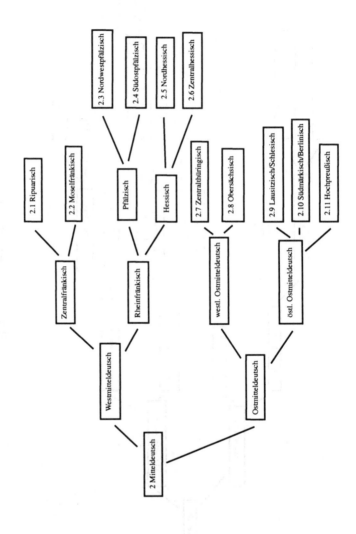

DIP: Central German Branches

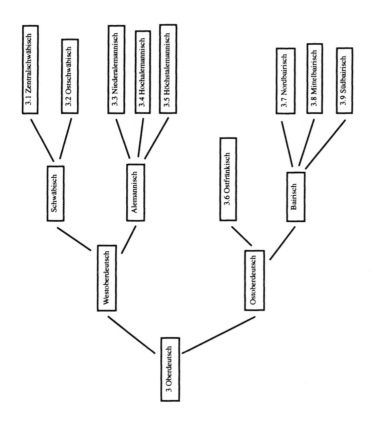

DIP: Upper German Branches

301

William D. Keel
University of Kansas
Lawrence, Kansas

Patterns of Shift in Midwestern German Speech Islands

Introduction

A survey of the American Midwest at the beginning of the twentieth century would have revealed numerous rural enclaves where spoken varieties of literary German and of dialects of German were heard almost to the exclusion of English.[1] Prior to the First World War, the use of German and its dialects in these "speech islands" for everyday social intercourse and for public activities was commonplace. The anti-German hysteria during and after the era of the First World War produced a time of uncertainty in these German-American speech communities and typically introduced a period of transition to English usage in a variety of public and even private domains. The post-Second World War era witnessed the rapid demise of these speech islands. By and large they have developed into what has been termed *Restsprachinseln*,[2] where the once commonly spoken varieties of German can only be recalled by the last generation of fluent or semi-fluent speakers. Heritage societies have typically become the only domain of use for these varieties of spoken German and German dialects. The only exception to this general trend is found in speech communities of the Old Order Amish and the Hutterian Brethren where religious and social isolation inhibit final accommodation to the dominant American English culture.

The near extinction in the second half of the twentieth century of the large number of German speech islands established during the course of the nineteenth century in the American Midwest by German-speaking immigrants from Central and Eastern Europe is an unparalleled linguistic event. As Heinz Kloss noted in 1966:

> This is a development whose epic proportions should not be underestimated. The linguistic assimilation of nine million German-Americans . . . is the most striking event of its kind in the annals of modern history. No other nationality group of equal numerical strength and living in one country has ever been so well nigh completely assimilated.[3]

From our vantage point at the beginning of the twenty-first century, we can examine a number of recent studies, primarily doctoral dissertations, whose focus has been such German-American speech islands with the goal of comparing the patterns of maintenance of German and especially the patterns of transition to the dominant English language as well as the apparent reasons for that transition. For our purposes, we will examine these studies with several questions in mind:

(1) What claims have been made in empirical studies of Midwestern German speech islands regarding the patterns of shift to English during the twentieth century?

(2) To what extent can we claim that the use of literary German in worship services, confirmation instruction, prayers, and other church-related activities fostered the use of German (or a German dialect) in the speech community?

(3) What role was played by community schools, whether public or parochial, in fostering the use of German (or a German dialect) in the speech community?

(4) What was the significance of the outbreak of anti-German hysteria after the entry of the U.S. into the First World War for the continued use of German (or a German dialect) in the speech community?

(5) Can the final shift to English be viewed as a radical decision to stop using German (or a German dialect) with the linguistic system largely intact—a system that in subsequent years could be revived for cultural or heritage purposes?

From our review of these individual studies a more general pattern of linguistic accommodation and attrition emerges. Social factors typically introduce English as the language of normal everyday usage by the beginning of the twentieth century. The number of fluent speakers of the immigrant language begins to be naturally reduced over time until the communicative network utilizing the immigrant language disintegrates. The effects of such distinegration are felt at different stages in different domains of use. We are left finally with a small group of individuals in the speech community, both fluent and semi-fluent, who attempt to revive the memory of the language through heritage activities. We will argue that this pattern can be applied with few if any exceptions to German-American speech islands in the Midwest which have made the complete transition to English usage. This pattern of shift may also have application in such speech communities throughout the world.

German Group Settlement in the Rural American Midwest, 1820-90

During the seventy years spanning the period from 1820 to 1890 millions of German-speaking immigrants coming from both the German linguistic homeland in

Central Europe and from German colonies in the Russian and Austrian empires crossed the Atlantic and headed for the available land on the American settlement frontier. Aside from several significant groups that settled in Texas most found new homes in the territories and states that have come to be known as the American Midwest, stretching in its broadest terms from the Appalachians in the east to the Rocky Mountains in the west and located generally north of the line formed by the Ohio River. Through chain migration and group settlement a number of German speech islands in this region emerged during the nineteenth century. A large number of the German-American speech islands in the Midwest have been able to survive well into the twentieth century. A brief survey of some of the most significant of these German-speaking settlements follows.

Prior to 1850 several pockets of German settlement emerged in the newly formed territories and states along the Ohio River, in Michigan and in Missouri. Low German-speaking German Catholics from Westphalia established themselves in the northwestern Ohio county of Auglaize beginning in 1833.[4] German Catholics from Baden, Hesse and Bavaria founded a major settlement in southwestern Indiana centered on Dubois County beginning in 1836.[5] Of particular interest are also the Lutheran settlements from Bavarian Franconia in Dubois County, Indiana, beginning around 1838, and in Michigan in the vicinity of Frankenmuth in 1845.[6] German Lutherans also established larger settlements from Saxony in Perry County, Missouri, in 1839 and from Hannover in Benton and Lafayette counties in western Missouri beginning around 1840.[7]

During the 1850s, the northwestern states of Iowa, Wisconsin and Minnesota attracted the majority of settlers from German-speaking areas of Central Europe. Notable are the Amana Colonies in southeastern Iowa established in 1855 and the massive immigration of Schleswig-Holsteiners to the Davenport and Scott County, Iowa, area in the aftermath of the failed revolt against Danish authority.[8] Wisconsin to this day boasts the highest percentage of German ancestry in its population—53% according to the 1990 U.S. census. Of special interest for our purpose are the settlements by the Swiss in Monroe County, primarily from the canton of Glarus, by Low German-speaking Lutherans in Sauk County, and by Catholic Rhinelanders northwest of Madison in Dane County.[9]

The post-Civil War era—the 1870s and 1880s—can be characterized by the immigration of German-speaking settlers from eastern and southeastern European German colonies in the Russian and Austrian empires to the states of the Great Plains: Kansas, Nebraska, and North and South Dakota. Following the enticements of the transcontinental railroads Volga German Catholics and Protestants as well as German Mennonites from Volhynian, Volga and Black Sea colonies in Russia flocked by the thousands to Kansas and Nebraska in the 1870s.[10] A decade later the Dakotas received the lion's share of German immigration from the Russian Empire.[11] At the same time German-speaking immigrants from Bohemia, Moravia, Galicia and especially Bukovina in imperial Austria were establishing larger settlements primarily in west central Kansas.[12] Of special interest are the Hutterian Brethren who settled in the Dakotas beginning in 1876.[13] Of course, immigration from regions now located in modern Germany continued during this period as well. A significant area of Low German speech developed in the border region between Kansas and Nebraska in the 1870s.[14]

Contemporaneous with the mid-nineteenth century immigration of German-speaking settlers from Central and Eastern Europe was the westward movement of settlers of earlier German ancestry, such as the Pennsylvania Germans. Pennsylvania Germans, in particular the Amish and "Old" Mennonites, continue to this day to establish new colonies throughout the American Midwest.[15] The settlement pattern of these groups interspersed with a variety of English-speaking settlements as well as smaller settlements representing other linguistic groups speaking such immigrant languages as Swedish, French, Italian, Czech and others created a crazy-quilt pattern of settlement that remained largely unchanged until the social and economic upheaval during and after the Great Depression and the Second World War. America's rural communities experienced such population loss to urban areas in the period following the Second World War that long-established rural German speech communities essentially ceased to exist, finding themselves now in the larger context of the American English culture.

Varieties of German and Domains of Usage in German-American *Sprachinseln*

The varieties of spoken German found in these Midwestern speech islands exhibit the same richness as in the dialects of the European homeland. Several major Low German communities have been documented with Westphalian, Eastphalian, North Low Saxon, Pommeranian and especially West Prussian "Mennonite" Low German well represented. Central German dialects, too, can be found throughout the area from Ripuarian to Upper Saxon, with Palatine and Hessian dialects being brought to the Midwest primarily by Pennsylvania Germans and Germans from Russia and Bukovina. Upper German dialect speech islands reflecting East Franconian and Swiss German date from the earliest settlement period, while Swabian and Bavarian groups more typically established themselves in the wave of secondary immigration from southeastern Europe near the end of the nineteenth century.

In some communities a type of linguistic accommodation to a spoken variety of written German apparently occurred. This phenomenon is attested for Dubois County in Indiana.[16] The assumption is that speakers of competing dialects accepted a spoken form of the written language as a koiné. Similar claims have been made for the emergence of *Ausgleichsmundarten* especially in the dialects of the Volga Germans and that of the Amana Colonies in Iowa.[17]

It is also clear that these were all spoken idioms, with usage restricted to certain domains: conversations within the family and among friends and acquaintances. Usage in more public circumstances especially in school or church tended in all communities to reflect a spoken version of written or literary German. Some groups developed somewhat elaborate patterns of usage. For the Hutterian Brethren a four-way pattern has been reported:

(1) Basic Hutterite reflecting the most restricted domains within the community and associated with the speech of women and children;

(2) Standard Hutterite used primarily by men discussing general matters, but understood by all members of the community;

(3) Preachers' Hutterite a specialized "high" form of the language, but identical with spoken written German; and

(4) a spoken realization of literary German.[18]

Printed and written forms of German appear to have been much more limited in the Midwestern German speech islands. Printed German in newspapers, magazines and books nearly always reflected usage in the German homeland, rather than some American variety. Often the rural German community was served by periodicals from larger cities such as Cincinnati, St. Louis, and Milwaukee. Personal letters, diaries and the like to the extent that they have been examined reflect the level of ability in producing literary German learned in school, rather than examples of the spoken dialect.

Dialects were the language of the home and were often referred to as "slopbucket Dutch" and not considered appropriate for written or public expression. Commenting on the difficulty in eliciting linguistic material in the base dialect in a Low German community in Kansas, Bonebrake notes:

. . . those informants who received schooling early enough to have been taught Standard German were difficult to convince that their spoken language, Low German, was the language desired for the interview. Those who had never learned Standard German were equally astonished that anyone could wish to transcribe their unwritten language. The most strenuous effort was needed to convince informants that their language was not considered inferior by an outsider, . . .[19]

Accommodation and Attrition: The Transition to English

The pattern of development in the German-language speech islands has been consistent. Early German settlers often established homesteads among English-speaking ones. Over the course of several years, the earlier English-speaking settlers moved on and were replaced by additional German speakers. By the end of the nineteenth century the German speech island was firmly established with German schools and German religious services providing strong support for the maintenance of the immigrant language. Labor intensive farming, large family size, and lack of mobility ensured a cohesive, isolated and concentrated speech community.

However, the schools in which German was used as the language of instruction became at a very early stage the focus of some controversy in the larger English-speaking community. Many states adopted legislation in the latter decades of the nineteenth century mandating English alone as the language of instruction in schools.[20] However, it is unclear to what extent such legal prohibitions on the use of German in the parochial schools of Lutherans and Catholics were enforced. As is well known, many state legislatures introduced bills during the 1919 session in the aftermath of the First World War banning German as a language of instruction in all elementary schools, whether public or church operated. It remains uncertain whether such legislation in effect wiped out German instruction or simply reinforced a process that was already lessening the need for German language instruction in both public and parochial domains. The reversal of that ban by the U. S. Supreme Court in 1923 apparently had little effect on changing the situation one way or the other.

Even in speech communities with a relatively long history of German-language instruction in the school, the chronology of shift appears to coincide with the first four decades of the twentieth century. Mennonites settling in Kansas had German schools beginning in the 1870s which soon became summer schools, while the regular school year was taught in English. In addition, Schmidt (1977) reports the existence of a secondary school (*Vereinsschule*) for Mennonite children in the community of Hoffnungsau in central Kansas from 1907 until 1927. Half of the subjects were taught in German (Bible history, church history, German reading, German grammar, and drawing) while the other half were taught in English (science, penmanship, music, English Bible, English and Classics). Yet, even with this long-term support of German in the schools, by the mid-1920s and 1930s the community was rapidly making the transition to English in all areas (see more detailed discussion below).

The second pillar of community support for the continued use of German, the church, faced no such legal prohibition of language use due to the constitutionally protected separation of church and state. However, the churches' desire to serve the needs of the younger members of the congregation who were being schooled in English contributed to the transition to English in all aspects of religious practice. Equally strong in directing the churches toward English usage was the hope of reaching an ever-expanding body of believers. The missionary zeal of the Protestant denominations, from the Lutherans to the Amish, has played a major role in the transition to English. Low German-speaking Lutherans in Kansas gave the following reason in 1924 for the use of English: "At this time God turned us—and shall we not recognize it as a dispensation of His wisdom—to the language of our country as a missionary medium."21 Thus, in the eyes of some, the accommodation of the immigrant language to English was divinely inspired.

Bonebrake's conclusions (1969) about the transition to English in Hanover, Kansas, find confirmation thirty years later in the recently completed M.A. thesis (2002) by Doris Dippold. Dippold investigated twenty-one religious congregations in Cole County, Missouri.22 The churches examined in Jefferson City and rural areas of the county included Roman Catholic, Missouri and Iowa Synod Lutheran, German Evangelical (now United Church of Christ) and German Methodist bodies. These congregations founded in the second half of the nineteenth century had been German-speaking initially. By the middle of the twentieth century all had made a complete transition to English usage in all areas (worship services, confirmation classes, organizations and parochial schools).

Dippold noted some correlation to the circumstances surrounding the First World War as well as in a few cases to those of the Second World War but her data do not support the often stated claim that the anti-German atmosphere during the wars led directly to the shift away from German. On the other hand, she was able to draw distinctions between largely rural homogenous congregations (with a significantly longer retention of German in all domains) and congregations in Jefferson City coexisting with many English neighbors (with an earlier shift to English). The driving factor in abandoning German, however, was the often explicitly noted need to accommodate the growing nearly monolingual (English) youth in the congregation. The near total use of English in school appears to be the cause for the shift to English among the younger generation. And, this use of English in schools had been the case at least one generation prior to the First World war. From Dippold's study it appears that the entry of the United States into the War merely coincided with the social accommodation to the younger English-speaking generation in these communities. The anti-German feelings may have supported, and in some cases accelerated the change, but the shift to English would have happened anyway.

Hand in hand with the loss of the high varieties of German in these speech islands went the gradual attrition of linguistic forms in the dialects. Whether the result of interference from or convergence with the dominant English language, the result of internal developments of linguistic simplification common to all dialects of German, or simply the result of incomplete learning, the spoken varieties still heard in the majority of German speech islands are viewed by most researchers as greatly simplified varieties of the European parent dialects or even dialects rapidly converging their linguistic structures with those of English.23 The *Sprachinseln* of the nineteenth century have become the *Restsprachinseln* of today.

The loss of immigrant dialects and the transition to English has been documented and analyzed in a number of dissertations and monographs treating the speech islands noted above. One of the most detailed of these studies involves the Hoffnungsau congregation of Mennonites from Russia in south central Kansas whose church is located in rural McPherson County. The primary area of Mennonite settlement in Kansas extends across four counties along the Santa Fe Railroad line including Marion, Harvey, McPherson, and Reno counties, with additional daughter settlements further west such as that found in Meade County.24 Although the Mennonite settlements in this region also exhibit Pennsylvania German (principally among the Old Order Amish in Reno County), Swiss German, West Prussian High German, and, in two communities known as "Schweitzer" Mennonites, a Palatine-type dialect, the largest and most widespread settlements speak varieties of West Prussian Low German or *Plautdietsch*.25

The group speaking West Prussian Low German migrated from the southern Russian Empire—now Ukraine—to Kansas and other areas of North and South America beginning in 1874. By 1880 some 3,000 had settled in south central Kansas. Their use of German in worship services and of Low German in everyday communication followed patterns similar to those discussed above. Until World War I the linguistic situation remained largely that of an isolated German speech island. The transition to English occurred gradually between 1920 and 1950 both for High German in church and school and for Low German in the home and among friends.26 Mary Schmidt's study of the linguistic transition from German and Low German to English in the Hoffnungsau community completed in 1977 offers us a number of insights into that process.

The German-language summer vacation school began in the 1890s with a four-month session. As the term for the regular, English-language, public school increased in length, the period for the German school was shortened. In the years immediately following World War I, the German summer school was only in session for four weeks and at times was only held for one or two weeks in a given summer. By 1927 training in the use of literary German for religious purposes in such summer schools had ceased.

Church services in Hoffnungsau were, however, held exclusively in German until 1932. Over a period of several years in the 1930s English was gradually introduced, first in the Sunday school classes, then in the worship services, and finally in the baptismal rites. It was not until 1941 that the actual number of English services began to be in the majority. The last totally German worship service was held in 1947, although German was still used for parts of the worship service until 1950.

The transition from the use of *Plautdietsch* to English parallels the transition of literary German to English. The maintenance of the Low German dialect, however, continues about twenty years—or one generation—beyond that of literary German. The real decline in the use of the dialect does not begin until the late 1930s or perhaps a few years later. J. Neale Carman in his detailed study of non-English languages found in Kansas claims that the use of Mennonite Low German in families with children reached what he refers to as "the critical year" about 1935. However, for some communities such as Goessel in Marion County he argues that the critical year was not reached until 1950. The "critical year" was based on Carman's estimate of when fewer than one-half of the families with children in the home were using the dialect in a given community.

Again, Schmidt provides an overview of the transition from *Plautdietsch* to English in the home for the Hoffnungsau community. Based on her interviews and research she divides the population into language-use groups by date of birth:

(1) Persons born prior to 1917: These individuals were raised in a nearly exclusive Low German environment. The dialect was used at home while literary German was learned in school and used in church. In the mid-1970s this group still enjoyed speaking Low German at gatherings of family and close friends.

(2) Persons born 1918-27: These individuals grew up with a mostly Low German home life with occasional use of English. They were still exposed to some formal training in literary German and attended church services in German until they reached adulthood. A critical difference in this group is that they used English in speaking to their children. This observation corresponds to Carman's estimate of the "critical year" for Mennonite Low German in Hoffnungsau falling between 1935 and 1940.

(3) Persons born 1928-47: These individuals grew up with some Low German in the home, but English predominated. They had no formal training in literary or standard German and can only recall attending German worship services as children. They may often have a good passive knowledge of the Low German dialect, but can typically speak only short phrases and individual words.

(4) Persons born 1948-57: These individuals typically did not hear Low German spoken in the home and lack the passive understanding of the preceding group. This group has had no experience with literary or standard German either in school or in church.

(5) Persons born 1958-67: These individuals have had virtually no experience

311

with Low German and yet have what Schmidt calls a "keen awareness" of their community's linguistic heritage.

While our fieldwork with numerous fluent informants in Kansas and Missouri over the past twenty years attests that hundreds of individuals in a given speech community are able to speak a German dialect, it is also clear that the communicative needs which were earlier served by German or a dialect of German are now served by English. As with the Hoffnungsau community, German dialects have become markers of a community's heritage and a signal of group identity, but they no longer are used for everyday conversation or interaction in the community.

Attempts at Linguistic Preservation: The Celebration of Heritage

Within two hundred miles of the University of Kansas in Lawrence the interested traveler can still locate numerous communities which were settled largely by Germans. To this day, some one hundred fifty years after the original settlements, the German dialects brought by those immigrants have persisted. One can still find hundreds of speakers of these dialects who now fondly recall them as the language of family and community in their youth. Anecdotes, children's rhymes, and reminiscences of those earlier years often can be recalled in the local dialect easier than in the now dominant English. In recent years, annual heritage events have begun to take place in western Missouri and south central Kansas, which might lead one to believe that German dialects and culture are alive and well. The same could be reported for other areas of German settlement in the Midwest.

The German linguistic heritage of the Midwest becomes quite visible each fall, especially during the month of October. For over a decade, Low German theater groups have been staging performances of skits in the local dialects in the communities of Concordia and Cole Camp in Missouri and as part of the annual "Fall Festival" at Bethel College in North Newton, Kansas.[27] In preparation for these events, community members offer language instruction in the Low German dialects (both *Plattdüütsch* and *Plautdietsch*, depending on the location) to participants in the skits and others interested in refreshing their knowledge of their mother tongue or learning the immigrant dialect of their forebears.[28] The "Fall Festival" at Bethel College also includes a "Schweitzer" Mennonite program featuring skits and anecdotes in the Volhynian Mennonite (Palatine) dialect.

The "Folk Festival" held each May in Hillsboro, Kansas, attracts visitors with "Music and Low German Entertainment." Another typical "heritage" event is the religious service conducted in the immigrant dialect. For instance, in May 1994 the Missouri Synod Lutheran St. Paul's Church in Concordia, Missouri, held its very first Low German church service featuring a choir singing favorite hymns translated into the Low German dialect.[29] Of course, the ancestors of the current members of the congregation could not have imagined using the dialect in church just as modern-day Catholic masses in German do not reflect the real heritage of those groups. Marysville, Kansas, has held a "Germanfest" in early June for a number of years, with a Low or High German worship service being the highlight of the weekend. It often seems that everywhere one looks a community or a church group in the Midwest is celebrating its German heritage. Are these events signs of resilience and even of a renaissance of immigrant dialects after almost a century and a half of acculturation and assimilation to the dominant American English culture?

The Low German service at Concordia, Missouri, in May 1994 provides some significant insights into the current situation. The attendance at the service was 378 which exceeded the expectations of the organizers. Some in attendance observed that they were glad to see the people of Concordia keeping Low German in use and making attempts to keep people interested in the language. Others found it refreshing to learn that people cared so much about their heritage. Local children, however, understood practically nothing of the Low German in the service. Many of the guests stated they enjoyed the service but understood nothing. Even those who grew up speaking Low German were often puzzled by the texts used in the service. Of course, the language was never a written language for these people, but rather only a spoken idiom.[30]

Similar remarks were made to the author regarding a recent "Schweitzer" Mennonite program at Bethel College in October 2001: The audience is dwindling and fewer people are able to understand the dialect texts. However, the larger audience of about 300 persons attending the Mennonite Low German (*Plautdietsch*) skit about making *Borscht* for the Fall Festival at Bethel and the audience reaction confirmed that passive understanding was still present among the many senior citizens in attendance.

Conclusion

In his study of the Low German community of Concordia, Missouri, Ballew (1997) noted that "although the dialect is in its last generation of speakers, they seem to have full command of usage, and therefore no need to fall back on borrowing from English. It [the dialect] will move from fluent speakers to non-existence in one moment. Concordia Low German was put into storage by default because it became easier to use English in everyday situations." Ballew proposes the following model for the life stages of the current generation of Concordia Low German speakers:

Stage 1.   Pre-school: monolingual learning of Low German.

Stage 2.   Early school years: bilingual English and Low German

Stage 3.　　End of school/early adulthood: suppression of Low German and near exclusive use of English.

Stage 4.　　Mature adulthood/senior citizen: revival of Low German as a heritage phenomenon; restricted to special heritage activities (clubs, worship services, skits, choir groups etc.).

While there are some details of this model that may vary from speech community to speech community, the pattern of accommodation during the early school years to English and the subsequent attrition of German and its dialects appears applicable to almost all of the communities studied. In most rural areas, the shift to instruction in English in the schools had the most telling effect on the first generation to be confronted with the rapid need to learn English to succeed in school. That generation in turn made a conscious decision not to use the immigrant language with its children to provide them with an easier start in school. This critical decision to use English in the home with small children is one confirmed in speech communities across the Midwest. With this decision the die was cast and the eventual disappearance of the Midwestern German speech islands a certainty.

Directly connected to the decision of parents to use English with their children and of perhaps even more importance for our understanding of the process of shift to English is an examination of family speech networks and domains in Midwestern German speech islands. In examining the shift to English we tend to look at the entire community as a whole and not individuals or family groups. As Huth and Seeger (2002) have shown in the Low German community of Marshall and Washington counties in Kansas, the individual networks involving the use of High German, Low German, and English within a family can have an incredibly determinative effect. A mixed-language marriage, first language of the father and of the mother as well as other close adult relatives, an older sibling starting school in English, the death of one or both parents, the move from the farm to town, all of these and other situations have an impact on the language use of the new generation. As Huth and Seeger have noted, we need to understand not only whether speakers of a community spoke a particular language, but also with whom, when, why and about what. What emerges is a more complex picture of interaction in both the immigrant language and the other varieties competing for existence in the community.

Returning to our other original questions, it now appears that the church represents an institution with little influence on the process of language transition. As long as the active members of a congregation or parish required German, it was used in a variety of situations (worship, confirmation, baptism, organizations). As soon as enough younger members required those services in English, the church had to conform or risk losing its younger members—the split of some churches into English and German bodies in the early years of this process is well known. And, the well-attested differences between the multilingual denominations such as Roman Catholic or Methodist, with earlier shift to English in the German congregations, and those largely German in their makeup, Lutheran, Reformed, Evangelical, with longer retention of German, only provides additional support for this thesis.

The impact of the First World War has also received far too much credit for the demise of German speech islands in the Midwest. How often has a fieldworker in a speech island heard the statement to the effect, that because of the anti-German feelings during World War I everybody stopped speaking German? Yet, we know that everybody, especially in a largely German community and even more so in an isolated rural German community, did not stop speaking or acquiring German or the local dialect. This typically did not begin to happen on a large scale until a couple of decades later, typically in the 1930s and 1940s. Again, study after study confirms this. If this were not so, we would now have only persons over eighty or ninety years of age with any fluency whatsoever.

Finally, the social and economic restructuring of American society during the Great Depression and World War II with massive redistribution of the rural population to towns and urban centers, not to mention the disruption of extended military service for males, needs to be explored in regard the entire complex of questions associated with the transition from vibrant speech communities with immigrant languages to the near ghost communities of today. The individual studies referenced in this essay taken together cast a very different light on the process of accommodation to English and attrition of the immigrant variety.

Despite the flurry of present-day activity in some German-dialect speech communities in Kansas, Missouri, and in the other German-American speech islands in the American Midwest, the now living generation of speakers will be the last to have any fluency in these dialects. Indeed, there is, in reality, no following generation of even partially fluent speakers. Those born after the period between the two world wars simply did not grow up in an environment where it was necessary to communicate in any form of German or a German dialect and thus did not have the opportunity or the need to learn that language. The efforts to preserve the various German dialects in the American Midwest will have modest success in that the dialects will be documented, described, tape recorded and even video recorded prior to the extinction of these dialects in the first half of the twenty-first century.

Notes

1See *Deutsch als Muttersprache in den Vereinigten Staaten: Teil I: Der Mittelwesten*, ed. Leopold Auburger, Heinz Kloss, and Heinz Rupp, Deutsche Sprache in Europa und Übersee, vol. 4 (Wiesbaden: Franz Steiner Verlag, 1979) for an attempt at an overview of the situation of German in the American Midwest.

2The term *Restsprachinsel* was used by Klaus Mattheier, University of Heidelberg, in a conversation with the author in Newton, Kansas, in October 1993, to characterize the linguistic situation in the German speech islands of the American Midwest in which German or a dialect of German is now primarily spoken (or can be recalled) by a final generation of fluent or partially fluent speakers and where English is the usual language of social intercourse.

3Heinz Kloss, "German-American Language Maintenance Efforts," in Joshua A. Fishman, ed., *Language Loyalty in the United States: The Maintenance and Perpetuation of Non-English Mother Tongues by American Ethnic and Religious Groups* (The Hague: Mouton, 1966), 249.

4Wolfgang Fleischhauer, "The German Dialects Spoken in Several Communities in Auglaize County, Ohio," in *The American Philosophical Society: Yearbook 1962* (Philadelphia, 1963), 533-35; Anne Aengenvoort, *Migration—Siedlungsbildung—Akkulturation: Die Auswanderung Nordwestdeutscher nach Ohio, 1830-1914*, Vierteljahreszeitschrift für Sozial- und Wirtschaftsgeschichte, 150 (Stuttgart: Franz Steiner, 1999).

5Peter Frank Freeouf, "Religion and Dialect: Catholic and Lutheran Dialects in the German of Dubois County, Indiana," Ph.D. diss., Indiana University, 1989

6Freeouf, "Religion and Dialect: . . ."; Daniel Nützel, "Case Loss and Morphosyntactic Change in Haysville East Franconian," in *The German Language in America, 1683-1991*, ed. Joseph C. Salmons (Madison, WI: Max Kade Institute for German-American Studies, 1993), 307-21; Renate Born, *Michigan German in Frankenmuth: Variation and Change in an East Franconian Dialect* (Columbia, SC: Camden House, 1994).

7Brad Grindstaff, "Saxon German in East Perry County, Missouri: Synchronic Analysis and Retention Study," M.A. thesis, Southern Illinois University, 1978, copy in the collection of the Max Kade Center for German-American Studies, University of Kansas, Lawrence, Kansas; William Noble Ballew, "The Low German Dialect of Concordia, Missouri," Ph.D. diss., University of Kansas, 1997; *Hier Snackt Wi Plattdütsch* (Cole Camp, Missouri, 1994); J. Neale Carman, "Foreign Language Units of Kansas," vol. 3, typescript, 1974, University of Kansas Archives, Spencer Research Library, Lawrence, Kansas, 3:406ff; [Rev. Alfred W. Rodewald and others], *Descending Love—Ascending Praise: St. Paul's Lutheran Church, Concordia, Mo., 18401990* [Concordia, Missouri, 1990], especially pp. 13-92; Hella Albers, "Niederdeutsch in den USA als Beispiel von Sprachkontakt: Feldforschung zum Niederdeutschen in Cole Camp/Missouri," Diploma thesis, Universität Hildesheim, 1999.

8Kurt Rein, *Religiöse Minderheiten als Sprachgemeinschaftsmodelle: Deutsche Sprachinseln täuferischen Ursprungs in den Vereinigten Staaten von Amerika* (Wiesbaden: Franz Steiner Verlag, 1977); Lawrence J. Rettig, "Grammatical Structures in Amana German," Ph.D. diss., University of Iowa, 1970; Philip E. Webber, "Betwixt and Between: The Tension of Language Contact in Iowa's Amana Colonies," in *The German Language in America, 1683-1991*, pp. 10323; Alfred P. Kehlenbbeck, "Die plattdeutsche Mundart in Iowa

County, Iowa," Ph.D. diss., University of Wisconsin, 1934; Birgit Mertens, *Vom (Nieder-) Deutschen zum Englischen: Untersuchungen zur sprachlichen Assimilation einer ländlichen Gemeinde im mittleren Westen Amerikas*, Sprachgeschichte, 2 (Heidelberg: Universitätsverlag C. Winter, 1994).

9Brian Lewis, "The Phonology of the Glarus Dialect in Green County, Wisconsin," Ph.D. diss., University of Wisconsin, 1968; Dale J. Donnelly, "The Low German Dialect of Sauk County, Wisconsin: Phonology and Morphology," Ph.D. diss., University of Wisconsin, 1969; Peter A. McGraw, "The Kölsch Dialect of Dane County, Wisconsin," Ph.D. diss., University of Wisconsin, 1973.

10William D. Keel, "On the 'Heimatbestimmung' of the Ellis County (Kansas) Volga-German Dialects," *Yearbook of German-American Studies* 17 (1982): 99-109; D. Chris Johnson, "The Volga German Dialect of Schoenchen, Kansas," Ph.D. diss., University of Kansas, 1994; Patrick Kaul, "Untersuchungen zum Deutsch in Kansas: Migration und Entwicklung des Wolgadeutschen in Ellis und Rush Counties," M.A. thesis, Universität Mannheim, 1996; Marjorie Baerg, "Gnadenau Low German: A Dialect of Marion County, Kansas," Ph.D. diss., University of Chicago, 1960; Robert H. Buchheit, " Mennonite 'Plautdietsch': A Phonological and Morphological Description of a Settlement Dialect in York and Hamilton Counties, Nebraska," Ph.d. diss., University of Nebraska, 1978; Rein *Religiöse Minderheiten*.

11Shirley Fischer Arends, *The Central Dakota Germans: Their History, Language and Culture* (Washington, DC: Georgetown University Press, 1989); Rein, *Religiöse Minderheiten*.

12William Keel and Kurt Rein, eds., *German Emigration from Bukovina to the Americas* (Lawrence, Kansas: Max Kade Center for German-American Studies, 1996); Gabrielle Lunte, "The Catholic Bohemian German Dialect of Ellis, Kansas," Ph.D. diss., University of Kansas, 1998.

13Rein, *Religiöse Minderheiten*.

14Veronica A. Bonebrake, "A Sociolinguistic and Phonological Survey of Low German Spoken in Kansas," M.A. thesis, University of Texas, 1969; Jan E. Bender, "Die getrennte Entwicklung gleichen niederdeutschen Sprachgutes in Deutschland und Nebraska," Ph.D. diss., University of Nebraska, 1971.

15An interesting case study of the demise of a Pennsylvania German community in Illinois is offered in a reprint of a 1937 article by Herbert Penzl, "The Pennsylvania German Dialect in Sterling, Illinois," *Journal of the Center for Pennsylvania German Studies* 3,5 (Winter 1996): 1718.

16Freeouf, "Religion and Dialect."

15Viktor Schirmunski, "Sprachgeschichte und Siedlungsmundarten," *Germanisch-Romanische Monatsschrift* 18 (1930): 113-22, 177-88; Rettig, "Amana Dialect"; Rein, *Religiöse Minderheiten*.

16Rein, *Religiöse Minderheiten*, especially pp. 271-76; Kurt Rein, "German Dialects in Anabaptist Colonies on the Great Plains," in *Languages in Conflict: Linguistic Acculturation on the Great Plains*, ed. Paul Schach (Lincoln, Nebraska: University of Nebraska Press, 1980), 102-4.

17Bonebrake, "Low German in Kansas," 12.

18Bonebrake, "Low German in Kansas," reports statutory restrictions on the use of German as early as the 1870s.

19J. W. Werling, *History of the Kansas District, Evangelical Lutheran Synod of Missouri, Ohio and Other States* (St. Louis: Concordia Publishing House, 1938), 36.

22Doris Dippold, "'It Just Doesn't Sound Right': Spracherhalt und Sprachwechsel bei deutschen Kirchengemeinden in Cole County, Missouri," M.A. thesis, University of Kansas, 2002.

23William D. Keel, "Reduction and Loss of Case Marking in the Noun Phrase in German-American Speech Islands: Internal Development or External Interference?" in *Sprachinselforschung: Eine Gedenkschrift für Hugo Jedig*, ed. Nina Berend and Klaus J. Mattheier (Frankfurt: Peter Lang, 1994), 93-104.

24Carman, *Foreign Language Units of Kansas: I. Historical Atlas and Statistics*, especially pp. 58, 164-65, 188-91, 192-95, 246-49; Harley J. Stucky, "The German Element in Kansas," chap. 15 of *Kansas: The First Century*, 4 vols., ed. John D. Bright (New York: Lewis Historical Pub. Co., 1956), 1:329-54; *They Live in Hope: A Guide to Hillsboro's Pioneer Adobe House Museum and the Mennonite Adobe House Culture of Central Kansas, 1874-1900* (Hillsboro, KS: Multi Business Press, n.d.).

25Robert H. Buchheit, "Language Maintenance and Shift among Mennonites in South-Central Kansas," *Yearbook of German-American Studies* 17 (1982): 111-21.

26Mary Schmidt, "Linguistic Transitions of the Russian-Mennonites in Kansas," M.A. thesis, Emporia State University, 1977; Buchheit, "Language Maintenance and Shift."

27The Concordia Low German Club "Hadn Tohopa" has performed its skits each October since the fall of 1990. The Cole Camp group evolved out of a 150th anniversary celebration of the founding of Cole Camp in 1989. Cole Camp has also produced a volume on the Low German heritage of the community *Hier Snackt Wi Plattdütsch* (Cole Camp, 1990) and offers video recordings of its skits for sale.

28Viola Mieser, a retired second grade teacher in Concordia, now deceased, produced a series of lessons for learning pronunciation and basic conversation in the Concordia Low German dialect (manuscript, n.d.). Lessons for Mennonite Low German were prepared by Marian Penner Schmidt and are available from the Alexanderwohl Mennonite Church Archives in Goessel, Kansas (manuscript, 1979). Xerox copies of these handwritten materials have been acquired by the Max Kade Center for German-American Studies, University of Kansas.

29Rev. Alfred Rodewald conducted the Low German worship service in Concordia on 22 May 1994. He had previously conducted a Low German service in Cole Camp in 1992.

30Ruth Rodewald, "Widespread Interest in First-Known Low German Service in Concordia, Mo.," news release, Concordia, Missouri, 25 May 1994.

References

Aengenvoort, Anne. 1999. *Migration—Siedlungsbildung—Akkulturation: Die Auswanderung Nordwestdeutscher nach Ohio, 1830-1914*. Vierteljahreszeitschrift für Sozial- und Wirtschaftsgeschichte, 150. Stuttgart: Franz Steiner.

Albers, Hella. 1999. "Niederdeutsch in den USA als Beispiel von Sprachkontakt: Feldforschung zum Niederdeutschen in Cole Camp/Missouri." Diploma thesis, Universität Hildesheim.

Arends, Shirley Fischer. 1989. *The Central Dakota Germans: Their History, Language and Culture*. Washington, DC: Georgetown University Press.

Auburger, Leopold, Heinz Kloss, and Heinz Rupp, eds. 1979. *Deutsch als Muttersprache in den Vereinigten Staaten: Teil I: Der Mittelwesten*. Deutsche Sprache in Europa und Übersee, 4. Wiesbaden: Franz Steiner Verlag.

Baerg, Marjorie. 1960. "Gnadenau Low German: A Dialect of Marion County, Kansas." Ph.D. diss., University of Chicago.

Ballew, William Noble. 1997. "The Low German Dialect of Concordia, Missouri." Ph.D. diss., University of Kansas.

Bender, Jan E. 1971."Die getrennte Entwicklung gleichen niederdeutschen Sprachgutes in Deutschland und Nebraska." Ph.D. diss., University of Nebraska.

Bonebrake, Veronica A. 1969. "A Sociolinguistic and Phonological Survey of Low German Spoken in Kansas." M.A. thesis, University of Texas.

Born, Renate. 1994. *Michigan German in Frankenmuth: Variation and Change in an East Franconian Dialect.* Columbia, SC: Camden House.

Buchheit, Robert H. 1978. "Mennonite 'Plautdietsch': A Phonological and Morphological Description of a Settlement Dialect in York and Hamilton Counties, Nebraska." Ph.D. diss., University of Nebraska.

Buchheit, Robert H. 1982. "Language Maintenance and Shift among Mennonites in South-Central Kansas," *Yearbook of German-American Studies* 17: 111-21.

Carman, J. Neale. 1962. *Foreign Language Units of Kansas: Volume 1, Historical Atlas and Statistics.* Lawrence, KS: University of Kansas Press.

Carman, J. Neale. 1974. "Foreign Language Units of Kansas." Typescript of volumes 2 and 3. University of Kansas Archives, Spencer Research Library, Lawrence, KS.

Dippold, Doris. 2002. "'It Just Doesn't Sound Right': Spracherhalt und Sprachwechsel bei deutschen Kirchengemeinden in Cole County, Missouri." M.A. thesis, University of Kansas.

Donnelly, Dale J. 1969. "The Low German Dialect of Sauk County, Wisconsin: Phonology and Morphology." Ph.D. diss., University of Wisconsin.

Fleischhauer, Wolfgang. 1963."The German Dialects Spoken in Several Communities in Auglaize County, Ohio." In *The American Philosophical Society: Yearbook 1962.* Philadelphia, 533-35.

Freeouf, Peter Frank. 1989. "Religion and Dialect: Catholic and Lutheran Dialects in the German of Dubois County, Indiana." Ph.D. diss., Indiana University.

Grindstaff, Brad. 1978. "Saxon German in East Perry County, Missouri: Synchronic Analysis and Retention Study," M.A. thesis, Southern Illinois University.

Hier Snackt Wi Plattdütsch. 1994. Cole Camp, MO.

Huth, Thorsten, and Scott Seeger. 2002. "Language Networks and Domains: A Sociolinguistic Study of the Low German Speech Island of Marshall and Washington Counties, Kansas." Paper presented at the Symposium of the Society for German-American Studies, Amana, Iowa, April 1821.

Johnson, D. Chris Johnson. 1994. "The Volga German Dialect of Schoenchen, Kansas." Ph.D. diss., University of Kansas.

Kaul, Patrick. 1996. "Untersuchungen zum Deutsch in Kansas: Migration und Entwicklung des Wolgadeutschen in Ellis und Rush Counties." M.A. thesis, Universität Mannheim.

Keel, William D. 1982. "On the 'Heimatbestimmung' of the Ellis County (Kansas) Volga-German Dialects." *Yearbook of German-American Studies* 17: 99-109.

Keel, William D. 1994. "Reduction and Loss of Case Marking in the Noun Phrase in GermanAmerican Speech Islands: Internal Development or External Interference?" In *Sprachinselforschung: Eine Gedenkschrift für Hugo Jedig*, ed. Nina Berend and Klaus J. Mattheier, 93-104. Frankfurt: Peter Lang.

Keel, William, and Kurt Rein, eds. 1996. *German Emigration from Bukovina to the Americas*. Lawrence, KS: Max Kade Center for German-American Studies.

Kehlenbeck, Alfred P. 1934. "Die plattdeutsche Mundart in Iowa County, Iowa." Ph.D. diss., University of Wisconsin.

Kloss, Heinz. 1966."German-American Language Maintenance Efforts." In *Language Loyalty in the United States: The Maintenance and Perpetuation of Non-English Mother Tongues by American Ethnic and Religious Groups*, Joshua A. Fishman, ed. The Hague: Mouton.

Lewis, Brian. 1968. "The Phonology of the Glarus Dialect in Green County, Wisconsin." Ph.D. diss., University of Wisconsin.

Lunte, Gabriele. 1998. "The Catholic Bohemian German Dialect of Ellis, Kansas." Ph.D. diss., University of Kansas.

McGraw, Peter A. 1973. "The Kölsch Dialect of Dane County, Wisconsin." Ph.D. diss., University of Wisconsin.

Mertens, Birgit. 1994. *Vom (Nieder-) Deutschen zum Englischen: Untersuchungen zur sprachlichen Assimilation einer ländlichen Gemeinde im mittleren Westen Amerikas*. Sprachgeschichte, 2. Heidelberg: Universitätsverlag C. Winter.

Nützel, Daniel. 1993. "Case Loss and Morphosyntactic Change in Haysville East Franconian." In *The German Language in America, 1683-1991*, ed. Joseph C. Salmons. Madison, WI: Max Kade Institute for German-American Studies, 307-21.

Penzl, Herbert. 1996."The Pennsylvania German Dialect in Sterling, Illinois." *Journal of the Center for Pennsylvania German Studies* 3/5 (Winter): 17-18.

Rein, Kurt. 1977. *Religiöse Minderheiten als Sprachgemeinschaftsmodelle: Deutsche Sprachinseln täuferischen Ursprungs in den Vereinigten Staaten von Amerika*. Wiesbaden: Franz Steiner Verlag.

Rein, Kurt. 1980. "German Dialects in Anabaptist Colonies on the Great Plains." In *Languages in Conflict: Linguistic Acculturation on the Great Plains*, ed. Paul Schach, 94-110. Lincoln, NE: University of Nebraska Press.

Rettig, Lawrence J. 1970. "Grammatical Structures in Amana German." Ph.D. diss., University of Iowa.

Rodewald, Rev. Alfred W., et al. 1990. *Descending Love—Ascending Praise: St. Paul's Lutheran Church, Concordia, Mo., 1840-1990*. Concordia, MO.

Schirmunski, Viktor. 1930. "Sprachgeschichte und Siedlungsmundarten." *Germanisch-Romanische Monatsschrift* 18: 113-22, 177-88.

Schmidt, Mary. 1977. "Linguistic Transitions of the Russian-Mennonites in Kansas." M.A. thesis, Emporia State University.

Stucky, Harley J. 1956. "The German Element in Kansas." In *Kansas: The First Century*, 4 vols., ed. John D. Bright, 1:329-54. New York: Lewis Historical Pub. Co.

They Live in Hope: A Guide to Hillsboro's Pioneer Adobe House Museum and the Mennonite Adobe House Culture of Central Kansas, 1874-1900. No date. Hillsboro, KS: Multi Business Press.

Webber, Philip E. 1993. "Betwixt and Between: The Tension of Language Contact in Iowa's Amana Colonies." In *The German Language in America, 1683-1991*, ed. Joseph Salmons, 03-23. Madison, WI: Max Kade Institute for German-American Studies.

Werling, J. W. 1938. *History of the Kansas District, Evangelical Lutheran Synod of Missouri, Ohio and Other States*. St. Louis: Concordia Publishing House.

Contributors

Nina Berend studied at the universities of Omsk and Lwow in the Soviet Union, where she earned the doctorate in German. Since 1990 she has been a researcher at the Institut für Deutsche Sprache in Mannheim. She earned *Habilitation* at the University of Heidelberg in 1998. She is the editor of the *Wolgadeutscher Sprachatlas* (1997). Her research interests include dialectology, sociolinguistics, and linguistic integration.

Renate Born is associate professor in the Department of Germanic and Slavic Languages at the University of Georgia in Athens, Georgia. She earned a doctorate in linguistics at Cornell in 1979 and teaches courses on contrastive grammar and language variation. Her research interest in morphological change in German-American dialects is reflected in her monograph *Michigan German in Frankenmuth* (Camden House, 1994). Her research has also focused on variation in early modern German.

Ludwig M. Eichinger is director of the Institut für Deutsche Sprache in Mannheim and professor of Germanic linguistics at the University of Kiel. He also directs the linguistic atlas of Upper Bavaria. His recent publications include *Deutsche Wortbildung: Eine Einführung* (2000). He serves as treasurer and member of the executive committee of the Internationale Gesellschaft für die Dialektologie des Deutschen.

Janet Fuller is an assistant professor of linguistics at Southern Illinois University at Carbondale. Her areas of research include bilingualism and language contact, discourse analysis, and gender studies.

Glenn Gilbert is professor of linguistics and adjunct professor of German and anthropology at Southern Illinois University at Carbondale. His specialties are sociolinguistics, pidgin and creole languages, and the study of German and other European languages brought by nineteenth-century immigrants to the United States. He compiled and published *The Linguistic Atlas of Texas German* (1972).

Göz Kaufmann is a lecturer in German at the Universidad Federale do Rio Grande del Sul in Porto Alegre, Brazil. He studied at the universities of Texas and Heidelberg where he earned the doctorate in 1998.

William D. Keel is professor and chair of Germanic Languages and Literatures at the University of Kansas. His research interests in German-American settlement dialects led to the establishment of the Linguistic Atlas of Kansas German Dialects at the Max

Kade Center for German-American Studies at the University of Kansas. He is also editor of the *Yearbook of German-American Studies*.

Steven H. Keiser is an assistant professor of linguistics at Marquette University in Milwaukee, Wisconsin. His teaching and research are concentrated in linguistics, especially language contact, change, and shift. His dissertation, "Language Change across Speech Islands," applies sociolinguistic analyses to the maintenance, use, and structural transformation of the language commonly called Pennsylvania Dutch.

Elisabeth Knipf-Komlósi studied German at the universities of Pécs and Szeged in Hungary. She earned the doctorate in 1983 at Szeged with a dissertation on morphology. She earned *Habilitation* in Budapest in 1993. She has held appointments at Pécs and Budapest where she is currently head of German Studies at the Eötvös Loránd University. Her research interests include German word formation, varieties of German, sociolinguistics and speech islands.

Achim Kopp is associate professor of German and Latin at Mercer University, Macon, Georgia. Since August 2002 he has served as chair of the Department of Foreign Languages and Literatures. He received his doctoral degree from the University of Heidelberg in 1994 and is the author of *The Phonology of Pennsylvania German English as Evidence of Language Maintenance and Shift* (Susquehanna University Press, 1999).

Mark L. Louden completed his Ph.D. in Germanic linguistics at Cornell University in 1988 with a dissertation entitled "Bilingualism and Syntactic Change in Pennsylvania German." From 1988 to 2000 he taught general and Germanic linguistics courses at the University of Texas at Austin. Since 2000 he has been on the faculty of the Department of German at the University of Wisconsin-Madison and is the director of the Max Kade Institute there. His teaching and research interests include the general areas of syntax, acquisition, language contact, and language change; specific languages he has worked on include Pennsylvania German and Yiddish.

Klaus J. Mattheier studied history and German in Bonn and Bochum and has been professor of German at the University of Heidelberg since 1981. He has held visiting appointments in the United States, China and other countries. His wide-ranging research interests include the history and varieties of German as well as sociolinguistics. He serves as vice-president and member of the executive committee of the Internationale Gesellschaft für die Dialektologie des Deutschen.

Joachim Raith is a lecturer and researcher in didactics, applied linguistics and technology enhanced language learning of the English Department at the University of Essen. His research includes the linguistic behavior of the Old Order Amish in Delaware.

Kurt L. Rein is professor emeritus of German at the Ludwig-Maximilians-Universität in Munich and held visiting appointments at U.S. universities. He has written extensively on the dialects of the Germans from Bucovina as well as in Anabaptist communities in the Midwestern United States. He is also engaged in the research program of the Bukowina-Institut in Augsburg.

Peter Rosenberg has been a member of the faculty in linguistics at the Europa-Universität Viadrina in Frankfurt an der Oder since 1993. He earned the doctorate in German at the Free University of Berlin in 1985. He has undertaken extensive research trips to both Russia and to Latin America. His research interests include comparative speech island research, linguistic minorities, dialectology, urban languages, applied linguistics, as well as linguistic varieties in East and West Germany.

Peter Wagener earned the doctorate at the University of Göttingen in 1986 with an emphasis in German and Low German philology as well as general linguistics. Since 1990 he has been a researcher at the Institut für Deutsche Sprache in Mannheim where he directs das Deutsche Spracharchiv. He is co-editor of the series Phonai: Texte und Untersuchungen zum gesprochenen Deutsch. His research interests include regional varieties of German and linguistic change.

Philip E. Webber is professor of German at Central College in Pella, Iowa, where he has been a member of the faculty since 1976. A major focus of his research has been patterns of ethnicity and language use in Iowa communities. He has prepared videotaped material on the orally transmitted culture of Swiss-Americans in Elgin, Iowa, and on the East Friesian Low German community in the Iowa counties of Butler, Franklin, Grundy and Hardin. His four books include *Pella Dutch: The Portrait of a Language and Its Use in One of Iowa's Ethnic Communities* and *Kolonie-Deutsch: Life and Language in Amana.*

Magda Stroiñska / Vittorina Cecchetto (eds.)

Exile, language and identity

Frankfurt/M., Berlin, Bern, Bruxelles, New York, Oxford, Wien, 2003.
250 pp., 8 fig.
ISBN 3-631-39484-5 · pb. € 37.80*
US-ISBN 0-8204-5972-0

'Exile' means a prolonged, usually enforced absence from one's home or country. There is no paradigm for an exilic existence and no prescription of how to heal the loss of one's home and one's identity. Exiles move in *space*, migrating from one place to another, but they are trapped in *time*. They long for what they have lost and fear what is yet to come. Like the Roman god Janus, they constantly look both ways, often lacking language that would help them to reconnect with the world. This volume examines the process of the exile's *self-translation* by rediscovering a way of expression for the ensnared experience. It requires a new language so that the self may take a new shape. By discussing the unavoidable losses wrought upon immigrants, exiles and refugees by the mere fact of being displaced, the authors hope to foster a better understanding of these problems and help to rebuild shattered identities and ruined lives.

Contents: An interdisciplinary perspective on language and identity loss in exile · Literary, sociolinguistic and social issues related to exilic experiences of 20th century · Nationalism, memories of the Holocaust · Alienation · Self-translation in exile · Immigration from Yugoslavia · Women survivors of torture or the reception of East German films in the West

Frankfurt/M · Berlin · Bern · Bruxelles · New York · Oxford · Wien
Auslieferung: Verlag Peter Lang AG
Moosstr. 1, CH-2542 Pieterlen
Telefax 00 41 (0) 32 / 376 17 27

*inklusive der in Deutschland gültigen Mehrwertsteuer
Preisänderungen vorbehalten
Homepage http://www.peterlang.de